An Introduction to Women's Writing

An Introduction to Women's Writing

From the Middle Ages to the Present Day

Edited by

Marion Shaw

PRENTICE HALL

London   New York   Toronto   Sydney   Tokyo   Singapore
Madrid   Mexico City   Munich   Paris

First published 1998 by
Prentice Hall Europe
Campus 400, Maylands Avenue
Hemel Hempstead
Hertfordshire, HP2 7EZ
A division of
Simon & Schuster International Group

Typeset in 10/12pt Ehrhardt
by Dorwyn Limited, Rowlands Castle, Hants

Printed and bound in Great Britain by
Hartnolls Ltd, Bodmin, Cornwall

Library of Congress Cataloging-in-Publication Data

Available from the publisher.

British Library Cataloguing in Publication Data

A catalogue record for this book is available from
the British Library

ISBN 0-13-206459-6

1 2 3 4 5   02 01 00 99 98

Contents

Notes on contributors   vii

Introduction: the life apart   1
Marion Shaw

1   Abandoned women: female authorship in the Middle Ages   9
Marion Wynne-Davies

2   Transgressing boundaries: women's writing in the Renaissance
and Reformation   37
Janet Clare

3   Usurping authority over the man: women's writing 1630–89   65
Elaine Hobby

4   'Publick view': women's writing, 1689–1789   94
Jane Spencer

5   A revolution in female manners: women writers of the Romantic period,
1789–1832   122
Harriet Devine Jump

6   A woman's business: women and writing, 1830–80   149
Lyn Pykett

7   Out of the attic . . .: women and writing at the *fin de siècle*   177
Viv Gardner

8   Looking within: women's writing in the modernist period, 1910–40   203
Clare Hanson

9   'Writing as re-vision': women's writing in Britain, 1945 to the present day   235
Diana Wallace

Index   264

The idea for this book was conceived by Jackie Jones: I am grateful to her. My thanks go to Christina Wipf-Perry and Jill Birch of Prentice Hall, and to Diana Wallace for valuable editorial assistance.

Notes on contributors

Marion Wynne-Davies is a Senior Lecturer in English Literature at the University of Dundee. Her books include *Women and Arthurian Literature: Seizing the Sword* (1996) and *The Tales of the Clerk and the Wife of Bath* (1992).

Janet Clare is a lecturer in English at University College Dublin. She is author of *Art Made Tongue-Tied by Authority: Elizabethan and Jacobean Censorship* (1990) and has published several articles on Renaissance drama, censorship and New Historicism, and drama in the English Republic.

Elaine Hobby is Reader in Women's Studies in the Department of English and Drama at Loughborough University. She has been working on seventeenth-century women's writing since being assured, as a new postgraduate student in 1978, that 'there weren't any women then'. Her publications include *Virtue of Necessity: English Women's Writing 1649–1688* (1988).

Jane Spencer is Senior Lecturer in English Literature in the School of English and American Studies, University of Exeter. Her publications include *The Rise of the Woman Novelist* (1986), *Elizabeth Gaskell* (1993) and an edition of Aphra Behn's *The Rover and Other Plays* (1995). She is currently working on the eighteenth-century reception of Aphra Behn's work, and on early women's periodicals.

Harriet Devine Jump is Senior Lecturer in English Literature at Edge Hill University College. She has edited and contributed to *Diverse Voices: Essays on Twentieth Century Women Writers in English* (1994), is author of *Mary Wollstonecraft: Writer* (1994) and editor of *Women's Writing of the Romantic Period, 1789–1837: An Anthology* (1996).

Lyn Pykett is a Professor of English and Head of Department at the University of Wales Aberystwyth. She is the author of *Emily Brontë* (1989), *The 'Improper' Feminine: The Women's Sensation Novel and the New Woman Writing* (1992), *The Sensation Novel from 'The Woman in White' to 'The Moonstone'* (1994), *Engendering Fictions: The English Novel in the Early Twentieth Century* (1995), and *Reading Fin de Siècle Fictions* (1996).

Viv Gardner is a Senior Lecturer in the Department of Drama at Manchester University. She is editor of *Sketches from the Actresses' Franchise League* (1985), co-editor with Linda Fitzsimmons of *New Woman Plays*, and with Susan Rutherford of *The New Woman and Her Sisters: Feminism and Theatre 1850–1914* (1992). She is currently working on a book on women theatre managers in the Victorian and Edwardian period.

Clare Hanson is Reader in English at the University of Leicester. Her publications include *Katherine Mansfield* (with Andrew Gurr) (1981), *Short Stories and Short Fictions, 1880–1980* (1985), *The Critical Writings of Katherine Mansfield* (ed.), *Re-Reading the Short Story* (ed.) and *Virginia Woolf* (1992). She has published articles and reviews on a range of feminist topics and women writers, and is currently working on a study of women and fiction after Virginia Woolf.

Diana Wallace is currently completing her PhD thesis, which focuses on female rivalry as a theme in inter-war fiction by women, at Loughborough University.

Marion Shaw is Professor of English and Head of the Department of English and Drama at Loughborough University. She has published on nineteenth-century writers, particularly Tennyson, and also on women writers of the inter-war period. She is currently completing a study of the novelist Winifred Holtby.

Introduction: the life apart

Marion Shaw

In her useful introductory text, *Literature and Feminism*, Pam Morris begins with 'some obvious questions. What is feminism? What does it mean to be a feminist? What is the purpose of feminist literary criticism? How can it affect the way we read?' (1993: 1). In answering the third and fourth of these questions, her argument is 'constructed round three thematic concerns: the question of a woman's identity, the formation of canons and the politics of aesthetic evaluation' (9).

An Introduction to Women's Writing: From the Middle Ages to the Present Day addresses these three thematic concerns: it discusses women's perception of themselves as women and particularly as women writers; it is a history and a description of women's writing during nearly a thousand years; and it registers the ways in which women's writing has been received and the values which have been attributed to and demanded of it. It is also, of course, an account of women's success as writers. Often against the odds, women have written an astonishing amount and though much has been overlooked and certainly much has been lost, there is a wealth remaining. As Ellen Moers wrote as long ago as 1963, to be a woman writer 'meant, may still mean, belonging to a literary movement apart from but hardly subordinate to the main-stream: an undercurrent, rapid and powerful' (1977: 42). *An Introduction to Women's Writing* measures that rapid, powerful undercurrent. It does so 'apart from' the mainstream because a separate measurement still needs to be taken.

In 1928 Virginia Woolf wrote that 'we think back through our mothers if we are women'. Although she believed this true of all aspects of women's lives, she was particularly concerned in *A Room of One's Own* with the woman writer. The problem as she saw it then was that women writers could find little trace of their literary mothers, they 'had no tradition behind them, or one so short and partial that it was of little help' (1945: 76). The supplying of this deficiency has been one of the aims and achievements of feminist criticism of the last twenty-five years. After Moers's pioneering book, itself now a classic of feminist criticism, came the iconoclastic writing of critics like Mary Ellmann (1968) and Kate Millett (1970), who attacked the masculine canon and its sexist and misogynist portrayal of women. They were followed by critics who sought, in the words of Maggie Humm, 'to give a *material* shape to, and [to] revalue women's culture and writing' (1994: 9). For feminist purposes it

1

was no longer adequate to condemn a tradition which had forgotten, neglected or trivialized women's writing; an alternative history was required, to show that women had written and could write. The recuperation of the recent past was undertaken by Elaine Showalter in *A Literature of Their Own: British Women Novelists from Brontë to Lessing* (1977) and Sandra M. Gilbert and Susan Gubar in *The Madwoman in the Attic: The Woman Writer and the Nineteenth-Century Literary Imagination* (1979). Then came the reclamation of earlier centuries – Elaine Hobby's *Virtue of Necessity: English Women's Writing 1649–88* (1988) and Jane Spencer's *The Rise of the Woman Novelist: From Aphra Behn to Jane Austen* (1986), for example. Such books grew out of and stimulated the growth in 'women's writing' courses in higher and further education in the United States and Britain. By the mid-1980s a 'women's writing' course was no longer remarkable but something of a staple in most institutions.

Those of us who taught or took such courses, which came into their heyday during the early 1980s, found, though, that constructing an alternative canon of women's writing involved many doubts and criticisms. Some of these doubts were political ones: what was the point of a separatist movement which left the 'mainstream' undisturbed? where were the black, working-class, lesbian writers (and students)? how does feminism, and feminist criticism, intersect with other political loyalties, with, for instance, Irish Republicanism or membership of the Conservative Party? Any assumption that there was a homogeneous feminist readership for whom an alternative tradition of writing could be established soon fractured into different feminisms and different feminist writing traditions. There were also the philosophical doubts: what do we mean by the category 'woman'? What is the difference between sex and gender? is a woman's identity biologically given or socially constructed? These debates proliferated into books as various as *Motherlands: Black Women's Writing from Africa, the Caribbean and South Asia*, edited by Susheila Nasta (1991), *Gender Trouble: Feminism and the Subversion of Identity* by Judith Butler (1990) and *The Straight Mind and Other Essays* by Monique Wittig (1992). A sign of the changing times was the 1,000 page collection of essays edited by Robyn R. Warhol and Diane Price Herndl called *Feminisms: An Anthology of Literary Theory and Criticism* (1991). The pluralism of the title, *Feminisms*, registered the multiplicity of both feminist criticism and feminism itself. The first of Pam Morris's questions, 'What is feminism?', has either to be answered very loosely, as something to do with the improvement of the lives of women, or it has to be recast as 'What feminisms are there, and how are they constructed and operative within specific historical and cultural contexts?' Feminist criticism likewise has to recognize its differences and specificities. There is neither a unitary theory nor a unitary practice; there are feminist criticisms.

An Introduction to Women's Writing: From the Middle Ages to the Present Day is a collection of new essays which, as its title indicates, constitutes an historical mapping, chronologically organized, with the purpose of describing and analyzing what women wrote, and the material and ideological conditions in which they wrote. It is divided into periods because, however arguable and blurred the divisions between one period and another may be, it is by chronological units of this kind that the study of literature is usually organized. Such an organization acknowledges the relationship between writing and its historical context.

With the exception of the Medieval period, *An Introduction to Women's Writing* is confined to texts in English and, for the most part, to writing in England; the authors it is concerned with are predominantly white and upper or middle class. As such it has national, ethnic and class limitations. To have widened the remit would have been to have produced a book of either gargantuan size or of crass superficiality. As it stands, it is unusual; although there are anthologies of extracts of women's writing, such as *An Anthology of British Women Writers* edited by Dale Spender and Janet Todd (1989), and reference books like Joanne Shattock's invaluable *The Oxford Guide to British Women Writers* (1994), it is difficult to think of another book which performs the critical overview that *An Introduction to Women's Writing* offers. It constitutes a survey and its purpose is to enable a present-day reader to take a perspective down the centuries of women's writing, to consider at large what has been done, to ponder the themes and issues that seem to the contributors to this book to be of importance, and then perhaps to move on to a more detailed and specific study of a particular period or an author or group of authors.

Looking backwards and seeing the forward march of women's literacy and literary production, it is apparent that certain concerns endure for women who attempt the pen even though society changes in other respects. From the thirteenth to the twentieth century the question of propriety persists in regard to women's writing. Immodesty may have been fiercely proscribed for the medieval woman writer but it also damagingly condemned a writer like Mary Elizabeth Braddon in the 1860s, and even now it can earn a poet such as Fiona Pitt-Kethley a scabrous reputation beyond what would attach to a male contemporary. Another enduring anxiety is that of lineage: 'England has had many learned women . . . and yet where are the poetesses? . . . I look everywhere for grandmothers and see none,' wrote Elizabeth Barrett Browning in 1845 (Kenyon, 1897: vol. I, 230–2) and although in prose at least there are now the great mothers and grandmothers to exhort and challenge, in poetry there is still an uneasy sense of thinness in those previous centuries, and the legacy of the label 'poetess' to embarrass and enfeeble.

The labels attached to women writers relate to the construction of traditions and canons and the way in which these have tended to exclude and diminish women writers or see them as on the edge of significant literary movements and periods. The Romantic period, dominated by a small group of male authors, is such a case and so is the Modernist movement early this century. By drawing attention, as *An Introduction* does, to the women who were also part of these movements, the intention is not to demote Wordsworth and Keats or Yeats and Joyce but to include another, female view of how life and writing was then. The intention is more than literary curiosity; it is to counterbalance the mainstream, to validate the 'movement apart', to show its strengths and anxieties and to establish its matrilineal tradition.

The title of Marion Wynne-Davies's opening chapter, 'Abandoned Women', brilliantly points to and puns on persistent aspects of this tradition. Medieval women writers are extreme examples of canonical neglect in that until recently they were for the most part left out of accounts of the period in the assumption that either they were illiterate and wrote nothing or that what they wrote was unworthy of remembrance. A related interpretation of abandonment reveals a loss of individual identity which, paradoxically, for many Medieval women writers was a desired, strategic surrender of the self, to the point of death in some cases, in order to write God's word. A mystical abandonment of this kind justified challenging church and state proprieties because it invoked a higher authority. A challenge could, of course, be mounted by abandoned women of another kind, loose women, who lost respectability by writing of love, or of secular matters in general. To write at all was to abandon the strictest codes of female passivity and subservience; as Marion Wynne-Davies points out, while women of the Medieval period did write, by doing so they were in direct rebellion against their own societies. How much more rebellious, then, to challenge the misogyny of both clerical authority and the courtly romances by writing, as Christine de Pizan did, of the realities of women's sexual experiences.

There is a tendency to homogenize the writing of the Middle Ages; history seems to have moved slowly so that two or three centuries have come to appear as one. The Renaissance and the Reformation, however, have more sharply delineated boundaries and within this period there are, to a modern perception, important shifts. One of these, Janet Clare suggests, is that in the early seventeenth century, when the Renaissance begins to give way to the Reformation, texts authored by women start to explore questions relating to female subjectivity and subjectification. In the sixteenth century, although literacy was acceptable for upper-class women, displays of learning and of opinion were viewed with suspicion. A woman's reading was directed towards the cultivation of obedient and pious behaviour in her personal life, and to exceed this, as, for instance, in the reading of political treatises, was to challenge standards of female decorum. So too was the reading of romance literature; its knightly matter was inappropriate for a woman and its erotic impulse dangerous to her chastity. To write, women had to negotiate these literary constraints: by indirect means, as translators, for instance, or with self-effacing anonymity, and only occasionally directly. With the Jacobean period came a more self-conscious challenge to patriarchy and patristic discourses and a remodelling of cultural representations of women. The increasing confidence of their public voices indicates a drift away from earlier ideals of exemplary femininity.

These public voices gain in audibility as the seventeenth century unfolds. Great social, religious and political disruptions seem to have been both cause of and justification for women's increased incursion into print. As Elaine Hobby shows, they wrote and published on war, love, politics, education, health, cookery, hare-coursing and debt, and in doing so they risked censure and punishment. The familiar apologies for 'immodesty' in taking up the pen are there, and so too is the abandonment to divine authority which justifies the spiritual polemic of a Quaker like Susanna Parr or the life-stories which are part of God-inspired conversion narratives of Baptists like Sara Davy and Hannah Allen. In secular writing, the change is more marked; no subject is safe from a woman's pen, and a more assertive, argumentative and opinionated female discourse emerges, with no voice more vigorous than that of Aphra Behn. As Jane Spencer says, Behn's legacy of public success and audacity was an important one for eighteenth-century women writers. To write in 'publick view', to earn money by the pen, had been pioneered by her.

The period of greater political stability after 1688 encouraged an increase in middle-class literacy and leisure, accompanied by a growth in the publishing trade. Women writers had opportunities as never before and although their participation in this expanding literary market was still limited by ideals of feminine decorum, both the amount and variety of their writing increased. By the end of the 1780s, women's writing in England was well established. Successful women dramatists, poets and novelists, such as Hannah Cowley, Charlotte Smith and Ann Radcliffe, were accepted by both men and women as established figures in the literary scene. Yet they too were soon to be abandoned, ironically enough by a historical phase which itself saw an upsurge in feminist discourse. What was rescued from the eighteenth century after the Romantic movement included few women writers, for although writing and publication by women reached unprecedented levels during the Romantic period, this has been occluded by the focus on the male Romantic poets. The two most famous women writers of the period, Jane Austen and Mary Wollstonecraft, are popularly remembered as lone voices: Austen as an anachronism at odds with Romanticism and Wollstonecraft as a solitary feminist polemicist. Yet as Harriet Devine Jump argues, women were Romantic poets too, were hugely prolific as novelists of all kinds, and also, like Joanna Baillie, were successful dramatists. Austen and Wollstonecraft put women's names into literary history yet the effects of this were mixed. Although Austen brought respectability and esteem to the woman's novel, her work confirmed the domestic sphere as the proper one for women; Wollstonecraft argued for women to be educated and treated as rational beings instead of the sexual, sentimental creatures of contemporary fashion yet the irregularities of her own life were used to discredit her views. The charge of immodesty receives another twist: although what a woman writes may be respectable, her life sits in judgement on her work and outstrips it in interest.

Biography posing as literary recognition casts a blight on women's writing of the nineteenth century. As Lyn Pykett shows, women entered the literary marketplace as professionals in increasing numbers; literature became their business. Yet of the many who earned successful livings out of writing, the few whose reputation survived their deaths were in some cases known more for their life-stories than their work. Elizabeth Barrett Browning is the chief example of this, her romance with Robert Browning obscuring her success as a poet, and the Brontë sisters' tragic deaths do as much to keep their names alive as the merits of their books. One of the achievements of twentieth-century feminist criticism is, as Pykett points out, to show such romanticized figures of the woman writer in a context of prolific women's writing, as members of a writing sisterhood.

The respectability of subject matter which earned the woman writer approval – 'doting mothers, and perfect wives, / Sublime Madonnas, and enduring saints', as Barrett Browning contemptuously put it – became also the critical put-down which framed women's writing as limited to the safely domestic. It is one of George Eliot's achievements in *Middlemarch* that she manipulates this limitation to create in Dorothea a Madonna, a saint, and an almost perfect wife whom criticism could not but find significant. But what fulfilled – or nearly so – a Dorothea could not satisfy her granddaughters at the end of the century. The title of Viv Gardner's chapter on this period – 'out of the attic' – refers, of course, to the figure of the first Mrs Rochester in *Jane Eyre* whom Gilbert and Gubar (1979) use as a trope for women's repressed desires in nineteenth-century fiction. If the woman writer comes out of the attic after 1880 it is in search of autonomy for the New Woman figure, and for herself as a new kind of writer. As Gardner argues, the *fin de siècle* produced significant changes in the representation of women generally, and for women writers in particular this was an innovative, unsettled and questioning time. The love-and-marriage plot no longer sufficed, the tensions between family responsibilities and creativity were more sharply polarized, gender roles were not the fixities they were previously assumed to be. The heroine in May Sinclair's novel *The Creators* (1910) expresses the conflicting demands made on a New Woman to fulfil new potentials: 'now she was beginning to feel the trembling of the perfect balance. . . . She moved with tense nerves on the edge of peril' (quoted herein page 198).

The 'voyage out' into new opportunities outside the domestic sphere continued into the twentieth century, accelerating during and after the 1914–18 war. Women's writing of this Modernist period reflected the growing diversity of the lives and experience of middle-class women. In the Modernist texts, like Dorothy Richardson's *Pilgrimage* (1915–67) or Virginia Woolf's *Mrs Dalloway* (1925), women's consciousness is the finely-tuned gauge of a modern subjectivity in which states of being and becoming are explored; in the non-Modernist texts, such as Winifred Holtby's *South Riding* or Sylvia Townsend Warner's *Summer Will Show*, both published in 1936, which Clare Hanson describes as 'writing otherwise', women not only have careers which absorb them but they look outwards towards society's needs and organizations for which, as women citizens after 1918 for the first time in history, they must share responsibility. The looking within of Modernism is balanced, Hanson suggests, by a return in the writing of the 1930s to 'the contingent [and] material constraints on women's lives'.

In the concluding chapter, 'Writing as re-vision: women's writing in Britain, 1945 to the present day', Diana Wallace maps a contemporary landscape of prose and poetry. As she points out, there has been a tendency in feminist criticism to concentrate on texts from previous times, leaving the contemporary, which includes the rebirth of feminism in the late 1960s and the 1970s, as unoccupied territory. The term 'abandoned', used by Marion Wynne-Davies in relation to Medieval women's writing, begins to assume a dangerous new relevance to the contemporary scene. Diana Wallace's chapter and her bibliography of primary sources seek to redress this but are necessarily selective and speculative. The contours of the landscape are not defined as they are, for good or ill, for the nineteenth century. Wallace's title borrows Adrienne Rich's term 're-visioning' to describe an overarching concern in twentieth-century women's writing to rework texts from earlier times – in some cases as early as the Classics and the Bible – in order to challenge the cultural myths which allowed women only male-defined identities. There are new myths too, or old myths so re-visioned that their meaning and significance are transformative. Fevvers, Angela Carter's bird-woman in *Nights at the Circus* – 'Is she fact or is she fiction?' – revolutionizes not only the Icarus story but the act of story-telling itself.

The overall impression of a collection of essays like *An Introduction to Women's Writing*, because it begins in the distant past and ends with the present day, is inevitably one of progression and development: the issues seem clearer, the choice wider and the obstacles less formidable the nearer to the present this evolution draws. But though it surely is the case that it is easier for women to write now than in the past – and to suggest otherwise seems to me both to deny history and to diminish the efforts of those who struggled to write in previous times – it is not the case that what women write now is 'better' than what was written earlier or that their lives are more interesting or more worth recording and studying than those of their predecessors. To suggest otherwise would be to impose a canonicity according to chronology, a modern and contemporary elitism which *An Introduction* by its very nature seeks to avoid. As Elaine Hobby has said in her chapter on seventeenth-century women writers, '[o]ne of the most powerful effects of reading these writings by women is the discovery that they give the lie to any assumption that women in the past were chaste, silent and obedient; or indeed that they were lascivious wastrels. They were as various, as witty, and as inventive as people in any period.'

Bibliography

Butler, Judith (1990), *Gender Trouble: Feminism and the Subversion of Identity*, London: Routledge.

Ellmann, Mary (1968), *Thinking About Women*, London: Macmillan.

Gilbert, Sandra M. and Susan Gubar (1979), *The Madwoman in the Attic: The Woman Writer and the Nineteenth Century Literary Imagination*, New Haven: Yale University Press.

Hobby, Elaine (1988), *Virtue of Necessity: English Women's Writing 1649–88*, London: Virago.

Humm, Maggie (1994), *A Reader's Guide to Contemporary Feminist Literary Criticism*, Hemel Hempstead: Harvester Wheatsheaf.

Kenyon, F.G. (ed.) (1897), *The Letters of Elizabeth Barrett Browning*, 2 vols, London: Smith, Elder.

Millett, Kate (1977) [1970], *Sexual Politics*, London: Virago.

Moers, Ellen (1977) [1963], *Literary Women: The Great Writers*, London: W.H. Allen.

Morris, Pam (1993), *Literature and Feminism*, Oxford: Blackwell.

Nasta, Susheila (ed.) (1991), *Motherlands: Black Women's Writing from Africa, the Caribbean and South Asia*, London: The Women's Press.

Shattock, Joanne (1994), *The Oxford Guide to British Women Writers*, Oxford: Oxford University Press.

Showalter, Elaine (1982) [1977], *A Literature of their Own: British Women Novelists from Brontë to Lessing*, London: Virago.

Spencer, Jane (1986), *The Rise of the Woman Novelist: From Aphra Behn to Jane Austen*, Oxford: Blackwell.

Spender, Dale and Janet Todd (eds) (1989), *An Anthology of British Women Writers*, London: Pandora Press.

Warhol, Robyn R. and Diane Price Herndl (eds) (1991), *Feminisms: An Anthology of Literary Theory and Criticism*, New Brunswick, N.J.: Rutgers University Press.

Wittig, Monique (1992), *The Straight Mind and Other Essays*, Hemel Hempstead: Harvester Wheatsheaf.

Woolf, Virginia (1945) [1928], *A Room of One's Own*, Harmondsworth: Penguin.

1

Abandoned women: female authorship in the Middle Ages

Marion Wynne-Davies

Introduction

A brief glance through the introductions to, essays about, and histories of Medieval women writers elicits a bleak view of a period in which few women could read, let alone write, and those who did 'compose' cannot be categorized as 'authors' in the twentieth-century understanding of that term. Even the most recent criticisms offer a cautious and circumspect vista; for example, Alexandra Barratt in her pathbreaking collection *Women's Writing in Middle English* (1992) concludes that,

> [the] assumption that 'authority', and therefore authorship, were incompatible with femininity . . . is responsible both for the lack of educational opportunities and for the relative paucity of women's texts. (5)

Similarly, Emilie Amt in *Women's Lives in Medieval Europe* (1993) complains that,

> Not enough of these [women's own writings] survive from the Middle Ages to enable us to build up an accurate picture of life from a purely female perspective. (7)

Indeed, Julia Boffey in 'Women Authors and Women's Literacy in Fourteenth- and Fifteenth-century England' (*Women and Literature in Britain, 1150–1500*, ed. Carol Meale; 1993) begins her argument tersely with the judgement that,

> compilers of biographical dictionaries of early English women authors, and of anthologies of their writing, have a hard and repetitious time. (159)

Finally, Carolyne Larrington in *Women and Writing in Medieval Europe* (1995) is forced to admit that,

> Medieval women may . . . have been as well-suited to artistic production as any man, but the evidence for this contention is hard to come by today. (215)

What is uniformly agreed upon, even in these specialist texts, is that there are very few surviving works – 'relative paucity', 'hard to come by' and 'not enough' – written by Medieval women. Moreover, although questions of lost authorship and anonymous writings are posited by contemporary feminists working in this area, the dangers of inaccurate attribution and literary hoaxes are too strong to allow the 'rediscovery' of a Medieval woman writer without detailed research and comprehensive verification. It was the overall barrenness, then, of this field, together with the disheartening conclusions of those involved in excavating the primary material, that allowed me to posit initially the notion of 'abandoned women', in the sense of literary neglect (abandoned as in forsaken or banished). Yet, while this might be a commonplace of feminist literary criticism, lamenting the lack or loss of women writers in any given period, it simply fails to do justice both to the radicalism and persistency of the original female authors, as well as to the revolutionary and assiduous research of their twentieth-century editors and critics. For example, any student of English literature might well have heard of Julian of Norwich or Margery Kempe, but how many know of Marguerite Porete?

The title of this essay initially derives from the heading Barratt uses for an excerpt from Marguerite Porete's *Le Mirouer des Simples Ames* (1296–1306): 'The Simple Soul Abandons Herself to the Will of God' (Barratt, 1992: 61–70). Here, of course, the word 'abandoned' is used in the sense of having given oneself up to God without resistance (to sacrifice, devote and surrender one's will) and, as such, places *Le Mirouer* firmly in the tradition of Medieval visionary literature. Marguerite Porete was a late thirteenth-century beguine from Flanders whose mystical treatise, *Le Mirouer*, was condemned and publicly destroyed; then, when she continued to circulate her work, the author was herself condemned as a heretic and was burnt at the stake. In her life and writings Marguerite Porete had challenged the conventions of both church and state. First, the group to which she belonged, the beguines, consisted of women who gathered together in small communities to live in a chaste, religious and self-supporting manner; they were initially condoned by the church, but their spiritual and economic independence gradually led to hostility from both the religious and secular authorities. Second, the content of *Le Mirouer*, in which a dialogue occurs between Lady Reason, Lady Love and the Free Soul, gave rise to the suspicion that the author was advocating the heresy of the Free Spirit, which claimed that those whose souls had been preferred by God were no longer bound by conventional moral codes. Within the parameters set by the Inquisition there appear to have been justifiable grounds for the accusation of this heresy, since Porete claims that the Free Soul 'giveth to nature al his askynges, withoute grucchyng of conscience', but it is also difficult to imagine that the author's sex was unimportant in such a trial (Barratt, 1992: 64). It is significant that, while unaware that the author was a woman, the Carthusian monk who translated *Le Mirouer* into English (*The Mirror of Simple Souls*) simply noted that the text was difficult and that it had been misunderstood, not that it was heretical. More recently, Porete's work has been included within the canon of Medieval women writers; she is, for example, anthologized by Barratt (1992: 61–70), Katharina M. Wilson in *Medieval Women Writers* (1984: 204–26) and Elizabeth Petroff in *Medieval Women's Visionary Literature* (1986: 280–3). Her popularity with feminists is both biographical and textual: she acted out in her own existence a direct challenge to the patriarchal authority of the church, from a refusal to withdraw her writings to the ultimate denouement of both life and text in the fire. Moreover,

Porete's use of three female protagonists in *Le Mirouer* who differ from their male-authored counterparts (Lady Reason is idealized in Boethius's *Consolation of Philosophy* yet denigrated by Porete, while her Lady Love is almost universally represented elsewhere by a male figure) predicates a textual vindication of women's importance within philosophical and spiritual discourses. It is, perhaps, ironic therefore that a woman who seems to a late twentieth-century readership to signify such radical female independence, in her own lifetime strongly advocated the destruction of the self, as the will surrendered itself to God, 'I shulde leie al this in him and go to nought' (Barratt, 1992: 67). Linking Porete to other self-abnegating Medieval women mystics, Barratt points out that,

> Marguerite Porete, the only medieval woman known to have been put to death for writing a book, carries this ideal of self-effacement to its logical conclusion, that of self-annihilation, becoming 'pure nought'. (Barratt, 1992: 10)

The valuable rediscovery of women writers such as Porete is in this manner rent by the conflicting voices within their texts, making the attempt to weave a coherent picture of Medieval female authorship often an inadequate two-dimensional representation of the inner threads of a gendered subjectivity which is both wrought by, and pulls against, the ideology which frames it.

An acceptance of mutual otherness offers a way in which such conflicts may be acknowledged and encompassed, although not brought to any easy resolution. Thus, the recuperation of the 'abandoned' female voices of the Medieval period requires a doubled perception, whereby the feminist reader of the late twentieth century 'hears' the revoicing of the older text through the ideology of a present independent female subjectivity, while at the same time, 'hearing' the earlier articulation of a woman whose desire for textual authority inevitably led to an 'abandonment' of her individuality. For example, Marguerite Porete may be upheld both as a radical exponent of a pre-feminist discourse, and as an example of the Medieval ideal of self-denying womanhood. Of course, there are certain impossibilities about such a theoretical proposition in that we can never fully encompass the realities of the Medieval world and that ultimately it is impossible to know exactly why Porete chose to write or why there were varying receptions to her work. But, by examining the gaps between the different perceptions, between the alternate voicings, between the surface picture and the tensions underneath, it becomes possible to suggest a way in which Medieval women's literature may be recuperated into the academic canon and even enjoyed by readers outside academe.

Before, however, moving on to a more detailed discussion of the texts themselves based upon the doubled readings suggested above, I should like to take up one further meaning for the word 'abandoned', that is, to be given up to immoral influences. For, while the spiritual writers of the Medieval world were giving themselves unreservedly to God, the secular authors of the same period were devoting their time to courtly love. This ethos has elicited parallel perceptions similar to those discussed above, since, although it is perfectly evident from the numerous narratives, lyrics and advice books that extramarital love was idealized, animating the modern romance conventions, at the same time, even the most rudimentary historical enquiry uncovers an absolute policing of female chastity and harsh punishments for proven adultery.[1] The radical shift of ideological positioning required to allow for both courtly love and married chastity seems antithetical to a late twentieth-century reader, but it has previously been suggested that no such obstacles presented themselves to the Medieval author. Nevertheless, one of the concerns of this essay is to explore the way in which women writers utilize courtly love and to question its representation within a specifically gendered text. Authors such as Marie de France (late twelfth century) and Margery Kempe (*c*.1373–*c*.1439) certainly employ the idea of extramarital love within their work but, interestingly, rarely to the benefit or joy of the female characters. For example, in Marie's Anglo-Norman lai, 'Laüstic', a noble wife has a lover about whom she thinks all the time even though their desire is not consummated. As a result she stands by the window of her bedchamber in order to see her beloved so often that her husband becomes jealous and asks her what she is doing. The lady explains that she is listening to the song of a nightingale, whereupon her husband traps the bird and confronts his wife:

> 'Lady,' he said, 'where are you? Come forward and speak to us. With bird-lime I have trapped the nightingale which has kept you awake so much. Now you can sleep in peace, for it will never awaken you again.' When the lady heard him she was grief-stricken and distressed. She asked her husband for the bird, but he killed it out of spite, breaking its neck wickedly with his two hands. He threw the body at the lady, so that the front of her tunic was bespattered with blood, just on her breast. (Marie de France, 1986: 94–6; 95)

The lady sends the dead bird to her lover who retains it, relic-like, in a golden casket. The short song focuses on a brief emotional exchange using traditional symbolism to represent the pure love and spiritual grief of the two lovers. Yet it also suggests the material difficulties faced by an honourable woman whose love is not directed towards her husband. In a period when arranged marriages were the norm such extramarital desires were supposedly an accepted aspect of the courtly ethos, yet Marie's lady is careful not to attract any blame and the relationship with the knight is never sexual, 'they could not meet and take their pleasure with each other'(94). Moreover, the dangers of such liaisons are made explicit by Marie through the violent reaction of the husband and the image of the blood-spattered dress. While this latter symbol signifies the lady's broken heart, at the same time the graphic picture of violence makes it clear that if the husband had known it was another man the lady wished to see, rather than a bird she wanted to hear, the woman's fate could have been equally as bloody. In Marie's lai the knight woos the lady requesting her love repeatedly, similarly, in *The Book of Margery Kempe* Margery explains how, even though she hates having intercourse with her husband she was tempted by another man:

> In the second year of her temptations it so happened that a man whom she liked said to her on St Margaret's Eve before evensong that, for anything, he would sleep with her and enjoy the lust of his body, and that she should not withstand him, for if he might not have his desire that time, he said, he would have it another time instead – she should not choose. . . . At last – through the importunings of temptation and a lack of discretion –

she was overcome and consented in her mind, and went to the man to know if he would then consent to have her. And he said he would not for all the wealth in this world; he would rather be chopped up as small as meat for the pot. (Kempe, 1985: 49–50)[2]

There are of course clear distinctions between the two narratives: Marie's poem is a courtly romance written about and for the nobility, whereas Margery's spiritual auto-biography concerns moral temptation and is set firmly in the lower classes. The encoding of desire in the two works contrasts love and lust, and the behaviour of the men is sharply distinct, the knight treasuring the memory of his lady's loss in a quasi-mystical fashion, and Margery's would-be lover spurning and mocking her, turning her 'temptation' into a coarse joke. The collapsing dialectic of spiritual and courtly love, which is a commonplace of Medieval literary criticism, is sustained in these two pieces, the secular love being elevated to the spiritual, and the spiritual being revealed as base and earthly. Yet, the gendered assumptions are not so dissimilar: Marie's lady is 'prudent' and does not make any overt sexual advances to the knight, whereas Margery acknowledges herself that she has lacked 'discretion' when offering her sexual favours so freely. It is tempting to add another voice to the view offered by these two women who themselves lived 200 years apart, that is, the advice of the twentieth-century mother who advises her daughter not to 'give in too easily' as men consider women who readily agree to have sex as 'cheap'. Although it is important to acknowledge that the construction of female identity into the neat dialectic of virgin/whore, good girl/bad girl, is a social formation and in no way 'natural' or 'universal', at the same time the depressing similarities between past and present are hard to ignore. Thus, in addition to the specific Medieval discourses of courtly love and spiritual temptation, the texts expose specifically gendered voices which open up the works to a present-day readership. In addition, while retaining an awareness of the ideals of courtly love within literary discourses, the examples of Marie and Margery make it clear that it is essential to uncover how Medieval women themselves constructed their roles within the secular world.

The structure of this essay has, I hope, now manifested itself: in the subsequent sections I intend first to examine the general background of 'abandoned' Medieval women writers, second to focus more specifically on the spiritual authors who 'abandoned' themselves to God, and third to discuss the supposedly morally 'abandoned' women of secular texts as they are inscribed by women rather than men. The play of meaning is thus encoded both within the essay's central linguistic trope as well as in its theoretical positioning, for although the aim of this exposition is to recuperate Medieval women writers for a modern readership, at the same time it carries within it inevitable strands of historical recalcitrance – voices will be heard and not heard, pictures seen and not seen.

Abandoned and forgotten: Medieval women writers

There are few women authors today whose claim to literary canonization in the cause of women's writing is as strong as that of Marguerite Porete who, after all, died for her book. Yet, there are moments when the divisions between Medieval and Modern constructions, and constrictions, of female articulacy are suddenly and startlingly bridged. One such closure occurred for me in 1986 when I visited Assisi as a tourist and joined a group wandering through the dark passages of the Medieval churches there. At certain points of interest the crowd slowed down and formed knots about the object of their awe or curiosity and, as I was at the tail end of the group, I often waited until the others had shifted on to a new marvel before taking my time to examine the cause of their excitement. Mostly I encountered gilded treasures gleaming through the shadows or strange relics smoothed with the constant pressure of hands, but one of the objects shocked me into a silent stasis, it was a Poor Clare. The dark and heavily shrouded figure of the nun sat in a small stone enclosure divided from the outer world with heavy iron bars; she remained immobile and silent, prohibited by her order from communicating with those gazing at her from beyond the grille. For the Western twentieth-century tourists she was a curious oddity, an anachronism from the past stranded in a modern society in which women could lay claim to an autonomous and articulate self.[3] But I was also aware of the fact that the rule which governed the nun's behaviour was the first to be written by a woman for her own convent, and in this sense it was important to acknowledge that the behaviour of the Poor Clares came to be governed by a text which both activated the independent female voice of their founder, while at the same time silencing those women who followed her example. Clare of Assisi (*c.*1193–1253) was the daughter of a wealthy family, who avoided the marriage arranged for her by her parents by entering a convent. She had been greatly influenced by Francis of Assisi and founded an order of religious women at the church of San Damiano which followed the Franciscan example of poverty and self-denial. Clare finally gained Papal acceptance for her rule in 1253, the year of her death, yet its self-limiting injunctions are still in use today. For example, the Poor Clare I saw in Assisi was bound by the rule which governed 'Silence, the Parlor, and the Grille':

> The sisters may not speak in the parlor or at the grille without the permission of the Abbess. . . . Let a curtain be hung inside the grille which may not be removed except when the Word of God is preached or when a sister is speaking with someone. Let the grille have a wooden door which is well provided with two distinct iron locks, bolts, and bars, so that it can be locked, especially at night, by two keys, one of which the Abbess should keep and the other the sacristan. Let it always be locked except when the Divine Office is being celebrated and for the reasons given above. (Amt, 1993: 240)[4]

The excessive constraints of Clare's dictates contrast strongly with her own determination to have her rule accepted by the patriarchal authorities of the church, forcing the reader/viewer to recognize the present-day nuns simultaneously as representative of a strikingly independent female will, as well as stereotypical objects of women's enforced silence.

My material experience of viewing the Poor Clare may be re-enacted through reading a text written by a Medieval woman: the difference of perception is striking, sometimes even shocking, but the way in which gender is constructed often appears oddly familiar and certainly accessible. For example, while the constraints upon Medieval women might appear at odds with our own lives, the basic structures and dominant discourses (education, marriage, motherhood) are quite similar. When female authors such as Christine de Pizan (*c.*1365–1434) defend women against misogynist attacks, she reminds us of the polemical responses of many twentieth-century feminists to entrenched patriarchal approaches. For example, at the beginning of Christine's *The Book of the City of Ladies* (1405) the Ladies Reason, Justice and Rectitude appear to the author and encourage her to build a city (write a book) which defends women against the male authors who have previously denigrated them. One of the questions Christine asks concerns the lack of female lawyers, to which Reason responds:

> If anyone maintained that women do not possess enough understanding to learn the laws, the opposite is obvious from the proof afforded by experience, which is manifest and has been manifested in many women . . . who have been very great philosophers and have mastered fields far more complicated, subtle, and lofty than written laws and man-made institutions. (Pizan, 1983: 32)

Today, the inability of women to break through the 'glass ceiling' in the British legal system is notorious and a focus for attack by numerous women; moreover, in 1998 the Bar is increasingly being denounced for its discrimination against female pupils. As already suggested, these similarities do not mean that the attitude towards women lawyers is timeless and unchangeable, indeed, Christine herself termed those who held such a view, especially men, 'foolish', but again, it appears that certain ideologies have persisted, particularly with regard to the oppression of female independence, and that women who challenge masculine authority are marginalized today just as they were in Medieval Europe.

This marginalization is particularly important in terms of its effect upon women writers in the field of English literature, yet, as this essay is intended to show, it is no longer sufficient excuse to proclaim that no Medieval women may be included on the curriculum, first, because they didn't exist, or only in negligible numbers, and second, because there are no contextual studies or modern editions of primary material available. The range of background information about women's lives in the Medieval period is extensive as may be seen from the bibliography at the end of this essay. Of more specific interest here are works which discuss female authorship in the period and those which anthologize their writings.[5] I have already referred to several studies which offer useful discussions of women's literacy and the ways in which they were able to gain access to textual articulation; in addition, Meg Bogin's *The Women Troubadours* (1976), Peter Dronke's *Women Writers of the Middle Ages: A Critical Study of Texts from Perpetua (+203) to Marguerite Porete (+1310)* (1984), and Carol Meale's *Women and Literature in Britain, 1150–1500* (1993) provide useful critical analyses of individual writers. Amt's *Women's Lives in Medieval Europe* (1993) and Larrington's *Women and Writing in Medieval Europe* (1995) are both source books which cover different aspects of women's lives (for example, marriage, love, sex and friendship, women and the arts) offering useful examples of how men and women of the Middle Ages wrote about their own lives. In terms of primary material anthologies are still more common than individual works; for example, Barratt's *Women's Writing in Middle English* begins with the early Trotula texts with their advice on how to recreate virginity ('Forto mak streyt the prive membre') and concludes with Margaret Beaufort's warning against lust ('Lechery is enmy to all vertues and to alle goodnes') (Barratt, 1992: 37 and 307). Other useful collections which provide translated versions of the originals and which cover the whole of Europe rather than Barratt's Middle English remit include: Wilson's *Medieval Women Writers* (1984) and Elizabeth Petroff's *Medieval Women's Visionary Literature* (1986). In addition, this essay refers to specific editions of individual works and criticisms of particular authors, bibliographical details of which are provided in the relevant endnotes. Indeed, it is quite possible to construct a comprehensive reading programme in Medieval women's literature, perhaps centring it about Barratt's anthology and several paperback translations, such as *The Book of Margery Kempe*, Julian of Norwich's *Revelations of Divine Love* (1966) and Christine de Pizan's *The Book of the City of Ladies* (1983), supplementing this with passages from Amt and Larrington and selected essays from Dronke and Meale. Therefore, although there is still an enormous amount of work to be done to produce the choices available in relation to nineteenth- or twentieth-century women writers (for example, it is not possible to locate Middle English versions in a reasonably priced paperback for all texts, making for an unsatisfactory mixture of original and translated material), enough does exist to make reading in this field both lively and interesting.[6]

Certain common themes emerge from the background information, and it is useful to indicate those which are particularly important for the practice of women's writing. Most importantly, the link between education and authorship is an essential aspect of why women failed to produce as many texts as their male counterparts. At the same time, however, it is important to remember that levels of scholarship were neither static nor steadily improving throughout the period in question. Before the thirteenth century women in convents could expect a good education in Latin, although subsequently, with the economic decline of women's foundations and the development of the university system, nuns came increasingly to rely on the vernacular. Hence, the Anglo-Saxon abbess Hildelith and her nuns at Barking, Essex, were able to read quite complex Latin, while even in the later twelfth century Clemence and another nun of Barking, respectively, translated the life of St Catherine of Alexandria into Anglo-Norman verse, and composed a life of St Audrey based on a Latin original (Larrington, 1995: 186–94; and Barratt, 1992: 3). But, by the fourteenth century it is clearly assumed that nuns will not be familiar with Latin and works for them were written in English or French. For example, we know that Julian of Norwich could read and write in English, but her knowledge of Latin is far from certain (Julian of Norwich, 1966: 17 and 63). There are two issues arising from this information. First, that the modern tendency to assume that education improved gradually to its most recent status is inaccurate when discussing women's learning. While men might have gained access to an increasingly sophisticated and widespread area of scholarship, although even this is questionable, women certainly cannot claim a similar providential history. There have been periods in Britain's history when women have been more autonomous, more articulate and more economically independent than at others; Anglo-Saxon women appear to have had more educational opportunities than their Medieval counterparts, and, similarly, women in the sixteenth century seem to have benefited from the advent of Protestant humanism. The education of women is, therefore, not a constant, even within the period discussed here, and it is therefore necessary to excavate the immediate historical circumstances which allowed individual women to lay claim to an independent authorial voice.

The second point to be made concerns the way in which women actually wrote, their material experience of authorship; for example, although Margery Kempe could neither read nor write she produced the earliest known autobiography in English. The Proem to Margery's account explains her difficulties:

> Afterwards, when it pleased our Lord, he commanded and charged her that she should have written down her feelings and revelations, and her form of living, so that his goodness might be known to all the world.
> Then the creature had no writer who would fulfil her desire, nor give credence to her feelings . . .

After a while, however, she finds a scribe but his text is so poor that it is hard to read and she subsequently entreats a priest to make a good copy:

> Then there was such evil talk about this creature and her weeping, that the priest out of cowardice dared not speak with her but seldom, nor would write as he had promised the said creature.

Eventually, after more delays and hindrances the priest accepts the task:

> The priest, trusting in her prayers, began to read this book, and it was much easier, as he thought, than it was before. And so he read over every word of it in this creature's presence, she sometimes helping where there was any difficulty. (Kempe, 1985: 35–6)

This is a graphic description both of the obstacles an illiterate woman had to overcome if she wanted to have her words written down, as well as the manner in which women were able to dictate their text to a scribe and even to 'edit' their own work. The assumption implicit throughout Margery's negotiations is, of course, that women should not write, as Julia Boffey points out:

> No one, over the course of the twenty years during which she awaited God's commandment to publish her visions, or during the course of the four or five years during which the priest struggled with the first scribe's handwriting, seems to have suggested the practical solution that she should learn to write. (Boffey, 1993: 163)

It was not just lower-class women such as Margery, however, who used scribes, as Larrington makes clear,

> the skills of reading (which many women were able to do) and of writing were regarded as separate. In twelfth-century England, for example, a well-educated noble lady would be expected to be able to read three languages: Latin, French and English, but writing was a skill for scribes, who earned their living by it. (Larrington, 1995: 222)

Nevertheless, scribes were not only employed by women, men also used others to write for them without any notion that this would in some way make the text less of a personal statement. The Medieval concept of 'authorship' must therefore be recognized as quite different from a twentieth-century view, in that while the men and women may be said to have 'authorized' the writing, they might not have wielded the pen themselves and their words might well have been interpreted, translated or amended by a scribe, clerk or spiritual advisor.[7]

The link between education and authorship is important, but as the above analysis has suggested, there is no consistency in female education throughout the Middle Ages, nor is there an automatic bond between literacy and women's ability to produce texts, although a noble, educated, literate woman, like Christine de Pizan had decidedly more opportunities as a writer than the unlettered, lower-class Margery Kempe. Clearly, therefore, Medieval women – at both ends of the social spectrum – could and did become authors. Why then are there so few works available? Barratt points to the practical difficulties, 'the lack of a carrel (the medieval equivalent of a room of one's own), of pens and parchment, of peace and quiet', and it is significant that the majority of female authors from this period wrote from within the sheltered atmosphere of the convent and not from the hectic domesticity of a house replete with husband, children and livestock. Yet Barratt also suggests that 'the real obstacles were as much psychological as practical' and that, since 'authorship' denoted 'authority' it was extremely difficult for a woman to extract herself from her interpellated position as an inferior within the dominant ideology (Barratt, 1992: 5). The women already quoted in this chapter support such a hypothesis: Marguerite Porete adopts the marginalized role of the heretic, remaining silent and refusing to defend herself when on trial, Marie de France while dabbling in the ethos of courtly love is careful to preserve the chastity of her heroine, Clare of Assisi composed a rule whereby the enclosing of women within safe boundaries is taken to an extreme, and Margery Kempe cautiously waits for God's command before she attempts to begin her textual activities. Only Christine de Pizan remains vibrantly autonomous in her gendered role and, yet, she too employs all her rhetorical skills and argumentative intricacies in order to present women in a radically new light. The impossibility of escaping one's own ideology is now a commonplace of historicist criticism and it is essential to recall that while women did write in the Medieval period, by doing so they were in direct rebellion with their own societies. The choices afforded those women who wished to become authors were therefore limited, increasingly so after the Anglo-Saxon period and before the sixteenth century. But certain strategies were employed to overcome the 'psychological' barriers referred to by Barratt, some of which have already been implied in the foregoing argument. For example, marginal and excessive positions (Porete and Clare) could be adopted, thereby stressing a difference and alienation from that which was the accepted convention, or a higher authority could be claimed (Margery) placing God's authority over the patriarchal laws of the secular world. In the subsequent two sections, on spiritual and secular literatures, I intend to examine the ways in which Medieval women were able to challenge social practices and gain an independent textual identity.

Abandoning oneself to God

Margery Kempe's quest for authentication of her spiritual experiences at one point took her to Norwich where she visited Julian:

> And then she was commanded by our Lord to go to an anchoress in the same city who was called Dame Julian. And so she did, and told her about the grace, that God had put into her soul, of compunction, contrition, sweetness and devotion, compassion with holy meditation and high contemplation, and very many holy speeches and converse that our Lord spoke to her soul, and also many wonderful revelations, which she described to the anchoress to find out if there were any deception in them, for the anchoress was expert in such things and could give good advice.

Julian's encouraging response is duly recorded:

> 'I pray God grant you perseverance. Set all your trust in God and do not fear the talk of the world, for the more contempt, shame and reproof that you have in this world, the more is your merit in the sight of God.' (Kempe, 1985: 77–8)

Margery is careful to note that it is God who authorizes her audience with Julian, but at the same time she endows the anchoress with her own authority; Julian is an 'expert' and offers 'good advice'. Interestingly, Julian reinforces Margery's dependence upon and assertion of God's will, and explicitly tells her not to worry about 'the talk of the world', in other words, the misogynistic attacks she has already been subjected to. Both women call upon the spiritual authority of God to override the patriarchal conventions of their own society, and both employ 'revelations' as a means to legitimize their own voices within the Christian discourse. As Petroff points out, the role of a female mystic offered considerable freedom to Medieval women:

> Visions were a socially sanctioned activity that freed a woman from conventional female roles by identifying her as a genuine religious figure. They brought her to the attention of others, giving her a public language she could use to teach and learn. . . . She could be an exemplar for other women, and out of her own experience she could lead them to fuller self-development. Finally, visions allowed the medieval woman to be an artist, composing and refining her most profound experiences into a form that she could create and recreate for herself throughout her entire life. (1986: 6)

Therefore, even if a woman lacked the scholarly education of a male clerk, her visionary experience was as legitimate as his textual authority. What I want to suggest here, however, is that the visions of individual women did not have to exist in isolation from one another, Margery's dialogue with Julian being a case in point. Indeed, Margery draws upon the works of other women mystics in the account of her own visionary experience; apart from the broad similarities between the spiritual experiences of Margery and the Italian mystic Angela of Foligno and the Prussian visionary Dorothea of Montau (Margery visited the areas where both had lived during her pilgrimages), there are explicit references to the lives of Bridget of Sweden, Mary of Oignies and Elizabeth of Hungary. Margery tells how a sympathetic priest read 'St Bride's book' to her and how in a vision God says to her,

'For in truth I tell you, just as I spoke to St Bridget, just so I speak to you, daughter, and I tell you truly that every word that is written in Bridget's book is true, and through you shall be recognised as truth indeed.' (Kempe, 1985: 182 and 183)

Moreover she would have been in Rome when Bridget was canonized. The resemblances between Margery, Mary of Oignies and Elizabeth of Hungary are considerable, particularly with regard to their constant weeping; indeed, when Margery is attacked by the church for obsessive crying, her priest/scribe is reconciled to these demonstrations partly because of the examples of Mary and Elizabeth:

he read of a woman called Mary of Oignies, and of her manner of life . . . of the abundant tears that she wept, which made her so weak and feeble that she could not endure to look upon the cross, nor hear our Lord's Passion repeated without dissolving into tears of pity and compassion. . . . Elizabeth of Hungary also cried with a loud voice, as is written in her treatise. (191–3)

Margery thus draws authentication for her visions and behaviour from other women mystics, she evokes their support, either verbally as in the case of Julian, or via their example as with Bridget, Mary of Oignies and Elizabeth of Hungary, in order to endorse her own spiritual work. There are a number of further parallels between women mystics and Margery affirming that she participated in a widespread visionary discourse that was specifically open to women, but the direct references in her text imply a more succinct and self-aware appropriation of a public female voice.[8] For example, Margery asserts that it is her particular duty to convey Bridget's words, and that only through her revoicing will the 'text' be recognized as true. Rather than accepting that Medieval women wrote in isolation with each authoress creating her own textual tradition, it appears that later writers drew upon a gendered discourse in which female voices could be called upon for authentication and verification.[9]

Such 'sisterly' support was, perhaps, necessary in a society which rejected female spiritual authority and where convention ensured that the truth of women's mystical experiences was always questioned. The priest who wrote down Margery's story only accepted her weeping as an outer manifestation of her inner holy state when he encountered the examples of Mary of Oignies and Elizabeth of Hungary, other female mystics, and Julian warns of the 'contempt, shame, and reproof' Margery will experience from a doubting world. Even if then, a woman could summon God's authority, even if there were female exemplars she could draw upon, by choosing to voice her own visionary experiences she challenged the dominant patriarchal ideology and constructed herself as a radical at the margins of her society.

Discussions of Margery Kempe's work have consistently located her radicalism in the personal vibrancy of her utterance; for example, Sidonie Smith comments that,

her text both imitated conventions of official life stories, accepting the ideological requirements of female purity and subordination to man, and somehow escaped them by wrenching the autobiographical form to serve the purposes of her own desire for power and authority. (1987: 83)

Thus, Margery Kempe activated the double-voiced identity necessary for her work, both personal and textual, to be accepted; she both conforms, 'female purity', and challenges, 'her own desire for power and authority'. Initially, therefore, it would appear that Julian and Margery were very different, in that the anchoress's measured utterances and enclosed lifestyle would have presented a far more acceptable identity than that of the garrulous and headstrong townswoman. Yet, in her own way, Julian was as radical as Margery Kempe.

Julian of Norwich (1342–*c.*1416) believed herself to be terminally ill at the age of 30/31 and gazing at the cross received fifteen 'showings' related to Christ; during the night she was assailed by devils, but in the morning banished her doubts and was granted a final confirmatory vision. Julian, of course, did not die, living to write down a short version of her mystical experience immediately, and then, some twenty years later, to enlarge upon her first endeavour with a longer and more meditative version, *Revelations of Divine Love.*[10] Julian's desire to suffer with Christ and her tripartite division of her experience into understanding, suffering and a material sign of God's grace is quite conventional, but she departs from the normal bounds of visionary literature in two important ways. First, Julian emphasizes God's love and fails to acknowledge that God can be wrathful; this assertion that souls will be saved is certainly not orthodox. More important for a feminist approach is Julian's second departure from the authorized church doctrine in her description of Jesus as a woman, or more specifically as 'mother' in relation to God the 'father':

> Thus in our Father, God almighty, we have our being. In our merciful Mother we have reformation and renewal. . . . In yielding to the gracious impulse of the Holy Spirit we are made perfect.

She then goes on to justify this gender allocation:

> A mother's is the most intimate, willing, and dependable of all services, because it is the truest of all. None has been able to fulfil it properly but Christ and he alone can. We know that our own mother's bearing of us was a bearing to pain and death, but what does Jesus our true Mother do? Why, he, All-love, bears us to joy and eternal life! (Julian of Norwich, 1966: 166 and 169)

The idea of Christ as 'mother' was not original to Julian and it is possible to support her ideas both from the Bible (Isaiah xlix: 1 and 15 and lxvi: 13, and Matthew xxiii: 37) and from the church fathers (St Anselm and St Bernard), yet the gendered attribution was hardly commonplace.[11] Moreover, by insisting upon the importance of motherhood, 'truest of all', and by linking the discussion to the material aspects of childbearing, 'pain and death', Julian asserts the importance of women to the origins of Christianity itself. Female significance is, however, skilfully entwined in the rhetorical strategies of the text; for example, Julian clearly privileges motherhood but at the same time says that only Christ may fulfil the role properly. Then, in a further twist she compares our bodily birth 'pain and death', with our spiritual birth into 'joy and eternal life'. This makes perfect sense in theological terms, in that the human mother produces a mortal child who must die (and, presumably the woman carries connotations of Eve whose original transgression led to the fall from grace), and in that Christ died on the cross in order to save humankind and so 'gives birth' to our immortal souls. Yet, the conjunction of 'pain and death' simultaneously with the concept of childbirth as well as with the image of the crucifixion, shifts the significa-tion to encompass both the mother's own suffering and possible demise, in addition to Christ's torment and anguish on the cross. While ostensibly adhering to the conventions of gender difference and to the hierarchical positioning of Christ before any woman, Julian manipulates her text in order to deconstruct the traditional roles she overtly supports, drawing male and female bodily experience into the same subjectivity and further emphasizing the equivalence of Christ and/as the mother. Although very different in their manner of radicalism, Julian and Margery form part of a strong and cogent discourse which proclaimed the importance of female roles and women's experience within the Medieval church.

The tradition of female spiritual literature in England was reinforced with transla-tions into Middle English of works originally written in Latin, and it is likely that Margery's references to 'St Bride's book', the life of Mary of Oignies and Elizabeth of Hungary's 'treatise' fell into this category; extracts from Bridget's *Revelations* and *The Revelations of Saint Elizabeth* are anthologized in Barratt's *Women's Writing in Middle English* (Barratt, 1992: 84–94 and 71–83).[12] Indeed, the most explicit reference, after Julian of Norwich, to another woman mystic in Margery's book is to Bridget of Sweden (*c*.1302–73). Bridget was a noblewoman who, after having been widowed in 1344, experienced a series of visions which encouraged her to establish a double order for nuns and monks and, as such, she became the first woman in the Western church to found a religious order. Although Bridget did not herself become a nun, she was active in papal circles and, due to her charity when alive and miracles attributed to her after her death, she was canonized in 1391. Bridget was a popular saint in Medieval England; apart from the reference to her by the unlettered Margery Kempe, who would only have had access to the well-known saints, a major Bridgettine house was founded by Henry V at Syon in 1415, which became conspicuous for its influence at court and for its scholarship. Bridget's *Revelations* participate in the maternal dis-course already voiced by Julian (this will also recur in the writing of Dame Eleanor Hull referred to below), but her visions offer a more experiential version of mother-hood in the depiction of the nativity:

> then I sawe that gloryus and blysshyd chylde lyinge upon the harde erth all nakyd, ful fayre, whyte and clene. The flesshe off hys moost gloryus body was then ful clene and pure frome al fylth and unclennes. . . . Then the wombe of the Vyrgyn that was very grete afore the byrth, yt swagyd and wythdrewe inwarde agayn to the state that yt was in afore she conceyvyd. And then her body was off a mervelus and off ryght grete beuty and fayrnes and ful plesaunt to beholde. (Barratt, 1992: 88)

Bridget, who had eight children herself, uses her own knowledge of childbirth in a manner impossible for the male cleric, commenting upon the, usual, 'fylth and unclennes' of the baby's body as it emerges from the womb, and on the, usual, distended form of a woman's 'belly' after pregnancy. What she offers is an idealized version in which the patriarchal condemnation of the womb as unclean is refuted, and the woman is returned to her maiden-like shape making her, once more, an ideal of beauty. Indeed, in this latter almost wish-fulfilment image Bridget does not veer far from the advice columns in twentieth-century magazines on pregnancy which strongly advocate pre- and post-natal exercises to 'return you to your shape'. The ideal female body, then, appears to have remained resolutely that of the flat-stomached girl, rather than the round-stomached mother. The combination of pat-riarchal convention and a challenge to male authority – medical, social and religious – in the passage above conforms with the strategies we have already noted in the works of Margery and Julian, where women writers must work within and at the edges of their own gendered construction.

The actual identity of Elizabeth of Hungary cannot firmly be ascertained although Barratt suggests that Elizabeth of Toess (*c.*1294–1336) is the most likely candidate for the authorship of the revelations. This Elizabeth was the daughter of the King of Hungary and a Dominican nun; the description of her visions was taken down by another nun and eventually translated into Middle English. Elizabeth's similarity with Margery is based mainly on her weeping, but her own independent voice and the dominance of the other women portrayed in her text also suggest a matching sense of individual autonomy. For example, when the Virgin Mary describes the annunciation to Elizabeth in a vision, the Virgin characterizes herself in a dynamic role, rather than as the passive woman of Christian convention:

> I beganne to thynke and desyre wyth wylfull brennyng herte yf I myght doo ony thyng or have in me for the whiche God wolde lette me never parte from hym. And whan I thought thus, I rose up and went to a book and beganne to rede in it. And in the fyrst openyng of the book came before my syght the worde of Esaye the prophete, *Ecce, virgo concipiet et pariet filium etc.* That is, 'Loo, a mayden shall conceyve and bere a sonne' etc. And as I bethought me, thynkyng that maydenhode pleased moche to God, sythen he wolde hys sonne sholde be born of a mayde, thenne I purposed in my herte, for the reverence of hym, to kepe maydenhode and, yf it befyll me to see hyr, forto serve hyr in maydenhede all my lyf tyme and, yf it nedyd, forto goo wyth hyr thorugh all the worlde . . . the next nyght folowyng . . . I herde a voyce clerely seyeng to me, 'Mayden of Davyd kynred, thou shalt bere my sonne.' (Barratt, 1992: 78–9)

On one level Elizabeth's version is perfectly traditional in that Mary only thinks this way because God is in the process of readying her to bear Christ, and the vision of her reading the book accords perfectly with the numerous artistic representations of the annunciation. However, the vocabulary hardly resembles that of a passive woman: the words 'thynke', 'desyre' and 'wylfull' linked to the persistent use of 'I' suggest a self-aware and purposeful subjectivity. Moreover, the suggestion that Mary wishes to remain a 'mayden' in order to serve the chosen 'mayde' sounds very much like a rhetorical device, a disclaimer which serves merely to uncover her active desire to bear the child herself, as of course Elizabeth the listener, as well as the reader, already knows she will do. In Elizabeth's version of the annunciation, therefore, Mary is an active participant in the Christian narrative, indeed, within the chronology of the text it appears as if the Virgin thought of her role as Christ's mother *before* the angel descends from heaven to tell her so. Again, Elizabeth articulates a double identity in which her voice may be read as conventional at the same time as it suggests a more radical view of female experience.

The women discussed so far in this section are relatively well known, Margery and Julian being staples of the Medieval literary canon and Bridget and Elizabeth being supported by Christian scholarship. Before moving on to secular writing, however, I should like to draw upon Barratt's anthology to suggest the inclusion of three further works which are interesting in themselves and would provide useful material for those studying this field. The first is an anonymous account of a dream, while the other two are attributed to noblewomen, Dame Eleanor Hull and Lady Margaret Beaufort (Barratt, 1992: 163–76, 219–31, 279–81 and 301–10). *A Revelation Showed to a Holy Woman* was written in the early fifteenth century but, although it is possible to verify several of the names mentioned in the text, the author remains anonymous. The work is a prose letter which recounts several dreams in which the author witnesses the suffering of her friend, the nun Margaret, in purgatory; Margaret asks the dreamer to offer up prayers for her soul and when this is done a final vision shows her taken up to heaven by the Virgin. The work itself is fascinating in its account of Margaret's sufferings which are detailed in a racy and sensational manner:

> . . . and me thoghte I sawe abowte hir seven devylles, and one of tham clede hir with a longe gown and a longe trayle folowyng hir, and it was full of scharpe hukes [hooks] withinn, and the gowne and the hukes me thoghte were alle rede fyre. And than the same devell tok wormes and pykk [pitch] and tarre and made lokkes [locks, of hair] and sete tham appon hir hede, and he toke a grete longe neddir [adder] and putt all bowte hir hede and that, me thoghte, hissed in hir hede, as it had bene hote brynnyng iryn in the colde water; and me thoghte scho cryed when scho was so arrayede, als me thoghte that alle the werlde myghte hafe herde hir. And the littill hounde and the catt forfette in sondir [chewed to pieces] hir legges and hir armes. (Barratt, 1992: 168)

The form of Margaret's punishment is suitably gendered; she is portrayed as a fashionable lady with a long train, a crown-like head-dress and attendant pets, the horror of her ordeal arising from the fact that the dress has hooks on its inside, the head-dress is a venomous snake and the dog and cat maul their mistress. The devil responsible identifies itself as 'foule stynkkyng pryde' and thus affirms the traditional representation of this vice, or its punishment, in the form of a woman. Margaret is also punished by the devils 'slewth' [sloth] and 'glotonye':

> And than me thoghte this devele and that other devele cutt awaye hir flesche and hyr lyppes, and thirste the huke into hir herte. And than thay drewe hir into a grete blake water [lake] and that semyd als colde als any ise [ice], and mekyll [much] therof was freside [frozen] to my syghte; and therin thay keste [cast] hir and possede [pushed] hir up and down . . . (Barratt, 1992: 170)

The tortures continue, here with the references to 'lyppes', 'herte' and the immersion of Margaret's body carrying an underlying voyeuristic eroticism not dissimilar to that employed in the early saints' lives.[13] Indeed, when Margaret is finally redeemed by the Virgin, her body symbolically washed clean and 'a crowne sett one her hede and a septre in hir hande' her story increasingly resembles that of the virgin martyrs such as St Margaret and St Katherine, transforming the sinful Margaret and the fallen womanhood she represents into an idealized and triumphal version of female saintliness and Christian perfection (Barratt, 1992: 175).[14]

The 'Holy Woman' whose dreams of purgatory are referred to above was almost certainly not a nun, but lived a devout existence in the secular world; the same may be verified about the last two authors, both of whom were noblewomen, active in the dynastic manipulations and political alliances of the later Middle Ages. Perhaps their worldly knowledge and their actual experience of motherhood gave them the impetus to concentrate upon female roles and bodies, especially that of the Virgin Mary, although both were translating rather than originating their material. At this point it is important to note that translation did not function in the same fashion as today; Medieval (and, indeed, Renaissance) translators were allowed to alter and reform their work, rather than search for as accurate and faithful a rendition as possible. Dame Eleanor Hull (*c*.1394–1460) was a member of the Lancastrian household who was deeply religious; she translated, from the French, two works, *The Seven Psalms* (the penitential psalms and a commentary upon them) and *Meditations upon the Seven Days of the Week* (supposedly selections from the writings of St Augustine, St Anselm and St Bernard). In the latter text the Saturday meditation is on the Five Joys of the Virgin and contains an account of the annunciation, which covers, in a manner not dissimilar to that of Bridget, a description of Mary's womb. Eleanor employs an authoritative tone in her repeated avowals of the Virgin's bodily cleanliness:

> . . . in the wombe of that *purist* vyrgyne clothyd it with here most *puryst* flesshe and bloode' . . . whan ye bare in your right *swete* and *clene* wombe . . . in that chambre that was moste *clene* and *pure* and beste arayed with chastyte . . . that it sholde be *clene* and *feyre* and fulle of beaute. [italics mine] (Barratt, 1992: 228–9)

In her commentary Barratt rightly points out that women's 'wombs, in the writings of Medieval gynaecologists were very far from "sweet and clean"', and she goes on to suggest that while Eleanor Hull idealizes the Virgin Mary's womb she merely identifies an exception to the conventional view of female anatomy, which means that the figure of Mary, simultaneously 'encourages and stifles women's aspirations' (Barratt, 1992: 220). Yet, if Eleanor Hull appears to lack the forceful and independent approach of the earlier religious female authors, such as Bridget and Margery, the last writer to be considered in this section might be seen as drawing a line at the end of female visionary radicalism before the advent of the Renaissance with its increased intellectual freedom for women. Lady Margaret Beaufort (1443–1509) occupied the most elevated social position of all the English women considered here, in that she was the mother of Henry VII, but her depictions of women in her translation, *The Mirror of Gold to the Sinful Soul* (from the French version of the Carthusian Latin text, *Speculum Aureum*) are almost misogynistic in tone.[15] Rapes are clearly seen to be the fault of the woman, and the womb, praised to excess by Eleanor Hull, is summarily dismissed as impure:

> And yf thou beholde and consyder well what mete thou art norisshed with in thy moders wombe, truly noon other but with corrupt and infect blod, as well is knowen by many phylosophers and other great clerkes. (Barratt, 1992: 306)

If this section commences with the repudiation of patriarchal authority by one woman (Julian) to another (Margery), then it concludes with the capitulation of a woman author (Margaret Beaufort) to male textual precedent – 'great clerkes'. Moreover, the argument with which I began has shifted in its remit, for instead of only identifying a mutually supportive female spiritual discourse, the absolute need of a tradition of women writers for other, subsequent, female authors has become apparent.

'Those ladies who have been abandoned for so long'

One of the most flamboyant and well-known Medieval women must surely be Joan of Arc (*c*.1412–31); perceived as a saint by the French and an unnatural, devilish woman by the English, she is a self-enclosed model of the double standards of female identity. Not only did she dress in men's clothes while simultaneously asserting her female sex as 'The Maid', but she also breached the divide between national politics and spiritual vision seeing no internal contradictions in her curious amalgam of worldly and holy, male and female, significations. A letter sent by Joan to the English at Poitiers makes this point clear:

> Return to the [Maid], who is sent by God, the King of Heaven, the keys of all the towns which you have seized and ravaged in France. (Larrington, 1995: 182)

Joan's perception of herself did not, however, extend to an identification with other women; like Elizabeth I in her Tilbury speech, Joan sets herself up as an exception to the accepted norms of gendered behaviour and not as an example of radicalism for other women to emulate. Nevertheless, these restrictions did not prevent Christine de Pizan (1365–1429) from transforming the martial maid into a 'feminist' ideal; in Christine's poem 'Ditié de Jehanne d'Arc' she praises Joan:

> Oh! What honour for the female sex! It is perfectly obvious that God has special regard for it when all these wretched people who destroyed the whole Kingdom – now recovered and made safe by a woman – something that five thousand men could not have done – and the traitors have been exterminated. Before the event they would have scarcely believed this possible. (Larrington, 1995: 163)

Christine transplants Joan's battle from the realm of national politics into the field of sexual politics; she is as much concerned to stress the way in which 'a woman' has accomplished more than 'five thousand men', as she is commenting upon the safety of the kingdom of France, and the indeterminate 'they' of the last line could refer equally to men and the English. Medieval examples of female accomplishment, power and fame, are relatively few and, even if the original rejected her sexual identity or indeed, was drawn from fiction and mythology, a woman writer interested in establishing a diachronic line of female influence or a synchronic plane of mutual activity by women, clearly felt free to employ whatever material came to hand. An example of this process of reworking may be found in Margery Kempe's evocation of Bridget of Sweden, but Christine de Pizan's accomplished manipulation of her textual authorities and material antecedents is supremely self-conscious in its political positioning and in its choice of literary form. Of all the women writers to be considered in this essay Christine is the most skilful and refined, and her works were popular during her own life, being copied many times, as well as being readily available today in paperback translations.[16]

Christine de Pizan received a good education and, when she was widowed and left penniless in 1390, she supported herself, her three children, her mother and a niece by becoming, first a copyist, and then a highly-regarded author, composing prose and poetry for members of the French court. As such, she was France's first professional woman writer. She is of interest to twentieth-century feminist criticism because of her attack against the misogynistic, but highly acclaimed, work, *Le Roman de la Rose*, which she accused of defaming and misrepresenting women, and because of her subsequent defences of women, the foremost of which is *The Book of the City of Ladies*.[17] While it is necessary to recognize that Christine cannot be termed a 'feminist' in the twentieth-century sense of the term, her literary forays in support of the female sex against the overwhelming forces of patriarchal textual authority cannot but be admired. Christine's trite moralisms might be unpalatable for today's readership, but her radical voice must be set alongside her more conventional, and probably more profitable, writings; she too has a doubled persona who exists within her own society as well as along the margins of change.

In *The Book of the City of Ladies* Christine maintains her dextrous balancing act between reasoned argument, which appears as traditionalist, and a forceful defence of women against male clerical authority. At the beginning of the work she adopts a fictional second-self who sits, in archetypal Medieval fashion, reading a book, on this occasion one by Matheolus, until she is interrupted by her mother who calls her to come to dinner. Yet, the following morning Christine is drawn reluctantly back to a consideration of the same work:

> But just the sight of this book, even though it was of no authority, made me wonder how it happened that so many different men – and learned men among them – have been and are so inclined to express both in speaking and in their treatises and writings so many wicked insults about women and their behaviour. Not only one or two and not even just this Matheolus (for this book had a bad name anyway and was intended as a satire) but, more generally, judging from the treatises of all philosophers and poets and from all the orators – it would take too long to mention their names – it seems that they all speak from one and the same mouth. They all concur in one conclusion: that the behaviour of women is inclined to and full of every vice. (Pizan, 1983: 3–4)

At first Christine is puzzled by this conclusion since her experience of female behaviour, her own and 'other women whose company I frequently kept', suggests that the male authorities are wrong, but she reluctantly bows to their superior knowledge since,

> it would be impossible that so many famous men – such solemn scholars possessed of such deep and great understanding, and so clear-sighted in all things, as it seemed – could have spoken falsely on so many occasions, (Pizan, 1983: 4)

and concludes by detesting herself 'and the entire feminine sex, as though we were monstrosities in nature', and finally turning to God in her anguish (Pizan, 1983: 5). At this point three ladies appear to Christine in a blaze of light proclaiming themselves to be Reason, Justice and Rectitude and informing the mortal woman that they have come to help her in her divinely ordained task of building a city (writing a book) to defend women,

> so that from now on, ladies and all valiant women may have a refuge and defence against the various assailants, those ladies who have been abandoned for so long, exposed like a field without a surrounding hedge, without finding a champion to afford them an adequate defense. (Pizan, 1983: 10)

Christine accepts her role as the defender of women and they set off to the 'Field of Letters' where the City of Ladies will be founded/written (Pizan, 1983: 4–16). Indeed, there is a wonderful Medieval illustration of Christine and Reason working on the Field of Letters, hoeing out the weeds of misogyny.[18] However, to return to the initial narrative of *The City*, I should like to indicate the way in which, while genuflecting to those 'many famous men', the author undermines male textual authority from the very beginning of her text. Matheolus's book is immediately rendered unimportant by the more important call to dinner by Christine's mother, but she underlines its negligible value further by saying it had 'no authority' and also had a 'bad name'. The condemnation is then broadened to all misogynistic writers who are seen to have made 'wicked insults' against women, and who are, with a skilful rhetorical turning of the tables ('one and the same mouth'), depersonalized and objectified. Christine's literary dexterity is employed to complete her attack when she ironically over-praises male authors ('so many . . . such . . . such . . . so'), only to twist this eulogy with the final words, 'as it seemed'. The basis of her argument in defence of women is surprisingly similar to those of the spiritual female writers discussed above, for she claims, first, that experience is as important as textual authority, and second, that her work is divinely inspired. However, perhaps it is the surprising number of women involved in such a short passage (Christine, her mother, her friends, Lady Reason, Lady Justice, Lady Rectitude and the other ladies and valiant women of the past and present), all working for, or desiring, the defence of women against misogyny, that ultimately divides the world into a gendered opposition with Christine as 'champion' of the female forces. As Maureen Quilligan points out in *The Allegory of Female Authority: Christine de Pizan's Cité des Dames* (1991), in her book,

> Christine de Pizan seriously begins not only to revise her *auctores*, but to rewrite history. (Quilligan, 1991: 68)

For, not only does Christine refute the misogynistic patriarchal textual tradition, she self-consciously founds an all-female counter-tradition in which women writers played an essential part.

In one of the quotations above Christine de Pizan refers to women as 'abandoned' in a manner similar to that employed in the first section of this essay; she points out that they have been forsaken by,

> those noble men who are required by order of law to protect them, who by negligence and apathy have allowed them to be mistreated. (Pizan, 1983: 10)

This is hardly the stuff of courtly love, that ideal by which the Medieval nobility were supposed to conduct their lives. But Christine's view of extramarital activity, of illicit love and of the flirtations of adultery bears little resemblance to the idyllic songs and entangled narratives of the romance authors. Several sections of *The City* are devoted precisely to challenging the view of marriage as constraining and loveless that allowed the ideal of courtly love to flourish. Rectitude gives examples of those women who have shown great love for their husbands, of those women who are both beautiful and chaste, and of those women who are constant. But, perhaps the most significant exchange occurs when Christine points out:

> I am . . . troubled and grieved when men argue that many women want to be raped and that it does not bother them at all to be raped by men even when they verbally protest,

to which Rectitude quickly responds,

> chaste ladies, who live honestly take absolutely no pleasure in being raped. Indeed, rape is the greatest possible sorrow for them. (Pizan, 1983: 160–1)

The sexual advances made to Margery Kempe (quoted at the beginning of this essay) would quickly be classified by Christine as offering 'absolutely no pleasure', although, of course, Margery finds the illicit approach erotically stimulating, and she later reinterprets her desire as a temptation of the devil. The rule for a woman who wishes to sustain her social position is clearly laid down by Christine, while Margery provides both an acknowledgement of such a dictum and a personal expression of how such strictures could be broken. Indeed, in *The Treasure of the City of Ladies*, a book which acts as a manual for female behaviour, Christine explicitly warns against being too friendly with men:

> there is absolutely no doubt that women, whoever they may be, who delight in being friendly with many men, and even if they do not think that there is anything wrong with it, but rather that it is for laughter and amusement, will scarcely be able to continue these friendships without their being talked about unfavourably, and not only by envious strangers who ceaselessly consider how they can abuse others, but, indeed, even by many of those same men with whom the women are friendly. For women do not suspect that before these men have frequented them for very long some or most of them will try to seduce them if they can. (Pizan, 1985: 115)

Rather than idealizing courtly love, Christine de Pizan emphasizes the dangers to the woman – both social and physical – of any relationship with a man that may be construed as informal. Instead of tracing the erotic path of romantic desire, she warns of the loss of social standing and the threat of rape.

In some ways this is a rather harsh judgement and should not be equally applied to all Medieval men! If we turn to the Paston letters, for example, the two brothers present very different forms of masculine behaviour. John II is, perhaps, one of those men of whom Christine cautions, for he certainly entered into a number of sexual dalliances, never marrying and constantly incurring his mother's (Margaret Paston) disapproval; one of her earliest letters instructs him to,

> beware of your expense better (than) ye have be before this time, and be your own purse-bearer. (Paston Family, 1983: 100)[19]

Meanwhile, John II's younger brother, John III, appears as a dutiful son and constant and loving husband; it is to John III that his mother appeals when she is in need of aid:

> . . . letting you weet that mine cousin Clere [Elizabeth Clere] hath sent to me for the 100 mark that I borrowed of her for your brother . . .. And send me an answer thereof in haste if ye will my welfare, for I shall never be in quiet till I know an end in this; for she hath therefor an obligation of £100, and it is not kept close – there been many persons now knowen it, which meseemeth a great rebuke to me that I departed so largely with your brother that I reserved not to pay that I was in danger for him, and so have divers said to me which of late have known it. And when I remembered it it is to mine heart a very spear, considering that he never gave me comfort therein, nor of all the money that he hath received will never make shift therefor. (Paston Family, 1983: 202–3)

Moreover, despite the plans for a noble alliance mooted by John II, John III appears to have made 'a love match'; certainly his wife-to-be, Margery Brews, addressed him as 'my very well-beloved Valentine' and assures him that,

> . . . if ye command me to keep me true wherever I go
> Iwis I will do all my might you to love and never no mo.
> And if my friends say that I do amiss, they shall not me let so for to do.
> Mine heart me bids evermore to love you
> Truly, over all earthly thing.
> And if they be never so wroth, I trust it shall be better in time coming.
> (Paston Family, 1983: 234)

It should be pointed out immediately, however, that the arrangement of the above lines into poetic form was undertaken by the editor, Norman Davis, and in the manuscript version they are written down as prose. Then, again, as Margery Brews used a scribe, Thomas Kela, the actual structure of the text ceases to belong solely to her as 'author', and, in any event, the discourse she employs is, regardless of form, that of courtly love. The presentation of herself in the role of servant, 'if ye command me', the suggestion of opposition, 'If my friends say that I do amiss', and her vocabulary, 'true', 'love', 'heart' and 'truly', all combine in a representation of the courtly lady writing to her lover. Margery was correct in her interpretation of opposition, since her father only reluctantly agreed to the match and John II was opposed since his mother had offered the young couple the manor of Sparham, which although hers to give, would at her death otherwise have gone to John II and not John

III. She was also accurate in her choice of discourse, since John III had been a retainer at court and would, as such, have been familiar with the language of courtly love, indeed, he uses it himself in another letter:

> please accept this note as my messenger to remember me to you most faithfully and to say that I above all other men wish to know that you are in good health . . . and, mistress, although I have given you little cause to remember me for lack of acquaintance, yet please do not forget me when you count up your suitors . . . and now farewell, my own fair lady. (Paston Family, 1981: 187)[20]

The 'mistress' addressed above, however, is not Margery Brews, but another woman called Anne, and is only one of a series of letters, all employing the language of courtly love, in which John III addresses potential brides. Of course, it is impossible to know whether Margery herself was the author of love letters to suitors other than John, and with so little evidence available, a gender distinction – women as true, men as fickle – is impossible to make. What is clear, however, is that for a skilful courtier like John III courtly love was a linguistic tool to be employed in the serious negotiations for a bride, and, incidentally, in letters of service to his lord and lady (Watt, 1993: 122–38). There is no question, for Margery and John III, of sexually consummating the relationship before marriage, and the overall impression given is that in making this politically advantageous union the woman and man involved were coincidentally lucky in that it matched their personal desires.

The Paston papers also contain an account of a more dramatic relationship, this time between Margery Paston, daughter to Margaret and sister to the two Johns, and Richard Calle, the family's bailiff. The first hint that something is wrong occurs when Margaret writes to John II asking him to remove Margery from the house to reside with 'my Lady of Oxford or with my Lady of Bedford', and it quickly emerges that Margery had fallen in love with Calle, her social inferior and therefore, for the Pastons, an undesirable match. Despite the opposition the two conducted a private and clandestine betrothal (legally binding in the Medieval period) and hence considered themselves married. Margaret called in the Bishop of Norwich to determine whether or not their pledges were binding, and when he reluctantly affirmed that they were, the family broke all contact with the disgraced couple. None of Margery's letters survive, if they existed at all, but one of Calle's to her remains extant in which he addresses her as 'Mine own lady and mistress', and bemoans their situation in courtly fashion,

> meseemeth it is a thousand year ago sin that I spake with you . . . Alas, alas, good lady, full little remember they what they do that keep us thus asunder. (Paston Family, 1983: 178–9)

When the material equivalent of courtly love entered the real world of marriage negotiations and threatened to disrupt political alliances, as well as economic and class status, the ideal was quickly thrust aside and the individual threatened with disgrace and social isolation.

From the examples of Medieval women's writing quoted here, those of Christine de Pizan and the Paston women in this section and those of Marie de France and

Margery Kempe at the beginning of the chapter, it becomes clear that courtly love was for women, at most, a rhetorical game. Indeed, even such verbal dalliance had to be carefully guarded or avoided in case a woman's character should be besmirched and her social standing subsequently diminished. The 'abandoned' women of courtly love in the Medieval period might have existed in the fictional world of the troubadour or romancer, but they are certainly not represented either by the women writers discussed in this chapter or in their works.

Conclusion

The overall purpose of this chapter has been to recover and recuperate Medieval women's literature for a present-day readership. While acknowledging the inevitable differences between past and present, the lacunae of perception between Medieval and Modern ideologies, I have tried to offer ways in which to negotiate these divides through a doubled awareness which encompasses otherness and similitude. The inescapable recalcitrance of the early texts must be accepted, but the possible range of access uncovered is both surprising and rewarding for the feminist critic as well as the general reader.

There are, of course, certain linking themes in the texts discussed, apart from the broad, and quite conventional, division into spiritual and secular works. For example, the difficulties encountered by women writers who attempted to challenge the confining limitations of their societies' ideologies recur again and again, creating martyrs like Marguerite de Porete, obsessives like Clare of Assisi, and even conformists like Margaret Beaufort. Yet, the majority of women discussed here – and undoubtedly far more could have been included – do not allow themselves to be 'abandoned' in any sense of the word. Instead, they become, in Christine de Pizan's terminology, 'champions' of their sex. They challenge patriarchal conventions and male textual control in diverse, and often idiosyncratic ways, but certain similarities may be discerned. Experience is set against authority in the usual dialectic, with Bridget of Sweden and Eleanor Hull focusing on motherhood, and Margery Kempe and Christine de Pizan highlighting the inequalities and dangers of male/female relationships. Analogously predictable is the assertion of God's superior authority which allows women to circumvent the earthly laws of men; the anonymous author of *A Revelation* presents a martyred nun, Julian of Norwich asserts Christ's role as mother, Elizabeth of Hungary rewrites the story of the annunciation, and Joan of Arc creates a curious amalgam of politics and religion.

However, unexpected strategies have also emerged from the analyses undertaken above. For example, a female tradition – whether of female writers, mystics, saints, warriors, or simply notable women – appears to have been an important tool in the construction of an authorial female subjectivity. Margery, Julian, Bridget, Elizabeth and Christine all call upon other women as exemplars, forming a mutually supportive network of Medieval women's voices. Moreover, these gendered articulations specifically challenge patriarchal conventions: Julian asserts the value of motherhood to

Christianity, while Bridget of Sweden and Eleanor Hull are in direct opposition to the male-authored medical authorities when they categorically describe the womb as clean and pure. In parallel, the ethos of courtly love with its tacit condoning of extramarital relationships, is vehemently challenged by Christine de Pizan who points out the dangers of such dalliances to women in no uncertain terms, while the possible disgrace devolving upon women from such liaisons is attested to by Marie de France, Margery Kempe and the Paston women. Moreover, these discourses – of parenthood, female bodies and romantic love – are as enshrined in patriarchy today as they were in the Medieval period. As such, it is essential that women's writing, past and present, is given adequate space to create a balanced view in terms of gender.

Finally, however, the individual voices of the authors, the specific tones, forms and themes of the works, offer a panoply of the experiences of Medieval women: Margery with her vibrant assertiveness, Christine with her clever arguments, Julian with her measured enlightenment, Elizabeth of Hungary with her self-confident knowledge, and even the anonymous author of *A Revelation* with her erotic voyeurism, all have a unique autonomy which resides alongside their representative historical and sexual roles. This combination of the individual and typical ensures that, while not of our own period, these Medieval women writers will never ultimately be abandoned.

Notes

1. For a discussion of courtly love in relation to women see Larrington, 1995: 39–53.
2. The quotation is taken from a modern translation of Margery's work. A Middle English version is available (Kempe, 1961) although it would have to be photocopied for student use, hence my decision to use the Penguin translation. Margery's book is a classic example of how women's writing may be 'abandoned' in that the whole text was lost until 1934. In my reading of Margery's autobiography I have been influenced by two Marxist accounts: Delany, 1983: 76–92; and Aers, 1988: 73–116.
3. It is important to make the point that the women in the tour group were from Western societies. Women from Islamic nations, of course, would not have found the Poor Clare shocking, although, dependent upon their own views, they might have approved or commiserated with her veiled and enclosed state.
4. See also: Clare of Assisi, Saint, 1982.
5. Of the books dealing with the lives of Medieval women the following list represents those I have found most useful: Amt, 1993; Anderson and Zinsser, 1988; Beer, 1992; Bennett et al., 1989; Bynum, 1987; Erler and Kowaleski, 1988; Labalme, 1980; Lucas, 1983; Millett and Wogan-Browne, 1990; Rose, 1986; and Shahar, 1988.
6. For the graduate student there are even more exciting possibilities since modern editions of Medieval women writers are needed to further the teaching canon.
7. For a general discussion see: Clanchy, 1993; and for a more specific account see: Staly, 1994: 1–38.
8. See: Mueller, 1984: 57–69; and Smith, 1987: 64–83.
9. In this point I differ from Jocelyn Wogan-Browne who has argued convincingly that women were not writing in a female tradition, although perhaps my qualifying note about later Medieval writers allows for this distinction.
10. The Wolters edition (Julian of Norwich, 1966) is a modernized version of the long account; for a Middle English version of both long and short texts see *A Book of Shewings to the Anchoress Julian of Norwich* (Julian of Norwich, 1978).

11. For a general discussion see: Bynum, 1982; for a more specific account see: Bradley, 1976.
12. For the complete version of Bridget's revelations see Bridget of Sweden, Saint, 1987, and for her *The Rule of St Saviour*, which is also quoted in Barratt and which reaffirms Bridget's assertion of female rights, see: Bridget of Sweden, Saint, 1978. For a full version of Elizabeth of Hungary's text see: Elizabeth of Hungary, Saint, *c*.1492. For the Middle English version of Mary of Oignies's life see: Mary of Oignies, 1884–5. I have chosen to focus on Bridget and Elizabeth because of their accessibility to present-day students.
13. See: Savage and Watson, 1991.
14. For the life of St Margaret see: Millett and Wogan-Browne, 1990: 44–85; and for St Katherine see: Katherine, Saint, 1981.
15. *The Mirror* was published in 1506, no modern edition of the complete text exists.
16. For example, I intend to refer to *The Book of the City of Ladies* (Pizan, 1983), but *The Treasure of the City of Ladies, or the Book of the Three Virtues* (Pizan, 1985) and *The Epistle of the Prison of Human Life* (Pizan, 1984) are readily available.
17. For a discussion of Christine's role as a 'feminist' see: Gottlieb, 1985: 337–64; and Delany, 1990.
18. *De lof der vrouwen*, Ms. Add. 20698, f.17 (London, the British Library), copied in Quilligan, 1991: 62. Quilligan's critical account of Christine's work has influenced me in my argument and is an outstanding example of an informative as well as thoroughly enjoyable piece of criticism.
19. For a translation of the late Middle English version see: Paston Family, 1981: 104.
20. This extract is not included in Paston Family, 1983. Diane Watt quotes another example of John III's courtly language – to yet another potential bride; see: Watt, 1993: 122–38.

Bibliography

Primary materials

Amt, Emilie (1993), *Women's Lives in Medieval Europe*, London: Routledge.

Barratt, Alexandra (1992), *Women's Writing in Middle English*, London: Longman.

Bridget of Sweden, Saint (1978), *'The Rewyll of Seynt Sauioure' and Other Middle English Brigittine Legislative Texts*, James Hogg (ed.), Salzburg: Salzburger Studien zür Anglistik und Amerikanistik, 6.

Bridget of Sweden, Saint (1987), *The Liber Coelestis of St Bridget of Sweden*, Roger Ellis (ed.), Oxford: Early English Text Society, o.s. 291.

Clare of Assisi, Saint (1982), *Francis and Clare: The Complete Works*, R.J. Armstrong and I. Brady (eds), London: SPCK.

Elizabeth of Hungary, Saint (*c*.1492), 'The Revelations of Saynt Elysabeth the kinges doughter of hungarye' in *Lyf of Saint Katherin of Senis* printed by Wynkyn de Worde.

Julian of Norwich (1966), *Revelations of Divine Love*, trans. Clifton Wolters, Harmondsworth: Penguin.

Julian of Norwich (1978), *A Book of Shewings to the Anchoress Julian of Norwich*, E. Colledge and J. Walsh (eds), Toronto: University of Toronto Press.

Katherine, Saint (1981), *Seinte Katerine*, S.R.T.O. d'Ardenne and E.J. Dobson (eds), London: Early English Text Society, s.s. 7.

Kempe, Margery (1961), *The Book of Margery Kempe*, S.B. Meech and H.E. Allen (eds), Oxford: Early English Text Society, o.s. 212.

Kempe, Margery (1985), *The Book of Margery Kempe*, trans. B.A. Windeatt, Harmondsworth: Penguin.

Larrington, Carolyne (1995), *Women and Writing in Medieval Europe. A Sourcebook*, London: Routledge.

Marie de France (1986), *The Lais of Marie de France*, G.S. Burgess and K. Busby (eds), Harmondsworth: Penguin.

Mary of Oignies (1884–5), *Prosalegenden*, Karl Horstmann (ed.), *Anglia* 7–8: 102–96.

Millett, Bella and Jocelyn Wogan-Browne (eds) (1990), *Medieval English Prose for Women*, Oxford: Clarendon Press.

Paston Family (1981), *The Pastons. A Family in the Wars of the Roses*, ed. and trans. Richard Barber, Woodbridge: Boydell Press.

Paston Family (1983), *The Paston Letters*, Norman Davis (ed.), Oxford: Oxford University Press.

Petroff, Elizabeth Alvilda (1986), *Medieval Women's Visionary Literature*, Oxford: Oxford University Press.

Pizan, Christine de (1983), *The Book of the City of Ladies*, trans. Earl Jeffrey Richards and foreword by Marina Warner, London: Pan Books.

Pizan, Christine de (1984), *The Epistle of the Prison of Human Life*, trans. J.A. Wisman, New York: Garland Library of Medieval Literature.

Pizan, Christine de (1985), *The Treasure of the City of Ladies, or the Book of the Three Virtues*, trans. Sarah Lawson, Harmondsworth: Penguin.

Savage, Anne and Nicholas Watson (trans. and eds) (1991), *Anchoritic Spirituality: Ancrene Wisse and Associated Works*, New York: Paulist Press.

Wilson, Katharina M. (1984), *Medieval Women Writers*, Manchester: Manchester University Press.

Secondary materials

Aers, David (1988), 'The Making of Margery Kempe: Individual and Community' in David Aers, *Community, Gender, and Individual Identity. English Writing 1360–1430*, London: Routledge, pp. 73–116.

Anderson, Bonnie S. and Judith Zinsser (1988), *A History of Their Own*, New York: Harper and Row.

Beer, Frances (1992), *Women and Mystical Experience In the Middle Ages*, Woodbridge: Boydell Press.

Bennett, Judith M., Elizabeth A. Clark, Jean F. O'Barr, B. Anne Vilen and Sarah Westphal-Wihl (eds) (1989), *Sisters and Workers in the Middle Ages*, Chicago: Chicago University Press.

Boffey, Julia (1993), 'Women Authors and Women's Literacy in Fourteenth- and Fifteenth-century England' in *Women and Literature in Britain, 1150–1500*, Carol M. Meale (ed.), Cambridge: Cambridge University Press, pp. 159–82.

Bogin, Meg (1976), *The Women Troubadours*, New York: Paddington Press.

Bradley, Ritamary (1976), 'The Motherhood Theme in Julian of Norwich', *14th Century English Mystics Newsletter* II(4), 25ff.

Bynum, Caroline (1982), *Jesus as Mother: Studies in the Spirituality of the High Middle Ages*, Berkeley: University of California Press.

Bynum, Caroline (1987), *Holy Feast and Holy Fast: The Religious Significance of Food to Medieval Women*, Berkeley: University of California Press.

Clanchy, Michael (1993), *From Memory to Written Record: England 1066–1307*, Oxford: Blackwell.

Delany, Sheila (1983), 'Sexual Economics, Chaucer's Wife of Bath and *The Book of Margery Kempe*' in Sheila Delany, *Writing Women*, New York: Schocken Books, pp. 76–92.

Delany, Sheila (1990), ' "Mothers to Think Back Through": Who Are They? The Ambiguous Example of Christine de Pizan' in Sheila Delany, *Medieval Literary Politics: Shapes of Ideology*, Manchester: Manchester University Press.

Dronke, Peter (1984), *Women Writers of the Middle Ages: A Critical Study of Texts from Perpetua (+203) to Marguerite Porete (+1310)*, Cambridge: Cambridge University Press.

Erler, Mary and Maryanne Kowaleski (eds) (1988), *Women and Power in the Middle Ages*, Athens: University of Georgia Press.

Gottlieb, Beatrice (1985), 'The Problem of Feminism in the Fifteenth Century' in *Women of the Medieval World*, Julius Krishner and Suzanne F. Wemple (eds), Oxford: Basil Blackwell.

Labalme, Patricia (1980), *Beyond Their Sex: Learned Women of the European Past*, New York: New York University Press.

Lucas, Angela M. (1983), *Women in the Middle Ages: Religion, Marriage and Letters*, Hemel Hempstead: Harvester Wheatsheaf.

Meale, Carol (ed.) (1993), *Women and Literature in Britain, 1150–1500*, Cambridge: Cambridge University Press.

Mueller, Janel M. (1984), 'Autobiography of a New "Cretur": Female Spirituality, Selfhood and Authorship in "The Book of Margery Kempe" ' in *The Female Autograph*, Domna C. Stanton (ed.), Chicago: Chicago University Press, pp. 57–69.

Quilligan, Maureen (1991), *The Allegory of Female Authority: Christine de Pizan's Cité des Dames*, Ithaca: Cornell University Press.

Rose, Mary Beth (ed.) (1986), *Women in the Middle Ages and Renaissance*, Syracuse: Syracuse University Press.

Shahar, Shulamith (1988), *The Fourth Estate: A History of Women in the Middle Ages*, London: Routledge.

Smith, Sidonie (1987), *A Poetics of Women's Autobiography: Marginality and the Fictions of Self-Representation*, Bloomington: Indiana University Press.

Staly, Lynn (1994), *Margery Kempe's Dissenting Fictions*, Pennsylvania: Pennsylvania State University Press.

Watt, Diane (1993), ' "No Writing for Writing's Sake": The Language of Service and Household Rhetoric in the Letters of the Paston Women' in *Dear Sister: Medieval Women and the Epistolary Genre*, Karen Cherewatuk and Ulrike Wiethaus (eds), Philadelphia: University of Pennsylvania Press.

2

Transgressing boundaries: women's writing in the Renaissance and Reformation

Janet Clare

While the term Renaissance was once regarded almost exclusively by cultural historians in terms of an epoch of humanist learning and courtly or aristocratic writing, its boundaries, temporal and ideological, are in the process of being remapped by New Historicist, Cultural Materialist, feminist and post-colonial critics. More materially based criticism has stressed social and political discontinuities, tensions and ruptures rather than the coherence and order which were associated with an earlier idealist criticism. The perpetuation of literary styles and forms has warranted a broader application of the cultural concept of Renaissance. Despite the obvious changes in aesthetic and ideological assumptions during the late Tudor and early Stuart period, the term Renaissance in England is now commonly perceived as extending to the early decades of the seventeenth century. At the same time, the canon of Renaissance literature has expanded to include texts which would not formerly have been judged literary, while familiar texts have been reappraised in the light of different ideologies of power and gender. A broader, culturally hybrid and less socially exclusive analysis of the English literary Renaissance is amenable to a study of contemporaneous women's writing. The writings of women, whether religious, popular, humanist or courtly, had in the mid-sixteenth to early seventeenth century at least one common aspect: women writers represented in their work an alternative culture which ran alongside the dominant culture. In writing as some did with a view to publication, they were transgressing boundaries.

'I perceive that learned women be suspected of many,' wrote Juan Luis Vives in his *Instructions of a Christian Woman* (Vives, 1529: D2v).[1] Vives is here articulating just one of the cultural assumptions which inhibited women's reading and, by extension, writing during the Renaissance. In positioning women as subjects, male humanists such as Vives, Erasmus, Thomas More, Thomas Elyot and Roger Ascham held comparatively advanced views on the education of women, specifically noblewomen; nonetheless the aim of female learning was narrowly perceived as personal cultivation rather than the acquisition of formal skills.[2] In *Instructions of a Christian Woman*, Vives' declared purpose is to provide 'precepts and rules howe to lyve' and his emphasis accordingly is on the practical application of knowledge in the constitution of a moral and pious life. Women were excluded from rhetorical training on the assumption that its performative element conflicted with notions of female decorum. Reading material was carefully regulated. Certain works – including, for example, romance literature, with its emphasis on knightly conduct – should be prohibited, for 'it can not lightly be a chaste mayd that is occupied thynknge of armour'. *Instructions of a Christian Woman* was commissioned by Catherine of Aragon for her daughter Mary, later Mary Tudor, but ideas directed at royal and aristocratic learning filtered gradually through to other social classes as the work became a popular conduct book, reaching its ninth edition in 1592.

Conduct books, aimed primarily at a middle-class audience, also reiterated the end to which female learning was to be directed. Thomas Salter's translation in 1579 of Gian Michele Bruto's *La Institutione di una Fanciulla Nate Nobilmente* as the *Mirrhor of Modestie* stresses the acquisition of the traditional female virtues of chastity, piety and humility. In the inculcation of male constructs of female virtue, the Bible, the teachings of the church fathers and narratives of virtuous women are judged appropriate reading material. Philosophy, poetry and rhetoric are considered inappropriate studies, as they may produce self-expression, seduce women away from simple Christian truths and activate a desire to participate in the public world. In these contexts, Bruto reserves his greatest opprobrium for romantic, chivalric fiction and plays.

In 1582 Thomas Bentley, a lawyer of Gray's Inn, assembled a collection of both male and female authored texts, *The Monument of Matrones*, which is illuminating because it exemplifies the texts specifically judged fit for a female readership. In his Introduction Bentley stresses female piety and natural subordination. The argument is once more supported by recourse to the Scriptures, but here Bentley is tellingly selective. He omits two verses from his Pauline texts (I *Corinthians* 11: 11–12) which stress the independence and even equality of men and women. As Suzanne Hull has commented, this is an example of the power of omission used to affirm the idea of submissiveness (Hull, 1982: 141). The selection of devotional works, prayers, pious meditations and biblical extracts is premissed on the understanding that this celebration of female piety from different ages corresponds with norms of current female virtue in which all women should rejoice.

We should not necessarily see exhortatory patriarchal discourse and female practice as homologous. The link between dominant cultural assumptions about learning and gender, as manifested most frequently in writing by men, and contemporaneous writing by women is at best tenuous. In the Renaissance, reading material was prescribed for both men and women and whilst women's entry into writing and into print was sometimes apologetic and cautious, the same could be said of male authors who apologized for publication or, by circulating their works in manuscript, disdained it altogether. Nevertheless, a sense of feminine literary decorum and the limits placed upon female education did contribute to the genres and subjects of women's literature during the early Renaissance. This consciousness, for example, would have precluded women from contributing to an emergent popular vernacular literature, primarily expressed in drama and prose fiction. Women's initial entry into print was largely through translation, a medium which allowed the female voice to co-exist with that of the original author. But the choice of text for translation, for instance John Jewel's *An Apologie or answere in defence of the Churche in England* undertaken by Anne Cooke in 1564, could be a politically controversial one (Beilin, 1987: 55). In other genres, women writers were more obviously obliged to negotiate inventively the re-straints, formal, social and moral, imposed upon them. Such strategies might take the form of a challenge to the authority of male readings of the scriptures. Another technique was the appropriation of the modesty topos. The apologetic or self-deprecating idiom of several of the texts which we will consider needs to be read at other than face value. Paradoxically, to draw attention to a lack of learning or seemingly to acquiesce in patriarchal notions of female inferiority could disarm the male reader and prove an enabling device for the publication of women's writing.

The term 'Renaissance', despite its familiar associations, nevertheless embodies a period of change rather than one which is culturally monolithic. Social and political conditions in Jacobean England seem to a limited degree less constrictive towards female literary discourse. In the early seventeenth century women appropriated the hitherto male-authored genres of romance, the love sonnet, political tragedy and polemical writing. Distinctions between the works of women in the early and the late Renaissance periods respectively can, however, be misleading when the writing of women outside or on the margins of the dominant discourse is considered. Going beyond culturally sanctioned writing practices, Anne Askew, Margaret Tyler and Isabel Whitney produced respectively a religious testimony, the translation of a romance and popular poetry.

The radicalism of Anne Askew (1521–46) is apparent in her Protestant conversion, her resistance to her Catholic landowner husband, Thomas Kyme, and in her auto-biographical record of opposition to the Henrician backlash against the reformers. When Kyme evicted her from the family home, Askew removed to London where she petitioned unsuccessfully for divorce and became associated with the circle of Catherine Parr, Henry VIII's sixth wife. The King's break with Rome and the suppression of the monasteries had not entailed changes to Catholic doctrine itself and in 1539 this position was reinforced by the Act of Six Articles which decreed severe penalties for denying the doctrine of transubstantiation, clerical celibacy, pri-vate masses and auricular confessions (Dickens, 1967: 247). First examined for heresy in 1545 concerning her refusal to accept Catholic doctrine in respect of the sacra-ments, Askew was released because of insufficient evidence. She was examined and released a second time before her final gruelling imprisonment in the Tower. Askew was subjected to intensive interrogation and, contrary to the usual understanding that women should not be tortured, was racked in an attempt to make her recant and incriminate Protestant women at court. Not only did Askew remain steadfast, but she left a remarkable written account of her interrogations and her spirited refutations of the charges made against her, and through her unwavering assertions of belief she presents a powerful self-portrait. *The First Examinacyon of the worthy Servant of God, Mistresse Anne Askewe* (1546) and *The lattre examinacyon of the worthye servaunt of God mastres Anne Askewe* (1547) conform to no easily identifiable genre.[3] They are part diary, part spiritual autobiography and part testimonial; as Askew records the questionings of her interlocutors and her responses, the texts also exhibit a dramatic quality derived from their origins in oral discourse.

Askew's testimonies of her examinations were published with an Introduction, interpolations – classified as 'elucydacyon' – and summaries written by the Protestant bishop and polemical playwright John Bale. Bale, in his address to the Christian readers of *The First Examinacyon*, valorizes Anne Askew's faith, whilst citing the commonplace argument that the strength of God is vindicated through the use of such a weak vessel:

> . . . concernynge her, it may wele be sayde, that Paul verefyeth 2 Cor 12. The strength of God is here made perfyght by weaknesse. When she semed most feble, than was she most stronge. And gladlye she rejoyced in the weakenesse, that Christes power might strongelye dwell in her. Thus choseth the lorde, the foolish of this worlde to confounde the wyse, and the weake to deface the myghtye. (1546: 9v)

Bale's displays of scripturalism are, however, technically surpassed by Anne Askew's skilful use of biblical statement, language and metaphor, with which she records her examinations at the hands of the bishops. Throughout her interrogation on matters of doctrine and of religious practice, Askew reclaims biblical teaching in advocating the Protestant position. She is questioned on the truth of a statement which she is alleged to have made, that she would rather read 'fyve lynes in the Bible, than to heare fyve masses in the temple'. In answer, she begins by cleverly and boldly subverting the question:

> I confessed, that I sayd no lesse. Not for the dysprayse of either the Epistle or Gospell. But because the one ded greatlye edyfye me, and the other nothinge at all. As Saynt Paul doth witnesse in the xiiii chaptre of his first Epistle to the *Cor* where as he doth say. If the trumpe geveth an uncertaine sounde, who wyll prepare hymselfe to the battayle?(3)

Later in the text, she records that she is rebuked by the Bishop's chancellor 'for uttering the scriptures when St Paul had forbidden women to speake or talke of the worde of God'. Here, she uses her more refined interpretation of the Epistles to correct her accuser:

> I answered hym that I knewe Paules meaninge so well as he, which is, 1 Corinthians xiiii that a woman ought not to speake in the congregacyon by the waye of teachinge. And then I asked hym, how manye women he had seane, go into the pulpett and preach. He sayde, he never sawe non. Then I sayd, he ought to find no faulte in poore women, except they had offended the lawe. (10r—10v)

In drawing this scriptural and legal distinction, Askew argues the weakness of the case against her and her innocence in the face of biblical authority. Later, when asked by the Bishop of London why she has so few words, she skilfully appropriates in her own defence the frequently cited cultural ideal of the silent woman: 'I aunswered, God hath given to me the gift of knowledge, but not of utterance. And Solomon sayth, that a woman of few words, is a gift of God.'

Repeatedly, Askew outwits the divines with her verbal skills. In the first *Examinacyon* she is questioned obliquely on the Catholic sacrament of Confession and on the status of the individual 'conscience'. In advocating the exposure of conscience to priestly counsel, the Bishop of London employs the simile of a wound, which must be revealed to the surgeon before he can act. Askew takes up the image and in response implicitly rejects confession: 'I answered that my conscience was clere in all thinges. And for to laye a playstre unto the whole skynne, it might apear moche folye' (23v). In the second *Examinacyon* she is relentlessly interrogated on the doctrine of transubstantiation, and, in her refutation, argues with sophistication that it rests on a selective literalism. If the communion bread is indeed the body of Christ, she asks, why are not other biblical metaphors so literally transformed? 'Ye maye not here (sayd I) take Christe for the materyall thynge that he is syngnfyed by. for than ye wyll make hym a verye dore, a vyne, a lampe, and a stone, cleane conttarye to the holye Ghostes meanynge' (21). There is a lightness of tone in the economical rejection of a doctrine which fuelled the major controversies of the Reformation.

The formal recall of dialogue in Askew's text gives it an immediacy of impact as well as a dramatic quality. Further, as she narrates the locations and conditions of her examination, the reader becomes conscious of the narrative of persecution. In the second *Examinacyon*, as the interrogation intensifies, Askew includes her meditations on the scriptures. Her circumstances change. She is removed from Newgate prison to the Tower. Her scorn for her questioners deepens: 'Master Ryche and the Bishopp of London with all their power and flatteringe wordes were about to persuade me from God. But I ded not esteme their glosynge pretences.' Later when she refuses to betray her female co-religionists, she records dispassionately:

> Then they ded put me on the racke, bycause I confessed no ladyes nor gentyllwomen to be of my opynyon, and theron they kepte me a longe tyme. And because I laye styll and ded not crye my Lord Chauncellor and mastre Ryche, toke peynes to racke me their owne handes, tyll I was nygh dead. (45)

The same stoical resilience is present in the ballad which Askew wrote and apparently sang when she was imprisoned in Newgate and which is printed after her prayer of forgiveness for those who have committed violence against her. Here Askew represents herself as the Christian knight with faith as both shield and weapon. The armour of faith – a popular image, culled from Paul's letter to the Ephesians – enables her to go among her foes:

> Faythe in the fathers olde
> Obtayned ryghtwysnesse
> Whych make me verye bolde
> To feare no worldes dystresse.
> I now rejoyce in hart
> And hope byd me do so
> For Christ wyll take my part
> And ease me of my wo.

The masculine imagery of crusading gives way to feminine as Askew draws attention to her testamentary act of writing:

I am not she that lyst
My anker to lete fall
For everye dryslynge myst
My shyppe substancyall
   Not oft use I to wryght
In prose nor yet in ryme,
Yet wyll I shewe one syght
That I sawe in my tyme.
   I sawe a ryall trone
Where Justyce shuld have sytt,
But in her stede was one
Of modye[4] cruell wytt
   Absorpt was ryghtwysnesse
As of the ragynge floude,
Sathan in hys excesse,
Sucte up the gyltlesse bloude
   (63–4; Travitsky, 1989: 185–6)

Askew defines her political act of defiance as a record of oppression which she feels impelled to make; she is determined to authenticate 'one syght' of her time. The verbal skills and the depth of knowledge revealed in the text, not to mention the evidence of physical and mental endurance, make the *Examinacyons* remarkable literary texts and historical documents. In the very act and manner of recording her experiences and convictions, Askew repudiates all conventional notions of woman's physical and moral frailty and intellectual inferiority.

Anne Askew's direct, self-conscious style is reflected in the poetry of Isabella Whitney, who uniquely for a woman in this period wrote and published popular poetry. Whitney produced two collections, *Copy of a letter, lately written in meeter, by a Yonge Gentilwoman to her unconstant lover* (1567) and *A sweet Nosgay, or pleasant Posye. Contayninge a hundred and ten Phylosophicall Flowers* (1573).[5] She may also have contributed, as the only female poet, to two popular anthologies published by Richard Jones, the publisher of *Copy of a letter* (Fehrenbach, 1981: 85–7). In one of her verse epistles attached to *A sweet Nosgay* and addressed to her sister, Whitney draws attention to her single state, which enables her writing: 'But til some household cares me tye / My bookes and Pen I wyll apply' (1573: D2r). The poetry often appears semi-autobiographical as Whitney alludes to economic hardship through loss of employment, personal illness and family relationships. Since so little is known of her life, however, the autobiographical constructions may serve as a different form of modesty topos.

Copy of a letter is interesting as an example of love poetry which is neither courtly nor neo-Platonic, written from a female perspective. In form, the poetry is loosely modelled on Ovid's *Heroides*, which comprised verse epistles written between legendary lovers, a genre later adopted by Aphra Behn. In Whitney's verse, the female voice is by turns jocular, teasing and sceptical, far removed from the plaintive tones of the dominant cultural form of male-authored Petrarchan love poetry. Whitney's female persona, in popular ballad metre, addresses a former lover who she has heard is to marry another. The poet seems to want to test the authenticity of the lover's vows made to her and to others:

> And if you cannot be content
> to lead a single lyfe.
> (Although the same right quiet be)
> then take me to your wife.
>
> So shall the promises be kept,
> that you so firmly made:
> Now chuse whether ye wyll be true,
> Or be of SINONS trade.

There follows a catalogue of unfaithful or destructive male lovers, Aeneas, Theseus, Jason and Paris, punctuated by allusion to the faithful Troilus, but without any of the customary misogynistic references to Cressida. The woman would like to cast the lover as Troilus, setting the ideal imaginary against the probable reality; but she is resigned to rejection, so long as she knows the truth:

> And unto me a Troylus be,
> if not you may compare:
> With any of these parsons that
> above expressed are.
>
> But if I can not please your mind
> for wants that rest in me:
> Wed whom you list, I am content,
> your refuse for to be.
> (Travitsky, 1989: 118–20)

Part of the interest and appeal of the poem lies in the ambiguous situation to which it alludes. The relationships, past and present, appear deliberately underwritten as the reliability of all words, including rumours and vows, is questioned. Despite the commonplace appeal to mythical lovers, there is a freshness and unconventionality in the voice of the unselfpitying subject.

In *A sweet Nosgay*, Whitney's second published collection of verse, the poet's voice is more obviously derivative. Whitney's dedication to George Mainwaring contains an apology for her borrowings: 'Though they be of anothers growing, yet considering they be of my owne gathering and makeing up: respect my labour and regard my good wil.' The dedication is followed by a prose and verse address to the reader. In the first she plays on the association of 'nosegay' as a protection against infection, but then disclaims any similar powers for her own poetic garnering. The verse epistle takes the form of autobiography, as Whitney, still drawing on the imagery of harvesting, alludes to her unemployment, illness and subsequent preoccupations:

> This harvest tyme, I harvestlesse
> and servicelesse also:
> And subject unto sicknesse, that
> abrode I could not go.

> Had leasure good, (though learning lackt)
> some study to apply:
> To reade such Bookes, whereby I thought
> my selfe to edyfye.
>
> (1573: A5v)

Yet she self-deprecatingly dismisses the scholarly disciplines as 'past this head of mine' and turns instead to popular poetic, from which she culls her verse maxims and moralizings. Later in the collection, however, she recovers her own voice in the verse epistles she directs to her brothers, sister and cousin and, most strikingly, in the long poem her 'Wyll and Testament' (Travitsky, 1980: 76–95), in which, making London her executor, she rhetorically takes her leave of the city.

The poem's originality lies in its anthropomorphic and phantasmagoric evocation of London occasioned by the poet's wish to make various bequests to the city and its inhabitants:

> I first of all to London leave
> because I there was bred:
> Brave buildyngs rare, of Churches store,
> And Pauls to the head. . . .
> I Goldsmithes leave, with Juels such,
> as are for Ladies meete.
> And Plate to furnysh Cubbards with,
> full brave there shall you finde:
> With Purle of Silver and of Golde,
> to satisfye your minde.

After describing in lively and ironic detail the various merchandise she will leave to the already wealthy city – fashionable clothes, boots, shoes, artillery, luxury foods, wines, medicines and the specific places where they can be sought – Whitney turns to the city's underclass, the criminals, the alleged lunatics of Bedlam, debtors and prisoners. To the debtors' prison, Ludgate, she initially decides to leave nothing because, she reasons in a moment of realism, she will need to keep a place there for herself while she lives:

> I am not now in case to lye,
> here is no place of jest:
> I dyd reserve, that for my selfe,
> if I my health possest.
> And ever came in credit so
> A debtor for to bee.
> When dayes of paiment did approach,
> I thither ment to flee.

The irony deepens as, reminding herself that no one is likely to offer her any credit and that she will therefore have no need of Ludgate, she decides to leave the prison a legacy of some bankrupts. The fantastic endowments completed, the poet's impecunious condition is now revealed, as she declares that she has no money for her own burial:

> And though I nothing named have,
> to bury mee withall:
> Consider that above the ground,
> annoyance bee I shall.
> And let me have a shrowding Sheete
> to cover mee from shame:
> And in oblivyon bury mee
> and never more mee name
> Ringings nor other Ceremonies,
> use you not for cost:
> Nor at my buriall, make no feast,
> your mony were but lost.
>   (Travitsky, 1980: 93)

The desire for self-erasure is contrasted with Whitney's earlier references in the poem, first to the bequest she would like to make to her printer and then to her books, which she wills her friends to buy. Whitney's feminism is apparent in the way she fashions herself as independent and free-thinking and establishes her identity through authorship.

In the act of writing and publishing popular verse, Whitney was breaking the bounds of both her class and sex. A similarly transgressive act was *A mirrour of princely deedes and knighthood*, a translation by Margaret Tyler of the first part of a Spanish romance by Diego Ortunez de Calahorra. The novelty of Tyler's work lay in her choice of the romance, a genre which, with its valorizing of sexual love, was viewed as *risqué* reading for women. Moreover, the lengthy translation is accompanied by a purposeful prefatory letter (Travitsky, 1989: 144–6) which is highly revealing about the restrictions imposed on female literary production. In an aside, Tyler comments that, amongst her ill-wishers, she hopes that there will be none who would wish her 'either not to write or to write of divinitie', but then adds, perhaps in mock self-deprecation, that she cannot comprehend such controversies. She draws attention to an apparent contradiction between the large number of books dedicated to women and the absence of female authorship. If women may read, why may they not 'farther wade in them to the serch of a truth. And then much more why not deale by translation in such arguments.' Translation, she suggests, is theoretically defensible as woman's work, since it does not require 'deep invention or exquisite learning', but after this apology she concludes on a much more assertive note: 'My perswasion hath bene thus, that it is all one for a woman to pen a story, as for a man to address his story to a woman.' Throughout the address, Tyler engages vigorously with the idea of feminine literary decorum. She recognizes that some will see her translated story as 'prophane' and a matter more manlike than becomes her sex; but, she remonstrates, 'every man holds not the plow, which would the ground were tilled: and it is no sinne to talke of Robinhoode though you never shot in his bow.' Tyler's prefatory material thus discloses the woman writer's awareness of the boundaries which circumscribed her work and acknowledges the gesture she is making, in her act of translating romance, against cultural authority.

It might be argued that whilst aristocratic women may have had more leisure to write and greater opportunity to circulate in manuscript or publish their work, their prominent social profile might render them more inhibited in the nature of their literary output. The work of Mary Sidney, Countess of Pembroke, most clearly exemplifies the Renaissance ideal of female authorship, imperfectly as that may have been understood (Hannay, 1990; Lamb, 1990). Apart from a few original poems – which include the pastoral 'Dialogue between two shepherds, Thenot and Piers', ostensibly in praise of Elizabeth I as Astrea, and the encomium to her brother, 'To the Angel Spirit of the Most Excellent Sir Philip Sidney', prefaced to her version of the *Psalms* – Mary Sidney was active in the field of translation. 'A Dialogue between two shepherds' was written in anticipation of a visit, which did not materialize, by the Queen to Wilton, the Pembroke estate, where Mary Sidney presided over a literary coterie. The short entertainment reveals a translator's preoccupation with words, their limitations and indeterminacies. One of the shepherds, Thenot, speaks an official language of praise: he claims that his panegyrical images will rightly convey the essence of Astrea's greatness. The other, Piers, disputes the claim and, when Thenot asks why his panegyric to Astrea should fail to convey his meaning, Piers's reply undermines the efficacy of language itself:

> Words from conceit do only rise,
> Above conceit her honor flies,
> But silence, nought can praise her.
> (Sidney, 1993: 1048)

This represents at one level a modest, but effective, dismantling of the rhetoric of compliment lavished on the Queen throughout her reign in lyrics, drama and courtly pastime. At another level, Piers's quasi-mystical approach proceeds from the premiss that human words can never seek to encapsulate the divinity of transcendence, which equates Astrea with God.

Generically varied, Mary Sidney's choice of texts for translation is characterized by their academic nature and by their links with the cause of international Protestantism. Following the death of her brother, killed in 1586 at Zutphen after he had volunteered against the Spanish, Mary Sidney completed his translation of the *Psalms*. The Countess's other translations were those of Robert Garnier's closet drama *Marc Antonie*; *discours de vie et de la Mort*, the work of Philippe de Mornay, a Huguenot and friend of her brother; and *Trionfo della Morte*, one of the *Trionfi*, Petrarch's six vernacular poems in *terza rime*.

Artistically and politically, the *Psalms* occupy an important place in Protestant poetics; their translation was perceived as both a literary and a devotional act. In his *Defence of Poesie* (1595), Philip Sidney had praised David's *Psalms* as representing exemplary poetry. As the psalmist had imitated 'the unconceivable excellencies of God', so must the translator elucidate the words of David. Studies of the Sidneian psalter have invariably drawn attention to its intra-lingual nature, that is, the harnessing of different translations from the Hebrew, interpretative additions, the borrowing of an image from one psalm for another and the careful selection of images from working models, all of which make it a creative endeavour.[6]

Like her brother, Mary Sidney consulted a range of translations of, and glosses on, the *Psalms* and adapted the stanzaic and metrical forms and rhyme schemes of the French psalter. Implicit themes are forcefully conveyed. Thus is she able to emphasize the foolish pretensions of earthly endeavours, the limits of human knowledge and, repeatedly, the Calvinist doctrine of the insufficiency of humankind unaided by God's grace, which is notably conveyed in the alliteration of the second stanza of Psalm 51: 'For I, alas, acknowledging do know / My filthy fault, my faulty filthiness / To my soul's eye uncessantly doth show' (Sidney, 1992: 48). The apprehension of unworthiness in this psalm, well known as neck-verse, is accompanied by the violence of the language which describes the fate of the psalmist's enemies and, by implication, the opponents of the Protestant cause. The third stanza of Psalm 58 opens with a ferocious apostrophe which is sustained in the destructive images which follow:

> Lord, crack their teeth, Lord, crush these lions' jaws,
> So let them sink as water in the sand.
> When deadly bow their aiming fury draws
> Shiver the shaft ere past the shooter's hand.
> So make them melt as the dishoused snail,

But the stanza concludes with the image of a still-born child:

> Or as the embryo whose vital band
> Breaks ere it holds, and formless eyes do fail
> To see the sun, though brought to lightful life.
>   (Sidney, 1992: 55)

The graphic description can be more fully appreciated when it is compared with the text in the Great Bible of 1539, translated by Miles Coverdale: 'like the untimely fruit of a woman and let them not see the sun'. Tension is created here by the interaction of the vehicle – the still-born child – and tenor – the destruction of the enemy – which constitute Mary Sidney's metaphor. The poetic urgency, vigorous syntax and the emotional intensity of the translation anticipate the lyrics of John Donne, who expressed his admiration of the Sidneian psalter.

The rendering of the *Psalms* into English by Protestant reformers was equally a political undertaking. Sung, set to music, read privately, or rewritten as consolatory exercises (as both Thomas Wyatt and Anne Askew did in prison), the *Psalms* enabled an exploration of subjectivity whilst representing the spiritual life of the Reformed church. In England the Reformers saw the state as a new Israel and the suffering, faith and joy recorded by the protagonists of the *Psalms* were a state of being with which they identified. Begun by a Protestant cultural hero in her brother, Mary Sidney's translations acquired an additional political significance in their dedication and presentation to Queen Elizabeth, who is likened to David. This is no empty praise, but carries with it an exhortation to the Queen to fulfil her obligations, defend the true faith and 'doo what men may sing'. Her essentially scholarly act thus has its motivation in upholding the Sidney tradition by stimulating an active Protestant and nationalist aristocracy.

It is possible to see the Jacobean period as a transitional moment for women seeking to gain access to the circulation, if not the publication, of literary works which were neither strictly devotional nor translations. Early seventeenth-century texts authored by women begin to explore questions relating to female identity, subjectivity and subjectification submerged in the act, if not the choice, of translation. Aemelia Lanyer, in her long poem partly concerned with the passion of Christ, *Salve Deus Rex Judaeorum* (1611), uses her biblical sources much more obviously to women's advantage. Elizabeth Cary's original closet drama *Mariam* (1613) is self-evidently female-centred; but in its representation of subjectivity as a *locus* of consciousness, it goes further than other dramas of female heroism. In the poetry and prose of Lady Mary Wroth there is some exposure of the cultural codes and networks which constrain women. Finally, and perhaps most significantly from a cultural point of view, women entered the formal controversy which had long surrounded the roles and alleged dispositions of the sexes.

Lanyer's poem *Salve Deus Rex Judaeorum*, comprising nearly two thousand lines, is at once a vivid narration of the Passion and Resurrection of Christ, at times echoing the Gospel of Matthew almost *verbatim*, and a moral vindication of women. The Passion constitutes only one component of a narrative described on the title page as also containing 'Eve's Apologie in defence of women', 'The Teares of the Daughters of Jerusalem' and 'The Salutation and Sorrow of the Virgine Marie'. The close reading of scripture is in keeping with Lanyer's Protestantism, but events are narrated so that the significance and nature of women's roles in the story are foregrounded. In her meditative repudiations of the cultural stereotyping of Eve and in her address to virtuous women, Lanyer is self-consciously writing against patriarchy and patristic discourse. The poem contains a number of novel perspectives on the feminine. It is unusual, for example, to approach Mary's virginity in terms of her 'being from all men *free*' (Lanyer, 1993: 97, my italics), as opposed to her being untouched, or unsullied, by man. Lanyer reverts to the medieval tradition in describing Christ through the imagery of female beauty, in contrast to a tradition which depicted Christ as the male lover wedded to his faithful (female) church. It is, moreover, provocative to depict the Countess of Cumberland receiving the keys of St Peter, with all the authority that bequest implies. Of all the virtuous women whom she could have chosen from the Old Testament, Lanyer chose Deborah, Judith, and Esther: three formidable figures who would not in any way approximate to contemporary notions of female passivity.[7] Such a questioning, feminine poetic consciousness in a religious text is a remarkable new departure in this period.

The work begins on a secular note with a nostalgic evocation of Elizabeth I as Cynthia, whose death has caused the poet to immortalize Margaret Clifford, Countess of Cumberland in her stead. After a meditation resonant with language from the Psalms and Gospels on the glory and ubiquity of God, represented in familiar images of monarch and bridegroom, Lanyer addresses and idealizes the countess. Her portrayal of Margaret Clifford's seclusion at Cookham is at odds with the material reality of the countess's seclusion: Cookham was a temporary refuge while she and her daughter were striving to retain lands willed by her husband to his brother. But in

Lanyer's text the countess, who through her virtue and piety shows her contempt for worldly things, shares the divine glory. Recalling pronounced anti-court sentiment in Jacobean satire and drama, Lanyer applauds Margaret for her withdrawal from the society of the court:

> Thou from the Court to the Countrie art retir'd,
> Leaving the world, before the world leaves thee:
> That great Enchantresse of weak mindes admir'd,
> Whose all-bewitching charmes so pleasing be
> To worldly wantons; and too much desir'd
> Of those that care not for Eternitie
>
> (Lanyer, 1993: 58)

There is nothing new in these representations of seclusion from the world, but in representing a woman as withdrawing from the essentially male world of court politics and preferring 'to serve a heav'nly King', Lanyer gives the motif a more feminist nuance. In these early stanzas she engages with other familiar poetic motifs, notably the idea in much neo-Platonic and courtly love poetry that beauty can be equated with virtue. Lanyer distances herself from other, male, poetry of praise: 'That outward Beautie which the world commends, / Is not the subject I will write upon.' Through the evocation of various women whose beauty led to distress and downfall, Lanyer returns to the supreme quality of grace which makes the countess pleasing in her maker's sight.

After this lengthy introduction, with its interrogation of conventional poetics, Lanyer addresses the reader and seeks to justify her involvement with her elevated theme. At first, she is apologetic, invoking the image of Icarus, fearing that her muse may be flying above its 'appointed strain'. But then, as did Askew, she appropriates the biblical commonplace that the weaker the vessel used for divine purposes, the more is God glorified:

> But yet the Weaker thou doest seeme to be
> In Sexe, or Sence, the more his Glory shines,
> That doth infuze such powerfull Grace in thee,
> To shew thy love in these few humble Lines; (63)

A modesty trope is rewritten so that the poet is able to claim (as did Milton in far more rhetorical terms in the invocation to *Paradise Lost*) that the poem is divinely inspired.

The biblical narrative begins with the intensely dramatic events of Gethsemane: at this point the narrator's voice is largely subsumed in the story. Her style, however, remains personal in its emotionally sympathetic descriptions and perspectives. In a style characteristic of the Baroque, Lanyer evokes the figure of the praying Christ at Gethsemane:

> Thou prayedst more earnestly, in so great feare,
> That precious sweat came trickling to the ground,
> Like drops of blood thy sences to confound. (69)

She differentiates between the patriarchal God and the Son: 'Loe here his Will, not thy Will, Lord was done'. She stresses Christ's innocence, his suffering, humility, gentleness and obedience – those virtues commonly associated with the female – while noting that his betrayers and persecutors are all men. Even the disciples forsake Christ, and 'do like men, when dangers overtake them'. Only Pilate's wife intervenes in an attempt to prevent the violation of justice, and her voice and that of the narrator intermix in their plea, 'Let not us Women glory in Mens fall / Who had power given to over-rule us all' (84).

The implication that men's involvement with the death of Christ is the equivalent of a second Fall represents a startling rewriting of traditional doctrine. Lanyer takes this further and, subverting centuries of misogynistic interpretations of the Fall, claims (as later would Rachel Speght) that Eve was less culpable than Adam. Again, she appropriates familiar concepts of the primal relationship. Since Adam was the physically stronger of the sexes and had more direct communication with God, it lay with him to resist temptation. Man's greater involvement in the act of Original Sin occasions a return to men's betrayal of Christ, culminating in the stanza in which the narrator makes an impassioned plea for female equality:

> Then let us have our Libertie againe,
> And challendge to our selves no Sov'raigntie;
> You came not in the world without our paine,
> Make that a barre against your crueltie:
> Your fault beeing greater, why should you disdaine
> Our beeing your equals, free from tyranny?
> If one weake woman simply did offend,
> This sinne of yours, hath no excuse, nor end. (87)

To reinforce the stanza's final bold assertion, Lanyer retells the events leading to the Crucifixion, in which the 'daughters of Jerusalem' assume a central significance. The poet addresses the women and in opulent language describes their empathic relation to Christ: 'Your tearefull eyes, beheld his eies more bright . . . Your Eagles eyes did gaze against this Sunne / Your hearts did thinke, he dead, the world were done' (93–4). The scene shifts to focus on Mary the woeful mother, 'all comfortlesse in depth of sorow drowned', then reverts to the other iconic representation of Mary, the virgin of the *Magnificat*. Here, Lanyer seems to revive the pieties of the later medieval religious lyric. Moreover, the *Magnificat*, with its destruction of the proud and its elevation of the lowly, is an appropriate verse for Lanyer to employ in her programme for the return of women's 'Libertie'.

Salve Deus Rex Judaeorum is ostensibly a religious poem which imports into a Protestant poetic some aspects of the long Passion lyrics of the fifteenth century. However, it also has to be read as a medium for Lanyer to express contentious ideas in a bid for female patronage. When the poem was originally published in 1611 it contained eleven elaborate dedications, all to women, including Queen Anne, and a further poem addressed to 'all vertuous Ladies in generall'. Among the dedicatees was Margaret, Countess Dowager of Cumberland: the poem opens and closes extolling her virtues, a motif which recurs throughout the text. From the country house poem 'The Description of Cooke-ham' which concludes the volume, it is apparent that Lanyer had resided with the countess and that she hoped, through her poetic offerings, that some economic favour might continue. There is, however, no evidence that Lanyer received any financial reward or preferment through her writing. While patronage was offered by women – and there are numerous tributes to female patrons from Daniel, Jonson and Donne – it was not yet open to them as writers and poets.

As a country house poem, 'The Description of Cooke-ham' is interesting in its female adaptation, rather than appropriation, of a male language of clientage. A useful comparison can be made with Ben Jonson's more well-known celebration of the Sidney family estate 'To Penshurst', which may post-date Lanyer's poem. In Lanyer's work, however, the house and the estate are subordinate to the presence of the countess and to the poet's memory of the countess's daughter, Anne Clifford, who has departed to marry the Earl of Dorset. As the verse moves towards the fragmentation of the female household, the language changes from its initial celebration of the countess and its appreciation of the house as vitalized by her presence. With Anne's departure the character of the estate is metamorphosed. Images of desolation body forth Lanyer's sense of loss at Anne's absence and presage her own imminent departure from the same privileged world. At one point, the poet's personal voice breaks through the patterns of conventional praise as Lanyer self-consciously complains about the social distance between herself and her would-be patrons:

> Unconstant fortune, thou art most too blame,
> Who casts us downe into so lowe a frame:
> Where our great friends we cannot dayly see,
> So great a difference is there in degree.
> (Lanyer, 1993: 134)

This sense of grievance about class distinctions is also conveyed in several of the dedications to the volume. In contrast, Jonson's voice in 'To Penshurst' is impersonal and assured, betraying nothing of Lanyer's insecurity in his role as poet/client. The fantasized notion of lower-class femininity as a site of greater freedom which subsists in both male and female authored texts of the period is far removed from the material reality of the socially subordinate writing woman.

Lack of access to publication may explain why Elizabeth Cary's original closet drama *The Tragedie of Mariam* was not published until 1613, nearly a decade after it was apparently composed. Written when she was 17, the play, based on Thomas Lodge's translation of Josephus's *Antiquities of the Jews*, exemplifies Cary's precocious scholarship, which was later demonstrated in her translation of a controversial Catholic work, *The Reply of the Most Illustrious Cardinall of Perron, to the Answeare of the Most Excellent King of Great Britaine* (1630) and in her political history *The History of the Life, Reign, and Death of Edward II*, published only in 1680.

Mariam draws on episodes from Josephus's account of early Palestinian history: the consolidation of Herod's power as King of the Jews, his marriage to his second wife Mariam, the murder of her brother and grandfather, the arousal of his jealousy fuelled by his sister Salome and the subsequent execution of Mariam. Josephus emphasizes the price paid by Herod within his own house for his public domination. It is this aspect of domestic relations played out against larger political events that engages Cary, but with the notable difference that Mariam is not represented merely as victim of Herod's jealousy, but as a subject who constructs herself in opposition to her husband's tyranny.

The play conforms to the conventions of neo-Senecan closet drama. As the final Chorus reminds the reader, the dramatic unities have been preserved in so far as all the vicissitudes of events have been compressed into one day. There is one location, that of Jerusalem, and the action is clearly focused on the domestic intrigues and emotions which contribute to Mariam's tragedy. In keeping with the convention of reporting rather than representing violent, climactic events, a messenger relays the news of Mariam's death while Herod's crazed grief and remorse are expansively articulated. At the end of each act, the Chorus offers a moralistic interpretation of events which is sometimes at odds with the tensions and complexities of the drama. Despite its formal adherence to the strictures of closet drama, *Mariam* is self-evidently more dramatic in its plotting and characterization and has more theatrical potential than earlier examples of the genre.[8]

The inner dynamics of the drama are boldly established in the first scene. This comprises Mariam's soliloquy, which is premissed on the presumptuous rumour that Herod has been executed by Caesar in Rome. Mariam's speech encapsulates a turmoil of feelings: she had begun to hate her husband for his cruelties while he lived, but now believing him dead, she recalls his love for her, which demands some kind of recognition. Emotions again fluctuate as she considers Herod's despotic order, re-layed to her by his counsellor Sohemus, that in the event of his death she is to be executed. Interestingly, Cary adds additional domestic intrigue and some parallelism to the plotting, which involves Salome's desire to rid herself of her husband in order to marry her lover Silleus, Prince of Arabia. Salome is an unambiguously malevolent character, resembling Iago in her manipulative skills; nevertheless she is given reson-ant lines about the unfairness for women of laws governing divorce. Her assertions that she means not to be ruled by precedent and that she will secure a divorce from her husband provoke an enraged response:

> Are Hebrew women now transformed to men?
> Why do you not our battles fight.
> And wear our armour? Suffer this, and then
> Let all the world be topsy-turvèd quite.
>
> (I.vi.421–4)

The means by which Salome acquires her freedom are, however, entirely reprehens-ible and as such they cast into relief the integrity of Mariam's expression of autonomy.

That the report of Herod's death is false merely serves to confirm Mariam's hatred of her husband. When Herod returns to Jerusalem, eagerly anticipating his reunion with Mariam, she has determined on opposition: 'I will not to his love be reconcil'd,

With solemn vows I have forsworn his bed.' In a defiant speech, she recognizes that she has power to beguile and manipulate Herod, but disdains to do so. She will maintain her own identity, depending on her reputation, which she believes – too confidently, as it turns out – will protect her from slander. Such bold assertions provoke a reaction from Sohemus – 'Unbridled speech is Mariam's worst disgrace' – and a more moralizing caution from the Chorus. When Mariam meets the returned Herod, she confronts him with his past crimes against her family. From there, with little preparation, Salome's plot against Mariam takes over. Manipulated by his sister, Herod's abrupt reversion from uxoriousness to distrustful jealousy to revenge is powerfully communicated. Mariam's response to Herod's accusation that she is plotting to poison him ('Is this a dream') anticipates Hermione's response in *The Winter's Tale* to the tyrannically jealous Leontes ('My life stands in the level of your dreams'), while Herod matches Leontes in his vituperation and obsessive jealousy. Yet at a psychological level, Cary's play is in some ways more complex. Mariam's only half-spoken antipathy towards Herod facilitates Salome's plotting and Herod's intuition of it works subliminally to make him believe something which he knows not to be true. His disordered thought is evident in his request to Salome to order Mariam's execution and then enact physical reparation:

> Why, let my love be slain,
> But if we cannot live without her sight
> You'll find the means to make her breathe again.
> (IV.vii.385–7)

The final scenes are dominated by Herod's remorse and self-recrimination, which are predicted by Mariam in the messenger's report to her husband: ' "By three days hence, if wishes could revive / I know himself would make me oft alive" '. Herod's self-lacerations contrast with the descriptions of Mariam's stoical death and the economy of her language. It is as if she had internalized the strictures on feminine silence earlier articulated by the Chorus and Sohemus. Her prison soliloquy in Act IV suggests some kind of retraction of her former assertion of self:

> Had not myself against myself conspir'd,
> No plot, no adversary from without
> Could Herod's love from Mariam have retir'd
> Or from his heart have thrust my semblance out. . . .
> Had I but with humility been grac'd,
> As well as fair I might have prov'd me wise:
> But I did think because I knew me chaste,
> One virtue for a woman might suffice.
> That mind for glory of our sex might stand,
> wherein humility and chastity
> Doth march with equal paces hand in hand.
> (IV.viii.533–65)

Here, Mariam seems at one level to be endorsing cultural prescriptions of feminine behaviour and accepting that transgression of such boundaries can only bring misfortune. It would be a mistake, however, to foreground the speech as conveying the play's central perspective on gender. Mariam's words are spoken with only partial knowledge of the extent of Salome's plot against her. However much she may try to rationalize her downfall as a consequence of 'unwomanly' behaviour, this is not endorsed by the play. Constabarus on his way to execution comments:

> But no farewell to any female wight
> You wavering crew; my curse to you I leave,
> You had but one to give you any grace:
> And you yourself will Mariam's life bereave.
>   (IV.vi.310–13)

This misogynist speech has, nevertheless, a ring of truth about it. Mariam is destroyed by another woman, as Othello is destroyed by another man. What Herod praises as Mariam's 'world-amazing wit' plays into the hands of Salome; but it does not in itself cause her tragedy.

In her redaction of early Jewish history, thereby giving Mariam a voice, Cary was reinterpreting historical material from a woman's perspective and achieving something quite novel. Unlike other plays of the period in which the female heroine is central – albeit plays performed in the public playhouse and not, as *Mariam*, read aloud – the conflict is here consistently presented from Mariam's position. Mariam's psychology, Herod's explosion of jealousy, the irony caused by the concealment for half the play that Herod is alive and the control of intrigue further reveal Cary's dramatic skills. Yet the drama to some extent remains inhibited by the formal constraints of its genre. The sententious Chorus and the stoical suffering and death of Mariam rest uncomfortably in a play where human conflicts are so fully realized.

Like Elizabeth Cary, Lady Mary Wroth broke new ground in writing within genres hitherto authored by men. Her prose romance *Urania*, and sonnet sequence 'Pamphilia to Amphilanthus', published in the same volume in 1621, are important as the first of their kind to be written by a woman, but they are also significant as late interventions in genres whose appeal had reached its peak during the previous century. The fact that these works are female authored and that they were composed with an aesthetic self-consciousness of out-moded conventions makes their writing strategies and perspectives particularly novel.

Urania, as a late Jacobean text, is quite different in narrative detail and in tone from the Elizabethan pastoral romance epitomized by *The Countesse of Pembroke's Arcadia* (1590), written by Wroth's uncle Philip Sidney for his sister Mary Sidney. *Urania* does not present a coherent world of moral mythology, but rather depicts the frailty of human emotion and purposes in continually shifting political and personal circumstances. Love and passion, treated humorously by Sidney, are often treated ironically by Wroth. Nevertheless, at a local level, *Urania* does recall aspects of its generic antecedents. The very title of Wroth's romance recalls the opening chapter of *Arcadia*, where the shepherds Claius and Strephon are mourning the absence of the recently departed shepherdess Urania. Wroth's romance, however, opens in the presence of Urania, who, having discovered that she is not, as she thought, the daughter of the shepherds, is mourning the loss of her identity.[9] Wroth, after Sidney, draws on Platonic and Protestant associations of Urania as the heavenly muse, the higher type of Venus. In Sidney's story, Urania had slipped from view and so, also, some way into Wroth's narrative Urania is for a considerable time abandoned by the narrator. While Urania is left imprisoned in the Tower of Love – an allegorical construct reminiscent of Spenser – the role of female heroine is assumed by Pamphilia, the daughter of the King of Morea, later Queen of Pamphilia and, most importantly in the context of Book One of *Urania*, lover of Amphilanthus. Thus, in its own way, Wroth's title is as misleading as that of Sidney, in so far as much of Sidney's story is located in the false pastoral idyll of Basilius's country court.

As representative of a genre which specializes in multiple narrative strands, numerous inset stories and apparently chaotic plotting, and which privileges the arbitrary and the contingent event over cause and effect, *Urania* excels. In its multiplicity of detail as well as its occasional use of allegory and symbolism, Wroth's romance is closer to Spenser's *Faerie Queene* than it is to *Arcadia*. Aspects of Shakespeare's late romances also seem to figure in the representation of the sundering of friends, family and lovers, although unlike Shakespeare's last plays there are few reunions and reconciliations signifying closure. Indeed, the last sentence of Book Four of *Urania*, which ends the published volume, is, like *Arcadia*, incomplete and, even as it again unites Pamphilia and Amphilanthus, suggests another journey:

> *Amphilanthus* must goe, but intreates *Pamphilia* to goe as far as *Italy* with him, to visit the matchles Queene his mother, she consents, for what can she denye him? all things are prepared for the journey, all now merry, contented, nothing amisse; griefe forsaken, sadnes cast off, *Pamphilia* is the Queene of all content; Amphilanthus joying worthily in her and

The romance ends formally on a provisional note. The journey will continue; Pamphilia will accompany Amphilanthus only 'as far as Italy'. Indeed, the sense that the reunion of the lovers is temporary only is borne out by Wroth's sequel, preserved in manuscript and never published, in which Amphilanthus and Pamphilia are married to others.

There is no real focal point to *Urania*, as the action shifts across Europe and Asia and encompasses the fortunes in love and adventure of the younger generation of royal children. The political world depicted in episodes of tyrannical rule and usurpation is harsher than the false pastoral idyll of Sidney's *Arcadia*. Love is often unrequited, or blighted by inconstancy. The unhappy love affair between Perissus and Limena which Perissus recounts to Urania at the beginning of the romance, is one of the few relationships to be ultimately fulfilled. Perhaps reflecting the sexual intrigues of Jacobean court circles known to Wroth, betrayal is common. Parselius, brother of Pamphilia, for instance, grieves over his separation from Urania, but readily betrays her when he encounters the charms of Dalinea:

> All this Parselius beheld, but most the princess who he so much admired as admiration wrought so far as to permit him to think that she equalled Urania. This was a sudden step from so entire a love as but now he vowed to his shepherdess, being an heresy, as he

protested, for any man to think there lived a creature like his love. But into this he is now fallen, and will lead the faction against her. Uncertain tyrant love, that never brings thy favourites to the top of affection but turns again to a new choice! Who would have thought any but Urania's beauty could have invited Parselius to love? . . . . He was not so struck with wonder when he first saw Urania (though with it he lost his liberty) as he was now wounded to death, losing life if no compassion succeeded. This first sight won him and lost his former bondage; yet was he freed but to take a new bond upon him. (Wroth, 1991: 149)

Love as bondage is a recurrent metaphor, but one which is more apt for women, who have limited modes of agency, than for men. Antissia, daughter of the King of Roumania, finds herself in love with Amphilanthus, a condition which, the narrator comments, leads to 'her lost liberty'. Separated from Pamphilia, Amphilanthus, whose name literally means lover of two, unthinkingly responds to her passionate feelings. The narrator's tone is dry and ironic as Amphilanthus's dalliance with Antissia is described: 'He, the more he saw her respect to him, answered it with his to her. Kindness then betrayed them, she showing it, he (as a kind hearted prince to ladies) receiving it' (Wroth, 1991: 74). In a syntactically complex sentence, the convention of chivalric love is again treated with wry understatement: 'He was not inexperienced, therefore soon saw remedy must be given, and cruelty he imagined it would be in him, who discerned he might by his art help, if he refused that good to one so fair and so kindly loving' (Wroth, 1991: 75). In contrast with this almost studied engagement of feeling, Antissia suffers the torments of jealousy and Pamphilia pain from the knowledge of Amphilanthus's faithlessness. Further, the inherent dishonesty of the knightly code can be contrasted with the directness of Pamphilia towards the love-making of Steriamus: 'Leave this folly and I will wish you well' (Wroth, 1991: 85).

Through the figures of Urania, Antissia and particularly Pamphilia, we have the first exploration in English romance literature by a woman writer of female subjectivity which initiates action. Urania's mode of agency is as a counsellor to others, whereas, interestingly, Pamphilia is presented as a writer. Authorship is seen as one of the few modes of self-expression available to her as a woman. Although Pamphilia tells Antissia that 'many poets write as well by imitation as by sense of passion' (Wroth, 1991: 114), it is clear that for Pamphilia, writing becomes a refuge for feelings which she is culturally conditioned to suppress. Even Antissia, who is far more uncontrolled in exposing her jealous feelings, recognizes that writing will enable her 'to put her thoughts in some kind of measure'.

As a romance, *Urania* explores female rather than male heroism, in so far as the challenges laid down are of love rather than of conflict. When male heroism is on display, as in the rescue of Limena, Wroth casts an oblique light on it. The description of Limena's bondage is erotic, apparently pandering to male voyeurism:

he tied her to it [a pillar] by the hair, which was of great length and sun-like brightness. Then pulled he off a mantle which she wore, leaving her from the girdle upwards all naked, her soft, dainty white hands he fastened behind her with a cord about both wrists, in manner of a cross, as testimony of her cruellest martyrdom. (Wroth, 1991: 101–2)

From this state of abjection Limena is rescued by Parselius, who is 'quickly put out of his admiration, hasting to revenge her wrong'. In the midst of the conflict, another knight arrives and unties Limena. With a light comic touch, Wroth conveys Parselius's offence at being thus upstaged: 'whereat Parselius was offended, thinking himself highly injured that any, except himself, should do that service, telling him he much wondered at his boldness'. Whereas men suffer love and desire as much as women, they are perceived to find self-expression in their public roles and martial exploits. Steriamus, who is in love with Pamphilia, is counselled by Amphilanthus to return to Albania because 'the rest of the world hath need of such princes' (Wroth, 1991: 85), and not to allow passion to overthrow a brave spirit. Women are seen to have no such recourse to action and, in addition, have to suffer the torment of male inconstancy.

Soon after *Urania* was published, Wroth was forced to withdraw it on the grounds that it contained covert allusions to contemporary court affairs. John Chamberlain, writing to Dudley Carleton, reported that Lord Denny had taken exception to allusions to himself and his family. According to contemporary opinion, relayed by Chamberlain, Wroth's audacity was displayed in her barely concealed purposes, which she had expected to pass unnoticed: she had taken 'license to traduce whom she please, and thincks she daunces in a net' (Lewalski, 1993: 249–50). Denny vented his anger in a satirical poem, in which he addresses Wroth as 'hermophradite in show, in deed a monster' and admonishes her to 'leave idle bookes alone / For wise and worthyer women have writte none'. In support of his censoring activity, Denny was able to invoke the notion of writing as an unwomanly activity. Wroth retaliated with her verses, chiding Denny, 'lett rauling rimes alone / For wise and worthier men have written none'. In this confrontation over a woman's text, the woman was silenced, but so was her male critic.

In the sonnet sequence, 'Pamphilia to Amphilanthus' (Wroth, 1992), composed before *Urania*, the persona of Pamphilia is consistent with the character of the romance. The early sonnets record her sufferings at her lover's inconstancy. Here Wroth expands the nature of the genre to explore the experience of love itself. Philip Sidney's 'Astrophel and Stella' might be regarded as a model for Wroth's work, in so far as she was consciously returning to a genre of Petrarchan love poetry which had been culturally displaced by the metaphysical style. There are, however, significant differences between the two. 'Astrophel and Stella' is dominated by a powerful subjectivity and dramatization of the self. The sequence creates the persona of the lover as a subject in a continual state of restless excitement; he is always on the verge of new feelings of hope or frustration. Stella, the unattainable woman, is evoked, but she remains the silent interlocutor. She is an absent presence. In 'Pamphilia to Amphilanthus', the personality of the subject is less dominant and there is no direct role reversal in the sense of a female lover's overt and passionate solicitation of the male beloved. The latter is displaced and silenced as the relationship and the feelings it elicits, rather than the beloved himself, becomes the focal point. Indeed, in none of the sonnets is Amphilanthus specifically evoked.

That love itself rather than the beloved is the stimulus to poetry is conveyed in the opening sonnet, 'When nights black mantle could most darknes prove'. Recalling

Petrarch's 'Trionfe d'Amore', Pamphilia experiences a dream vision in which Cupid and Venus triumph over her heart:

> Butt one hart flaming more than all the rest
> The goddess held, and putt itt to my brest,
> Deare sonne, now shutt sayd she: thus must wee winn;
> Hee her obay'd, and martir'd my poore hart,
> I, waking hop'd as dreames itt would depart
> Yett since: O mee: a lover I have binn.
>
> (Wroth, 1992: 85)

Later, in subsequent sonnets, the persona struggles to free herself from the will of the gods and discover the nature of love for herself. The closing couplet of Sonnet 7 is an address to Cupid and an assertion of self: 'Yett this Sir God, your boyship I dispise; / Your charmes I obay, but love nott want of eyes'. This rejection of the familiar idea of love rendering its victim blind and helpless is only momentary and the struggle between states of surrender and autonomy becomes the thread throughout the sonnets. Sonnet 14, for instance, opens with a despairing recognition of the paradoxical nature of enslavement: 'Am I thus conquer'd? have I lost the powers / That to withstand, which joy's to ruin mee?' But, although the persona attempts to assert her freedom, love is more coercive: 'I love, and must: So farwell liberty'. The opposition of love and liberty in Wroth's sonnets replaces, for most of the sequence, the more familiar conflict in the male-authored sonnet between physical desire and neo–Platonic notions of love leading to virtue and supreme reason: although, in 'A Crowne of Sonnets dedicated to Love', which completes 'Pamphilia to Amphilanthus', love is represented as enhancing reason.

Wroth recalls a whole discourse of passionate, unrequited love to explore female subjectivity. Although she exploits the conventions associated with Petrarch and the familiar images of night, sleep, grief and absence, she often uses such tropes in a subtle, skilfully sustained manner. Sonnet 43 is one of a group of sonnets conveying a sense of loss at what is presumably the absence of Amphilanthus. In the opening lines the poet builds up conventional associations of eyes as supreme, 'lights and guids of love', but then reverses such associations. In the absence of the beloved, eyes are no longer associated with light: they become 'poore lost roomes' possessed by darkness. Skilfully weaving the literal and the symbolic, Wroth demands an abnegation of all light in sympathy with the lover:

> Soe bee all blessed lights from henceforth hid
> That this black deed of darknes have excess,
> For why showld heaven afford least light to those
> Who for my misery such darknes chose

Here, and elsewhere, Wroth reworks and revises standard tropes in the service of a poetics of love designed not to court a lover or to express the physical charms of a desired object, but to enact a drama of love, desire and loss in the consciousness of the woman-lover-poet.

In the history of the literary Renaissance, the work of Cary, Lanyer and Wroth significantly marks the female appropriation of male-authored genres so as to offer fuller expression of female agency and subjectivity. Of equal cultural significance were the women who had no connection with writing through birth or patronage, but who intervened as authors in the formal debate about the nature of women. Rhetorically constructed attacks upon and defences of women, sometimes by the same author, were popular reading material throughout the sixteenth century and presumably contributed to essentialist concepts of the sexes.[10] Whatever the motivation for entering into the debate, the premiss of this literary genre was a gendered one. Certain assumptions were held about female nature, regardless of any cultural influences on behaviour and of class and social differences between women. Whether in the form of denunciation or defence of women, tracts were authored by men.

One early exception may have been 'Jane Anger', who published *Jane Anger Her Protection for Women* in 1589; although the name is certainly a pseudonym, it seems likely, in view of its sustained lambasting of misogynist attitudes, that the text is female-authored. It is difficult to assess the qualities of a work belonging to a genre which had never been associated with integrity and sincerity. As Linda Woodbridge has commented, overt sincerity and righteous indignation can themselves be sophisticated poses (1984: 57). Nevertheless, Anger's pamphlet is witty and vigorous in her puncturing of crude male prejudices against women and also in exposing some of the inherent contradictions in male polemic. Adopting the structures of formal indictments of women, men are attacked for inherent vices – notably, lust, deceit and malice – and a catalogue of both exemplary and unexemplary men is offered. The argument might be simple – if there are bad women in history, there are also bad men – but it needed to be voiced. In shifting some of the ground of the controversy, Anger's pamphlet represents a key text.

One particularly virulent attack on women in the Jacobean period, by Joseph Swetnam, a fencing teacher, provoked other female authors to enter further into the formal debate. The title of Swetnam's tirade *The Arraigment of Lewd, Idle, Froward, and Unconstant Women; or the vanity of them, Choose You Whether. With a Commendation of Wise, Virtuous, and Honest Women* published in 1615 was misleading, since it contained no commendation of women whatsoever. Instead, the pamphlet consists of invective, replete with fantastic allusions to women's sexuality and their alleged desire to dominate and usurp power in the household. Men are oppressed, women are the vocal sex with tongues that cause terror and wreak utter confusion on their sorry victims. Clearly, Swetnam was exploiting the lucrative market for anti-feminist polemic, and the replies of Rachel Speght, and of the pseudonymous Ester Sowernam and Constantia Munda, fuelled interest in the controversy.[11] Of the responses, Speght's *A Mouzell for Melastomus* is the most interesting for the author's sense of mission, her self-proclaimed authorship (at 19), and the lucidity of her refutation of Swetnam's polemic.

Speght's Calvinism is apparent in her self-fashioning as God's warrior, a revealing appropriation of a religious image for an ostensibly secular purpose, and as a protective guise against the popular charge of woman's unruly speech. She continues to express her objectives in biblical terms, claiming that she will expose the speciousness of Swetnam's use of scripture and in so doing 'comfort the mindes of all *Hevah*'s sex', so that they need not 'fear the darts of envy or obtrectators' (A3v). Confuting the popular prejudice of woman's irrationality and lack of control, Speght's argument is reasoned, logical and cleverly scriptural. In her Preface she had accused Swetnam of 'wresting and perverting everie place of Scripture' (B2v), and her text reveals a lucid exposition of Swetnam's misconstructions. Like Lanyer, Speght shows an awareness of how the Bible has been misappropriated to legitimate a view of woman's moral inferiority and subordination. Revising the conventional idea of woman's weakness, she argues that men and women must take equal responsibility for the Fall:

> [Eve] being the weaker vessell was with more facility to be seduced: Like as a Cristall glasse sooner receives a cracke than a strong stone pot. Yet we shall finde the offence of *Adam* and *Eve* almost to paralell: For as an ambitious desire of being made like unto God, was with the motive which caused her to eate, so likewise was it his. (4)

Again, like Lanyer, Speght is writing purposefully against the popular and misogynist construction of Eve; it is particularly interesting that she is doing so within the limited scope of the satirical pamphlet, which was often regarded as a salacious and scandalous medium.

Four years after Speght had entered the arena of the formal controversy, she published her second and quite different work, a verse meditation, *Mortalities Memorandum, with a Dreame Prefixed, imaginarie in manner; reale in matter* (1621). The well-established genre of the allegorical dream vision is here used creatively to expose the educational restrictions placed on women and the morally destructive aspects of misogyny as represented by Swetnam. *A Dreame* begins with a speaker in an ailing condition which has been caused by the disease of ignorance:

> My grief, quoth I, is called *Ignorance*,
> Which makes me differ little from a brute.
>
> I hungry am, yet cannot seeke for foode;
> Because I know not what is bad or good
> (Speght, 1621: 2)

Experience, personified, tells her that only true knowledge which 'by labour is attain'd' in Erudition's garden can help her. The anti-feminist position is expressed by 'Disswasion', who points to alleged personal difficulties of attaining knowledge, including the speaker's dullness and defective memory, and then, tellingly, her 'time and sex'. Disswasion is silenced by Desire, supported by Industry and then by Truth, who tells the speaker that according to Paul both men and women have 'bodie, soule and spirit' and thus that 'a Woman have her intellect in vaine / Or not endevour *Knowledge* to attaine' (5). Again, a woman writer has deftly reclaimed St Paul for her own purposes. The 'journeyes end' of the speaker is an Edenic paradise, where she tastes of all types of knowledge and where intellectual desire is represented as 'lawfull avarice'. The visionary, allegorical nature of the poem allows Speght the freedom to imagine a utopia in which female learning is venerated. The experience of the dream is, however, shattered by the intrusion of the present and the speaker's recollection of her opposition to Swetnam:

> I therefore to that place return'd againe.
> From whence I came, and where I must remaine.
> But by the way I saw a full fed Beast,
> Which roared like some monster, or a Devill,
> And on *Eves* sex he foamed filthie froth;
> As if that he had had the falling evill;
> To whom I went to free them from mishaps,
> And with a *Mouzel* sought to binde his chaps.

The inter-textual allusions draw attention to Speght's self-identity as a writer, even though she acknowledges that it was not she, but Constantia Munda, who had succeeded in silencing her opponent. The sequence continues with allusions to the depredations of death as greater even than those inflicted on women by Swetnam and the poem becomes more personal as it concludes with the author's grief over the death of her mother.

Mortalities Memorandum, with its biblical maxims and sermonizing tone, lacks the originality and daring of *A Dreame*. The structural imbalance between the challenging *Dreame* and the ideological commonplaces of *Mortalities Memorandum* may in part be due to the position of the female writer discovering strategies for public expression. Despite the pedestrian nature of *Mortalities Memorandum*, Speght continues to consolidate her Christian defence of women: death was inflicted as a curse, but 'womans seede hath brooke the serpants head'. With its emphasis on the familiar *contemptus mundi* theme, the work might be interpreted as an appropriate leave-taking of a literary, creative life, a departure, referred to in passing in *A Dreame*. In the latter text Speght had alluded to some unspecified 'occurance' which called her away from the pursuit of knowledge. From the outspokenness of *A Mouzell* through the female consciousness of the visionary *Dreame* to the retreat into the anti-worldliness of *Mortalities Memorandum*, Speght defines her ambitions as polemicist and poet.

Speght's work provides an illuminating comparison with that of Anne Askew. Both women wrote as part of their Christian duty and regarded their faith as sanction for their public testimonies. But, whereas Askew's *Examinacyons* were endorsed because they could be harnessed to the Protestant cause, the reception of Speght's Christian defence of women was less favourable. She records in the opening address of *Mortalities Memorandum* that she has been both censured for her intervention in popular controversy and deprived of authorship:

> I know these populous times affoord plentie of forward Writers, and criticale Readers; My selfe hath made the number of the one too many by one; and having bin toucht with the censures of the other, by occasion of my *mouzeling Melastomus*, I am now, as by a strong motive induced (for my right's sake) to produce and divulge this of spring of my indevour, to prove them further futurely who have formerly deprived me of my due, imposing my abortive upon the father of me, but not of it.

The reason for publishing a second time is to claim rightful authorship of *A Mouzell*, which, despite Rachel Speght's name on the title page, seems to have been accredited to her father. Evidently some readers could not accept that a satirical pamphlet in defence of women had been written by a woman.

This is a salutary reminder that, despite the emergence of original writing by women in the Jacobean period, a female author was more open to censure than her male counterpart. Speght's perception of women in terms of their Christian mission was not shared by a society which allowed numerous re-printings of Swetnam's tract. *Urania* was suppressed, while court satire in Jacobean drama was allowed some freedom. Lanyer's bid for patronage appears to have failed, whereas male poets could earn some remuneration or combine writing with a professional life. Nevertheless, the remodelling of cultural representations of women which we find in all the texts of Jacobean women writers and the increasingly confident articulation of public speaking voices were contributory factors in the gradual shift away from Renaissance ideals of exemplary femininity.

Notes

I would like to thank Danielle Clarke, John Flood and John Gallagher for reading and commenting on this chapter. I am also grateful to students at Goldsmiths' College, particularly Lucy Tunstall, and MA students at UCD who contributed enthusiastically to courses on women's writing in the early modern period.

1. Where pages have not been numbered the early modern practice of indicating page by signature (for example, A-A4v (verso)) has been observed.
2. See Jardine, 1983: 49–57; Grafton and Jardine, 1986: 29–58; Janis Butler Holm, 'The Myth of a Feminist Humanism: Thomas Salter's *The Mirrhor of Modestie*' in Levin and Watson, 1987: 197–205.
3. All quotations, page and signature references are from the original texts. Extracts from both *The First Examinacyon*, *The lattre examinacyon*, and 'The Balade which Anne Askewe made and sange while she was in Newgate' are in Travitsky, 1989.
4. Askew appears to be employing 'modye', a variant on moody, in the sense of 'proud' or 'arrogant', as a deliberate poetic anachronism. I am grateful to Alan Fletcher for this information.
5. Whitney's verse will appear in *Three Renaissance Women Poets: Isabella Whitney, Mary Sidney, Amelia Lanyer*, ed. Danielle Clarke, Penguin Classics.
6. See, for example, Zim, 1987: 152–210, and Hannay, 1991: 65–81.
7. I am grateful to John Flood of the Archdiocesan Seminary of Dublin, Holy Cross College, for advising me on Lanyer's feminist theology.
8. There was a production of *Mariam* at Bradford Alhambra Theatre on 22 October 1994.
9. The discussion of *Urania* mostly refers to Book One, which appears in *An Anthology of Seventeenth-Century Fiction*, ed. Paul Salzman, World's Classics, Oxford: Oxford University Press, 1991.
10. For a detailed account and analysis of the formal debate over women, see Woodbridge, 1984.
11. For replies to Swetnam see Shepherd, 1985.

Bibliography

Primary materials

Anger, Jane (1985), *Jane Anger her Protection for Women* in *The Woman's Sharp Revenge: Five Women's Pamphlets from the Renaissance*, Simon Shepherd (ed.), London: Fourth Estate.

Askew, Anne (1546), *The first examinacyon of the worthy Servant of God, Mistresse Anne Askewe . . . lately martyred in Smith-fielde, by the Romish Antichristian Broode.*

Askew, Anne (1547), *The lattre examinacyon of the worthye servaunt of God mastres Anne Askewe.*

Bacon, Anne Cooke, (trans.) (1564), *An Apologie or answere in defence of the Church of Englande with a briefe and plaine declaration of the true Religion professed and used in the same.*

Bentley, Thomas (1582), *The Monument of Matrones*, London.

Cary, Elizabeth (1994), *The Tragedy of Mariam, the fair queen of Jewry, Elizabeth Cary, Lady Falkland, with, The Lady Falkland, her life, by one of her daughters*, Barry Weller and Margaret W. Ferguson (eds), Berkeley: University of California Press.

Cerasano, S.P. and Marion Wynne-Davies (1995), *Renaissance Drama by Women: Texts and Documents*, London: Routledge.

Greer, Germaine, Jeslyn Medoff, Melinda Sansome and Susan Hastings (eds) (1988), *Kissing the Rod: An Anthology of 17th Century Women's Verse*, London: Virago.

Lanyer, Aemelia (1993), *Salve Deus Rex Judaeorum*, Susanne Woods (ed.), Oxford: Oxford University Press.

Sidney, Mary (1592), *Discourse of Life and Death. Written in French by P. Mornay. Antonius, a Tragedie written in French by R. Garnier. Both done in English by the Countesse of Pembroke*, London.

Sidney, Mary (1912), 'The Triumph of Death' Translated from the Italian by the Countess of Pembroke, ed. Frances B. Young, *PMLA* 27, 47–65.

Sidney, Mary, Countess of Pembroke (1992), *The Sidney Psalms*, R.E. Pritchard (ed.), Manchester: Carcanet.

Sidney, Mary, Countess of Pembroke (1993), 'A Dialogue betweene two shepherds, Thenot and Piers in praise of Astraea' in *The Norton Anthology of English Literature*, sixth edition, vol. I, New York: Norton.

Sidney, Philip (1939), *The Countesse of Pembroke's Arcadia*, Albert Feuillerat (ed.), Cambridge: Cambridge University Press.

Speght, Rachel (1621), *Mortalities Memorandum with a Dreame Prefixed, imaginarie in manner reall in matter*, London. Extract in Germaine Greer et al. (eds) (1988), *Kissing the Rod: An Anthology of 17th Century Women's Verse*, London: Virago.

Speght, Rachel (1985), *A Mouzell for Melastomus* in *The Woman's Sharp Revenge: Five Women's Pamphlets from the Renaissance*, Simon Shepherd (ed.), London: Fourth Estate.

Travitsky, Betty (1980), ' "The Wyll and Testament" of Isabella Whitney', *English Literary Renaissance* 10, 83–94.

Travitsky, Betty (ed.) (1989), *The Paradise of Women: Writings by English women of the Renaissance*, New York: Columbia University Press.

Tyler, Margaret (trans.) (1989), *A mirrour of princely deeds and knighthood* in *The Paradise of Women: Writings by English women of the Renaissance*, Betty Travitsky (ed.), New York: Columbia University Press.

Vives, Juan Luis (1529), *Instruction of a Christian Woman*, trans. Richard Hyrde, London [*c.*1540].

Whitney, Isabella (1567), *Copy of a letter, lately written in meeter, by a Yonge Gentilwoman: to her unconstant lover*. Extracts in *The Paradise of Women: Writings by English women of the Renaissance*, Betty Travitsky (ed.), New York: Columbia University Press.

Whitney, Isabella (1573), *A sweet Nosgay, or pleasant Posye. Contayning a hundred and ten Phylosophicall Flowers.*

Wroth, Mary (1621), *The Countesse of Montgomeries Urania.*

Wroth, Mary (1991), *Urania*, Book One in *An Anthology of Seventeenth-Century Fiction*, Paul Salzman (ed.), Oxford: Oxford University Press.

Wroth, Mary (1992), *The Poems of Lady Mary Wroth*, Josephine Roberts (ed.), Baton Rouge: Louisiana State University Press.

Secondary sources

Armstrong, Nancy and Leonard Tennenhouse (eds) (1987), *The Ideology of Conduct: Essays on Literature and the History of Sexuality*, New York and London: Methuen.

Beilin, Elaine V. (1987), *Redeeming Eve: Women Writers of the Renaissance*, New Jersey: Princeton University Press.

Brant, Clare and Diane Purkiss (1992), *Women, Texts and Histories 1575–1760*, London: Routledge.

Bridenthal, Renate and Claudia Koonnz (1977), *Becoming Visible: Women In European History*, Boston: Houghton Mifflin.

Callaghan Dympna, (1994), 'Re-reading Elizabeth Cary's *The Tragedie of Mariam, Faire Queene of Jewry*' in *Women, 'Race' and Writing in the Early Modern Period*, Margo Hendricks and Patricia Parker (eds), London: Routledge.

Dickens, A.G. (1967), *The English Reformation*, London: Fontana.

Fehrenbach, Robert J. (1981), 'Isabella Whitney and the Popular Miscellanies of Richard Jones', *Cahiers Elisabethains* 19, 85–7.

Grafton, Anthony and Lisa Jardine (1986), *From Humanism to the Humanities*, London: Duckworth.

Hannay, Margaret (1985), *Silent but for the Word, Tudor Women as Patrons, Translators, and Writers of Religious Works*, Kent, Ohio: Kent University Press.

Hannay, Margaret (1990), *Philip's Phoenix: Mary Sidney Countess of Pembroke*, Oxford: Oxford University Press.

Hannay, Margaret (1991), ' "Wisdome the Wordes": Psalm Translation and Elizabethan Women's Spirituality', *Religion and Literature* 23:3, 65–81.

Haselkorn, Anne M. and Betty Travitsky (1990), *The Renaissance Englishwoman in Print, Counterbalancing the Canon*, Amherst: University of Massachusetts Press.

Hull, Suzanne W. (1982), *Chaste, Silent and Obedient: English Books for Women 1475–1640*, San Marino, Calif.: Huntington Library.

Jardine, Lisa (1983), *Still Harping on Daughters: Women and Drama in the Age of Shakespeare*, Hemel Hempstead: Harvester Wheatsheaf.

Krontiris, Tina (1992), *Oppositional Voices: Women as Writers and Translators of Literature in the English Renaissance*, London: Routledge.

Lamb, Mary Ellen (1990), *Gender and Authorship in the Sidney Circle*, Madison: University of Wisconsin Press.

Levin, Carole and Jeanie Watson (eds) (1987), *Ambiguous Realities: Women in the Middle Ages and Renaissance*, Detroit: Wayne State University Press.

Lewalski, Barbara Kiefer (1993), *Writing Women in Jacobean England*, Cambridge, Mass.: Harvard University Press.

Logan, George M. and Gordon Teskey (eds) (1989), *Unfolded Tales: Essays on Renaissance Romance*, Ithaca and London: Cornell University Press.

Montrose, Louis (1986), 'Renaissance Literary Studies and the Subject of History', *English Literary Renaissance* 16: I, 5–12.

Shepherd, Simon (1985), *The Woman's Sharp Revenge: Five Women's Pamphlets from the Renaissance*, London: Fourth Estate.

Waller, Gary (1979), *Mary Sidney, Countess of Pembroke: A Critical Study of her Writings and Literary Milieu*, Salzburg: Institut für Anglistik und Amerikanistik, Universität Salzburg.

Woodbridge, Linda (1984), *Women and the English Renaissance: Literature and the Nature of Womankind 1540–1620*, Hemel Hempstead: Harvester Wheatsheaf.

Zim, Rivkah (1987), *English Metrical Psalms: Poetry as Praise and Prayer, 1535–1601*, Cambridge: Cambridge University Press.

3

Usurping authority over the man: women's writing 1630–89

Elaine Hobby

The years between 1630 and 1689 witnessed extraordinary changes in Britain. Transformation in economic and social life accelerated as people moved from the countryside to towns and cities, especially London (Coward, 1980: 26–30). As more men
took waged work and set up businesses outside the home, it became increasingly
difficult for single women to support themselves (Amussen, 1988; Clark, 1968; Jackson, 1992; Middleton, 1983). During those same years, a number of specific events
affected wider social structures. Throughout the 1630s, Charles I battled to centre
power in his own person, ruling without Parliament. In 1642, divisions over this
conduct erupted into two periods of civil war, culminating, in 1649, in the king's
execution. Just as Charles had sought to justify his autocratic behaviour by claiming
that as a divinely appointed sovereign he should be unchallengeable, so those who
fought and argued against him – who included many women – cited God's direct
command as the source of their actions. For the next eleven years, Britain, now a
republic, struggled to establish what God might want, and radical religio-political
groups, such as Baptists and Quakers, proliferated. State control over public debate,
and particularly over publishing, became fractured and ineffectual, and those previously excluded from such activities – including women – fought to make their
voices heard (Coward, 1980; Hill, 1975; Hobby, 1988; Mack, 1992; McGregor and
Reay, 1984).

1660 saw the Restoration of the Monarchy in the person of Charles II. This 'Merry
Monarch' presided over attempts to forge an alliance between the old, landowning
elite and the increasingly important money-making merchants and entrepreneurs, in
order to restore a stable hierarchy (Hutton, 1985; MacLean, 1995). This was the time
of the last Great Plague and of the Great Fire of London (1666), and of mounting
anxiety that despite the king's extremely public promiscuity, he seemed unlikely to
produce a legitimate heir. At his death in 1685 he was, indeed, succeeded by his
brother, James II, whose probable future accession had caused such outrage by the
late 1670s that Charles II, like his father, had finished his reign without a Parliament.
The opposition to James was widespread: he was an avowed Catholic, and Catholic
monarchs – the clearest living example was Charles and James's cousin, Louis XIV –
were reputedly domineering and autocratic. James II indeed managed only three years

on the throne before being ousted in a bloodless coup, the so-called Glorious Revolution. He was succeeded in 1689 by his Protestant daughter, Mary, and her husband, William of Orange (Coward, 1980; Kenyon, 1974).

Where were the women in all this? According to statute, common law, the church, and conduct books of the day, they were supposed to be chaste, silent and obedient. Their role was to guard the family's 'honour' through maintaining their chastity (virginity, followed by sexual fidelity to a husband), their identity defined primarily by the designations maid (virgin), wife, or widow, rather than by their occupation or social rank. A woman began life as her father's property, and subsequently she and all that she earned and owned became her husband's. By nature, it was claimed, women were sexually voracious, overly talkative, and spendthrifts; control and self-control had to be exercised resolutely if they were not to wreck both family and nation (Fraser, 1985; Hobby, 1993).

Such a picture distorts. Whilst it is true that men had extensive legal and economic power over women, and that this was endorsed ideologically, it would be wrong to assume that women created no room for manoeuvre, or did not consider themselves to be full members of the nation. In practice many women, at least for parts of their lives, worked in or managed businesses or held land (Prior, 1985).[1] Widowhood was a particularly free time, as the marriage system itself allowed: in return for her dowry, a wife was entitled to an inheritance, for her lifetime, if her husband predeceased her. In addition, widowed mothers of underage children might oversee family concerns until heirs reached maturity. A striking example of this is the fact that one of the two London theatre companies was under the 'Rule and Dominion' of Lady Henrietta Maria Davenant ('Dame Mary') from 1668 to 1673: the period during which Elizabeth Polwhele's only published play, *The Frolicks*, was performed by them, and when Aphra Behn's first three plays were staged (Howe, 1992: 26–7; Milhous and Hume, 1977; Pearson, 1988: 31–3). Behn was not being merely whimsical when she shows Isabella in *The History of the Nun* obtaining from her mother and her aunt the money that keeps her alive (Salzman, 1994: 167, 171).

Where the personal experience of widowhood made many women's economic activity visible at least for a while, the national upheavals of the 1640s and 1650s had particularly wide-ranging effects. Whether or not it was Bathsua Makin who wrote *The Malady and the Remedy* (1646), an anonymous pamphlet calling for the abolition of imprisonment for debt, where the author speaks as 'a free commoner of England . . . in the name and on the behalf of myself and many thousands free-born of this nation' (Mahl and Koon, 1977: 122),[2] we know that many women petitioned Parliament over personal grievances and public matters during those years. A group of women calling for the release of the radical John Lilburne in July 1653, for instance, insisted in print that 'it is ours and the nation's undoubted right to petition, although an Act of Parliament were made against it', advising the republic's government to

> consider the readiness and willingness of the good women of this nation, who did think neither their lives, nor their husbands' and servants' lives and estates to be too dear a

price for the gaining of your's [*sic*] and the nation's ancient rights and liberties out of the hands of encroachers and oppressors.[3]

The impact on women's lives of the belief that God had called them to participate in the great remaking of his nation can be seen in a number of texts. Susanna Parr, for instance, although in some ways quite conservative, was a founder member of a new church in Exeter committed to 'liberty of conscience and freedom from that yoke of being servants unto men [i.e. people]' (Graham et al., 1989: 103). Anna Trapnel, on trial in Truro in 1654 for disturbing the peace and being a witch, reports that, aided by God's inspiration, she turned the supposed shame of her single state into a freedom. Challenged by the judge, 'I understand you are not married', she claims to have retorted, 'Then having no hindrance, why may not I go where I please, if the Lord so will?' (Graham et al., 1989: 81). The following year, Hester Biddle threatened to burn to the ground the university towns of Oxford and Cambridge for being 'full of filth' in their role as educators of the nation's elite (Hobby, 1991b: 165). Many hundreds of women were prosecuted for such activities during the 1650s, and thousands more joined the groups they were part of. It is the writings of these activists that form the great majority of women's published texts in the early part of the period (Hobby, 1992). They are, I suspect, the ghost haunting Milton's Eve in *Paradise Lost*: these are the women who insist on working on their own in the garden, who eat the fruit of knowledge but refuse to see this as sin.[4] Meanwhile, on the royalist side of the conflict, the best-known women authors of the period – Katherine Philips, Margaret Cavendish, Aphra Behn – all made use of the social disruptions of war and Restoration to justify their writing.

Between 1630 and 1689, then, in the face of injunctions to silence and modesty, more than 250 women made their way into print. With each decade, their numbers increased, as they embarked on explorations of war and love, politics and romance, cookery, education and debt.[5] In doing so they jeopardized their reputations as good women, and most of their works are filtered through the need to excuse this 'immodest' behaviour (Crawford, 1985; Goreau, 1980; Hobby, 1988). Even Aphra Behn, one of the most highly praised authors of either sex in her generation, had her most successful (and sixth) play, *The Rover* (1677), performed and published anonymously, and with her gender disguised.[6] This subterfuge is all the more notable because it was unusual for women to use a pseudonym or to write anonymously, and Behn's first five plays, most of which had been successful, had all been brought out under her own name.

In 1929, addressing female students at Cambridge University, Virginia Woolf urged all women 'to let flowers fall upon the tomb of Aphra Behn . . . for it was she who earned them the right to speak their minds' (Woolf, 1977: 63). A similar sentiment is gathering momentum in higher education today, as reading of women's texts increases (Hobby and Overton, 1994), and a great number of studies, especially of Behn's work, have appeared. Women's writing is also being included in mainstream anthologies of seventeenth-century works, and collections dedicated to women's texts are growing in number. Following the lead set by Elaine Showalter's pioneering *A Literature of Their Own: British Women Novelists from Brontë to Lessing* (1978), it is possible to see connections and continuities among these works. The names of Philips and Behn, for instance, were specifically evoked by many of their contemporaries and successors, including Ephelia, Anne Killigrew, Jane Barker, Anne Wharton, and a host of unnamed followers (Greer et al., 1988; Medoff, 1992). Although a convention quickly grew up of associating Philips's name with maidenly virtue, and Behn's with a shocking bawdiness – reputations which misrepresent both writers, as is discussed below – there is evidence that Behn knew not only Philips's name (Salzman, 1994: 249), but also her verse. Behn's 'On Mr J.H. in a Fit of Sickness' (Salzman, 1994: 233–6), often cited as evidence that she had a humiliating love affair with John Hoyle (a topic I shall return to), is an extended reworking of Philips's 'Orinda to Lucasia' (Bernikow, 1974: 60; Fullard, 1990: 65; Thomas, 1990: 226), containing many direct verbal echoes.[7] Orinda's longing for intimacy with another woman, Lucasia, becomes Behn's meditative, teasing reflection on women's impossible sexual desire for John Hoyle, a man whose sexual preferences were homoerotic.

Although the changes in present-day perceptions of seventeenth-century literature brought about by feminist intervention are striking, the focus still tends to be narrow. The drive to discover, in Showalter's terms, 'the links in the chain that bound one generation [of women writers] to the next' (Showalter, 1978: 7), has tended to confine attention to the 'literary' genres of plays, poetry and prose fiction, works which also sit most easily in traditional undergraduate curricula. This emphasis omits the forms in which most seventeenth-century women published: political pamphlets and conversion narratives dealing with their involvement in the public upheavals of their time.[8] It can also conceal how deeply injunctions to silence were internalized. A clear indication of how unacceptable women's publishing remained is found in a letter written in May 1653 by Dorothy Osborne to her fiancé William Temple. She says that, having seen Margaret Cavendish's *Poems and Fancies* (1653), she is convinced 'there are many soberer People in Bedlam, i'le swear her friends are much to blame to let her goe abroade [out and about]' (Parker, 1987: 79).[9] This chapter will proceed, therefore, by making a brief case for the interest of the kinds of writing which are still rarely written about, before indicating some routes into the most-cited women's works of the 1630–89 period: writings on romantic love and marriage, and modern editions of texts by Katherine Philips, Aphra Behn and Margaret Cavendish.

Writings on politics and religion

Traditional definitions of the female role might invite the assumption that early women's writing would have been concerned with love and marriage. Readers of *Kissing the Rod*, on the other hand, could draw the conclusion that the major preoccupation of female authors was death (Greer et al., 1988). In fact, in terms of both the preponderance of writers and the numbers of texts they produced, by far the most common impetus to a woman's publishing between 1630 and 1689 was her activities and opinions concerning national, even international, issues of politics and religion. There are many interconnections between the neglected pamphlets these women produced, because the sects' collective organizational structures meant that members knew each other's ideas and published works, and engaged with one another's arguments (Hobby, 1994, 1996). Ironically, this means that the one relatively well-known pamphlet to emerge from the Quaker movement, Margaret Fell's *Women's Speaking Justified* (1666, 1667), is not the ground-breaking work it is usually described as: many of her arguments had earlier been developed by her sisters, whose work is forgotten whilst hers is reprinted (Ferguson, 1985; Latt, 1979).

Throughout the period 1630 to 1689, religion and politics were so interconnected that it does not make sense to speak of them separately. This is partly due to the social upheavals outlined above: the king, and those resisting him, understood themselves to be guided by God, and political arguments, especially in the middle of the century, were conducted in terms of 'what God wants'. Strong convictions were seen as emanating not from the self, but from divine guidance. In a period when governments of various political complexions tried to control society in part through the regulation of religious behaviour, the Bible was also a peculiarly well-known book, available as a store of symbolic narratives and promises. For the modern reader scriptural echoes might at first create an obstacle to approaching these writings, but in the mid-seventeenth century the familiarity of many Bible stories meant that this feature of their construction had a democratizing effect. People were far more likely to recognize Cain and Abel, the Woman clothed with the Sun and the activities of St Paul, than they were to pick up the allusions to classical learning scattered through the writings of well-schooled men.

In *Susanna's Apology Against the Elders* (1659; Graham et al., 1989: 101–15), for instance, Susanna Parr does a lot more, through her use of scriptural allusion, than defend herself against defamation from her Baptist minister, Lewis Stuckley. The pamphlet's title alludes to the story of Susanna and the Elders which, though excluded from the Authorised Version of the Bible, had long formed part of the Book of Daniel and was still well known. In the Apocryphal tale, evil religious elders try to blackmail the virtuous Susanna into responding to their sexual advances. When she refuses they bring a false charge of immodesty against her. Parr models her own vindication narrative on these events. Just as the Elders create a situation in which Susanna appears to be immodest in the sense of unchaste, so Stuckley, a man of 'serpentine subtlety' (106), first insists that Parr speak out in church, and then uses her doing so to suggest that she is too forward. Where the Apocryphal Susanna's vindication is dependent on Daniel's intervention, however, Parr can manage her own. Insisting that 'my sex, my natural and sinful infirmities . . . made me unfit to speak unto others' (108), she publishes a pamphlet which includes her acerbic judgments on many of her fellow church members (107). Her right to do so is presented as a duty, as her pamphlet climaxes with incontrovertible evidence that her experiences are part of a divine plan. A child of hers dies, and 'upon the borders of hell' in her pain (110), she comes to believe that Stuckley's congregation is as dead to God as her child is to her, and causing him as much pain. What choice do her readers have, if they are not to seem unmoved by the death of a child, but to find her beliefs vindicated? Through her use of the modest Susanna, Parr demonstrates her right to be seen as virtuous and conventionally feminine at the very time she is insisting that she knows the correct way forward for the national church.

Where Parr's pamphlet is angry, moving, self-assertive in its ostensible self-effacement, the work of her fellow Baptist, Anna Trapnel, is positively rollicking. It is unlikely that the account she gives of her trial in *Her Report and Plea* (1654; Graham et al., 1989: 71–86) bears close relation to what was actually said in court: she is too cutting in her responses not to have been jailed for contempt if events had occurred exactly as she describes them. The resulting pamphlet, however, is excellent propaganda, inviting readers to join those outside the courtroom in applauding her acquittal (84); prompting them, even, to join the radical Fifth Monarchy movement. Like Parr, she uses biblical allusions to strengthen her case. The trial scene, for instance, echoes the persecution of both Christ and St Paul, using the reader's assumed knowledge of these Bible stories to justify her unseemly behaviour. Smiling at her accusers, she points out the parallel between her reaction and that of Paul when threatened by Felix (Acts 24: 10ff): 'this servant of the Lord looked cheerfully all the time of his accusations charged upon him' (79). Paul was in the right, and so is she. She, like Paul, has good reason to smile, as she provokes her reader to find her opponents ridiculous.

St Paul, the first important popularizer of Christianity, was commonly used by seventeenth-century women to vindicate their unfeminine actions and writing. The consistency with which they cite him indicates that their use of scripture was analytical, or, it might be said, selective: it was, after all, St Paul who called for women's silence (1 Corinthians 14: 34–5), adding, 'I suffer not a woman to teach, nor to usurp authority over the man' (1 Timothy 2: 11–12). In 1658, Katharine Evans and Sarah Cheevers made a particularly bold use of St Paul's example: they left their husbands and children at home and set off for Alexandria to retrace one of the apostle's evangelizing journeys. The message they spread in Christ's name was the Quaker principle that God's truth, or Light, resides in everyone, making church and social hierarchies unnecessary. When they broke their journey at Malta, then under the control of the Inquisition, they were arrested, and spent the next three years in prison.

This is a short Relation Of some of the Cruel Sufferings (for the Truths sake) of Katharine Evans & Sarah Cheevers (1662) is, therefore, compelling just for the tale it tells of the women's steadfastness and courage (Graham et al., 1989: 116–30). Also remarkable is the way in which the authors use the story of their experiences to make a case for their ideas. In Quaker theology, the crucial evidence that someone is acting from divine inspiration, and should therefore be respected, comes from the fact that others recognize the presence of God in their words and deeds. Authority comes not from a church hierarchy, or from the Bible, but from the collective recognition of God's presence (Bauman, 1983). The *short Relation* is therefore presented to 'a child of wisdom' (120), 'the wise reader' (122), who is encouraged to agree with its 'Truth' through the way it is told. In this drama, the friars are mere bit-players, ineffectual fools, whose arguments are easily countered (121–3), and who are irrational enough to engage in self-flagellation 'till the blood come' (125). The measured, ironic narrative also incorporates a moment of ecstasy, where the prose breaks apart and sentence rolls upon sentence, each beginning 'And' (123). Here is a vision of warfare, of a woman giving birth, of a dragon and angels. The language and events are those of the Book of Revelation, but it is crucial to Evans and Cheevers's political aims that the passage is not interpreted as a mere literary borrowing. Evans insists, 'in obedience to the Lord I have written the things which I did hear, see, tasted and handled of the good word of God' (124). Their story is a personal narrative, but it is also a symbolic and incalculably important one. Presenting themselves, as so many of their contemporaries did, as God's mere instruments, they invent selves who can travel and write, and whose significance must be acknowledged by the 'wise reader'.

A major literary form in the latter part of the seventeenth century was the Baptist conversion narrative, which records the author's transition, through God's grace, from despair to redemption. Since the formula required believers to identify significant events in their lives, and show how these evidenced their acceptance by God, a format which might be expected to produce predictable patterns actually enabled the writing of some remarkable life stories. Sarah Davy's *Heaven Realized* (1670; Graham et al., 1989: 165–79), for instance, traces the author's journey from the isolation of a lonely, guilt-ridden childhood to a God-given intimacy with a female friend. In *Satan His Methods and Malice Baffled* (1683; Graham et al., 1989: 197–210), Hannah Allen makes a comparable transition from a living death as a widow – in the autobiography's opening words, she describes herself not as Hannibal Allen's widow, but as his 'late wife' (200) – to a new life as a wife and author. Despite Allen's repeated urging of the reader to see her life as evidence of a battle between God and Satan, the incidents she narrates also invite the interpretation that the 'deep melancholy' (201) that drives her to a series of suicide attempts is the culmination of years of neglect. In childhood she is passed back and fore between her Midlands home and her London school before being 'disposed of in marriage' (201) in her late teens to a husband who was hardly ever there. The subject of the text is a broken sinner, whose life, though worthless without God, also vindicates the decision to write; its author is a new Hannah Allen, one who can creatively re-present her life, and her old diary entries (202–3), to demonstrate that even despair like this can be recovered from.

These texts have much to tell us: it is worth getting our Bibles out and learning some religious history so that we can begin to understand them.[10]

Writings on love and marriage

Deadpan, the narrator of Behn's *The Fair Jilt* opens a tale where assault, deceit and murder are undertaken in the name of 'love' with the words, 'As love is the most noble and divine passion of the soul, so is it that to which we may justly attribute all the real satisfactions of life' (Salzman, 1994: 75; Todd, 1992: 29). As this macabre joke itself indicates, where romantic love appears in writings by women in this period – and whilst it is not the major topic in works published between 1630 and 1689, it is certainly central in material currently available – it is rarely noble or divine, and marriage does not of itself bring life's 'real satisfactions'.

Anne Wentworth's escape from the dynamics of earthly 'love' is made with the help of God. The story she tells in her autobiographical *Vindication* (1677; Graham et al., 1989: 180–96), is an extreme one. She began to publish her writings after her *'hard-hearted yoke-fellow* . . . of eighteen years' (183) had run away with her manuscripts (187). In a period when men were legally entitled to beat their wives, Wentworth looks to a future where such behaviour will no longer be tolerated, declaring that her husband 'has in his barbarous actions towards me a many times over done such things as not only in the *spirit* of them will be one day judged a murdering of, but had long since *really* proved so, if God had not wonderfully supported and preserved me' (186). She insists, too, that her own marriage is not a matter of mere personal significance, but a symbol of the wider relationship between men and women. Where earlier sectaries – Wentworth was a Baptist – had interpreted the biblical battle between evil Babylon and blessed Zion as representing a general struggle between right and wrong, or even as symbolizing the specific contrast between king and parliament, Wentworth suggests another way of understanding these scriptural figures. God has shown her that her husband and the Baptist church she has left are Babylon, she Zion, so 'my *oppressions* and *deliverance* had a *public ministry* and *meaning* wrapped in them' (193). This *Vindication* is not to be read as the story of a conflict between one man and one woman. It is against brutal men and their 'abettors' (186) that God is speaking when he deplores Babylon.

It was not uncommon in the seventeenth century for poets to make use of romantic love language when writing about a relationship between the soul and God (Lewalski, 1979). Two examples are the anonymous *Elizas Babes* (1652), and An Collins's *Divine Songs and Meditations* (1653). The events of Collins's *Songs* take place in a garden evocative of that in the Bible's great love poem, the Song of Solomon. Here, the Saviour woos the soul, 'Open to me my love', promising her that his 'firm fruition' is only available to 'single hearts' ('A Song expressing their happiness who have communion with Christ', Graham et al., 1989: 62–6). The product of this passionate 'union with the Lord' (63) is an extraordinarily experimental book of poems. In 'Another Song', for instance, an extended metaphor comparing a woman's life to the seasons of the year shows how barren conventional existence is (Graham et al., 1989: 67–9; Greer et al., 1988: 151–4). Having not experienced 'flowers' (menstruation), she cannot bear babies, the 'fruit' of the body, but she has something better. Her garden brings with it 'safety' from the 'storm and blast' of normal female existence, making her

> Apt to produce a fruit most rare,
> That is not common with every woman
> That fruitful are.

Elizas Babes, by contrast, uses not Bible echoes but the language of courtly love to produce a series of joyful, funny poems demonstrating the freedom that can be found through being 'affianced' to God rather than trapped in the 'slavery' of human marriage. Shot by 'heav'n's dart', not Cupid's ('The Dart', Greer et al., 1988: 142), Eliza cheerfully anticipates her own death, which will remove her from her husband to union with her 'Lover', Christ ('To my Husband', Greer et al., 1988: 144–6; Woodhuysen, 1992: 659–60; 'The Lover', Greer et al., 1988: 146–7).

Mary Carleton explores gender relations through a very different literary formula. *The Case of Madam Mary Carleton* (1663; Graham et al., 1989: 131–46) is a light-hearted pastiche of rogue literature and romance writing, in which Carleton presents her own account of being accused and acquitted of a capital offence, bigamy. With Mary Carleton casting herself in her tale as a desirable Lady being courted by the supposedly love-sick John, who 'would make away with himself' (136) if refused by her, *The Case* works in the same way as her self-presentation as a princess appears to have done. The reader is invited to share her amusement at 'this "love-killing" story' (137), and to want, like Samuel Pepys, to believe her.[11] Her witty scepticism makes for a very entertaining tale, but it was not enough to save the historical Mary Carleton. Not guilty of bigamy, she was her husband's property, and had no legal redress against his confiscating her belongings. Ten years later, having already once been deported for theft, Mary Carleton was hanged.

A comparable awareness of the limitations of the discourse of love features in a wide range of love poetry in the day. Because Anne Bradstreet emigrated to America in her teens, her work is usually omitted from anthologies of British writing. The fact that her first book, *The Tenth Muse Lately Sprung Up in America* (1650), was published in London, and appeared on a best-seller list there in 1657, perhaps justifies a glance at one of her poems. 'A Letter to my Husband Absent on Public Employment' (Greer et al., 1988: 137–8) is typical of the provocative way she engages with the social and poetic conventions of romantic love. At one level, the poem seems to affirm the traditional relationship of husband and wife. He is 'My head, my heart, mine eyes, my life'. Appropriately, he is represented by the glorious sun, whilst she is the lowly earth, dependent on his warmth to dispel her 'frigid colds', and, in his absence, is effectively 'dead'. Running athwart these assertions, though, the 'Letter' has another dimension. She is not, in fact, immobilized by his absence, but writing this intricate poem, deftly managing an extended conceit in which the sun/husband moves through the skies to return to her. The very fact of his distance from her also serves to prove that the platitudes spoken about marriage are untrue:

> If two be one, as surely thou and I,
> How stayest thou there, whilst I at Ipswich lie?
> So many steps, head from the heart to sever
> If but a neck, soon should we be together.

If husband and wife really were one person, he could not be absent. If the common comparison of man to head, with its associated authority and rationality, and woman to heart, with its emotionality, were accurate, they could not be separated. Since he is so far away, the implication goes, the equivalence of man/head and woman/heart is false. What the poem offers, instead, is a different kind of relationship: as she longs for his presence, she also writes poetry; at his return he will not be her master, but her 'dearest guest'. He is, indeed, more than her head: he is 'my joy'. Simultaneously, the poem refuses traditional gender relations and endorses a new basis for intimacy.[12]

Later in the century, many of the works of the pseudonymous Ephelia are poems addressed to Strephon or J.G., a factor which has sometimes led to the assumption that *Female Poems on Several Occasions* (1679) innocently narrates the story of the poet's own passion (Fowler, 1992: xli). In fact, though, the variability of stances, situations and tones makes it clear that *Female Poems* is an exploration of the conventions of both poetic and social versions of gender relations. These are literally occasional poems, as the volume's title indicates. In 'To J.G.', for instance, the Lady regrets having believed her lover's professions of affection. She has lost the shield afforded by the public performance of indifference which Mary Carleton describes so wittily, having trusted in his 'Soft amorous tales' (Greer et al., 1988: 276–8; Fowler, 1992: 742). 'To One That Asked Me Why I Loved J.G.' then uses the conventional belief that women eagerly explain their romantic obsessions to friends in private, to delightedly malign 'this false, this worthless, man' (Fowler, 1992: 743). Meanwhile, a poem written in the voice of a faithless lover, 'Upon His Leaving His Mistress', pushes male recommendation of sexual 'liberty' to an absurd and self-revealing limit. He recommends his mistress to model herself on 'the kind seed-receiving Earth', and make her womb, the planet's poetic equivalent, welcoming to allcomers (Fowler, 1992: 744).[13]

Law and convention might have dictated that a woman's life should be circumscribed by her role in relation to man, but women writers had other ideas.

Katherine Philips, 'Orinda' (1632–64)

Well into the eighteenth century, the most frequently praised woman writer of the period 1630 to 1689 was Katherine Philips, 'Orinda'. Complimented in her lifetime by, among others, Henry Vaughan, Abraham Cowley, Jeremy Taylor, Edward Dering, Roger Boyle, Earl of Orrery, and Wentworth Dillon, Earl of Roscommon, after her death she was regularly apostrophized (Hobby, 1988; Thomas, 1990). Especially praiseworthy, it was claimed, was the feminine horror she demonstrated when her poetry appeared in print in 1664. Such approval misleads, since her works were circulated widely in manuscript before this: an older form of publication than print, and at that time of higher status. Some details of the circumstances in which she wrote and disseminated her poems provide a more accurate sense of what is at stake in her poetry.

In 1648, at the age of 16, Katherine Fowler left her London boarding school to join her widowed and recently remarried mother in south-west Wales. There she was married to James Philips, a 54-year-old widower who was a relative of her new stepfather. Their age difference, and the marked contrast between England's capital city and life in rural Wales, were not the only factors separating husband and wife: where he was a prominent Parliamentarian, she had well-developed royalist sympathies. In these circumstances Katherine Philips established a network of friends and acquaintances, to whom she wrote verse encoding her royalist perspective. As a result, when her poetry was published in an unauthorized edition in 1664, her work was already known in literary and court circles, and her translation of Corneille's play *Pompée* had been well received at performances in Dublin and London (Van Lennep et al., 1965: xxxix–xl).

One of Philips's earliest published poems, 'Friendship's Mystery. To my dearest Lucasia', is also her most commonly anthologized work (Greer et al., 1988: 193–4; Ferguson, 1985: 103–4; Fullard, 1990: 64; Thomas, 1990: 90–1; Woodhuysen, 1992: 517). Whilst its very title makes it clear that this is a poem about friendship, its first appearance in print also signalled the anonymous author's politics. It was published in Henry Lawes's *The Second Book of Ayres and Dialogues* (1655), a collection with an avowedly royalist sub-text.[14] After the Restoration, Philips was to write a number of overtly monarchical poems, and these open the posthumous edition of her work published in 1667 (Thomas, 1990: 69–83). In 'Friendship's Mystery', however, like most of the works of the 1650s, the royalism is covert, presented in a manner akin to that adopted by Philips's close neighbour and political fellow-traveller, Henry Vaughan (Wilcher, 1983). This can be seen not only in the implicitly approving use of the relation between 'Princes' and 'subjects', and the reference to the greatness and innocence of thrones, but also in the description of the world as 'dull' and 'angry'. Lucasia is summoned to an 'election' superior to that espoused by the radical sectaries, who believed themselves 'elected' by God and therefore righteous in their opposition to the monarchy; the 'election' in this royalist alliance between Orinda and Lucasia is 'free/As angels'. A comparable sub-text inhabits other poems. In 'L'Amitie: To Mrs M. Awbrey', for instance, friends 'let the dull world alone to talk and fight', deciding together 'To pity kings, and conquerors despise' (Fowler, 1992: 697–8; Greer et al., 1988: 191–3; Thomas, 1990: 142).[15] Similarly, the first stanza of 'Orinda to Lucasia' communicates, through its description of a garden just before dawn, a longing for the absent sun/king to return, alluding to the 'murmur' of royalist protest which is taking place more 'Openly' (Bernikow, 1974: 60; Fowler, 1992: 698; Fullard, 1990: 65; Thomas, 1990: 226).[16]

The second stanza of 'Orinda to Lucasia', however, indicates a further important feature of Philips's poetry. Whilst the absence of the sun/king is dreadful, it is still the case that 'Thou, my Lucasia, art far more to me/Than he to all the under-world can be'. There is, in the words of 'Friendship's Mystery', 'a religion in our love': a new value-system which provides compensation. The qualities of this love are re-iterated and defined constantly, for instance in 'A Friend' (Fullard, 1990: 68–70; Thomas, 1990: 150–1), and 'To Mrs M. A. at Parting' (Fullard, 1990: 66–7; Thomas, 1990: 145–7). Borrowing from the neo-Platonic tradition of lovers exchanging their hearts, in 'Friendship's Mystery' Philips describes a mutual, life-affirming commitment, where 'both diffuse, and both engross'; 'We are ourselves but by rebound'. The interdependence and interchangeability of the lovers here contrasts significantly with the conventions of male love poetry: where Donne's lover in 'The Sun Rising' crows 'She is all states, and all princes, I' (Smith, 1971: 80), Orinda insists they are 'Both princes, and both subjects too'.[17]

The contrasts between the characteristics of this female intimacy and the gender distinctions which mar heterosexuality are indeed repeatedly indicated by Philips. In 'To my excellent Lucasia, on our friendship' (Bernikow, 1974: 61; Fowler, 1992: 696–7; Kaplan, 1975: 44; Thomas, 1990: 121–2; Woodhuysen, 1992: 518), the poet describes her state as merely mechanical before the beginning of this loving relationship:

> For as a watch is wound to motion
> Such was mine, for never had Orinda found
> A soul, till she found thine.

In a world where a woman can be another's 'joy, and life, and rest', a bridegroom is likened to a usurping 'crown conqueror'; a metaphor wittily extended into outrage at the very idea of marriage in 'An Answer to another perswading a Lady to Marriage' (Bernikow, 1974: 63; Woodhuysen, 1992: 378).[18]

It is possible, then, that Philips's poetry encodes not only royalism, but also lesbianism (Ballaster, 1995; Donoghue, 1993; Hobby, 1991a). What is certain is that her politics divided her from women called by God to enter female partnerships: Sarah Davy, Katharine Evans and Sarah Cheevers.

Aphra Behn, 'Astrea' (d. 1689)

A number of Aphra Behn's plays, poems and short stories are now available in print, and her work has received far more attention in the last few years than any of her contemporaries'. Almost nothing is known about her, despite the extensive research of her biographers (especially Duffy, 1989), and, in the place of fact, myths abound. What we do know is startling. It seems certain that, like the narrator of *Oroonoko*, she spent time in Surinam (Guyana). There is also proof that she worked as a British spy for Charles II: like the narrator of *The Fair Jilt*, she lived in Antwerp, though not arriving until after the botched execution of Prince Tarquin that the novella's narrator witnessed. Like so many of those who worked for Charles II, she was not paid for her services, and on her return to London in 1667 she was imprisoned for debt. There is no evidence who arranged for her release, or how; but in 1670, her first play, *The Forced Marriage*, was staged by the Duke of York's Company. By the time of her death in 1689 she had become one of the most prolific and successful authors of the day, having had performed and published some eighteen or twenty plays. There is also an epistolary novel, some novellas and short stories, many translations, and dozens of poems, in some of which her Tory politics are overt (Greer, 1991; see also Hutner, 1993 and Salzman, 1994).

We do not know, however, when or where she was born, who her family were, whether she was single or widowed, or how she became involved in the theatre. Many, including her first biographer, 'a Young Lady', who might have been Charles Gildon, the publisher of works posthumously attributed to her, have asserted that they know the answers, and used their speculations, deduced from her writings, to then 'prove' their critical interpretations. The most frequently repeated 'fact' of this kind is that Behn had a long, unhappy relationship with John Hoyle, who at his death in a fight in 1692 was described by Bulstrode Whitelock as 'an atheist, a sodomite professed, a corrupter of youth and a blasphemer of Christ' (Duffy, 1989: 139). Whilst it is clear from Behn's poems that she knew Hoyle well, and teased him about their intimacy, it is a mistake to assume that the historical Aphra Behn is identical with the speaker of these poems. Critics' insistence on Behn's desperate passion for an unresponsive, homosexual man seems driven by a desire to put her in her place: no one should be allowed to be as witty about love and sexuality as she was and not suffer. This critical assumption has also produced the repeated assertion that Miranda in *The Fair Jilt* is a manifestation of Behn, as she forces her sexual attentions on the unwilling Friar, Prince Henrick; and that Angelica Bianca's threats against the eponymous Rover, Willmore, are motivated by the same design (Duffy, 1989: 147; Morgan, 1981: 20–2; Munns, 1991: 203; Salvaggio, 1993: 264; Woodcock, 1948: 105, 113–18). It is also generally assumed, again without evidence, that *Loveletters to a Gentleman*, published in a posthumous collection of Behn's prose fiction, does not constitute the opening pages of an epistolary novel, but is a selection of Behn's letters to Hoyle (Salvaggio, 1993; Todd, 1992).

The distance between this impression of Behn's achievements and the evidence provided by her writings might appropriately be illustrated by her translation of one of the *Fables of Aesop*, 'The Young Man and His Cat':

> A youth in love with puss, to
> 　　Venus prayed
> To change the useless beauty to
> 　　A maid.
>
> Venus consents, but in the
> 　　Height of charms
> 'A mouse!' she cried, and leaves
> 　　His ravished arms.
>
> 　*Moral*
> Ill principles no mercy can reclaim,
> And once a rebel still will be the same.
> 　　　　　　　(Salzman, 1994: 250)

The wit here works on the side of the 'rebel' cat/woman: the man is 'in love with puss' (the pun is wicked), and of 'ill principles', finding a female 'useless' if she is not sexually available to him. The cat has her own agenda: mice are more interesting than men. The contrast between this and the translation of the same fable by Behn's contemporary, Roger L'Estrange, could hardly be sharper. In L'Estrange's version, it is the cat who wants to be made into something better than herself, and who is made to look ridiculous at her instinctive response to a mouse, 'whereupon the goddess, provoked at her conduct, turned her into a Cat again, that her manners and person might be consistent with each other' (L'Estrange, 1882(?): 239–40).

Central to Behn's oeuvre, in addition to her wit, is the fact of her being a playwright. This is not only because she made her fame as a dramatist, but also because of an inherent characteristic of plays: having no narrator, they allow for the representation 'in their own words' of widely differing characters, requiring the audience or reader to engage actively and analytically to decide what sense to make of them. This structural element of drama is harnessed by Behn in both her poetry and her fiction, which is all provocatively resistant to fixed positions or interpretations on the reader's part.[19]

One example of this is a single episode from the extremely complex story *The Fair Jilt* (Salzman, 1994; Todd, 1992), where Miranda attempts to seduce a friar. This is an early immoral act in a career which includes stealing the inheritance of her sister, Alcidiana; marrying Prince Tarquin for his status; and using her charms to persuade first a pageboy and then her husband to try to murder Alcidiana, both of them being sentenced to death for the attempt. Although on the final page the narrator reports that 'they say Miranda has been very penitent for her life past' (119), the last remark in the story gives another possible reason for her 'perfect . . . state of happiness': 'Prince Tarquin died about three-quarters of a year ago'. Throughout, Miranda, not the men who worship her, is in control, and in the end she is a rich widow, and free.

What is figured in her domination of those around her, though, is complex. Her energy and sheer success are dazzling. She is, in a sense, a heroine; or, perhaps more accurately, a hero. Just as men in Behn's society conventionally sought out wealthy brides, so Miranda is fixated on 'quality'. In her courtship of the friar – a 'man of quality' (87) – she positions herself in a masculine role, him in a feminine one. It is he who is 'charming' (87), and she fantasizes him out of his 'coarse, grey, ill-made habit' into 'the bed, the silent gloomy night, and the soft embraces of her arms' (88). 'She burnt, she languished, and died for the young innocent, who knew not he was the author of so much mischief' (89), courting him with letters and gifts. He, with his vow of chastity, is the meek virgin, she the lover 'in an agony of passion' (93). In its role-inversion, this episode highlights the conventions of gender by defamiliarizing them. At this level, it is not Miranda, but the male behaviour she mimics or parodies, which is revealed as predatory. Simultaneously, though, details in the passage make it impossible to forget that Miranda is a woman taking control of her position, doing so by displaying herself as an object of desire (91–2), and insisting that her own passions are as real as any man's. Both meanings of the episode intertwine, and it is necessary to see Miranda as both glorious and terrible.

Another example of Behn's deft refusal to allow her reader to occupy a fixed position is the short, deceptively slight *Adventure of the Black Lady* (Salzman, 1994). Here, the pregnant, single Bellamora escapes to London to have her child in secret. Unknown to her, she is recognized by the sister of the child's father, and he hurries to London to marry Bellamora before the baby is born. This resolution is helped by Bellamora's landlady, who delights in ridiculing the parish officials who pursue the reputedly unmarried mother. The plot, then, might seem to show the triumph of love and friendship ('bell amor') over the mean-mindedness of those who condemn unmarried mothers.

The Adventure of the Black Lady refuses any such simple reading through the way it is told, and a series of narrative misdirections indicate the danger of assuming that things are as they seem. For instance, at her arrival in London, Bellamora seems an ingenue ('bella mora'), 'being utterly unacquainted with the neat practices of this fine City' (191). The reader is invited to be more knowing, to assume that the porter who helps her is tricking her, and that the landlady whose house she settles in and who is so reluctant to let her send out for wine (192) will turn out to be a bawd.[20] Since the porter is honest and the landlady moral, it might seem the reader is wrong to doubt, Bellamora right to trust. But further details indicate that neither a romantic nor a cynical interpretation will do.

The major, though submerged, question addressed by this narrative is the connection between female sexuality and money. The father of Bellamora's child, the ironically named Fondlove, has taken advantage of her repugnance at being forced into an advantageous match with a wealthier man: he 'urged his passion with such violence' (194) that she acquiesced. After her sexual experience with him, however, she has 'abhorred the sight of him' (194). Her motivation to marriage at the story's conclusion is, perforce, financial, the clinching argument being that if she fails to accept Fondlove, their child will not be able to inherit either of their estates (196). The weight of this consideration is increased by the fact that, throughout her stay in London, all who know Bellamora conspire to make her believe she is the penniless victim of theft (195). Had her trunk been returned to her, she would have had no need to fear the overseers of the poor, and Fondlove might not have caught himself a wealthy wife. The landlady is not a bawd, but she has helped to sell Bellamora, motivated by the best, conventional beliefs: that it is better for a child to have two parents.

The interconnections of sexuality and money in a society where marriage entailed a financial transaction, and a wife's property usually became her husband's to dispose of at will, is a key context for understanding many of Behn's works. Several of her novellas have nuns as their central characters, and these women's desirability to men in their wealth and virginity means that they can represent, in exaggerated form, the lot of the marriageable woman in Restoration Britain.

The History of the Nun (Salzman, 1994) has all the appearance of a romantic tale: about half the story is concerned with the overwhelming emotions Isabella feels when, despite her resolve to remain single, she falls in love with Henault, and elopes with him. What is peculiar about the novella, though, is that its second half extends beyond the longed-for marriage, and shows that the pastoral idyll she had expected to inhabit is an illusion: the animals die and the crops fail. Marriage, it would appear, including marriage for love, is not the goal of life, but one of its conundrums. As the story's narrator grimly remarks, wives find themselves having 'to make the best of a bad market' (141). In Isabella's case, the experience of wedded bliss does not end with the economic disaster of following her heart to Henault. Some years after his reported death in battle she marries Villenoys, this time consciously motivated by economic considerations (177). She lives the life of a perfect lady, caring for the local poor and gaining a virtuous reputation: she has supposedly achieved every woman's desire, but marriage, once again, is only a stage in the narrative, not her conclusion. The 'dead' husband returns, as is necessary in romance; her solution is to murder both men. A brief look at how this is presented shows once again how Behn refuses her reader a fixed position or moral interpretation.

Having smothered Henault, Isabella gains Villenoys's assistance to dispose of his body through a feminine fit of fainting and tears (184–5). He puts it in a sack and, unbeknownst to him, she stitches the sack to his clothing when he picks it up. As Villenoys sets off to throw the body into the river from a nearby bridge, her parting advice to him is ghoulish:

> 'When you come to the bridge', said she, 'and that you are throwing him over the rail, which is not above breast high, be sure you give him a good swing' . . .. 'I'll warrant you', said Villenoys, 'I know how to secure his falling.' And going his way with it, love lent him strength, and he soon arrived at the bridge, where, turning his back to the rail, and heaving his body over, he threw himself with all his force backward the better to swing the body into the river, whose weight (it being made fast to his collar) pulled Villenoys after it and both the live and dead man falling into the river which, being rapid at the bridge, soon drowned him, especially when so great a weight hung to his neck, so that he died without considering what was the occasion of his fate. (186)

The desperate irony that 'love lent him strength', and the inexorable, forward-moving detail of this passage, which drives the reader onward with the falling of Villenoys, jostle against each other, making it impossible either simply to laugh at the effects of love and Isabella's training as a competent needlewoman, or to be appalled at her husbands' fates.

The heroine of Behn's most famous fiction, *Oroonoko*, is a very different figure from her nuns (Salzman, 1994; Todd, 1992). Throughout the narrative of her sexual assault and sale into slavery, and her being informed by her beloved Oroonoko that, in her own interests, he has decided to kill her, Imoinda remains an archetypally virtuous woman, modest and long-suffering, her fate decided by the men who desire and own her. In this, like Oroonoko himself, she works more as a representative of British culture than as the African she supposedly is. As many critics have argued in different ways, it is an act of will rather than analysis to see this novella simply as an early, perhaps the first, anti-slavery tract: its concerns with the Stuart dynasty, and with European conventions of gender relations, are too overt for that (Ballaster, 1992; Ballaster, 1993; Ferguson, 1992; Overton, 1992; Sussman, 1993). At the same time, it would be a mistake to identify the opinions and behaviour of the tale's narrator as straightforwardly presenting the narrative's perspective. As the narrator herself reflects in the midst of mounting tragedy, as a white person in a slave colony she cannot avoid responsibility for what ensues (64). Indeed, she colludes in persuading Oroonoko to trust his captors (45–6). As in all of Behn's fictions, the narrator is not a neutral figure, but a character who conceals as much as she reveals: in this case, a character finally more concerned with establishing her reputation as a story-teller, and with her status in Surinam and Britain, than with the lives and deaths of the characters she makes use of.

Where *Oroonoko* ends with the name of its modest heroine, who is accorded little inner life and no control over her fate, Behn's most famous and successful play, *The*

Rover (1677; Duffy, 1990; Link, 1967; Russell, 1994; Todd, 1992) opens, startlingly, with women alone on stage, plotting their futures (Pearson, 1988: 146). *The Rover* is contemporaneous with two of the best-known plays by Restoration men: William Wycherley's *The Country Wife* (1675), and George Etherege's *The Man of Mode* (1676). Even the briefest of comparisons between the three shows how different Behn's perspective is from theirs.[21] The action and humour of *The Country Wife* depend on and prove the 'truth' of Horner's assertion that women are sex-mad. This is clinched through the actions of the supposedly 'natural' woman Margery Pinchwife: woman's voracious sexual appetite is inherent, she demonstrates; all culture adds is a gloss to disguise this. The world of *The Man of Mode* is equally, though differently, vicious. The drive to achieve and maintain a place in a competitive hierarchy is the main motor of action. The key plotters are men, and three of the play's central female characters end up under the dominion of the arch wit, Dorimant.

The Rover could hardly be more different. The women certainly have a very active sexual appetite, but one only has to consider the female teasing about love and desire which opens the play to recognize a warmth missing in the works of Wycherley and Etherege. Here, as elsewhere, Behn makes a witty intervention in the stage conventions of the Restoration. Not for her the cross-dressed Margery Pinchwife, whose outfit only serves to show off her shape and make her available for Horner to ogle and paw. Behn's cross-dressed heroines – Hellena in *The Rover*, Laura, Cornelia and Marcella in *The Feigned Courtesans* (1679; Lyons and Morgan, 1991), the Widow in *The Widow Ranter* (1690; Duffy, 1990; Todd, 1992) – have other matters on their minds. The bodies displayed to the audience in a state of undress are not those of the actresses, but are instead those of men, and ridiculous men at that: Blunt crawling out of the sewer in his underwear in *The Rover*, Sir Feeble unable to consummate his marriage in *The Lucky Chance* (1686; Duffy, 1990). Many specific echoes in Behn's drama of other plays are also of note. For instance, *The Lucky Chance* opens with a jokey evocation of *Romeo and Juliet*, as Belmour gazes up at Leticia's balcony, sighing, 'Sure 'tis the day that gleams in yonder East'. In his subsequent inability to trust his beloved, he is a running commentary on the Romeo figure. *Abdelazer, or the Moor's Revenge* (1676; Duffy, 1990) can be read in part as a reinvention of the most famous of theatrical Moors, Othello; Abdelazer is driven to use his sexual prowess to avenge himself on the Europeans who have usurped him in his homeland and made him one of their soldiers.[22] The skill with which Behn cut and reworked the material on which she based her best-known plays has received some attention (Hobby, 1988: 117–19). The connections between her plays and others popular on the stage in her day are also well worth exploring.

If the opening scene of *The Rover* is compared with its second one, where a ribald group of men also discuss love and sex, further elements of Behn's gender-consciousness emerge. In both 1 i and 1 ii a single-sex group is interrupted by the arrival of a character or characters of the other sex. For the women, this produces a need to co-operate with one another so as to resist being dominated. When women appear in the men's scene, by contrast, they are responded to solely as sex objects. Where for the women their desires and their social subordination are in conflict, the men can do as they please, as long as other men consent.[23] The difference between men's and women's position is apparent not only to the audience: repeatedly in the play, and most famously when Angelica and Moretta stand symbolically above the men who are fighting over Angelica's picture (2 i), women watch and then comment on male behaviour.

Women's wit and determination, and their support for one another, are not however enough to overcome the significance of men's social domination and economic power. Although Valeria can intervene to prevent the disguised Florinda's rape by her own brother (5 i), and Angelica turns not on her rival, Hellena, but on Willmore himself on discovering his perfidy (4 ii, 5 i), it is the men who win. Antonio gets the whore he wants without even having to fight for her. Florinda trusts her Belvile, whom the audience has seen behaving like one of the lads, and obeys unquestioningly his instruction that she forgive his friends for trying to rape her. Hellena's fate is in some ways the worst of all, because she believes she has won: the Rover has agreed to marry her before bedding her. What Hellena doesn't know, but the audience does, is that Willmore has discovered she is a wealthy heiress. Her wit and beauty have inspired his lust, but so has the look of almost every woman he meets; it is when Angelica reveals to him Hellena's wealth that he resolves to marry her (4 ii). In all manner of ways it is the courtesan, Angelica, who is right (2 ii): the fact that men marry for money, and then own their wives' goods, makes the world a dangerous place for women.

Curiously, this sombre element of the play's plot has been overlooked by critics, who perhaps expect the equation of witty hero plus witty heroine to equal the triumph of youthful desire over parental control (Kavenik, 1991; Langdell, 1985; Link, 1967). (It is notable that there are no parents in *The Rover*: domination comes from men, not from the older generation's desire to arrange marriage.) A similar misconstruction is also regularly applied to *The Lucky Chance*. It is argued that Julia and Gayman are a well-matched pair, each in turn tricking the other into a disguised sexual encounter. Julia's angry recoil at her beloved's deceit in the play's last scene is accordingly interpreted as an act that Horner's sexual partners would be proud of (Gallagher, 1993). In fact, though, as Julia says in the play's closing moments, she never intended Gayman to be able to have intercourse with her in her guise as an old woman: the scene's interruption before consummation was always arranged. She was testing his fidelity, and finding it wanting, having not seen, as the audience has, his callous exploitation of sex with his landlady for money (2 i). Once more, where women are motivated by love, desire and honesty, men's crucial concern is shown to be finance.[24]

These brief observations on Behn's two best-known plays might give the misleading impression that gender relations are the main focus of her drama. It would be more accurate to observe that Restoration culture is at issue. *The Rover* centres on the nastiness of Cavalier values: the egocentric, dangerous hero is explicitly located as a member of the king's retinue during Charles's time in exile (1 ii). Whilst Behn was a Tory, her alliance with her brothers was anything but uncritical. *The Rover*, though, was written in 1677, when the stability of the monarchy seemed relatively assured. By 1679 the Exclusion Crisis was in full swing, and Behn's Tory commitments were of more pressing significance.[25] Consequently *The Feigned Courtesans*, markedly similar to *The Rover* in some of its plot devices of disguise and cross-dressing, and in the witty pairing of Galliard and Cornelia, has a completely different emphasis and resolution.[26] Most of the characters in this play work as a coded reference to the Popish Plot. Just as the Plot was not a Catholic conspiracy at all, but a Protestant attempt to produce the illusion that Catholics were conspiring to replace Charles II with his Popish brother James (Kenyon, 1974), so everyone in *The Feigned Courtesans* is something other than they appear to be. But beneath the massive, multiple, mistaking of identity, plotting and counter-plotting, the play's resolution insists that legitimacy and stability can prevail. This is shown most clearly in the fact that, despite themselves, Julio and Laura Lucretia come to recognize that the marriage that has been arranged for them by their parents is also their rightful fate. This conservatism is emphasized by the play's dedication to Charles II's most famous mistress, Nell Gwyn, whom Behn praises for her wit and virtue. In the play, Nell Gwyn is, in a sense, figured in the witty heroine, Cornelia. As 'feigned courtesan', Cornelia captures the rakish Galliard through her wit and actual chastity, just as Nell Gwyn 'has subdued the most powerful and glorious monarch of the world' (4), and has borne him two sons. In this play everything connected with monarchy, even its 'illegitimate' offspring, is legitimized.

In 1681, as the political crisis deepened, Behn wrote a play almost devoid of women. Most of the female characters in *The False Count* (Duffy, 1990) are indistinguishable from one another, and are smiling pawns in plots designed by men. The male characters, by contrast, are sharply delineated. Each represents a man of a different social status: Don Carlos is old wealth, his friend Antonio a member of the new elite. Francisco embodies the emergent new money, having made his wealth through his trade; in exchange for being admitted to the periphery of the elite, he is happy not to push to rise further. Guiliom, a day labourer and the eponymous false Count, appears to be a different matter altogether. He freely mimics and mocks his superiors, changes the plot they are trying to make use of him in, and gets both money and the woman of his choice. The play asks whether, beneath their status differences, these men are all the same: is there anywhere new for a country in political confusion to go to?

Abroad, is the answer of *The Widow Ranter* (1690). In the New World, where everything is in flux, and deported criminals form the ruling Council, Ranter can pass as a man and by the end of the fourth act win Daring, the partner of her choice. Strikingly, she spends the remainder of the action cross-dressed, fighting by her lover's side as his equal. In parallel to this, and in a series of scenes which echo and implicitly comment on it, is the tragic, heroic plot of General Bacon and his beloved Semernia. They are trapped within the language and logics of romantic convention; it is deeply fitting that when Semernia dresses as a man, Bacon accidentally kills her before dying of grief (5 iii).[27]

Margaret Cavendish, Duchess of Newcastle (1623–73)

In 1643, the 20-year-old Margaret Lucas, youngest child of an Essex gentry family, left home to join the court of Queen Henrietta Maria in Oxford (Grant, 1957; Jones,

1988). In 1644 she moved with them to France, where she married William Cavendish, Marquis (later Duke) of Newcastle, who had himself fled England after the defeat of his royalist troops. Throughout the interregnum, like many of their political allies, they lived on the Continent, mostly in Antwerp. According to her biographical accounts, he spent his time in schooling horses, she in writing. Her first two books, *Poems and Fancies* and *Philosophical Fancies*, were published in London in 1653, during Margaret Cavendish's unsuccessful attempt in a visit there to regain some of her husband's confiscated property. By the time of her death in 1673, she had published a further ten folio volumes, each running to several hundred pages. She sent copies of most of these not only to the English universities but to continental ones as well, determined to ensure her lasting fame.

Like Mary Carleton, she makes an appearance in Samuel Pepys's *Diary*. On 30 March 1667 he records going to the theatre to see *The Humorous Lovers*, a play he believed to be her work, though in fact it was her husband's. He declares it was

> the most silly thing that ever came upon a stage. I was sick to see it, but yet would not but have seen it, that I might the better understand her. (Pocock, 1927, vol. 2: 207; see also entries for 11 and 26 April 1667)

This mixture of fascination and deprecation was echoed nearly three centuries later in *A Room of One's Own*, where Virginia Woolf reflects on the

> vision of loneliness and riot the thought of Margaret Cavendish brings to mind! As if some giant cucumber had spread itself over all the roses and carnations in the garden and choked them. What could bind, tame, or civilise for human use that wild, generous, untutored intelligence? It poured itself out, higgledy-piggledy, in torrents of rhyme and prose, poetry and philosophy which stands congealed in quartos and folios that nobody ever reads. (59–60)

This combination of assumptions – that whilst the author was a fascinating spectacle, her works were confused, even mad – has characterized most references to Margaret Cavendish until very recently. Now, as modern editions of her writings appear, she is starting to be appraised, instead, as an experimental artist. David Norbrook, for instance, has pointed out that her extraordinary vivifying of the natural world pre-dates Marvell's (Woodhuysen, 1992: 51). Her poem 'The Hunting of the Hare' speaks mockingly, devastatingly, against blood sports:

> Men hooping loud such acclamations make
> As if the devil they did prisoner take,
> When they do but a shiftless creature kill,
> To hunt, there needs no valiant soldier's skill . . .
> As if that God made creatures for man's meat,
> And gave them life and sense, for man to eat;
> Or else for sport, or recreation's sake,
> Destroy those lives that God saw good to make;
> Making their stomachs graves, which full they fill
> With murthered bodies that in sport they kill.
> (Fowler, 1992: 636; Greer et al., 1988: 168–72)

Although Cavendish's biographers, and many of her critics, have tended to read her work as if her life and her writings are interchangeable, what emerges from her pages is a riot of voices. This is nowhere more true than in her autobiography, which first appeared as the thirteenth part of her baker's dozen of fictions, *Nature's Pictures Drawn by Fancies Pencil to the Life* (1656; Graham et al., 1989: 87–100).[28] There, whilst claiming

> I think it no crime to wish myself the exactest of nature's works, my thread of life the longest, my chain of destiny the strongest, my mind the peaceablest, my death the easiest, and the greatest saint in heaven, (97)

she also represents herself as 'dull, fearful and bashful' (90, 98). The autobiography's closing paragraph indicates one source of this consistently inconsistent self-depiction. Whilst claiming to have as much right to write her own life as Caesar or Ovid (98), she catalogues the reasons she might be forgotten by history:

> I was daughter to one Master Lucas of St John's near Colchester in Essex, second wife to the Lord Marquis of Newcastle; for, my lord having had two wives, I might easily have been mistaken, especially if I should die and my lord marry again. (99)

There is no coherent subject position available for a woman in a society where her identity, her status, her very name, are dependent on the man she is attached to by birth or marriage.

In many of Cavendish's fictions, the heroines have multiple selves, each one identified by a different name. In *Assaulted and Pursued Chastity* (1656; Lilley, 1994), the abandoned Miseria refuses to be tempted into prostitution, and becomes the virtuous Affectionata. She in turn metamorphoses into the cross-dressed hero, Travellia, who is so successful in his/her guise that s/he not only wins wars but is adopted as a son by a man with whom s/he lives closely for many years. On being told by Travellia that s/he is a woman, the old man is untroubled: the son's identity is not dependent on gender.

It is interesting to compare with the similar event in *Twelfth Night* the incident in this story where the cross-dressed Travellia is sent on a king's behalf to woo a woman. Shakespeare's Cesario is hopeless with a sword, embarrassed and amused by Olivia's instant infatuation. Olivia transfers her affections to Viola's twin brother inevitably, and without realizing she is doing so. Travellia, by contrast, forms a happy alliance with the queen she courts by proxy, who, on first being told Travellia is a woman, is 'moved by her mixed passions, anger and love; angry that she was deceived, yet still did love, as wishing she had been a man' (112). Subsequently the queen invites the king to be glad for her earlier passion for Travellia:

> The Queen told him that she was likelier to love him now, than if she had never been a lover before; for, said she, there is something pleasing in lovers' thoughts, be their fortunes never so adverse. (113)[29]

In *The New Blazing World* (1666; Lilley, 1994; Salzman, 1991) the heroine changes her name and status as she floats in a ship off the end of her world and on to another one. Her presence on the boat is due to a rich merchant's having forcibly abducted her. It is typical of Cavendish's work that this aspiring rapist and the sailors who abet him should first freeze to death, and then be left stinking on the vessel by their would-be victim as they thaw out in the Blazing World (125–6). The heroine's shift in identity from apparently helpless victim to adored Princess of the Blazing World is further complicated when the soul of the 'plain and rational' Margaret Cavendish, Duchess of Newcastle, comes to live in her body to work as her scribe. The souls of the two women become 'platonic lovers', a union welcomed by the princess after her adviser has cautioned her that 'husbands have reason to be jealous of platonic lovers, for they are very dangerous, as being not only very intimate and close, but subtle and insinuating' (181). Their subsequent adventures include travelling by submarine to save from hostile invasion the princess's homeland (203–8); and inventing their own imaginary worlds (183–9). This is the life available to women who escape 'love' of the kind threatened at the story's opening.

New directions

The brief summary given above of Cavendish's *Blazing World* misrepresents the story in ways symptomatic of recent accounts of women's writing in the 1630–89 period. I have described the work as if it would fit into a tradition of utopian writing. In fact, though, more than half of *The Blazing World* consists of philosophical disquisitions which seek to discredit empiricism and other scientific theories, and to recommend in their place Cavendish's own ideas about the nature and purpose of human life. It is this philosophizing which constitutes most of her published work. Because such material does not fit into modern conceptions of 'literature', none of it is in print and available for study.[30]

A recurrent concern in seventeenth-century women's writing is with the stifling impact of received authority. Hester Biddle would burn the universities to the ground; Aphra Behn suggests that if critics are really determined to impose conventions, they should confine themselves to the harmless task of inventing rules for children's games. Mary Trye, Hannah Wolley, Jane Sharp, Margaret Cavendish, Dorothy Osborne, An Collins, all mock, and refuse, in their various ways, the idea that there are objective standards against which their works can be judged, and found wanting (Hobby, 1988: 169–203; Hobby, 1996; Keller, 1995). One of the most powerful effects of reading these writings by women is the discovery that they give the lie to any assumption that women in the past were chaste, silent and obedient; or indeed that they were lascivious wastrels. They were as various, as witty, and as inventive as people in any period. In *The Blazing World*, the princess asks philosophers

> whether our forefathers [and, let's add, our foremothers] had been as wise, as men were at present, and had understood reason, as well as they did now? They answered, that in former ages they had been as wise as they are in the present, nay wiser; for, said they,

many in this age do think their forefathers have been fools, by which they prove themselves to be such. (Lilley, 1994: 170)

Indeed.

Notes

1. See also Bell et al., 1990: 287–93; Hobby, 1995.
2. The attribution to Makin of *The Malady and the Remedy* is speculative. See also her *An Essay to Revive the Antient Education of Gentlewomen* (1673; Mahl and Koon, 1977; Ferguson, 1985), which is presented in a male voice. Makin is regularly wrongly identified. Her maiden name was not Pell, but Reynolds. Tutor to Princess Elizabeth in the 1640s, as a teenager she had published a collection of poems in Greek, French, German and Spanish, *Musa Virginea* (1616). See Blain et al., 1990.
3. *Unto every individual Member of Parliament: The humble Representation of divers afflicted Women-Petitioners*, 1653. See Hobby, 1988: 13–18.
4. Recent feminist criticism on Milton approaches the Eve figure differently; see Duncker, 1991; Nyquist and Ferguson, 1987. Political writings by women in the 1630s and 1640s, which tended to be conservative, are not currently in print, excepting a few examples in Greer et al., 1988.
5. See Crawford, 1985, though her attribution of some works is inaccurate, and her statistics are distorted for the 1640s by her counting texts rather than authors, since the majority of female-authored works published in that decade were by Lady Eleanor Davies (see Cope, 1992). 1649 is therefore a more significant watershed for the increase in women's published writing than Crawford realizes.
6. The Prologue refers to the author as 'he'. In the third issue of the play, the phrase 'especially of our sex' was added to the Postscript, giving a specifically woman-centred focus to Behn's attack on the critics.
7. Fowler, 1992: 698 also includes the poem, but has a misprint in line 14, 'That' for 'Than'.
8. Ezell, 1993 seeks to point out the importance of the sectaries, but she is hampered by unfamiliarity with the materials, and by the limitations of French feminist theory. For other readings, see Hinds, 1992; Wiseman, 1992, 1993.
9. In 1663, Katherine Philips also consulted Osborne over how to prevent the publication of her *Poems* bringing her into disrepute (Thomas, 1990: 19).
10. See also Wilcox, 1992.
11. Pepys records arguing with Lady Batten in defence of Mary Carleton 29 May and 7 June 1663. Twentieth-century critics insistently believe John Carleton's defamation of her: see for instance Chalmers, 1992, where the story told by John of Mary's origins is treated as fact.
12. See also 'To my dear and loving husband' in Kaplan, 1975: 35–6, which delicately parodies the convention of comparing the lover to a hunter and the beloved to a deer. Here, both are deers/dears.
13. See also Elizabeth Taylor in Greer et al., 1988: 294–8.
14. Philips's first published poem, an elegy on William Cartwright, had already identified her royalism, as does her use of précieuse convention; see Thomas, 1990: 6–11.
15. Greer et al., 1988 wrongly suggest that an alteration in the poem's last line from 'factious' to 'sullen' reverses the meaning. The OED sense 1(a) of 'sullen' implies that Puritan politics (factious politics, in Philips's view) were regularly described as 'sullen' by their opponents.
16. The sun metaphor is also prominent in her poem lamenting the result of the Battle of Worcester, 'On 3 September 1651' (Thomas, 1990: 82–3; Woodhuysen, 1992: 171–2); and

in 'To the Excellent Mrs A.O. upon her receiving the name of Lucasia' (Greer et al., 1988: 191–3; Thomas, 1990: 101–2).

17. 'Friendship in Emblem, or the Seal' (Thomas, 1990: 106–8; Woodhuysen, 1992: 518) also echoes and implicitly criticizes Donne's compasses conceit in 'A Valediction: Forbidden Mourning'. In Donne's version, the foot of the compasses representing the woman is 'fixed', its purpose to control the behaviour of the male 'wanderer'. In Philips's poem, 'Each follows where the other leans/And what each does, this other means'.

18. See also 'Against Love' (Bernikow, 1974: 62–3; Fullard, 1990: 95; Kaplan, 1975: 43; Thomas, 1990: 214); 'a married state' (Greer et al., 1988: 188–9); Jane Barker, 'A Virgin Life' (Greer et al., 1988: 360–3).

19. Zimbardo, 1991 argues that Behn escapes from plays to write (implicitly more important) prose fiction. Much recent Behn criticism avoids the complications of her plays, focusing on the relatively simple Prefaces, Prologues and Epilogues. See Hutner, 1993 and Schofield and Macheski, 1991.

20. For a landlady who does turn out to be a bawd, see *The Unfortunate Happy Lady* (Salzman, 1991: 531–53). There, the 'innocent' heroine Philadelphia is revealed as devastatingly manipulative, soundly punishing the brother who has tricked her into a bawdy house, and marrying off to him a young woman who has irritated her.

21. I borrow this argument from work-in-progress of Bill Overton's. The contrast between Behn and Etherege is also provocative if one juxtaposes her poem 'The Disappointment' (Fowler, 1992: 724–7; Salzman, 1994: 223–7; Todd, 1992: 331–5) with the one it is answering: Etherege's 'The Imperfect Enjoyment' (Fowler, 1992: 708–9).

22. *Othello* was popular on the Restoration stage, and Thomas Betterton, who played Abdelazer, later became a famous Othello (Rosenberg, 1961).

23. See also 3 i and 4 iii, where women are alone, and 2 i and 3 iv, where men are.

24. Many of Behn's poems explore the attractions and dangers of love, for example: 'The Disappointment', 'Song. Love Armed', 'The Dream. A Song', 'Song. The Surprise', 'A Pindaric to Mr P. Who Sings Finely', 'To Alexis in Answer to His Poem Against Fruition', in Salzman, 1994. There are good discussions in Duyfhuizen, 1991 and Gardiner, 1993.

25. Parliament's attempt to exclude the Catholic Duke of York from the throne resulted in a long-running conflict; see Coward, 1980: 285–9. For Behn's involvement with Tory pamphleteering, see Duffy, 1989: 184–96.

26. These arguments have been developed in conversation with Liz Bridges.

27. Some of this play, which was posthumously published and so lacked Behn's close supervision, should be set in verse. The alternation between prose and verse in Behn's plays is always worth analyzing, since it often marks ironic shifts in perspective. See, for example, the confrontation between Angelica and Willmore in *The Rover* 2 ii.

28. The autobiography is also usually appended to editions of her biography, *The Life of the Duke of Newcastle*.

29. Compare the romance between Lady Happy and a mysterious princess in *The Convent of Pleasure* (1668; Rowsell, 1995; extracts in Ferguson, 1985). It is only after many scenes of pastoral courtship and passionate kissing that the princess is revealed to be a prince: a fact hidden from the reader/audience as well as from the infatuated Lady Happy, who had earlier proclaimed, 'Men are the only troublers of women, they cause their pain, but not their pleasures'. She establishes her 'convent of pleasure', a women's university, to enable women to have another choice in life.

30. See, though, the good account of Cavendish's philosophy in Sarasohn, 1984, and the philosophical poems in Fowler, 1992: 630–4.

Bibliography

Primary materials: modern editions of writings 1630–89

Bernikow, L. (ed.) (1974), *The World Split Open: Women Poets 1552–1950*, London: Women's Press.

Duffy, M. (ed.) (1990), *Aphra Behn: Five Plays, The Lucky Chance, The Rover Part I, The Widow Ranter, The False Count, Abdelazer*, London: Methuen.

Ferguson, M. (ed.) (1985), *First Feminists: British Women Writers 1578–1799*, Bloomington and Old Westbury: Indiana University Press and the Feminist Press.

Fowler, A. (ed.) (1992), *The New Oxford Book of Seventeenth Century Verse*, Oxford and New York: Oxford University Press.

Fullard, J. (ed.) (1990), *British Women Poets 1660–1800: An Anthology*, New York: Whitston Publishing.

Graham, E., H. Hinds, E. Hobby and H. Wilcox (eds) (1989), *Her Own Life: Autobiographical Writings by Seventeenth-Century Englishwomen*, London and New York: Routledge.

Greer, G. (ed.) (1991), *The Uncollected Verse of Aphra Behn*, Essex: Stump Cross.

Greer, G., J. Medoff, M. Sansome and S. Hastings (eds) (1988), *Kissing the Rod: An Anthology of 17th Century Women's Verse*, London: Virago.

Kaplan, C. (ed.) (1975), *Salt and Bitter and Good: Three Centuries of English and American Women Poets*, New York and London: Paddington Press.

Latt, D. (ed.) (1979), *Women's Speaking Justified (Margaret Fell) 1667*, California: Augustan Reprint Society.

L'Estrange, R. (trans.) (1882?), *The Fables of Aesop*, London: Frederick Warne.

Lilley, K. (ed.) (1994), *Margaret Cavendish: The Blazing World and Other Writings*, London and New York: Penguin.

Link, F. (ed.) (1967), *Aphra Behn: The Rover*, Lincoln: University of Nebraska Press.

Lyons, P. and F. Morgan (eds) (1991), *Female Playwrights of the Restoration: Five Comedies*, London and Rutland, Vermont: Dent.

Mahl, M. and H. Koon (eds) (1977), *The Female Spectator: English Women Writers Before 1800*, Bloomington and London: Indiana University Press; Old Westbury: The Feminist Press.

Milhous, J. and R. Hume (eds) (1977), *Elizabeth Polwhele: The Frolicks or The Lawyer Cheated (1671)*, Ithaca and London: Cornell University Press.

Morgan, F. (ed.) (1981), *The Female Wits: Women Playwrights of the Restoration*, London: Virago.

Parker, K. (ed.) (1987), *Dorothy Osborne: Letters to Sir William Temple*, London and New York: Penguin.

Pocock, G. (ed.) (1927), *The Diary of Samuel Pepys*, 2 vols, London and Toronto: Dent.

Rowsell, J. (ed.) (1995), *The Convent of Pleasure, A Comedy Written by the Thrice Noble, Illustrious, and Excellent Princesse, the Duchess of Newcastle*, Oxford: Seventeenth Century Press.

Russell, A. (ed.) (1994), *Aphra Behn: The Rover*, Toronto: Broadview.

Salzman, P. (ed.) (1991), *An Anthology of Seventeenth-Century Fiction*, Oxford and New York: Oxford University Press.

Salzman, P. (ed.) (1994), *Aphra Behn: Oroonoko and Other Writings*, Oxford and New York: Oxford University Press.

Smith, A. (ed.) (1971), *John Donne: The Complete English Poems*, London and New York: Penguin.

Thomas, P. (ed.) (1990), *The Collected Works of Katherine Philips the Matchless Orinda*, vol. 1: The Poems, Essex: Stump Cross.

Todd, J. (ed.) (1992), *Aphra Behn: Oroonoko, The Rover and Other Works*, London and New York: Penguin.

Woodhuysen, H. (ed.) (1992), *The Penguin Book of Renaissance Verse*, selected and with an introduction by David Norbrook, London and New York: Penguin.

Secondary materials

Amussen, S. (1988), *An Ordered Society: Gender and Class in Early Modern England*, Oxford: Basil Blackwell.

Ballaster, R. (1992), 'New Hystericism: Aphra Behn's *Oroonoko*: The Body, the Text, and the Feminist Critic' in *New Feminist Discourses: Critical Essays on Theories and Texts*, I. Armstrong (ed.), London and New York: Routledge, pp. 283–95.

Ballaster, R. (1993), '"Pretences of State": Aphra Behn and the Female Plot', in *Rereading Aphra Behn: History, Theory, and Criticism*, H. Hutner (ed.), Charlottesville and London: University Press of Virginia, pp. 187–211.

Ballaster, R. (1995), '"The Vices of Old Rome Revived": Representations of Female Same-sex Desire in Seventeenth and Eighteenth Century England' in *Volcanoes and Pearl Divers: Essays in Lesbian Feminist Studies*, S. Raitt (ed.), London: Onlywomen, pp. 13–36.

Bauman, R. (1983), *Let Your Words Be Few: Symbolic Speaking and Silence among Seventeenth Century Quakers*, London: Cambridge University Press.

Bell, M., G. Parfitt and S. Shepherd (eds) (1990), *A Biographical Dictionary of English Women Writers 1580–1720*, Hemel Hempstead: Harvester Wheatsheaf.

Blain, V., P. Clements and I. Grundy (eds) (1990), *The Feminist Companion to Literature in English: Women Writers from the Middle Ages to the Present*, London: Batsford.

Brant, C. and D. Purkiss (eds) (1992), *Women, Texts and Histories 1575–1760*, London and New York: Routledge.

Chalmers, H. (1992), '"The Person I Am, Or What They Made Me To Be": The Construction of the Feminine Subject in the Autobiographies of Mary Carleton', in *Women, Texts and Histories 1575–1760*, C. Brant and D. Purkiss (eds), London and New York: Routledge.

Clark, A. (1968), *Working Life of Women in the Seventeenth Century*, London: Frank Cass.

Cope, E. (1992), *Handmaid of the Holy Spirit: Dame Eleanor Davies, Never Soe Mad a Ladie*, Ann Arbor: University of Michigan Press.

Cotton, N. (1991), 'Aphra Behn and the Pattern Hero' in *Curtain Calls: British and American Women and the Theater, 1660–1820*, M. Schofield and C. Macheski (eds), Athens: Ohio University Press, pp. 211–19.

Coward, B. (1980), *The Stuart Age: A History of England 1603–1714*, London and New York: Longman.

Crawford, P. (1985), 'Women's published writings 1600–1700' in *Women in English Society 1500–1800*, in M. Prior (ed.), London and New York: Methuen, pp. 211–82.

Donoghue, E. (1993), *Passions Between Women: British Lesbian Culture 1668–1801*, London: Scarlet Press.

Duffy, M. (1989), *The Passionate Shepherdess: Aphra Behn 1640–89*, London: Methuen.

Duncker, P. (1991), 'Reading Genesis', in *What Lesbians do in Books*, E. Hobby and C. White (eds), London: Women's Press, pp. 205–25.

Duyfhuizen, B. (1991), '"That which I dare not name": Aphra Behn's "The Willing Mistress"', *English Literary History* 58, 63–82.

Ezell, M. (1993), *Writing Women's Literary History*, Baltimore and London: Johns Hopkins University Press.

Ferguson, M. (1992), *Subject to Others: British Women Writers and Colonial Slavery, 1670–1834*, London and New York: Routledge.

Fraser, A. (1985), *The Weaker Vessel: Woman's Lot in Seventeenth-century England*, London: Methuen.

Gallagher, C. (1993), 'Who Was That Masked Woman? The Prostitute and the Playwright in the Comedies of Aphra Behn', in *Rereading Aphra Behn: History, Theory, and Criticism*, H. Hutner (ed.), Charlottesville and London: University Press of Virginia, pp. 65–85.

Gardiner, J. (1993), 'Liberty, Equality, Fraternity: Utopian Language in Behn's Lyric Poetry', in *Rereading Aphra Behn: History, Theory, and Criticism*, H. Hutner (ed.), Charlottesville and London: University Press of Virginia, pp. 273–300.

Goreau, A. (1980), *Reconstructing Aphra: A Social Biography of Aphra Behn*, Oxford: Oxford University Press.

Grant, D. (1957), *Margaret the First: A Biography of Margaret Cavendish the Duchess of Newcastle 1623–1673*, London: Rupert Hart-Davis.

Grundy, I. and S. Wiseman (eds) (1992), *Women, Writing, History 1640–1740*, London: Batsford.

Hill, C. (1975), *The World Turned Upside Down: Radical Ideas During the English Revolution*, Harmondsworth and New York: Penguin.

Hinds, H. (1992), '"Who may Bind where God hath Loosed?": Response to Sectarian Women's Writing in the Second Half of the Seventeenth Century', in *Gloriana's Face: Women, Public and Private, in the English Renaissance*, S. Cerasano and M. Wynne-Davies (eds), New York and London: Harvester Wheatsheaf, pp. 157–69.

Hobby, E. (1988), *Virtue of Necessity: English Women's Writing 1649–1688*, London: Virago.

Hobby, E. (1991a), 'Katherine Philips: Seventeenth-Century Lesbian Poet', in *What Lesbians do in Books*, E. Hobby and C. White (eds), London: Women's Press.

Hobby, E. (1991b), '"Oh Oxford Thou Art Full of Filth": The Prophetical Writings of Hester Biddle, 1629(?)–1696', in *Feminist Criticism: Theory and Practice*, S. Sellers (ed.), New York and London: Harvester Wheatsheaf, pp. 157–69.

Hobby, E. (1992), '"Discourse so Unsavoury": Women's Published Writings of the 1650s', in *Women, Writing, History 1640–1740*, I. Grundy and S. Wiseman (eds), London: Batsford, pp. 16–32.

Hobby, E. (1993), 'The Politics of Gender', in *The Cambridge Companion to English Poetry Donne to Marvell*, T. Corns (ed.), Cambridge and New York: Cambridge University Press, pp. 31–51.

Hobby, E. (1994), 'Handmaids of the Lord and Mothers in Israel: Early Vindications of Quaker Women's Prophecy', *Prose Studies* 17: 3, 88–98.

Hobby, E. (1995), 'A Woman's Best Setting Out is Silence: The Writings of Hannah Wolley', in *Culture and Society in the Stuart Restoration: Literature, Drama, History*, G. MacLean (ed.), Cambridge and New York: Cambridge University Press, pp. 179–200.

Hobby, E. (1996), 'The Politics of Women's Prophecy in the English Revolution', in *Sacred and Profane: Secular and Devotional Interplay in Early Modern British Literature*, H. Wilcox, R. Todd and A. MacDonald (eds), Amsterdam: VU University Press, pp. 295–306.

Hobby, E. and B. Overton (1994), '"There is Not Space for Margaret Cavendish and Dryden": Higher Education Teaching 1640–1700', *Women's Writing: The Elizabethan to Victorian Period* 1: 3, 257–75.

Howe, E. (1992), *The First English Actresses: Women and Drama 1660–1700*, Cambridge and New York: Cambridge University Press.

Hutner, H. (ed.) (1993), *Rereading Aphra Behn: History, Theory, and Criticism*, Charlottesville and London: University Press of Virginia.

Hutton, R. (1985), *The Restoration: a Political and Religious History of England and Wales 1658–1667*, Oxford and New York: Oxford University Press.

Jackson, S. (1992), 'Towards a Historical Sociology of Housework: A Materialist Feminist Analysis', *Women's Studies International Forum* 15: 2, 153–72.

Jones, K. (1988), *A Glorious Fame: The Life of Margaret Cavendish Duchess of Newcastle 1623–1673*, London: Bloomsbury.

Kavenik, F. (1991), 'Aphra Behn: The Playwright as "Breeches Part"', in *Curtain Calls: British and American Women and the Theater 1660–1820*, M. Schofield and C. Macheski (eds), Athens: Ohio University Press, pp. 177–92.

Keller, E. (1995), 'Mrs Jane Sharp: Midwifery and the Critique of Medical Knowledge in Seventeenth-century England', *Women's Writing The Elizabeth to Victorian Period* 2: 2, 101–11.

Kenyon, J. (1974), *The Popish Plot*, Harmondsworth and New York: Penguin.

Langdell, C. (1985), 'Aphra Behn and Sexual Politics: A Dramatist's Discourse with her Audience', in *Drama, Sex and Politics*, J. Redmond (ed.), Cambridge: Cambridge University Press, pp. 107–28.

Lewalski, B. (1979), *Protestant Poetics and the Seventeenth-Century Religious Lyric*, Princeton: Princeton University Press.

McGregor, J. and B. Reay (eds) (1984), *Radical Religion in the English Revolution*, Oxford and New York: Oxford University Press.

Mack, P. (1992), *Visionary Women: Ecstatic Prophecy in Seventeenth-Century England*, Berkeley and Oxford: University of California Press.

MacLean, G. (ed.) (1995), *Culture and Society in the Stuart Restoration: Literature, Drama, History*, Cambridge and New York: Cambridge University Press.

Medoff, J. (1992), 'The Daughters of Behn and the Problem of Reputation', in *Women, Writing, History 1640–1740*, I. Grundy and S. Wiseman (eds), London: Batsford, pp. 33–54.

Middleton, C. (1983), 'Patriarchal Exploitation and the Rise of English Capitalism', in *Gender, Class and Work*, E. Gamarnikow et al. (eds), London: Heinemann, pp. 11–27.

Munns, J. (1991), ' "I by a Double Right Thy Bounties Claim": Aphra Behn and Sexual Space', in *Curtain Calls: British and American Women and the Theater, 1660–1820*, M. Schofield and C. Macheski (eds), Athens: Ohio University Press, pp. 193–210.

Nyquist, M. and M. Ferguson (eds) (1987), *Remembering Milton: Essays on the Texts and Translations*, London and New York: Methuen.

Overton, B. (1992), 'Countering Crusoe: Two Colonial Narratives', *Critical Survey* 4, 302–10.

Pearson, J. (1988), *The Prostituted Muse: Images of Women and Women Dramatists 1642–1737*, Hemel Hempstead and New York: Harvester Wheatsheaf.

Prior, M. (ed.) (1985), *Women in English Society 1500–1800*, London and New York: Methuen.

Rosenberg, M. (1961), *The Masks of Othello: The Search for Identity of Othello, Iago, and Desdemona by Three Centuries of Actors and Critics*, Berkeley and Los Angeles: University of California Press.

Salvaggio, R. (1993), 'Aphra Behn's Love: Fiction, Letters, and Desire', in *Rereading Aphra Behn: History, Theory, and Criticism*, H. Hutner (ed.), Charlottesville and London: University Press of Virginia, pp. 253–70.

Sarasohn, L. (1984), 'A Science Turned Upside Down: Feminism and the Natural Philosophy of Margaret Cavendish', *Huntington Library Quarterly* 47, 289–307.

Schofield, M. and C. Macheski (eds) (1991), *Curtain Calls: British and American Women and the Theater, 1660–1820*, Athens: Ohio University Press.

Showalter, E. (1978), *A Literature of Their Own: British Women Novelists from Brontë to Lessing*, London: Virago.

Sussman, C. (1993), 'The Other Problem With Women: Reproductive and Slave Culture in Aphra Behn's *Oroonoko*', in *Rereading Aphra Behn: History, Theory, and Criticism*, H. Hutner (ed.), Charlottesville and London: University Press of Virginia, pp. 212–33.

Todd, J. (1989), *The Sign of Angellica: Women, Writing and Fiction, 1660–1800*, London: Virago.

Van Lennep, W., E. Avery and A. Scouten (eds) (1965), *The London Stage 1660–1800, Part 1 1660–1700*, Carbondale: Southern Illinois University Press.

Wilcher, R. (1983), ' "Then keep the ancient way!": A Study of Henry Vaughan's *Silex Scintillans*', *Durham University Journal* 76, new series 45, 11–24.

Wilcox, H. (1992), 'Private Writing and Public Function: Autobiographical Texts by Renaissance Englishwomen', in *Gloriana's Face: Women, Public and Private, in the English Renaissance*, S. Cerasano and M. Wynne-Davies (eds), Hemel Hempstead: Harvester Wheatsheaf, pp. 205–27.

Wiseman, S. (1992), 'Unsilent Instruments and the Devil's Cushions: Authority in Seventeenth-century Women's Prophetic Discourse', in *New Feminist Discourses: Critical Essays on Theories and Texts*, I. Armstrong (ed.), London and New York: Routledge, pp. 176–96.

Wiseman, S. (1993), 'Read Within: Gender, Cultural Difference and Quaker Women's Travel Narratives', *Baetyl: The Journal of Women's Literature* 1: 2, 82–103.

Woodcock, G. (1948), *The Incomparable Aphra*, London and New York: T.V. Boardman.

Woolf, V. (1977), *A Room of One's Own*, London and New York: Granada.

Zimbardo, R. (1991) 'Aphra Behn: A Dramatist in Search of the Novel', in *Curtain Calls: British and American Women and the Theater, 1660–1820*, M. Schofield and C. Macheski (eds), Athens: Ohio University Press, pp. 371–82.

4

'Publick view': women's writing, 1689–1789

Jane Spencer

Aphra Behn died in April 1689, shortly after the 1688 Revolution that had led to the reign of William and Mary and set the scene for growing parliamentary domination of English political life. In 'A Pindaric Poem to the Reverend Doctor Burnet', written shortly before her death, she lamented a change that had left her stranded 'on the forsaken barren shore' of Stuart absolutism and Tory propaganda (Behn, 1992: 309). To many literary historians since then, Behn has seemed to be on the losing side of more than one conflict. The century following her death was notable not only for the Whiggery she detested and the growth of the City commerce she satirized, but for the development of new bourgeois literary and theatrical tastes which toned down and eventually outlawed her comedies along with many others of the Restoration. Outraged by libertine ideals and offended by bawdy words and actions, the new moralists, such as the influential Richard Steele, playwright and co-author of the *Tatler* and *Spectator* papers, created a climate in which the name of the most successful female playwright of the seventeenth century became a synonym for immorality. This mattered to women far more than the corresponding criticism of Etherege, Wycherley or Rochester for similar offences mattered to men. Facing the application of the still-familiar principle of taking individual women as representative of 'the sex', potential women writers after Behn had to prove that they were not like her, but on the contrary modest, chaste, properly feminine. Rejecting Behn's example became a route to feminine literary respectability (Ballaster, 1992: 198–211; Medoff, 1992).

But this was not the whole story. Behn also left eighteenth-century women writers the legacy of her professional success. Her plays frequently performed for much of the period, her novels reprinted, her works covertly admired and imitated by many, Behn remained an influence (Pearson, 1993). As a fictional innovator in particular she was important to the development of the novel, and as a woman 'forced to write for Bread and not ashamed to owne it' she was the forerunner of a growing number of versatile, professional women writing during the eighteenth century (Behn, 1678).

The century between the Settlement of 1688 and the French Revolution of 1789 was a time of steady commercialization and colonial expansion for a country that was beginning (after the 1707 Act of Union incorporating Scotland) to think of itself as Britain. The early years were characterized by strong Whig–Tory struggles, the middle and later years by Whig rule under the Hanoverian kings. While conflicts, foreign and domestic, were never far away, with involvement in European wars of succession, the Seven Years' War with France in 1756–63, the Jacobite uprisings of 1715 and 1745, and the loss of the American colonies after the 1775 American Revolution, the period was one of relative political stability after the upheavals of the seventeenth century. Throughout the century, the expansion of commerce and the growth of the bourgeois public sphere both enabled and were facilitated by a huge growth in the publishing industry. The readership expanded, though there is no consensus on its size or how fast it was growing; some historians argue for a rapid growth of the literacy rate, especially in urban areas, in the late seventeenth century, continuing into the eighteenth, while others contend that the expansion was not so much in numbers of readers as in the amount of their reading (Cressy, 1977; Shevelow, 1989: 29–32; Stone, 1969). Certainly those who were literate had more to read. Religious works, moral treatises, political pamphlets, volumes of poetry and plays were published in increasing numbers; relatively new forms like newspapers, periodicals, and novels, underwent particularly strong expansions. After 1750 changes in the commercial organization of the book trade led to fiercer competition and sharp rises in publication rates (Raven, 1992: 42–55).

Women as writers and readers played an important part in this growth, and in some specialized fields, like fiction, women writers, by the end of the century, were entering the market at a higher rate of increase than men (Stanton, 1991). At the same time women were continuing to write (and probably writing more) literature not intended for sale on the market: private letters, diaries, journals, poems and stories. Such forms were considered particularly appropriate for modest femininity, though paradoxically when they were published their air of privacy was their selling point. Women's participation in literature and the literary market was shaped by gendered custom and expectation; in particular, during the second half of the century the growing ideology of sentimentality and domesticity encouraged the development of certain feminized genres – the magazine specifically for the ladies, the female-authored children's book, the novel of sensibility. Yet women's writing in the period cannot be simply slotted into gendered categories. What strikes most about it is its rich variety. Women wrote scandalous political propaganda disguised as memoirs, witty epistles circulating in manuscript, confessional autobiographies, respected works of history, hymns, letters to the press, odes, sentimental novels, political propaganda, translations from Greek, literary criticism, periodicals, and much more.

With so much to choose from, it is impossible to do justice to it all in a chapter; but selection inevitably involves excluding interesting material. I have tried to describe a wide enough spread of writing to give an indication of general trends, while paying more detailed attention to a number of writers and works, chosen to give a sense of the variety of kinds of writing women were engaged in throughout the century. I have not tried to select a canon of most important women writers. Only one woman writer of this period, Frances Burney, used traditionally to be accorded a secure place in the university-taught canon (though Lady Mary Wortley Montagu usually got a mention); in recent years more have been added. Charlotte Lennox, whose novel *The*

Female Quixote (1752) has had a good deal of recent attention, now seems to be admitted, and Anne Finch, Sarah Fielding, and Anna Letitia Barbauld are surely on their way in. But feminist literary history seeks to do more than add women to the canon; it challenges canonical judgements and pays attention to the full range of women's writing. My own emphasis in this chapter is on the extent of women writers' participation in an expanding literary culture. Much has been written, and with good reason, of the external and internalized checks to female creativity at this time: the unequal access to education, time to write, and the means to publish, or be staged; the gendered shame attached to publicity, and the self-censorship enjoined by feminine modesty. Yet the statistical studies keep on revealing the increasing numbers of women writers, and criticism of their work keeps broadening our sense of its scope. There is some justification for Anne Messenger's celebratory conclusion that eighteenth-century women's literature is 'not derivative . . . nor is it peripheral . . . it belongs' (Messenger, 1986: 225).

In contrast, Ruth Salvaggio has questioned the value of trying to find a place for women writers to belong in an Enlightenment tradition which she analyzes as constituting itself on the suppression of a femininity defined in terms of darkness. Why should we 'want to recover women writers at all if we cannot locate in their writings a profound critique of exclusive systems' (Salvaggio, 1988: 116)? Perhaps because, whatever we can or cannot locate there, we want to know our history; if all we could find was complicity with the patriarchy, it would be depressing but necessary to know. And unless we do recover women writers, and give them a close attention that takes into account their historical difference from us, we will not know what profound critiques they may have in store for us.

We should not forget the barriers women faced as writers, but it can be useful to focus elsewhere sometimes. There is one barrier that critics and historians can do something about, and that is the barrier to recognition. Where recognition is concerned, the important concern for eighteenth-century women writers is not so much their original conditions of production, nor the biased treatment their contemporaries gave them; it is our reading of their work in the light of these considerations. If women writers are read as automatically and inevitably marginal, whatever they say and do, we will fail to understand their achievements, overstating the exceptional nature and challenge of some, overlooking the effectiveness of many more. In this chapter I look at eighteenth-century women's writing as a central part of English culture. However, although women writers were interested in many things besides articulating their own position, I have not escaped emphasizing their treatment of gender and writing. A work singling out women as writers needs to consider the issue, and the writers treated here did find themselves of necessity dealing in their work with 'the inescapable central term' of gender (Mermin, 1990: 336).

To what extent women writers should be seen as an integral part of their culture, implicated in its thought-systems, and to what extent they can be interpreted as oppositional, even disruptive forces, is a question that has been at the centre of much feminist criticism. The concept of a power-shattering *écriture féminine*, put forward in the 1970s by Hélène Cixous and others, has been more influential among critics of modernist and postmodernist writers than in criticism of earlier periods. Cixous's pronouncements that 'after plowing through literature across languages, cultures, and ages', she found that there has been very little 'writing that inscribes femininity'; that there has been a 'ridiculously small' number of women writers, and that of the ones that exist, 'the immense majority' show a 'workmanship . . . in no way different from male writing' (Cixous, 1981: 248), encouraged seekers of subversive feminine writing to look to the avant-garde, and historicist feminists to ignore a theoretical position that seemed to dismiss out of hand the women whose work they were discovering. This was a loss for eighteenth-century feminist criticism, since Cixous's notion of a feminine text that will 'blow up the law . . . break up the "truth"' (Cixous, 1981: 258) must be relevant to a century of Enlightenment whose writers, concerned for truth and law, often portrayed femininity as a threat to these values. More recently, feminist work has begun to apply notions of *écriture féminine* to this period. Ruth Salvaggio, for example, reads Anne Finch's writing about shade as creating a feminine space which 'does not simply oppose the light of man or the darkness associated with woman. It splits that duality from within' (Salvaggio, 1988: 106). In her reading, Finch's work is profoundly subversive, undermining the gendered oppositions on which Enlightenment ideas were based, and recording her own 'displacement, as a woman, in and from the Enlightenment world of men' (Salvaggio, 1988: 110).

Much more influential, however, in the recent development of feminist criticism of the eighteenth century have been the various approaches deriving from Marxist and New Historicist work. This very varied criticism shares a concern to place gender among other analytical categories, most notably race and class. The resulting analyses tend to place women writers by no means unproblematically, but certainly centrally, within a developing capitalist and imperialist culture, contributing to its formation and often complicit in its creation of unequal power-structures. These might be called integrationist readings of women's position in culture, as distinct from the separatist readings derived from the idea of *écriture féminine*. Particularly important here is the work of Nancy Armstrong, whose *Desire and Domestic Fiction* (1987) argued that the female authority of the domestic woman underpinned and enabled the rise of middle-class hegemony in the late eighteenth and early nineteenth centuries. This allowed for an understanding of women writers as (under certain circumstances) the authorized and power-bearing spokeswomen for their culture rather than its perpetual rebels, and made it easier to make sense of, for example, the conservatism of a writer like Hannah More. Recently Catherine Gallagher has extended this integrationist approach with her analysis of women's centrality to the development of the literary marketplace and new kinds of authorship in the eighteenth century, an analysis that places women as 'representatives of the condition of the author in the eighteenth century', only 'special in their extreme typicality' (Gallagher, 1994: xv). In contrast, other integrationist work focuses on the interaction of race and gender as formative categories in eighteenth-century thought. With the advent of the new-historical emphasis on the centrality of colonialism and imperialism, there has been analysis of the connection made between women and empire in eighteenth-century literary representations (Brown, 1993), and there is great interest in European women's representations of women of other cultures and races. Recent criticism of Behn's late novel *Oroonoko* (1688) focuses on the significance of her treatment of the African heroine, Imoinda (Brown, 1987; Ferguson, 1994). More generally, Felicity Nussbaum describes Englishwomen's use of the image of the foreign woman as their 'Other', arguing that writers as diverse as Anna Falconbridge, Lady Mary Wortley Montagu, and Mary Wollstonecraft 'consume the Other woman through their gaze and their texts' (Nussbaum, 1994: 154).

If the Foucauldian approach adopted by Armstrong and some others can some-times lead to overstating women writers' position as emblematic of general trends, and understating their capacity to criticize their culture, the most interesting of recent feminist work – by, among others, Donna Landry, Catherine Gallagher and Laura Brown – offers subtle analyses of the intertwining of cultural complicity and cultural critique to be found in women's writing of the period. Such integrationist readings, when complicated by the inclusion of feminine opposition as a possible stance, seem to me more fruitful than separatist ones. However, we do need to beware of grand narratives which too neatly plot the development of eighteenth-century women's writing on to a map of other trends such as the rise of bourgeois domesticity. In this chapter I have tried to generalize as little as is consistent with treating a great deal of writing in a small space. I have tried to indicate the variety of women's writing and its refusal to be confined to any singular feminine identity; to show that women writers were part of, and contributors to, central literary developments of their time; and to show that, from within their culture, they often articulated specific critiques of it derived from their various feminine positions.

Women writers often took a strongly defensive line against their critics, a tactic which may have led modern critics to exaggerate the hostility they faced. For ex-ample, Anne Finch, later Countess of Winchilsea (1661–1720), pondered on the reception of her writing in 'The Introduction':

> Did I my lines intend for publick view,
> How many censures would their faults persue,
> Some wou'd, because such words they do affect,
> Cry they're insipid, empty, uncorrect.
> And many, have attain'd, dull and untaught
> The name of Witt, only by finding fault.
> True judges, might condemn their want of witt,
> And all might say, they're by a Woman writt.
> Alas! a woman that attempts the pen,
> Such an intruder on the rights of men,
> Such a presumptuous Creature, is esteem'd,
> The fault, can by no virtue be redeem'd.
> They tell us, we mistake our sex and way;
> Good breeding, fassion, dancing, dressing, play
> Are the accomplishments we shou'd desire;
> To write, or read, or think, or to enquire
> Wou'd cloud our beauty, and exaust our time,
> And interrupt the Conquests of our prime;

Whilst the dull manage, of a servile house
Is held by some, our outmost art, and use.
(Finch, 1903: 4–5)

Finch held this poem back from publication, circulating it instead among her friends as the first in a manuscript collection of poems (McGovern, 1992: 33). Her fear of being attacked as presumptuous and unwomanly, and her insistence that her lines are not intended for the public, lend some credence to the view that for women writers in the early modern period, publicity and proper femininity were mutually exclusive. Angeline Goreau, in a discussion which has influenced recent feminist criticism, argues that publication of a woman's writings made her a public woman – in symbolic terms, a prostitute:

> To publish one's work . . . was to make oneself 'public': to expose oneself to 'the world'. Women who did so violated their feminine modesty both by egressing from the private sphere which was their proper domain and by permitting foreign eyes access to what ought to remain hidden and anonymous. (Goreau, 1980: 150)

Goreau's argument rests on a very clear distinction between public and private spheres, which recent work suggests does not apply to the seventeenth and eighteenth centuries. The re-examination of public and private, prompted by the work of Jürgen Habermas (Habermas, 1989), has led to the undermining of the notion that there were clearly demarcated, gendered public and private spheres in eighteenth-century discourse (Goodman, 1992). The manuscript circulation favoured by Finch certainly suggests the inadequacy of the idea of a strict public/private divide. As Margaret Ezell has pointed out, early modern women whose work circulated in this way often achieved an honourable fame and were acknowledged as part of the literary culture of their society (Ezell, 1992: 34–8). Anne Finch, as her recent biographer demonstrates, was well-received in her lifetime, and publication of her poems came after they had gained her a reputation in manuscript (McGovern, 1992: 95). Finch was not hiding from publicity in 'The Introduction', but choosing her public; read in this light, her complaint about attacks on women writers is less a reflection of her own anxiety and uncertainty than a contribution to her contemporaries' debate about women's qualities. 'They tell us, we mistake our sex and way', but the poems so introduced are there, in part, to show that 'they' are wrong.

Finch's concern with women's position is shared by many writers of the 1690s and early 1700s. It was a time of lively feminist and anti-feminist argument, taking place in the context of controversies between absolutist theories of government and emergent liberal political theory. '*If all Men are born free*, how is it that all Women are born slaves?' wondered Mary Astell in her 1700 essay, *Reflections Upon Marriage* (Astell, 1986: 76). Locke's characterization of the mind at birth as a *tabula rasa* and his tracing of ideas and the mind's qualities to its history of sense-impressions was not lost on women formulating arguments for a natural intellectual equality between the sexes (*Essay*, 1696: 11). From a more conservative political and religious standpoint, Mary Astell also blamed faulty education for women's shortcomings. In *A Serious Proposal to the Ladies* (1694) she used biblical references to underscore the point, echoed by women throughout the century, that 'Women are from their very Infancy debar'd those Advantages, with the want of which they are afterwards reproached, and nursed up in those Vices which will hereafter be upbraided to them. So partial are Men as to expect Brick where they afford no Straw . . .' (Astell, 1986: 143). Astell's Christian scorn of the world and its customs lent itself to the development of a feminist analysis of gender socialization:

> 'Twou'd puzzle a considerate person to account for all the Sin and Folly that is in the World (which certainly has nothing in it self to recommend it) did not Custom help to solve the difficulty. . . . 'Tis Custom therefore, that Tyrant Custom, which is the grand motive to all those irrational choices which we daily see made in the World, so very contrary to our *present* interest and pleasure, as well as to our Future. . . . When a poor Young lady is taught to value herself on nothing but her Cloaths and to think she's very fine when well accoutred; When she hears say that 'tis Wisdom enough for her to know how to dress her self, that she may become amiable in his eyes, to whom it appertains to be knowing and learned; who can blame her if she lay out her Industry and Money on such Accomplishments, and sometimes extends it farther than her misinformer desires she should? (Astell, 1986: 147–8)

Astell's *Serious Proposal* advocated convent-like colleges for women, an idea that did not come to fruition during the eighteenth century but which captured the imaginations of many eighteenth-century women. The work inspired a number of her female contemporaries and encouraged them in their commitment to education, writing and feminism: Judith Drake, Lady Damaris Masham, Elizabeth Elstob, the Anglo-Saxon scholar; Lady Mary Chudleigh and Elizabeth Thomas, who both wrote poems in anagrammatical praise of 'Almystrea'; and Lady Mary Wortley Montagu (Perry, 1986: 106–12). Astell's later *Reflections Upon Marriage* analyzed the institution as seriously disadvantageous to women, and if her religious and political affiliations prevented her arguing against established authority, even that of husbands, she made it scornfully clear that men did not hold their superior position through natural pre-eminence. Social subordination did not imply natural inferiority or a less direct relation to reason, goodness and God. The only good thing about marriage for women, she wrote, was that it allowed them ample scope for 'heroic Action' and 'Martyrdom', bringing glory to God; in worldly terms there was no advantage in being employed as a man's 'Upper-Servant' (Astell, 1986: 130). 'Wife and Servant are the same', agreed Mary Chudleigh in 1703 (Chudleigh, 1993: 83); years later, Sarah Fielding made one of the characters in *The Adventures of David Simple* (1744) reject a suitor with the observation that she 'had no kind of Ambition to be his *upper Servant*' (Fielding, 1969: 109). Mary Chudleigh shows Astell's influence in *The Ladies Defence* (1701), one of a number of feminist replies to John Sprint's *The Bride-Woman's Counsellor* (1699), a sermon, originally preached at a wedding, advocating extremes of wifely submission. Fourteen-year-old Sarah Field (later Fyge and Egerton) wrote an angry poem in reply (Medoff, 1982). Chudleigh's contribution to the debate was a poem in dialogue, allowing Melissa to reply to churlish husband Sir John Brute, chivalrous Sir William Loveall, and a parson who undermines Sprint's arguments for husbandly authority even as he tries to enforce them:

If he's a Fool, you must not think him so;
Nor yet indulge one mean, contemptuous Thought,
Or fancy he can e'er commit a Fault. . . .

And do not rudely too familiar grow:
Nor like some Country Matrons call him Names,
As *John*, or *Geffrey, William, George* or *James*;
Or what's much worse, and ne'er to be forgot,
Those courser Terms of Sloven, Clown or Sot;
For tho' perhaps they may be justly due,
Yet must not, Madam, once be spoke by you:
Soft winning Language will become you best;
Ladies ought not to Rail, tho' but in Jest.
Lastly, to him you Fealty must pay,
And his Commands without dispute obey.
A blind Obedience you from Guilt secures,
And if you err, the Fault is his, not yours.

(Chudleigh, 1993: 27)

The feminism of Astell and her contemporaries does not offer programmes for change: radical change in women's status is beyond their hope. They concentrate on demystifying marriage, supposedly woman's highest destiny, and undermining male dignity, adapting the satiric tradition, with its emphasis on human pride, to make a quietly cutting attack on pride's specifically masculine manifestations. Astell is at her most dangerous when ostensibly admitting male pre-eminence. 'All famous Arts have their Original from men, even from the Invention of Guns to the Mystery of good Eating' (Astell, 1986: 130).

This period was also one of expanding commercial opportunities for women writers, especially in the theatre. Delarivier Manley, Catherine Trotter and Mary Pix wrote tragedies and comedies, following the prevailing tastes for heroic tragedy based on historical material, and comedy of London life or based on Spanish intrigue. Mary Pix was the most prolific, producing twelve plays in the years 1696–1703 (Pearson, 1988: 171). Two of her comedies, *The Innocent Mistress* (1697) and *The Beau Defeated* (1700) are available in modern editions (Morgan, 1981; Lyons and Morgan, 1991). Both she and Catherine Trotter professed themselves in favour of the contemporary movement for reform of the stage, and claimed that as women they could be both moving and moral. Trotter's *Agnes de Castro* (based on a story by Behn), *The Unhappy Penitent* and *The Fatal Friendship* feminized the heroic drama with their emphasis on women's instead of men's conflicts between love and honour (Pearson, 1988: 187–8). Like most women playwrights of the time Trotter worked in other genres too: a juvenile production was an early novel, *Olinda's Adventures* (1696), and after retiring from the stage she continued, as Catherine Cockburn, to write on philosophy and morals. Delarivier Manley's dramatic works were only a small part of her writing career, which included journalism and most notably the Tory scandal chronicles, *Queen Zarah* (1705), *The New Atalantis* (1709) and *Memoirs of Europe* (1711). Manley's comedy *The Lost Lover* was given a poor reception in 1696; she complained in the Preface about the standard of the acting. The same year she tried a tragedy, *The Royal Mischief*, and complained that people had objected to its erotic warmth. Undeterred, Manley continued to portray passionate and outspoken women in heroic plays with strong erotic elements. *Almyna*, influenced by *The Arabian Nights* in its story of a sultan who has vowed to kill his bride after the wedding night, has been called 'the most explicitly feminist play presented in the period in the commercial theatre' (Pearson, 1988: 199) because it shows a woman educating a man into decency, but equally prominent is its eroticization of the hero's threat to the heroine and its expression of the masochistic desire that draws her into marriage with him. More clearly feminist in intent is *She Ventures and He Wins* (1695) by a woman known only by her pseudonym 'Ariadne'. This is a comedy of role-reversal that allows the heroine to steer the action (Spencer, 1994), and has been recently reprinted (Lyons and Morgan, 1991).

More successful than any of these playwrights was Susanna Centlivre (*c.* 1670–1723), one of the most prolific and popular dramatists of the early eighteenth century. Centlivre wrote nineteen plays between 1700 and 1722, as well as poems and letters. Though she encountered prejudice against female playwrights (Bowyer, 1952: 89–91), and in one famous rehearsal incident the actor Robert Wilks threw his part in *The Busy-Body* in the pit as 'a silly thing wrote by a woman' (Lyons and Morgan, 1991: xx), her plays consistently pleased the audiences of her time, and three of her comedies, *The Busy-Body* (1705), *The Wonder: A Woman Keeps a Secret* (1714) and *A Bold Stroke for a Wife* (1718) held the stage throughout the eighteenth century and remained popular in the nineteenth. Though she was no stage reformer, sharing with her predecessor Aphra Behn the belief that comedies were for amusement, not instruction, her plays followed the temper of the times by being more decorous than those of the Restoration, eschewing adultery and most bawdy. This made her plays survive longer than Behn's in the late eighteenth and nineteenth centuries, but has made her a less attractive proposition in the twentieth, and so far, at least, she has not had the theatrical and critical revival accorded to Behn. Another reason for this is the absence from her work (as from much early eighteenth-century drama) of a strong satiric edge. As a Whig writing in the early years of the century, she knew party opposition, but her party-political writing took the form of panegyric: praise of the Whig principle of Liberty, praise of Marlborough, praise of the Duke of Cumberland. (This last bore fruit when, after his accession to the throne as George I, he patronized her work.) Too often her Whig beliefs are translated on the stage into complacent patriotism. As one character announces in the first scene of *The Wonder*: 'the English are by nature what the ancient Romans were by discipline, courageous, bold, hardy, and in love with liberty' (Morgan, 1981: 331).

Yet she is an underrated dramatist, who works deftly with the conventions of Spanish intrigue comedy. Tricks, disguises, misunderstandings and confusions abound, and young lovers as always are united in the face of parental opposition. The humour lies in the layering of character awareness as the audience watches different characters being fooled to different degrees. In *The Wonder* Centlivre offers an interestingly feminist twist to the usual complicated intrigue, centring the play on Violante, who out of female solidarity shelters her friend Isabella, who is fleeing an unwanted marriage, and later Isabella's lover, Colonel Briton. This loyalty nearly costs her her relationship with Isabella's brother Don Felix, who jealously believes she is harbouring a lover of her own. To complicate matters Felix is himself in hiding after wounding a man in a duel; and Violante's maid Flora is pursuing a parallel intrigue with Don Felix's footman. Don Felix, whose conventional masculine honour has led to duels and jealous rage, has to learn to appreciate that women too have their code of honour, centring on female friendship (Pearson, 1988: 227–8). The bluff and amorous Colonel Briton, and the perky, convent-despising heroines, owe something to Behn's *The Rover* (1677), still very popular on stage at the time Centlivre was writing. Like Behn, Centlivre enjoys complicated misunderstandings and inventive heroines. In Act 5 Scene 2 of *The Wonder*, Violante is trying to placate Don Felix without revealing that Isabella is hidden in her closet. They are interrupted by her father, Don Pedro, from whom they must both conceal their love. Violante rises to the occasion, combining Isabella and Don Felix in a story that fools her lover and her father in different ways, and draws them in to collude with her. First she enlists her father on behalf of an unknown lady:

Don Pedro: Felix? Pray, what's your business in my house? Ha, Sir?
Violante: Oh, Sir, what miracle returned you home so soon? Some angel 'twas that brought my father back to succour the distressed. This ruffian here, I cannot call him gentleman, has committed such an uncommon rudeness as the most profligate wretch would be ashamed to own.
Don Felix: (Ha, what the devil does she mean?)
Violante: As I was at my devotion in my closet I heard a loud knocking at our door, mixed with a woman's voice, which seemed to imply she was in danger. (Morgan, 1981: 382)

Then she accuses Don Felix of drunkenly attacking the lady, glaring at him to make him support her story. He takes her hint, without any idea that there is really a lady in the closet to verify her tale. While he pretends to be drunk, Don Pedro promises to shield the unknown lady from Don Felix, and Isabella is able to come out of the closet and leave the stage, veiled. Violante soon follows her, quietly promising Don Felix an explanation later. 'The devil never failed a woman at a pinch!' comments Don Felix, bemused but beginning to follow her lead (Morgan, 1981: 383). Scenes like this ensured Centlivre's success with audiences and actors. Violante's role was popular with actresses including Kitty Clive, and the jealous Don Felix was a favourite role with the actor-manager David Garrick, who played it sixty-five times between 1756 and 1776 and chose it for his retiring performance (Bowyer, 1952: 183).

Susanna Centlivre's theatrical prominence forms a strong contrast with the more retired existence of her older contemporary, Anne Finch. As nonjurors, Finch and her husband had to withdraw from court life after the 1688 Revolution, and her poetry in praise of rural retreat is thus given a political edge. Finch, much of whose work has only recently been rediscovered (McGovern, 1992: 6–7), is undergoing a critical revival, and the variety of her work is being emphasized (McGovern, 1992; Mermin, 1990; Salvaggio, 1988). One recently anthologized poem is 'Adam Posed':

Could our first father, at his toilsome plough,
Thorns in his path, and labour on his brow,
Clothed only in a rude unpolished skin,
Could he a vain, fantastic nymph have seen,
In all her airs, in all her antic graces
Her various fashions, and more various faces;
How had it posed that skill, which late assigned
Just appellations to each several kind,
A right idea of the sight to frame;
T'have guessed from what new element she came,
T'have hit the wavering form, or given this thing a name!

(Lonsdale, 1989: 12)

Here Finch displays her ambivalence towards one prevailing satirical stereotype of femininity, the fashionable and frivolous young lady, frequently called a nymph. She comments on the nymph from her own, implicitly contrasted position, of steadfast, constant (and therefore both socially and politically unfashionable) woman of virtue. At the same time the lines convey a sense of delight in the protean nymph who so puzzles the original father of mankind, who is supposed to name and have dominion over all creatures: the poem contains 'a subtle assertion that women cannot be categorized nor molded into structures created and dominated by male rationality' (McGovern, 1992: 145).

Women's poetry in the eighteenth century has been given much more attention recently, especially since the publication of Roger Lonsdale's landmark *Eighteenth-Century Women Poets: An Anthology*. Critics of women poets in the late seventeenth and the eighteenth centuries have written about their adoption of strategies to allow them to speak in the high cultural language of verse. Margaret Doody has suggested that women found it hard to be Augustan poets because the classical learning and political interest typical of Augustanism were supposed to be closed to women; satire seemed unfeminine in attitude and the heroic metre of iambic pentameter too masculine in sound. They tended to adopt the more casual, less daunting, iambic tetrameter (Doody, 1985: 130, 241–2). Dorothy Mermin suggests that Aphra Behn, Katherine Philips and Anne Finch preferred informal verse and 'small and ordinary themes' (Mermin, 1990: 336). This approach certainly allows for a better understanding of poetry that used to be ignored as not grand enough. Doody notes the impudence that accompanies unpretentious form in a number of Augustan women writers (Doody, 1985: 244), while Lonsdale writes appreciatively of the 'informality, immediacy, and humour', as well as the 'earthiness and vigour', of women's verse in the eighteenth century (Lonsdale, 1989: xxxi, xxxvi). Still, it is possible that too much stress on their unpretentiousness risks belittling these writers – failing to notice where they are being ambitious in form and theme, and missing some of the challenges in informal verse.

Finch was best-known in her time for her pindaric ode 'The Spleen', which analyses the ailment of spleen or melancholy and was used in 1723 as an introduction to a medical treatise on the subject (McGovern, 1992: 161). The poem had both a public and a personal dimension. Finch herself was afflicted with the spleen, and describes its effects on her in one stanza of the poem:

> O'er me, alas! thou dost too much prevail:
> I feel thy force while I against thee rail;
> I feel my verse decay, and my cramped numbers fail.
> Through thy black jaundice I all objects see
>   As dark, as terrible as thee,
> My lines decried, and my employment thought
> An useless folly, or presumptuous fault:
>   Whilst in the Muses' paths I stray,
> Whilst in their groves, and by their secret springs,
> My hand delights to trace unusual things,
> And deviates from the known and common way;
>   Nor will in fading silks compose
>   Faintly th'inimitable rose,
> Fill up an ill-drawn bird, or paint on glass
> The Sovereign's blurred and undistinguished face,
> The threatening angel and the speaking ass.
>   (Lonsdale, 1989: 6)

These lines suggest a complex relationship between Finch's malady, attitudes to female artistry, and her own views of the function of poetry. The spleen's effects are ambiguously evoked: does it ruin her writing or just make her believe her poetry is failing? It is the distorting 'black jaundice' of the spleen that tells her she is thought useless and presumptuous for writing, but these imagined attacks on her take on the force of reality from their implicit connection to well-established conventional responses to women's art. These attacks provoke, in the second half of the stanza, a spirited defence of her refusal to be ordinary and to adopt the accepted modes of feminine art. There is a joyous defiance here, sharply contrasting with the gloom of the first seven lines. The act of describing her fear of criticism calls up an image of the activity criticized – wandering with the Muses – and the contemplation of this wandering restores delight. The mood-swing perhaps reflects Finch's personal experience of the spleen; and the syntax suggests not merely that the swing is rapid but that somehow both moods are held in place together, creating a startlingly dual image of the poet. 'Whilst' she blackly suffers her splenetic fears she is simultaneously elsewhere, in a secret and delightful poetic world. In some of her most famous words, she refuses the 'fading silks' of embroidery. Sewing being at this time not only a practically universal female employment but an emblem of female subordination, this refusal gives a feminist slant to Finch's allegiance to the muses, though one sadly dependent on a hint of scorn for the ordinary woman. Finch goes beyond simple comment on women's expected employments, however, to offer the female poet's perspective as a comment on current artistic theories. It is not just a case of sewing versus writing. All the arts mentioned, including Finch's, are arts of tracing with the hand: the issue is what and how the hand should trace. Finch refuses the silks, not because it is preferable to describe the rose in writing, but because the rose is 'inimitable'; the art she prefers is not an art of imitation but a search for the uncommon. Read in conjunction with Pope's recommendations to the poet, in his *Essay on Criticism*, to 'follow Nature' and convey 'what oft was thought, but ne'er so well expressed' (Pope, 1970: 146, 153), Finch's lines suggest her turning away from neoclassical standards in favour of imaginative pursuit of the unusual. Her feelings of oddity as a woman poet are transformed into a theory of the necessary oddity of poetic art.

Women novelists, at least in the early years of the century, did not have to deal as women poets did with the sense of their difficult relation to a prestigious masculine tradition. Daniel Defoe, Penelope Aubin and Eliza Haywood were all exploring themes of travel and women's sexual adventures in the 1720s, but Defoe did not become the women writers' reference point in the way that Samuel Richardson and Henry Fielding did for a later generation. While Anne Finch was attempting 'to redefine women's position in poetry' (Mermin, 1990: 351), her contemporary Delarivier Manley was turning from drama to fiction and making a name for herself as an erotic writer of politically motivated scandal, thinly disguised as fiction. *The New Atalantis* (1709) attacked the Whig ministry by disseminating accounts of the corruption and sexual peccadilloes of prominent Whigs; it was a huge success, and Manley was arrested, defending herself by insisting that she wrote only fiction. This work, along with *Queen Zarah* (1705), *Memoirs of Europe* (1710) and Manley's writing in *The Examiner*, contributed a great deal to Tory propaganda in the years leading up to the Tory ministry. They also established a particular kind of persona for the female novelist, combining eroticism with public participation in party politics (Ballaster, 1992).

It was Eliza Haywood (1693–1756), however, who did most to establish the idea of the commercial woman novelist in the early years of the eighteenth century. Though, like Manley, she wrote some 'scandal-fiction' (her *Memoirs of a Certain Island*, 1725, owing much to the inspiration of *The New Atalantis*), she concentrated more on fictional stories. She made her name with the extremely popular, three-volume *Love in Excess* (1719), and throughout the 1720s wrote a large number of shorter novels. The graph for production of novels by women in the eighteenth century shows a minor peak in the 1720s, largely due to her prolific output (Stanton, 1991). Even today Haywood tends to be read through the lens of the scandal and immorality she was associated with in her lifetime, largely through the efforts of Pope, who famously portrayed her in *The Dunciad* as the prize in a pissing competition between two booksellers (Pope, 1970: 384–6); and it is all too easy to polarize eighteenth-century women writers as 'Daughters of Behn' and 'Daughters of Orinda' (Katherine Philips) and to envisage a moral and an immoral female tradition (Williamson, 1990). It is true that eighteenth-century commentary very often divides women writers in this way, and that many women (on both sides of the divide) helped to build this rhetorical construct. As recent work has shown, however, Haywood has a great deal in common with Penelope Aubin, who presented herself as a moral writer very different from her immoral contemporary. Both write a fiction that mingles eroticism with a concern for moral choices for women who live in a world in which their virtue is inevitably understood in sexual terms (Prescott, 1994).

Other women writing novels in the early years of the century include Jane Barker, who adapted romance conventions for the semi-autobiographical *Love Intrigues* (1713), and published two collections of tales, *A Patch-Work Screen for the Ladies* (1723) and *The Lining of the Patchwork Screen* (1726), and Mary Davys, whose work includes comedies and several novels. One of these, *Familiar Letters Betwixt a Gentleman and a Lady* (1725) is one example of the strong development of the epistolary tradition in the early eighteenth century. The anonymously published and very influential *Lettres Portugaises*, translated into English as *Five Love-Letters From a Nun to a Cavalier* in 1678, had established the idea of the female writer as an enamoured woman writing desperately to her lover – though, ironically, the work was probably written by a man (Deloffre and Rougeot, 1962; Miller, 1981). In her ironic novel *Love Letters Between a Nobleman and his Sister*, Aphra Behn had adapted this convention by making the love-letters of Philander and Sylvia reveal the mingled scandals of their affair and his involvement in the Monmouth Rebellion. Davys also mixes amatory and political discussion, but in her *Familiar Letters* the tone is cooler and gentler, as Berina and Artander move gradually from friendship to desire through epistolary correspondence. Artander, a Tory dissatisfied with the Whig administration, has chosen country retirement, and corresponds with Berina, a Whig who remains enjoying the social life of the town. Each mingles expressions of friendship with worry about the other's politics. Artander finds Berina's 'only Weakness' her Whig views:

> Methinks the very Name, so hated and despis'd, should give your Inclinations a turn: then do but look back to our English Annals, and see the Practice of those Men, from whom the Name first took its Rise: look at the Block, the Ax, the sacred bleeding Head. (Davys, 1973: 270)

Berina retorts with reminders of the cruelties suffered by Protestants in Queen Mary's reign, and complains about present-day Tories' hankering for a return of the Stuarts. At his desire they turn to less contentious subjects, she regaling him with stories her friends have told her, he telling stories of the people he meets in the country. A note of urgency enters Artander's correspondence when he fails to hear from Berina: 'Is Berina's want of Health the Cause? Or is she grown weary of her Friendship and Correspondence? I wish you do not at last play the Woman more than the *Platonick*, and quit your Friendship for a Husband' (Davys, 1973: 286). She responds by complaining of the tiring round of social pleasures that has prevented her writing, and adds a snippet of news about the king retaining his *Corps du Guard*. Artander is pleased with the news, reassuring her that he is loyal to King George: 'since we have made him our King, we ought to use him like his Predecessors, and give him the Honour due to the Kings of *England*' (291). Artander having shown that his Toryism is not Jacobitism, and Berina beginning to hint that her Whig allegiances do not indicate that she would reject country retirement with a Tory, the story moves towards a political and amatory settlement. By the end, Artander is professing love and hastening back to town to see Berina, who remains cautious but holds out hopes of 'a kind Reception' (307). As in the French romance, love is earned through discussion of true friendship.

In its tone and its variety of topics, with polite discussion of political principles, and current news interspersed with comments on fashionable life illustrated by fictional anecdotes, *Familiar Letters* bears a great similarity to contemporary periodicals. Recent feminist criticism in this area has concentrated on the creation of a specific kind of address to the female reader in *The Tatler* and *The Spectator*, and the development of periodicals focused on domesticity and aimed at a female audience (Ballaster et al., 1991; Shevelow, 1989). However, Eliza Haywood's *The Female Spectator* (1744–6) is not part of any domestic or private ghetto for women. The title implies not a complement to the more famous periodical – a *Spectator* for women instead of for men – but a presentation of a woman's views on a variety of contemporary issues. Marriage, masquerades, gambling, drama and fashion are discussed in readers' letters and fictional anecdotes. A grumpy male correspondent who complains that the female spectator has not lived up to her promise of reporting current events is undermined by a dramatized discussion between an English lady and a Hanoverian one, which serves the double purpose of criticizing George II's foreign policy and demonstrating that women share the public right, which periodical literature at this time was instrumental in enforcing, to comment on affairs of state (Haywood, 1745: 100–3, 123–37).

Lady Mary Wortley Montagu was another woman who exercised that right in a varied literary oeuvre. Though she kept aloof from the world of commercial writing that supported Eliza Haywood and preferred to publish anonymously, she took a definite part in public debate. Her periodical, *The Nonsense of Common Sense*, which ran to nine numbers in the late 1730s, supported the Walpole administration in opposition to the periodical *Common Sense*. Most interestingly today is the sixth number, dated 24 January 1738, in which she expresses a feminism influenced by the earlier work of Mary Astell:

> Amongst the most universal Errors I reckon that of treating the weaker sex with a
> contempt, which has a very bad Influence on their conduct, who, many of them, think it
> excuse enough to say, they are Women, to indulge any folly that comes into their Heads.
> (Wortley Montagu, 1977: 131)

After her visit to Turkey while her husband was English ambassador to the Turks, she publicized the Turkish practice of inoculation for smallpox, having both her children inoculated and writing an anonymous 'Plain Account' of the operation for the newspaper *The Flying-Post* in 1722. To her contemporaries she was best known as a poet; her poems circulated in manuscript and some were printed. She also wrote a play adapted from Marivaux, *Simplicity, A Comedy*, which was not printed or performed in her lifetime.

Lady Mary is best known today for the brilliant letters which she wrote to various correspondents over the years, and which have been collected in three volumes. Those written during her travel to and stay in Constantinople show the fascination, shared by many of her fellow-Europeans, for the exotic Orient, and also her ability to analyze and compare different societies. She delighted to shock English expectations by declaring Turkish wives, because of the discretion afforded by their veils, much freer than English ones, and remarking sardonically that they 'don't commit one Sin the less for not being Christians' (Wortley Montagu, 1965: 327). To the Abbé Conti she offered comparisons between Mahometism and Christianity, adding her reflections on 'the natural Inclination of mankind to make Mysterys and Noveltys. The Zeidi, Kadari, Jabari, etc. put me in mind of the Catholic, Lutheran, Calvinist, etc. and are equally zealous against one Another' (Wortley Montagu, 1965: 317); to Alexander Pope, she wrote of Turkish poetry and sent some translations with her commentary, noting 'The Epithet of Stag-Ey'd (tho the Sound is not very agreable in English) pleases me extremely, and is, I think, a very lively image of the fire and indifference in his mistrisse's Eyes' (335); to Sarah Chiswell, she described the smallpox inoculation and her hope 'to bring this usefull invention into fashion in England' (339). To Lady Mar she described her encounters with Turkish ladies. One account of a visit to 'the Grand Vizier's Lady' in Adrianople shows her skill in evoking the exotic beauty associated for Europeans with the Orient, and a defence of the erotic aspect of her own aesthetic response.

> She was dress'd in a Caftan of Gold brocade flowerd with Silver, very well fited to her Shape and shewing to advantage the beauty of her Bosom, only shaded by the Thin Gause of her shift. Her drawers were pale pink, Green and silver; her Slippers white, finely embrodier'd; her lovely Arms adorn'd with bracelets of Diamonds, and her broad Girdle set round with Diamonds; upon her head a rich Turkish Handkercheif of pink and Silver, her own fine black Hair hanging a great length in various Tresses, and on one side of her Head some bodkins of Jewells. I am afraid you will accuse me of extravagance in this Description. I think I have read somewhere that Women allways speak in rapture when they speak of beauty, but I can't imagine why they should not be allow'd to do so. I rather think it Virtue to be able to admire without any Mixture of desire or Envy. The Gravest Writers have spoke with great warmth of some celebrated Pictures and Statues. The Workmanship of Heaven certainly excells all our weak Imitations, and I think has a much better claim to our Praise. For me, I am not asham'd to own I took more pleasure in looking on the beauteous Fatima than the finest piece of Sculpture could have given me. She told me the 2 Girls at her feet were her Daughters, tho she appear'd too young to be their Mother. (351)

For all the versatility of her talents, Lady Mary did not become the influential woman of letters she might have been; as Roger Lonsdale remarks, the social status that might have encouraged such a role also provided an inhibition against it (Lonsdale, 1989: 56).

In complete contrast to Lady Mary's high social position was the status of her younger contemporary Mary Leapor, one of a small but significant number of women from the labouring classes (others included Mary Collier and Ann Yearsley) who made their name as poets during this century (Landry, 1990). Born in 1722, Leapor lived her short life (she died of measles at the age of 24) in Northamptonshire, where her father kept a nursery garden, and for some time she was cook-maid in a gentry family. The friendship and patronage of Bridget Fremantle, a clergyman's daughter, brought her writing to the attention of the world beyond her own community. Leapor's work is now being reassessed, and she is recognized as an important, and critical, imitator of Pope (Greene, 1993; Landry, 1990; Thomas, 1994). Landry argues that her work, especially her ambitious 'plebeian country-house poem', *Crumble-Hall*, demonstrates that 'the limitations of a plebeian woman's education can be turned to good use, if what is generated is very close – and critical – reading of a few inspiring texts' (Landry, 1990: 107–10).

As a female imitator, Leapor both adopts a voice based on Pope's and, at times, puts herself in the place of his feminine subject-matter. In 'An Epistle to a Lady' Leapor's poetic persona, Mira, is self-mockingly created in imitation of Martha Blount, Pope's addressee in his 'Epistle to a Lady': without Martha Blount's advant-ages of beauty and fortune, Mira presents herself as a 'Martha manqué' (Thomas, 1994: 200). In her 'Essay on Woman', Leapor attempts to occupy both Pope's position and the position of a woman. Like Pope's 'Epistle to a Lady', the poem offers axioms in heroic couplets about woman-kind, beginning:

> Woman, a pleasing but a short-liv'd flower,
> Too soft for business and too weak for power.
> (Lonsdale, 1989: 207)

Mira, who again is the persona adopted here, is of course inescapably implicated in the anatomization of 'woman'. If the poem appears at the outset to define woman and sum her up from the outside, as the epistle develops Mira's position inside woman-hood is made clear.

The poem contains echoes of the famous toilet-scene in Pope's *Rape of the Lock*, but with a significant variation. While Pope mockingly reveals that Belinda's (nev-ertheless genuinely enchanting) beauty owes a great deal to the make-up that 'calls forth all the Wonders of her Face' (Pope, 1970: 222), Leapor's similar description of a much-courted nymph anatomizes, not female vanity but male greed:

> 'Tis wealth alone inspires every grace,
> And calls the raptures to her plenteous face.
> What numbers for those charming features pine,
> If blooming acres round her temples twine!
> Her lip the strawberry, and her eyes more bright
> Than sparkling Venus in a frosty night;
> Pale lilies fade . . .

> (Lonsdale, 1989: 207)

Here the woman's charms are firmly placed in the suitor's mind, and the raptures apparently displayed in her face are also his falsely poetic raptures about her. Her 'plenteous' face is both too big for beauty, and an indication of the only beauty the suitor really cares for, plenteous money. As the nicely ambiguous 'numbers' (of admirers, and poetic numbers or verses) indicates, the wealthy woman attracts not just mercenary suitors, but their bad writing, and the bathetic clash of poetic cliché and mercenary reality is wittily expressed in the ludicrous image of whole acres twining round her temples.

In the second verse Mira addresses Artemisia (her patron and frequently the addressee of her verse-epistles) with examples of unhappy women – Pamphilia, whose

intellect subjects her to 'The scornful eyebrow and the hated sneer' of her neighbours, and Sylvia, whose beauty has won her a husband who now tires of her. These
are treated with sympathy: only Cordia, the miser, is criticized. Pamphilia's story is
disturbing for Mira, raising as it does the question whether intellect is of any use to
women. 'Who would be wise, that knew Pamphilia's fate?' The answer offered is that
the pain of censure and ostracism, so keenly evoked in the verse and felt by Pamphilia, can be 'overlooked' by 'Simplicus and me' – the man's name indicating a
laudable simplicity of heart that presumably allows him to ignore foolish censure.
Simplicus complicates the issue: if Pamphilia earns censure specifically for being an
intellectual *woman*, his ease in dealing with the matter is not much help to her. Yet
Mira wishfully joins herself to Simplicus, claiming to share his immunity from the
world's malice.

Thus Leapor, like Pope, paradoxically claims to be protected from the very abuses
that most animate her verse. In lines strongly reminiscent of Pope's opening to the
Epistle to Arbuthnot, in which poet and friend conspire to keep out a wicked world, she
creates a safe position for Mira in home, friendship and poetry:

> If this be wealth, no matter where it falls;
> But save, ye Muses, save your Mira's walls:
> Still give me pleasing indolence and ease,
> A fire to warm me and a friend to please.
>   (Lonsdale, 1989: 208)

Mira is not only renouncing any desire for wealth, but implicitly, for the conventional
female role: she wants neither the admiration wealth may bring nor the marriage to
which it might lead. Indeed she does not want to be a woman at all: in the final lines of
the poem, women (for the first time) are charged with the traditional faults of cunning
and wilfulness, but the stress is on their misery rather than their folly:

> Though nature armed us for the growing ill,
> With fraudful cunning and a headstrong will;
> Yet, with ten thousand follies to her charge,
> Unhappy woman's but a slave at large.
>   (Lonsdale, 1989: 208)

A pessimistic ending, part of that tradition of female complaint about the female
position that is almost as much a feature of men's writing as women's, is here given a
different inflection by the position of the female speaker. She attributes female faults
to herself as well as others, yet still creates in her poem a rhetorical escape from
female slavery for herself and Artemisia. A woman who, like Mira, chooses a domestic
retirement and female friendship, can be free in her small space: a limited freedom,
but linked to that of the male satirist whose stance she echoes. Poetry allows Mira to
be as free as Pope; and his freedom, too, is revealed as a matter of domestic retreat.
The Augustan trope of happy retirement is given a fresh turn.

Another of Leapor's poems, the apparently naive 'The Epistle of Deborah Dough'
deals teasingly with the issue of a working-woman's writing and the place of literature

among the rural poor. Deborah Dough is what a genteel and unwary reader might
assume Mary Leapor, a cook-maid poet, to be – a garrulous gossip rattling off easy
rhymes about low subjects:

> Dearly beloved cousin, these
> Are sent to thank you for your cheese;
> The price of oats is greatly fell:
> I hope your children all are well . . .
>   (Lonsdale, 1989: 209)

The poet, however, is not Deborah but the object of her censure: 'our neighbour
Mary' who 'throws away her precious time/In scrawling nothing else but rhyme'
(209), as Deborah notes with a fine disregard of her own rhyming activities. She
compares 'Mary' unfavourably to her own taller, healthier daughter Cicely, who is
accomplished in all the feminine household arts. The next verse-paragraph intro-
duces a third poet: a local dairyman, put forward by Deborah as a rival to eclipse
Mary. He is a mysterious figure with a hint of magical powers, though Deborah tries
to maintain her scepticism about things literary: 'Things wonderful they talk of
him, / But I've a notion 'tis a whim' (209). The imagery describing his writing links
poetry and puddings rather than opposing them, as critics of women's writing so
regularly did. It is 'certain he can make / Your rhymes as thick as plums in cake'
(209). The country people apply the soothing powers of poetry with comic literalness,
sticking his papers on their feet to cure corns and round their ears to cure toothache.
While the male poet is ignorantly revered, the female poet is as ignorantly scorned. It
is assumed that a cook-maid cannot write verse and be a good cook, while a man's
prowess in writing matches his mastery of the domestic realm (he drinks scalding
porridge without harm, and he can throw a cheesecake without damaging it). The
domestic labour of women supports him (his wife makes the resilient cheesecake) and
reproaches her. Leapor records with pain-deflecting mockery the higher value placed
on men's endeavours, and satirizes common expectations about a cook-maid's writing, from the censoriousness of Deborah Dough, spokeswoman for village opinion, to
the condescension of the educated reader who would expect Deborah Dough to
epitomize the countrywoman writer.

   Many of the concerns that Leapor expressed in her poems were shared by women
writing in other genres. Women novelists of the mid-century were particularly interested in defending female writing and learning, and satirizing conventional expectations about female delicacy and domesticity. In *The Cry: A New Dramatic Fable*
(1754) Sarah Fielding and Jane Collier create a heroine who can acknowledge her own
desires while remarking tartly on those women 'who assert that they are married quite
accidentally, and without having once thought of it' (Fielding, 1754: II, 29). Favourite creations are the misunderstood young woman of learning, like Cynthia in Sarah
Fielding's *The Adventures of David Simple*, who is told 'reading and poring on Books,
would never get me a Husband' (Fielding, 1969: 101), and the obtusely unapprecia-
tive suitor, like Mr Arnold in Frances Sheridan's *Memoirs of Miss Sidney Bidulph*
(1761), who thinks the heroine so lovely that she need make no apology, even for

reading Horace: 'An apology, I'll assure you! did not this look, my dear, as if the man thought I ought to beg his pardon for understanding Latin?' (Sheridan, 1987: 73). Of course he did: women's understanding of Latin (and Greek) was understood as an assault on masculine prerogative. Unapologetically, Elizabeth Carter, the most famous woman of learning in the mid-century, translated the works of Epictetus (1758); while Sarah Fielding translated Xenophon's memoirs of Socrates (1762) and used a variety of classical sources for her *Lives of Cleopatra and Octavia* (1758), which offered a rereading of the historical accounts from a female viewpoint.

That women have a different view from men of what constitutes history is the premiss of Charlotte Lennox's novel *The Female Quixote* (1752), which contrasts the extravagant expectations of Arabella, who takes the feminocentric romances of seventeenth-century France to be relations of fact, with her suitor Glanville's allegiance to male historians who accord women little importance. Arabella's spirited defence of the reputation of women, from Thalestris of the Amazons and Cleopatra to her neighbour Miss Groves, makes her quixotism attractive; it is even successful, in so far as it turns the initially sceptical Glanville into an adoring hero. Still, there is more than a touch of resignation about the 'happy' ending in which Arabella accepts the fictitious nature of romance, and a marriage that will mean the end of adventure.

The sententious clergyman who cures Arabella of her delusions in a lecture clearly shows the influence of Samuel Johnson on Lennox, whose work he encouraged (Lennox, 1989: 419–28). Lennox can be seen to be troubled by Johnsonian authority in the same way that her heroine is troubled by the male authorities who separate her romances from historical truth. Other male contemporaries, especially Henry Fielding and Samuel Richardson, had a strong influence on the women novelists of the middle and later years of the century; their work was often subject to revisionary imitation. One of Eliza Haywood's later novels, *The History of Miss Betsy Thoughtless* (1751), recast the idea of Tom Jones, the erring young everyman, as the follies of the errant young woman. Sarah Fielding both learned from and influenced her brother's work in *The Adventures of David Simple*, with its mingled sentimental and satirical analysis of the trials of a man of feeling. Richardson, himself partly the product of an already existing tradition of women's fiction, was particularly important to women writers. They commented on his famous *Pamela* in their own plots; Charlotte Lennox's Sophia indignantly rejecting the man who, like Mr B–, follows up seduction attempts with marriage proposals. Frances Sheridan's *Memoirs of Miss Sidney Bidulph* was the most sustained and ambitious attempt to imitate Richardson's *Clarissa Harlowe*. Sidney is the dutiful daughter who (unlike Clarissa) does marry the man recommended by her family, despite her preference for a man whom her mother (unjustly, as it turns out) believes to be a rake of Lovelacian guilt. The duties of a daughter and a wife, and the extent of maternal authority, are examined in a novel that concludes that virtue brings no reward.

The sentimental novel of the middle and later years of the eighteenth century developed the presentation of the thinking and feeling heroine. Dramatic precedents influenced the lively dialogues, comic characters and emotional scenes of novelists like Sheridan, Lennox and Burney, while the epistolary tradition fed their development of the heroine's introspection. The development of the heroine's interiority made for a new examination of the old theme of courtship and marriage. Many novels took as their centre the feelings of a woman in dealing with her oppression within an unhappy marriage. While the restrictions imposed by the expectations of feminine decorum discouraged women from attempting to portray illicit passion in the manner of Rousseau's influential *Julie: ou La Nouvelle Héloise*, the idea of adultery haunts some of the most virtuous fictional wives. Sidney Bidulph, uneasily married to Mr Arnold, anxiously observes the reappearance of the man she once loved:

> Oh! my dear! I am mortified to the last degree, lest Mr Arnold should, from some indiscreet tongue, have received a hint of my former engagement; he may think me disingenuous for never having mentioned it, especially since Mr Faulkland has been in the neighbourhood: I think his nature is too open to entertain any suspicions essentially injurious to me; yet may this affair, circumstanced as it is, make an unfavourable impression on him. (Sheridan, 1987: 119)

Elizabeth Griffith's Lady Barton, married to a man who believes 'that women should be treated like state criminals, and utterly debarred the use of pen and ink', uses her letters to her sister to agonize about her guilty feelings for another man: 'if passion is involuntary it cannot be criminal . . .. Flattering sophistry! Alas! I would deceive myself, but cannot! Have I not vowed, even at the altar vowed, to love another? Yet can that vow be binding, which promises what is not in our power, even at the time we make it?' (Griffith, 1773: I, 2 and II, 108–9).

Partly because of the mingled emotionalism and moral concern of sentimental novels like Griffith's, women writing in the later years of the eighteenth century are sometimes seen as much more confined and less challenging than their predecessors. The greater emphasis on feeling in later eighteenth-century literature did, however, also encourage women to develop new ways of writing; and the influence of poets like Charlotte Smith and Anna Letitia Barbauld on nascent Romanticism is beginning to be recognized. One of the most ambitious of late-century writers was Anna Letitia Aiken, later Barbauld (1743–1825), who grew up at the Dissenting Academy in Warrington, where her father was a tutor. An early poem, 'To Dr. Aiken', addressed to her brother John, looks back to their close childhood bond and laments the divided path of brother and sister, while he pursues 'The nobler labours of a manly mind' and she is left feeling guilty about her own yearning for 'the tree of knowledge' (Barbauld, 1994: 18). Her attempt to claim 'nobler labours' for herself through writing can be seen in an ambitious public poem like 'Corsica', written in praise of General Paoli, who had led the failed revolt of Corsicans against Genoa. Written in lofty blank verse, the poem imagines Paoli as a hero of Miltonic proportions, with his 'eye sublime', his 'searching glance' and the 'brow / Serene, and spacious front', which bears 'the broad seal / Of dignity and rule'. Paoli, the 'rough sons of freedom' who fight with him, and the 'savage forests' and 'herds untam'd' of the island itself, contribute to the creation of a masculine sublime, anticipating the work of male Romantics and giving rise to contemporary concerns about the writer's unfemininity (Barbauld, 1994: 24, 22). However, the poem also implies the inclusion of the feminine in the heroic. What Dorothy Mermin has called 'the literalizing effect of the female voice' (Mermin,

1990: 349) operates here to revitalize common abstractions. Virtue is conventionally personified as feminine; but when she is invoked by a female poet, the reader tends to pay more attention to the femaleness of virtue, taking it at face value. Thus the poem claims a female share in the physical sensations and mental glories of heroic action:

> 'Tis not meats, and drinks,
> And balmy airs, and vernal suns, and showers
> That feed and ripen minds; 'tis toil and danger;
> And wrestling with the stubborn gripe of fate;
> And war, and sharp distress, and paths obscure
> And dubious. The bold swimmer joys not so
> To feel the proud waves under him, and beat
> With strong repelling arm the billowy surge;
> The generous courser does not so exult
> To toss his floating mane against the wind,
> And neigh amidst the thunder of the war,
> As Virtue to oppose her swelling breast
> Like a firm shield against the darts of fate.
>
> (Barbauld, 1994: 25)

Equally, the ending, which records Cyrnus's (Corsica's) fall, uses the conventionally feminine images of moon and muse to portray its failure. The failure is shared by the poet, conflated here with the muse: 'a British muse, / Though weak and powerless, lifts her fervent voice, / And breathes a prayer for your success' (Barbauld, 1994: 25). The prayer fails, and the poet apologizes for her mistakes in reading destiny and predicting virtue's triumph. Simultaneously, this failure, shared with the noble Paoli, is glorious. If failure is imagined in feminine terms, so too is the free mind which remains beyond failure:

> So vainly wished, so fondly hoped the Muse:
> Too fondly hoped: the iron fates prevail,
> And CYRNUS is no more. Her generous sons,
> Less vanquished than o'erwhelmed, by numbers crushed,
> Admired, unaided, fell. So strives the moon
> In dubious battle with the gathering clouds,
> And strikes a splendour through them; till at length
> Storms roll'd on storms involve the face of heaven
> And quench her struggling fires. Forgive the zeal
> That, too presumptuous, whispered better things
> And read the book of destiny amiss.
> Not with the purple colouring of success
> Is virtue best adorned: th'attempt is praise.
> There yet remains a freedom, nobler far
> Than kings or senates can destroy or give;
> Beyond the proud oppressor's cruel grasp
> Seated secure; uninjured; undestroyed;
> Worthy of Gods: The freedom of the mind.
>
> (Barbauld, 1994: 26)

Barbauld's editors note her great eminence at the end of the eighteenth century, and suggest that her reputation later fell in part because of the male Romantics' tendency to exclude women from their critical and poetic manifestos. The young S.T. Coleridge admired her, walking forty miles from Stowey to Bristol to meet her; but in later years he scorned her (Barbauld, 1994: xxii, xxxiii).

Wordsworthian Romanticism, with its emphasis on the manly poet's high calling, can be seen as creating a new set of difficulties for women trying to become, and be accepted as, poets (Lonsdale, 1989: xl–xli; Ashfield, 1995: xi–xiv). Barbauld's work is evidence of women's poetic contribution to Romanticism; but increasingly, in Barbauld's time, it was in prose that women were achieving recognition, and especially in the novel. The late-century novel offered women writers both commercial possibilities and the chance of critical prestige. Especially influential in raising the status of women's novels was the work of Frances Burney (1752–1840). Her first novel, *Evelina* (1778), delighted its readers and critics with its naive epistolary heroine, its gallery of comic characters, its satiric thrusts at social absurdities, and its tender scenes, notably the heroine's reunion with her father. It was her second, longer and more ambitious novel, *Cecilia* (1782), which made the most substantial contribution to the development of the novel and the tradition of female authorship.

Focusing on the experiences of a thoughtful young heiress, Burney is able both to present an analysis of the class- and money-obsessed society she encounters and reflect on the possibilities and limitations of a woman's attempts to better the world she lives in. Burney's sympathetic attention to the poor, her analysis of the corrupting effects of fashionable living and old-fashioned family pride, mark a new social breath and seriousness in the eighteenth-century novel; her creation of mixed characters and her refusal of unambiguous moral messages or happy endings enrich the fictional tradition. Her contemporaries compared her to Samuel Richardson and Henry Fielding; today her work can be seen to anticipate that of Charles Dickens and George Eliot (Burney, 1988: xxxviii). Central to the work is Cecilia's inheritance and the contrast between the power she supposes it brings her – power to act benevolently and redress the wrongs of society – and the way it actually imprisons and controls her.

As a young woman inheriting a large estate Cecilia Beverley is treated as an anomaly, hedged around by the provisions of her uncle's will, which requires her husband to take her name if the estate is to be retained, and consigns her until she comes of age to the care of three guardians, one chosen to provide a London home, one to take care of her fortune, one to give her connections with high social rank. None of them thinks her money her own: Mr Harrel tries in effect to sell her to his friend, and expects her to pay his huge debts; when she tries to withdraw some money to help this first guardian, the second, Mr Briggs, refuses to let her have it: 'Keep it for your husband; get you one soon: won't have no juggling' (Burney, 1988: 180); the third, Mr Delvile, refuses to intervene: 'Six hundred pounds . . . is a very extraordinary demand for a young lady in your situation' (185–6). Cecilia herself considers her uncle's fortune to be held in trust for others, but instead of thinking in terms of passing the estate on to a husband she feels a 'universal obligation' to use it to help everyone (Gallagher, 1994: 203).

She does manage to do some good, especially in her support of the labourer's widow, Mrs Hill, but more often she is placed in situations where from the best of her motives she wastes her fortune. Before his suicide Mr Harrel manages to sink the independent fortune she had from her parents in his own debts; eventually, renunciation of the larger fortune is called for by her love for Mortimer Delvile, whose family pride cannot bear the loss of his surname. Even then their marriage is secret – agreed to by his mother (but not by his father) on the understanding that Cecilia will take Delvile's name – and shortly afterwards, Cecilia finds herself through a series of persecutions and misunderstandings alone in London, with no money and nowhere to go. When she temporarily loses her reason and is taken in at a pawnbroker's house, she is advertised in a newspaper, a 'crazy young lady' with no money and no name of her own, who only 'talks much of some person by the name of Delvile' (901). When Delvile finds her, she does not recognize him:

> 'Why, why,' cried Cecilia, with a look of perplexity and impatience,
> 'will you not tell me your name, and where you come from?'
> 'Do you not know me?' said he, struck with new horror; 'or do you mean to kill me by the question?'
> 'Do you bring me any message from Mr Monckton?'
> 'From Mr Monckton? – no; but he lives and will recover.'
> 'I thought you had been Mr. Monkton yourself.'
> 'Too cruel, yet justly cruel Cecilia! – is then Delvile utterly renounced?
> – the guilty, the unhappy Delvile! – is he cast off for ever? have you driven him wholly from your heart? do you deny him even a place in your remembrance?'
> 'Is your name, then, Delvile?'
> 'O what is it you mean! is it me or my name you thus disown?'
> ''Tis a name,' cried she, sitting up, 'I well remember to have heard, and once I loved it, and three times I called upon it in the dead of night. And when I was cold and wretched, I cherished it; and when I was abandoned and left alone, I repeated it and sung to it.' (906–7)

Ophelia-like young women who have lost their reason are a common object of pathos in the sentimental literature of Burney's time. In *Cecilia* it is the patrilineal inheritance structures which have reduced her to this state: without a name of her own, without her reason, able only to repeat the name the Delvile family would preserve at all cost. She recovers, is reconciled to her husband, and even regains a measure of benevolent power when Delvile's aunt leaves her some money; but the happiness of the ending is muted, sober: Cecilia remains: 'portionless, tho' an HEIRESS' (941).

Other women novelists became heiresses through *Cecilia*. Charlotte Smith's first novel, *Emmeline* (1788), owes its wide social sweep, satirical tone, and concentration on the moral life of an intelligent and feeling heroine, to Burney's example. For Charlotte Smith, Mary Wollstonecraft, Elizabeth Inchbald, and other novelists of the 1790s, Burney's *Cecilia* was an important source; later, Maria Edgeworth and Jane Austen were influenced by it. The philanthropic heroine, who looks outward to society and faces conflict between her wide ambitions and the circumscribed social power of women, became a key figure in the English realist tradition (Doody, 1988: 127; Epstein, 1989: 159).

By the end of the 1780s, women's writing in England was well-established and highly regarded. Hannah Cowley was one of the most popular writers on the stage, writing sprightly comedies like *The Belle's Stratagem* (1780), which replaced the scheming Restoration rake with a contriving eighteenth-century lady. Elizabeth Inchbald's comedies were also extremely popular, and she was to take the sprightly heroine from stage to novel in *A Simple Story* (1791). Clara Reeve had published poems, an early Gothic novel, and a pioneering work of novel criticism, *The Progress of Romance* (1785), in which the work of women writers was especially praised (and Reeve's spokeswoman declared herself in favour of Aphra Behn, despite the famous immorality, out of solidarity with her sex). Anna Letitia Barbauld, Charlotte Smith and Hannah More were well-known poets. Ann Radcliffe's Gothic novels were starting to appear, with *The Castles of Athlin and Dunbayne* in 1789; Mary Wollstonecraft published the tentative philosophical novel *Mary, A Fiction*, in 1788. Great changes were about to hit political and literary life: the French revolutionary decade would bring, among much else, an upsurge in feminist discourse, and the beginnings of a Romanticism that was to place many of the writers discussed in this chapter in long obscurity.

Bibliography

Primary materials

Ashfield, Anthony (ed.) (1995), *Romantic Women Poets 1770–1838: An Anthology*, Manchester: Manchester University Press.

Astell, M. (1986), *The First English Feminist: Reflections Upon Marriage and other Writings by Mary Astell*, B. Hill (ed.), Aldershot: Gower.

Barbauld, A.L. (1994), *The Poems of Anna Letitia Barbauld*, William McCarthy and Elizabeth Kraft (eds), Athens: University of Georgia Press.

Barker, J. (1713), *Love Intrigues: or The History of the Amours of Bosvil and Galesia*, London: E. Curll and C. Crownfield.

Barker, J. (1723), *A Patch-Work Screen for the Ladies*, London: E. Curll and T. Payne.

Barker, J. (1726), *The Lining of the Patch Work Screen*, London: A. Bettesworth.

Behn, A. (1678), *Sir Patient Fancy: A Comedy*, London: Richard Tonson and Jacob Tonson.

Behn, A. (1992), *The Works of Aphra Behn*, vol. I, Janet Todd (ed.), London: William Pickering.

Burney, F. (1968) [1778], *Evelina, or the History of a Young Lady's Entrance into the World*, E.A. Bloom (ed.), London: Oxford University Press.

Burney, F. (1988) [1782], *Cecilia, or Memoirs of an Heiress*, M. Doody (ed.), Oxford: Oxford University Press.

Chudleigh, M. (1993), *The Poems and Prose of Mary, Lady Chudleigh*, M. Ezell (ed.), Oxford: Oxford University Press.

Davys, M. (1973), *Familiar Letters Betwixt a Gentleman and a Lady* (1725), in *The Reform'd Coquet and Familiar Letters by Mary Davys, and The Mercenary Lover by Eliza Haywood*, J. Grieder (ed.), New York and London: Garland.

Essay (1696) [Anonymous; possibly by Judith Drake], *An Essay in Defence of the Female Sex*, London.

Fielding, S. (1754), *The Cry: A New Dramatic Fable*, London: R. and J. Dodsley.

Fielding, S. (1762), *Xenophon's Memoirs of Socrates. With the Defence of Socrates Before his Judges*, translated from the Greek, Bath: A. Millar.

Fielding, S. (1969) [1744], *The Adventures of David Simple*, M. Kelsall (ed.), London: Oxford University Press.

Fielding, S. (1994) [1758], *The Lives of Cleopatra and Octavia*, C.D. Johnson (ed.), London and Toronto: Associated University Presses.

Finch, A. (1903), *The Poems of Anne Countess of Winchilsea*, M. Reynolds (ed.), Chicago: University of Chicago Press.

Griffith, E. (1773) [1771], *The History of Lady Barton*, London.

Haywood, E. (1719), *Love in Excess; or the Fatal Enquiry*, London: W. Chetwood.

Haywood, E. (1725), *Memoirs of a Certain Island*, London: Booksellers of London and Westminster.

Haywood, E. (1745), *The Female Spectator*, vol. 2, London: T. Gardner.

Haywood, E. (1986) [1751], *The History of Miss Betsy Thoughtless*, London: Pandora.

Inchbald, E. (1988) [1791], *A Simple Story*, J.M.S. Tompkins (ed.), London: Oxford University Press.

Jones, V. (ed.) (1990), *Women in the Eighteenth Century: Constructions of Femininity*, London: Routledge.

Lennox, C. (1989) [1752], *The Female Quixote: or The Adventures of Arabella*, Margaret Dalziel (ed.), Oxford: Oxford University Press.

Lonsdale, R. (ed.) (1989), *Eighteenth-Century Women Poets: An Oxford Anthology*, Oxford: Clarendon.

Lyons, P. and Morgan, F. (eds) (1991), *Female Playwrights of the Restoration: Five Comedies*, London: Everyman.

Manley, D. (1696), *The Lost Lover; or the Jealous Husband: A Comedy*, London.

Manley, D. (1696), *The Royal Mischief: A Tragedy*, London: R. Bentley, F. Saunders and J. Knapton.

Manley, D. (1707), *Almyna: or, The Arabian Vow. A Tragedy*, London.

Manley, D. (1710), *Memoirs of Europe*, London: J. Morphew.

Manley, D. (1972) [1705], *The Secret History of Queen Zarah*, J. Bosse (ed.), New York and London: Garland.

Manley, D. (1991) [1709], *The New Atalantis*, R. Ballaster (ed.), Harmondsworth: Penguin.

Morgan, F. (ed.) (1981), *The Female Wits: Women Playwrights of the Restoration*, London: Virago.

Pope, A. (1970), *The Poems of Alexander Pope*, J. Butt (ed.), London: Methuen.

Reeve, C. (1785), *The Progress of Romance*, Colchester: W. Keymer.

Sheridan, F. (1987) [1761], *Memoirs of Miss Sidney Bidulph*, London: Pandora.

Smith, C. (1971) [1788], *Emmeline, the Orphan of the Castle*, A.H. Ehrenpreis (ed.), London: Oxford University Press.

Wollstonecraft, M. (1976), *Mary, a Fiction and The Wrongs of Woman*, G. Kelly (ed.), London: Oxford University Press.

Wortley Montagu, Lady M. (1965), *The Complete Letters of Lady Mary Wortley Montagu*, vol. 1 1708–20, R. Halsband (ed.), Oxford: Oxford University Press.

Wortley Montagu, Lady M. (1977), *Essays and Poems and 'Simplicity, A Comedy'*, I. Grundy and R. Halsband (eds), Oxford: Clarendon.

Secondary materials

Armstrong, N. (1987), *Desire and Domestic Fiction: A Political History of the Novel*, Oxford: Clarendon.

Ballaster, R. (1992), *Seductive Forms: Women's Amatory Fiction from 1684–1740*, Oxford: Clarendon.

Ballaster, R., M. Beetham, E. Frazer and S. Hebron (1991), *Women's Worlds: Ideology, Femininity and the Woman's Magazine*, Basingstoke: Macmillan.

Barker-Benfield, G.J. (1992), *The Culture of Sensibility: Sex and Society in Eighteenth-Century Britain*, Chicago and London: University of Chicago Press.

Bowyer, J.B. (1952), *The Celebrated Mrs Centlivre*, Durham, N.C.: Duke University Press.

Brant, C. and D. Purkiss (eds) (1992), *Women, Texts and Histories 1575–1760*, London: Routledge.

Brown, L. (1987), 'The Romance of Empire: Oroonoko and the Trade in Slaves' in *The New Eighteenth Century*, L. Brown and F. Nussbaum (eds), London: Methuen, pp. 40–61.

Brown, L. (1993), *Ends of Empire: Women and Ideology in Early Eighteenth-Century English Literature*, Cornell: Cornell University Press.

Cixous, H. (1981), 'The Laugh of the Medusa' in *New French Feminisms*, E. Marks and I. de Courtivron (eds), Hemel Hempstead: Harvester Wheatsheaf, pp. 245–64.

Colley, L. (1992), *Britons: Forging the Nation 1707–1837*, London: Pimlico.

Cressy, D. (1977), 'Literacy in Seventeenth-century England: More Evidence', *Journal of Interdisciplinary History* 8:1, 141–50.

Deloffre, F. and J. Rougeot (eds) (1962), *Lettres Portugaises Valentins et Autres Oeuvres de Guilleragues*, Paris: Garnier.

Doody, M.A. (1985), *The Daring Muse: Augustan Poetry Reconsidered*, Cambridge: Cambridge University Press.

Doody, M.A. (1988), *Frances Burney: The Life in the Works*, Cambridge: Cambridge University Press.

Epstein, J. (1989), *The Iron Pen: Frances Burney and the Politics of Women's Writing*, Bristol: Bristol Classical Press.

Ezell, M. (1992), *Writing Women's Literary History*, Baltimore: Johns Hopkins University Press.

Ferguson, M. (1994), 'Juggling the Categories of Race, Class and Gender: Aphra Behn's Oroonoko', in *Women, 'Race', and Writing in the Early Modern Period*, M. Hendricks and P. Parker (eds), London: Routledge, pp. 209–24.

Gallagher, C. (1994), *Nobody's Story: The Vanishing Acts of Women Writers in the Marketplace, 1670–1820*, Oxford: Clarendon.

Goodman, D. (1992), 'Public Sphere and Private Life: Toward a Synthesis of Current Historiographical Approaches to the Old Regime', *History and Theory* 31, 1–20.

Goreau, A. (1980), *Reconstructing Aphra: A Social Biography of Aphra Behn*, Oxford: Oxford University Press.

Greene, R. (1993), *Mary Leapor: A Study in Eighteenth-Century Women's Poetry*, Oxford: Clarendon Press.

Habermas, J. (1989), *The Structural Transformation of the Public Sphere: An Enquiry into a Category of Bourgeois Society*, trans. T. Burger, Oxford: Polity Press.

Hendricks, M. and P. Parker (eds) (1994), *Women, 'Race', and Writing in the Early Modern Period*, London: Routledge.

Landry, D. (1990), *The Muses of Resistance: Laboring-Class Women's Poetry in Britain, 1739–1796*, Cambridge: Cambridge University Press.

Langbauer, L. (1990), *Women and Romance: The Consolations of Gender in the English Novel*, Ithaca: Cornell University Press.

McGovern, B. (1992), *Anne Finch and Her Poetry: A Critical Biography*, Athens and London: University of Georgia Press.

Medoff, J. (1982), 'New Light on Sarah Fyge (Field, Egerton)', *Tulsa Studies in Women's Literature* 1: 2, 155–75.

Medoff, J. (1992), 'The Daughters of Behn and the Problem of Reputation' in *Women, Writing, History 1640–1740*, I. Grundy and S. Wiseman (eds), London: Batsford, pp. 33–54.

Mermin, D. (1990), 'Women Becoming Poets: Katherine Philips, Aphra Behn, Anne Finch', *ELH* 57, 335–55.

Messenger, A. (1986), *His and Hers: Essays in Restoration and Eighteenth-Century Literature*, Lexington: University of Kentucky Press.

Miller, N. (1981), "'I's" in Drag: The Sex of Recollection', *The Eighteenth Century* 22, 42–67.

Nussbaum, F. (1994), 'The Other Woman: Polygamy, *Pamela*, and the Prerogative of Empire' in *Women, 'Race', and Writing in the Early Modern Period*, M. Hendricks and P. Parker (eds), London: Routledge, pp. 138–62.

Pearson, J. (1988), *The Prostituted Muse: Images of Women and Women Dramatists 1642–1737*, Hemel Hempstead: Harvester Wheatsheaf.

Pearson, J. (1993), 'The History of The History of the Nun' in *Rereading Aphra Behn: History, Theory, and Criticism*, H. Hutner (ed.), Charlottesville and London: University Press of Virginia, pp. 234–52.

Perry, R. (1986), *The Celebrated Mary Astell: An Early English Feminist*, Chicago and London: University of Chicago Press.

Prescott, S. (1994), 'Penelope Aubin and The Doctrine of Morality: A Reassessment of the Pious Woman Novelist', *Women's Writing: The Elizabethan to the Victorian Period* 1: 1, 99–112.

Raven, J. (1992), *Judging New Wealth: Popular Publishing and Responses to Commerce in England 1750–1800*, Oxford: Clarendon.

Ross, D. (1991), *The Excellence of Falsehood: Romance, Realism, and Women's Contribution to the Novel*, Lexington: University Press of Kentucky.

Salvaggio, R. (1988), *Enlightened Absence: Neoclassical Configurations of the Feminine*, Urbana: University of Illinois Press.

Schofield, M.A. and C. Macheski (eds) (1986), *Fetter'd or Free? British Women Novelists, 1670–1815*, Athens, Ohio and London: Ohio University Press.

Schofield, M.A. and C. Macheski (1991), *Curtain Calls: British and American Women and the Theater, 1660–1820*, Athens: Ohio University Press.

Shevelow, K. (1989), *Women and Print Culture*, London: Routledge.

Spacks, P.M. (1990), *Desire and Truth: Functions of Plot in Eighteenth-Century English Novels*, Chicago and London: University of Chicago Press.

Spencer, J. (1986), *The Rise of the Woman Novelist: From Aphra Behn to Jane Austen*, Oxford: Blackwell.

Spencer, J. (1994), 'Not Being a Historian: Women Telling Tales in Restoration and Eighteenth-century Literature' in *Contexts of Pre-Novel Narrative*, E. Ericksen (ed.), Berlin: Mouton de Gruyter.

Spender, D. (ed.) (1992), *Living By The Pen: Early British Women Novelists*, New York and London: Teachers College Press.

Stanton, J. (1991), 'The Production of Fiction by Women in England, 1660–1800: A Statistical Overview', paper given at the Eighth International Congress on the Enlightenment, Bristol.

Stone, L. (1969), 'Literacy and Education in England 1640–1900', *Past and Present* 42, 69–139.

Thomas, C.N. (1994), *Alexander Pope and His Eighteenth-Century Women Readers*, Carbondale and Edwardsville: Southern Illinois University Press.

Todd, J. (1989), *The Sign of Angellica: Women, Writing and Fiction, 1660–1800*, London: Virago.

Todd, J. (ed.) (1985), *A Dictionary of British and American Women Writers 1660–1800*, New Jersey: Rowman and Allanheld.

Turner, C. (1992), *Living By The Pen: Women Writers in the Eighteenth Century*, London and New York: Routledge.

Williamson, M. (1990), *Raising Their Voices: British Women Writers 1650–1750*, Detroit: Wayne State University Press.

5

A revolution in female manners: women writers of the Romantic period, 1789–1832

Harriet Devine Jump

Most literary periods are defined by their dates, as is the eighteenth century, or by reference to some historical parameter, like the 'Victorian' period. Rather oddly wedged between these two is the 'Romantic' period, which is defined by neither. The construction of the term Romantic, so far as British literature is concerned, is based almost entirely on the writings of a group of male poets (Blake, Wordsworth, Coleridge, Byron, Shelley and Keats) who were inspired by the American and French revolutions, who were reacting against the intellectual ideas of the eighteenth-century Enlightenment, and who placed a high value on individuality, imagination and the transcendental. In the work of their female contemporaries, Enlightenment thinking, with its emphasis on rationality, was not so wholeheartedly rejected, nor were the transcendental and imaginative values so fully embraced. Revolutionary ideology did, however, have powerful repercussions for women writers as well as for men. For this reason, a history of women's writing can justifiably consider a separate literary period to have begun in the first year of the French Revolution, 1789, and to have ended at the beginning of the 1830s when Victorian values were becoming widely established.[1]

The production and publication of literature by female writers reached unprecedented levels during the Romantic period. As Cheryl Turner's important research has shown, the production of fiction by women escalated greatly as the eighteenth century drew to a close. In 1778, the year Fanny Burney published *Evelina*, only two other women novelists had novels published. Eleven years later, in 1789, the year this chapter begins, twenty-six women novelists were responsible for a total of twenty-eight novels. The numbers decreased a little over the next few years – 1792 was a low point, with only seventeen novels by fourteen novelists – but then they started to rise again until in 1796 (the last year for which these figures exist) there were thirty-three female novelists published, responsible between them for thirty-nine novels (Turner, 1992: 212–16). Although this must be seen as part of general escalation in the publishing trade as a whole (Turner, 1992: 40), the figures are still striking.

That women continued to dominate the production of fiction throughout the Romantic period could be attributed to the fact that the novel had become a traditionally 'feminine' genre by this time. But women succeeded remarkably well in other genres as well. The two most successful playwrights of the Romantic period were both female. Elizabeth Inchbald (1753–1821) was responsible for more than twenty original plays, and translations or adaptations of European drama (including Kotzebue's *Lover's Vows* (1798), notorious for its scandalous production in Jane Austen's *Mansfield Park*). She also became a literary editor, and between 1808 and 1811 edited three collections of plays, the first of which was in twenty-five volumes and included biographical and critical introductions. While Inchbald's dramatic talent was mainly for comedy, serious drama and tragedy was dominated by Joanna Baillie (1762–1851). Her *Series of Plays; in which it is attempted to delineate the Stronger Passions of the Mind* (3 vols, 1798–1812) was undoubtedly the most important and influential dramatic literature of the period. Although not all the plays, each of which dealt with a particular 'passion', were produced, several were put on to great acclaim. *De Montfort*, a tragedy on the subject of hatred, was produced at Drury Lane in 1800 with Kemble and Mrs Siddons in the leading roles, and *The Family Legend*, a Scottish tragedy, was performed in Edinburgh in 1810 with a prologue by Baillie's great admirer Sir Walter Scott. The 'Introductory Discourse' to the first volume of Baillie's plays sets out her views on the importance of drama as a genre. The 'centre and strength' of drama, she argues, is its ability to depict human nature directly, through the characters, who must be true to nature, or 'we feel we have been imposed upon' (Baillie, 1798–1812: vol. i, 23, 25). Thus, it will naturally convey moral instruction without the need for overt didacticism, since it 'improves us by the knowledge we acquire of our own minds, from the natural desire we have to look into the thoughts, and observe the behaviour of others' (37).[2]

In poetry, too, women writers were becoming increasingly well established. Thirty collections of poetry by female poets were published in the last decade of the eighteenth century alone, and it has recently been pointed out that 1,402 first editions of women's poetry appeared between 1770 and 1835 (Jackson, 1993: xxii). Among the most successful poets were Charlotte Smith, whose *Elegiac Sonnets* went through ten editions between 1784 and 1800, and, later in the period, Laetitia Landon and Felicia Hemans, who both earned considerable incomes from poetry alone and also achieved public recognition and enormous popularity.

In fact the Romantic period saw the beginning of an appropriation, by women writers, of many 'public' genres: not only novels and 'tales', poetry and drama, but also non-fictional prose. Having already, by the last few decades of the eighteenth century, begun to be accepted as writers of travel literature and educational works, they went on to engage with more traditionally masculine genres such as critical essays and political commentary, progressively 'feminizing' discourses, such as philosophy as social critique, and political debate, that had previously been gendered masculine.[3]

The dates of the period that has come to be called Romantic have always been somewhat arbitrary. If, however, it is acknowledged that literary movements come into being as a reaction to the events and conditions of their time, then 1789, the year of the French Revolution, seems a logical beginning. It has long been recognized that the male writers of the period wrote as they did in direct response to the events which were taking place at this time, even if those events did not form a direct part of their discourse. Women writers were affected as well, although their response was, naturally enough, modified by the fact of their gender.

'The French Revolution produced a conspicuous effect in the progress of Mary's reflections. . . . Her respect for establishments was undermined' (Holmes, 1987: 229). So wrote William Godwin in his biography of his late wife, the professional writer and pioneering feminist Mary Wollstonecraft (1759–97). But while all radicals rejoiced in the overthrow of the *ancien régime*, viewing the Revolution, at least initially, as a huge advance of progress towards a putative golden age in which humankind would at last enjoy its birthright of 'freedom', the reaction of women to the event was more complex. Wollstonecraft's response is a case in point. While greeting the new government of France with cautious optimism, she quickly became disillusioned by the fact that the French Assembly's Declaration of Rights did not mention the rights of women. Specifically, she was distressed to find that their educational charter, drawn up by the liberal politician Talleyrand, failed to extend its new proposals to the education of girls, who were not, in its terms, to receive a formal education after the age of 8. This appears to have been the direct spur to her writing *Vindication of the Rights of Woman* (1792), a work which brought her instant literary celebrity and which had an enormous and lasting impact on almost all the female writers of the age. In the debate concerning the position of women in a society whose prevailing ideology afforded them no status beyond that of wife, mother and homemaker – a debate which dominated women's literature of the Romantic period – Wollstonecraft's writings, and her life-history, are a central, though usually unspoken, presence.

Wollstonecraft began her literary career as an educational writer, and in one sense the *Rights of Woman* can be seen as part of a debate on women's education which had already been in progress for a number of years. Several important women writers, among them Hannah More and Catharine Macaulay, had written on the subject before her; but none had done so as polemically – or as politically – as Wollstonecraft.[4] Her text is revolutionary both in that it was inspired by a revolution and that it calls for one: a 'REVOLUTION in female manners' (Wollstonecraft, 1989: vol. v, 265).

Many of her arguments are aimed at demonstrating that society has constructed a false and degraded model of femininity: 'Everything [a woman] sees or hears serves to fix impressions, call forth emotions, and associate ideas, that give a sexual character to the mind' (186). She derides the notion that women 'were created rather to feel than to reason' (131). Men and women, she argues, were certainly created equal so far as the capacity to reason is concerned, but man has 'from the remotest antiquity, found it convenient to exert his strength to subjugate his companion' (95), keeping women in a state of artificial ignorance.

Aware that marriage is one of the few ways in which women can establish themselves in comfort in a society which denies them any financial or moral independence, she argues that it is degrading for them to be always 'subservient to love or lust' (96). Instead of romantic love, she recommends a companionate marriage of equals, based on 'the calm tenderness of friendship [and] the confidence of respect' (99). Ideally, she would like to see some future date when women could be educated for 'more extensive plans of usefulness and independence': careers in medicine, in business, even in politics could 'save many from common and legal prostitution' (217–18). Even if such ideas seem impossibly distant, society will benefit from better-educated women as the mothers of future citizens.

Wollstonecraft's attack, deliberately designed to undermine the ideology on which notions of femininity had been predicated throughout the eighteenth century, had enormous repercussions. But any chance the *Rights of Woman* might have had of gaining wide acceptance, or of initiating real change in society, was effectively dealt a death-blow by the revelations made by William Godwin in his *Memoirs of the Author of the Rights of Woman* (1798). Written shortly after Wollstonecraft's untimely death, a result of childbirth complications, in 1797, Godwin's book was intended to demonstrate her admirable attempts to live according to the truth of her revolutionary feminist principles. But coming in the wake of a major swing to conservative, or anti-Jacobin,[5] politics – the result of the excesses of revolutionary France – and revealing as it did the fact that she had made two suicide attempts and had lived with a lover outside marriage, giving birth to an illegitimate child, the *Memoirs* effectively destroyed not only Wollstonecraft's reputation, but also any chance for her feminist principles to be accepted for many generations to come.

The debate on female education and gender roles in society continued throughout the Romantic period, but it necessarily became more covert. Several of Wollstonecraft's friends and disciples published feminist texts in the years immediately after her death, but the political climate was such that they had either to do so anonymously, as did Mary Hays (*Appeal to the Men of Great Britain on Behalf of the Women* (1798)), and Mary Ann Radcliffe (*The Female Advocate: or An Attempt to Recover the Rights of Women from Male Usurpation* (1799)) or to use a pseudonym, like Mary Robinson, who published her *Letter to the Women of England on the Injustice of Mental Subordination* (1799) as Anne Frances Randall. Even these voices fell silent as the nineteenth century dawned, bringing with it a shift from the revolutionary feminism of the first part of the period to a more restrained programme of post-revolutionary transformation through reason and the politics of domestic ideology. Works on female education such as Hannah More's *Strictures on the Modern System of Education* (1799) and Elizabeth Hamilton's *Letters on Education* (1801) are early examples of the cautious, conservative reformism which replaced the radical polemics of the revolutionary decade.

One of the best known women writers of the age, however, appears to have been little affected by the polemics of her more public-minded contemporaries. Writing privately in her *Journals* in the late 1790s and early 1800s – she had a horror of appearing in public as an author – Dorothy Wordsworth (1771–1855) steered a course which seemingly had little or no reference to the debate which dominates the period. However, although she became increasingly absorbed into domesticity in later life, the early years of the *Journals* show her existence to have been relatively free of some of the constraints which bound most women of the period. She was, at least, at unusual liberty to walk and to talk with the men of her household and acquaintance.

Valued for many years only for what they could tell readers of her brother's life and poetry, her *Journals* recount with sensitivity and precision the everyday details of her life in Somerset and in Grasmere. She documents not only the changes she sees in the natural world but also, with much compassion, tells of the poor and disadvantaged social outcasts she encounters almost daily in and around her village. Immersed as few other women writers of the period were in male Romanticism, she became neither a political feminist nor a late-Romantic 'domestic woman', but persisted quietly in following her own isolated, but wholly individual track.[6]

The shifting ideologies which are found in much female-authored non-fictional prose can also be clearly seen in the women's fiction of the period. Indeed, the writers of the early part of the period frequently turned to the novel as another means of disseminating their ideas.

Mary Wollstonecraft used her second novel, *The Wrongs of Woman; or, Maria* (1798) to expand on some of the ideas in her earlier *Rights of Woman*. In this fiction, she suggests not only that women's position in the legal system is so radically disadvantaged that they cannot be said to have a country – they are 'the *out-laws* of the world' (Wollstonecraft, 1989: vol. i, 146) – but also that women have a right to sexual fulfilment even outside marriage. Wollstonecraft's heroine, Maria, has made an injudicious early marriage to George Venables, a man who wastes the money she has brought to the marriage on drink and promiscuous sexual encounters. Maria's principles revolt against a patriarchal hegemony which dictates that she must submit herself sexually to a man for whom she has no feelings, and she speaks out forcefully against the prevailing sexual ideology which holds that a frigid woman is a virtuous woman. A woman who gives herself to her husband only to please him may be harmless, says Maria, but she will lack 'that fire of the imagination, which produces *active* sensibility, and *positive* virtue'. A woman is entitled to sexual pleasure, and 'we cannot, without depraving our minds, endeavour to please a lover or husband, but in proportion as he pleases us' (144–5).

Her principles eventually lead her to leave her husband, but he pursues and catches up with her, and incarcerates her in a lunatic asylum. Here she meets a fellow captive, Darnford, with whom she falls in love. In a scene that contributed greatly to the destruction of Wollstonecraft's reputation when the unfinished novel was published after her death, Maria makes the apparently rational decision to consummate the relationship physically without the sanction of marriage ('As her husband she now received him . . .' (181)). In the final chapter of the novel as it stands, Maria is in court, defending Darnford against her husband's action against him for seduction and adultery. Her passionate speech sets a woman's 'conscience' and 'sense of right' against 'the policy of an artificial society' (180). She pleads with the judge to give her the freedom that she already considers herself to have 'in the sight of heaven' (181), so that she may divorce Venables and marry Darnford. Unsurprisingly, the judge rejects her plea, with much patriarchal blustering about French principles. It seems, however, that Wollstonecraft intended to make Maria's second choice prove to be as ill-founded as her first: her projected endings are uniformly unhappy and show her trust in Darnford to have been misplaced.

It is difficult to see how Wollstonecraft would have managed to leave her heroine with her belief in her own conscience and 'sense of right' undiminished. The projected endings appear to point towards the conclusion that women do not, after all, possess the rationality for which the body of the work argues so passionately. The decision Maria makes proves after all to be informed less by reason than by the same old ill-founded emotionalism that had led her to marry Venables. Perhaps Wollstonecraft intended this as an indictment of the limited educational opportunities open to women. As she argued in the *Rights of Woman*, women cannot be expected to develop as fully moral beings if they are not given the opportunity for intellectual growth. As the novel stands, its message seems to be that rationality itself proves powerless in the face of a society so far from ideal that it can produce a flawed individual such as Darnford, whose very plausible exterior was, apparently, going to prove to be entirely specious.

The howls of anti-Jacobin outrage that greeted the publication of *The Wrongs of Woman* ensured that no woman novelist would again dare to make suggestions as radical as Wollstonecraft's. But beneath its revolutionary exterior, the novel's agenda is that of many, perhaps most, female-authored fictions of the period: an examination of a rational heroine's attempts to negotiate her place within a society and culture that failed to recognize her right to, or even possession of, rationality.

Mary Hays (1760–1843), born into a middle-class Dissenting family, became a writer in the 1790s. Deeply impressed by Wollstonecraft's *Rights of Woman*, she devoted most of her long professional writing life to the 'masculine' discourse of non-fictional prose. If she is remembered at all as a writer today, however, it is probably for her Jacobin novel, *Memoirs of Emma Courtney* (1796). In this work Hays scandalized the readers of her day by openly mingling autobiography with fiction, drawing on her own rejection by the Unitarian academic William Frend and including portions of her correspondence with William Godwin.

Like Wollstonecraft's heroines, Emma has developed an excessive sensibility as a result of a faulty education and an avid appetite for novel reading (she is reading between ten and fourteen novels a week at one stage). Her father attempts to counteract the ill effects of this by introducing her to historical and philosophical texts, but she also manages to read Rousseau's passionate love story *La Nouvelle Héloïse* (1761), a work to which she attributes 'a long chain of consequences, that will continue to operate till the day of my death' (Hays, 1987: 25). Under the influence of Rousseau's story, Emma develops a passionate attachment to Augustus Harley in which respect for the beloved's mind soon develops into a frankly physical desire. She writes to Harley, confessing her feelings and offering herself to him, supporting her right to do so by reference to Wollstonecraft's *Rights of Woman*. Harley rejects her, a 'moral martyrdom' (135) that she believes initially to be the result of her advanced principles. Later she discovers that he is already married to another, and immerses herself in a correspondence with the philosopher Mr Francis which Hays based on her own letters to Godwin. In her letters Emma attempts a philosophical vindication of her own actions, arguing that women's 'miserable' condition is a direct result of the repression of female desire (146–7). Social conditioning makes women into creatures of sensibility, but denies them an outlet for the sexual passion into which, she argues, sensibility readily converts. Failing even to persuade Harley to become her 'friend', Emma marries another suitor, only to discover as she nurses Harley on his deathbed that he has loved her all along. She devotes the last years of her life to raising Harley's son, hoping that her own hard-won lessons may help him to escape 'the tyranny of the passions' and to live a life of virtue and self control (199).

Hays claimed that her novel was intended 'as a *warning*, rather than as an example' (xviii), and her heroine's offer to live unmarried with Harley is not accepted. Nevertheless, *Memoirs of Emma Courtney* gained its author an enduring reputation for immorality and appeared to lend weight to the perceived connection, in the public mind, between female philosophy and unchastity. Undeterred, Hays published a second novel, *The Victim of Prejudice*, in 1799. In this equally radical work she confronts emotive issues of seduction, illegitimacy and rape as they affect the lives of a mother and her daughter. True to her political beliefs, Hays places the blame for her heroines' plights on the evils of a patriarchal hegemony, both individual ('man's despotism' and his 'vices') and social ('a sanguinary policy [which] precludes reformation' (Hays, 1799: vol. i, 167–8)). At issue here is not chastity itself but the reputation for chastity: like Hardy's Tess, Hays's heroines suffer from society's rejection of them for something which has been done to them against their wills.

The novels of Hays and Wollstonecraft were certainly the most outspokenly polemical of the women's fictions of the 1790s, though several other members of their circle produced moderately radical contributions to the debate. Elizabeth Inchbald's *A Simple Story* (1791) contrasts an impulsive, flighty heroine with her more serious and obedient daughter, only to show how both are crushed by patriarchal authority. Inchbald's later *Nature and Art* (1796) offers a harsher critique of male-dominated society in its story of an innocent heroine who is condemned to death for her loss of chastity by the same man who had seduced her years earlier. Mary Robinson's feminism and her radical politics are visible in her later novels, especially, perhaps, *The Natural Daughter* (1799), and Charlotte Smith's reforming political views are evident in *Desmond* (1793).

The politics of protest offered one way in which female authors could explore, and criticize, the patriarchal hegemony. Other writers, less outspoken, chose more covert means. One such was the newly popular Gothic novel, a genre which appealed to women both as writers and as readers.

Ann Radcliffe (1764–1823) was one of the most successful and popular woman novelists of the Romantic period, as the unprecedentedly large advances – £500 and £800 – she was paid for *The Mysteries of Udolpho* (1794) and *The Italian* (1797) clearly show. Radcliffe was not the first woman writer to explore the possibilities of the Gothic, but she was the first to gain widespread recognition for her fictions in this mode.

Twentieth-century readers may not be able to recapture the enthusiasm of Jane Austen's Catherine Morland for *The Mysteries of Udolpho*, but it is easy to understand why a 17-year-old with little interest in 'history, real solemn history' (Austen, 1974: vol. v, 108) becomes so absorbed in a novel which is centred almost entirely in the consciousness of its female protagonist. *Udolpho* tells the story of an orphan, Emily St Aubert, who is imprisoned by the villainous Montoni, her uncle by marriage, in a remote Apennine castle. Subjected to numerous threats, both human and (apparently) supernatural, she escapes at last and, after further trials and tribulations, is finally united with her lover Valancourt.

Like all Radcliffe's heroines, Emily is possessed of a keen and highly developed sensibility which is the source both of her trials and of her ability to transcend them. She has 'uncommon delicacy of mind, warm affections, and ready benevolence', but these go hand in hand with 'a degree of susceptibility too exquisite to admit of lasting peace' (Radcliffe, 1980: 5). In this she may be said to resemble many another eighteenth-century heroine: those of Fanny Burney's novels, evidently admired by Radcliffe, offer an obvious parallel. But while the trials endured by Evelina, Cecilia and Camilla are of the realistic world of society and its mores, Radcliffe's protagonists are tested in a fantasy world of the imagination whose threats and terrors are on an altogether larger scale.

Undoubtedly one of the things that made the Gothic genre particularly attractive to women writers was the fact that it allowed for the exploration of hidden and unnameable fears about the world, especially, perhaps, those of a sexual nature.[7] Radcliffe's male villains, patriarchal tyrants to a man, are frightening in their power, their intelligence, and their manipulativeness. Above all, the intensity of the threats which they pose derives from the fact that they are family members: Schedoni, in *The Italian*, is Ellena's uncle (although for a time he thinks he is her father), as Montoni, in *Udolpho*, is Emily's. It is this fact, as much as the supernatural terrors, which emphasizes the reader's sense of the heroine's extreme vulnerability.

In any case, in Radcliffe's novels, the supernatural elements are invariably revealed at the end to have a logical explanation. Radcliffe's purpose is well served by this device. Certainly the ghastly corpse behind the black silk veil, which terrifies Emily so much that she drops senseless on the floor (Radcliffe, 1980: 249), proves in the end to be only a wax figure (662). It is Emily's overdeveloped sensibility that has prevented her from discovering this earlier: a more robust, or less imaginative, girl would have 'dared to look again, [when] her delusion and her fears would have vanished altogether' (662). But Emily's imagination has also been her salvation, as, imprisoned within the castle which holds so many horrors, both real and imagined, she is able to transcend the terrors of her surroundings through a vividly experienced appreciation of the 'wild grandeur' of the surrounding countryside. The heightened emotion she experiences in the presence of 'the sublimity of nature' revives her, elevates her thoughts, and allows her mind to recover its strength (242). Similarly, in *The Italian*, Ellena's experience of 'gazing upon the stupendous imagery around her' enables her to see 'beyond the awful veil which obscures the features of the Deity'. As a result, her anxieties diminish, and she can view man, 'the giant who now [holds] her in captivity, [shrunk] to the diminutiveness of a fairy', as she realizes 'that his utmost force [is] unable to chain her soul, or compel her to fear him' (Radcliffe, 1991: 90–1). The female sublime, characterized by Patricia Yaeger in an influential essay as 'negative' or 'failed' (Yaeger, 1989: 201), becomes in Radcliffe's novels a wholly positive and helpful trope which enables vulnerable young women to survive in a frightening and hostile patriarchal environment.

Hays, Wollstonecraft and their radical female contemporaries came in for their share of criticism in the anti-Jacobin press – in 1800, the *Anti-Jacobin Review* referred to Elizabeth Inchbald, the most moderate of the female radicals, as 'the scourge of democracy' (*Anti-Jacobin Review*: vol. v (February 1800), 152). They were also criticized, both explicitly and implicitly, in the fictions of more conservative women novelists of the day. Mary Hays was memorably burlesqued by the novelist Elizabeth Hamilton as Brigetina Botherim, the man-chasing 'female philosopher' in *Memoirs of Modern Philosophers* (1800). Novelists like Jane West (in, for example, *The Advantages of Education* (1793)) and Hannah More, in *Coelebs in Search of a Wife* (1809), attempted to demonstrate the values of modesty, chastity and fidelity in conservative fictions which arguably succeed less well than those of their political opponents in convincing the reader of the strength of their position.

More interesting, and seemingly more durable as far as the modern reader is concerned, are those novels which do not overtly take either side in the political argument. This is, in fact, true of practically all of the women's fiction of the first three decades of the nineteenth century. This is not to suggest that the debates ceased. Rather they went underground, and took another form. In exploring issues concerning love, courtship and marriage, women novelists were necessarily continuing to conduct increasingly complex and subtle analyses of the same issues that had preoccupied Wollstonecraft in the revolutionary decade: a woman's role in society, the relation of the domestic sphere to public life, and the advantages of marriages of equality. That they did so with less polemicism should perhaps be seen as a tribute to their increasing artistry.

In fact, feminist arguments do appear fairly regularly in women's fiction of the second part of this period. They appear however not as direct polemicism but as ideological debate, and sometimes seem to be ironized or discredited within the text. In the more conservative novels, such as Hamilton's, and in Maria Edgeworth's *Belinda* (1801), which shows its author's disapproval of the more extreme aspects of feminism through the character of Harriot Freke, the cross-dressing campaigner for women's rights, the female philosophers are made to appear fairly ridiculous. *Belinda* is not such a conservative novel as this may suggest, however. Like one of Burney's heroines, Belinda is thrust out into the world and forced to make her own way there. But it is her own independence of spirit that sees her through, rather than the submission to authority which is characteristic of Burney's plots. Harriot Freke is only one of several unsatisfactory role models Belinda is presented with: Lady Delacour, intelligent, witty, but morally reprehensible, and Virginia, brought up on the educational principles set out in Rousseau's *Emile* (1762) to be innocent, docile and empty-headed, offer her more opportunities to assess, and reject, modes of being female in a patriarchal society.

Direct parody or burlesque of radical feminists naturally became less viable as the nineteenth century went on: Wollstonecraft, and her follower Mary Robinson, had died, Hays had largely abandoned polemics. But the debate continued. In Amelia

Opie's *Adeline Mowbray* (1804), Fanny Burney's *The Wanderer* (1814) and Susan Ferrier's *Marriage* (1818), more complex and subtle strategies are at work.

Opie's novel, loosely based on the life of Wollstonecraft, whom she knew, appears to offer a critique of Godwinian principles. Adeline is an emancipated woman who makes a supposedly rational choice to live unmarried with her lover, but finds herself increasingly isolated and ostracized from society. By the end she has been forced to renounce her principles, and concludes that marriage is, after all, 'beneficial to society' (Opie, 1986: 243). Nothing in the novel supports this view, however: all the marriages that are depicted are extremely unsatisfactory ones. *Adeline Mowbray* is a difficult novel to pin down, from an ideological perspective, precisely because the arguments it seeks to condemn appear more convincing and attractive than those it appears to endorse.

Fanny Burney's *The Wanderer; or, Female Difficulties* – published in 1814 but set at the time of the French Revolution – has received considerably less attention than her early novels. This fact is, perhaps, a legacy of its very poor initial reception. John Wilson Crocker wrote a vitriolic attack on it in the *Quarterly Review*, and William Hazlitt believed that it was a 'perversion' of Burney's talent.[8] It is a work which thoroughly deserves wider recognition, however. The most vulnerable of all Burney's heroines, Ellis is forced onto her own resources in a society which relegates independent single women to the lowest rung of the social ladder and where making a living by honest means proves almost impossible. Ellis is modest and orthodox, and never complains about the prevailing patriarchal hegemony which has ostracized her. A great deal of complaining is done in the novel, however; but it is done by a supposedly discredited character, the voluble feminist Elinor. Like Wollstonecraft, of whom she is obviously a follower, Elinor has acquired her advanced principles as a result of 'the late glorious revolutionary shake given to the universe' (Burney, 1991: 154). She is an ardent advocate of women's rights: 'Rights . . . which all your sex, with all its arbitrary assumption of superiority, can never disprove, for they are the Rights of human nature; to which the two sexes equally and unalienably belong' (Burney, 1991: 175). Like Hays's Emma Courtney, Elinor frankly declares her love for the hero, Harleigh, and refuses to take no for an answer even when it becomes clear that he prefers Ellis. Again like Wollstonecraft, she attempts suicide when she finally has to acknowledge that she cannot have Harleigh. Elinor's persistence comes to seem obsessive and self-centred, but her feminist arguments are allowed to go unchallenged, and it is clear that Burney herself has some sympathy with them. Indeed, her presence in the text allows Burney to question the prevailing ideology by indirect and subversive means.

Similarly, in Susan Ferrier's *Marriage*, the central character is the modest and virtuous Mary Lennox. Educated by her exemplary aunt to be an independent and rational thinker, she has imbibed Christian principles of benevolence and piety which sustain her and give her strength to endure the pain and humiliation that results from her reunion with her selfish and ignorant natural mother. Her cousin Emily, less ideally educated, consequently occupies less certain moral ground. But Emily's honesty, outspokenness, intelligence and wit make her a highly attractive character. Mary invariably wins the ideological arguments in which the two engage, but her conservative orthodoxy is inevitably subverted by her cousin's appealing shrewdness. Emily's belief that marriage should be an 'equitable division' and that man must acknowledge woman's possession of rationality (Ferrier, 1986: 384) seems subversively to endorse Wollstonecraft's arguments while allowing Ferrier to distance herself from the undesirable associations of feminist polemicism.

The one woman writer of the Romantic period who has been unequivocally awarded 'greatness', and its accompanying status as a syllabus author, Jane Austen (1776–1817) was long considered to be a profoundly a-historical novelist. Her own declared preference for '3 or 4 Families in a Country Village' as the ideal milieu for the novel (Austen, 1969: 100) was hauled up again and again to serve as evidence that the momentous political and social upheavals of her day were irrelevant to the study of her writing.[9] In the last two decades, all this has changed. Austen remains firmly established in the literary canon, certainly, but it is no longer possible to study her writing in isolation from the political and intellectual context of her time.

The change in Austen studies has been largely attributable, in the first instance, to Marilyn Butler's groundbreaking *Jane Austen and the War of Ideas* (1975). Butler's book has come under attack since its first appearance in 1975 for presenting an Austen so staunchly conservative and anti-Jacobin that she can be described as having a 'preconceived and inflexible' morality (Butler, 1987: 298). Nevertheless, *Jane Austen and the War of Ideas* was a publication of undeniable value to scholars of Austen and students of the Romantic period alike. It was the first work to place Austen's writing in the context of her time, and in doing so it opened the possibility of debate and generated many useful and interesting books on Austen and her relation to the cultural, political and gender issues of her society.[10] A literary critic from the middle of the twentieth century might be surprised to read of her as 'the representative Romantic novelist', one who deals with the central issues of the novel in this period:

> the gentrification of the professional classes and the professionalization of the gentry, the place of women in a professionalized culture that denies them any significant role in public or professional life . . . the re-siting of the authentic self in an inward moral and intellectual being so cultivated as to be able to negotiate successfully the varieties of social experience and cultural discriminations. (Kelly, 1989: 19)

Such, or something not too dissimilar, however, has Austen become for many critics and readers at the present time.

To call Austen a feminist, or to acknowledge her debt to the writings of Wollstonecraft, is not to suggest that she was a radical.[11] Nowhere in her novels does she recommend a revolution in society. Nevertheless, a 'REVOLUTION in female manners' such as Wollstonecraft called for (Wollstonecraft, 1989: vol. v, 265) is indubitably the agenda behind all her fiction. Above all else a pragmatist, she recognized that women must find a way of working within a status quo which afforded them no opportunities for engagement in the public sphere, and must do so without self-compromise. Unmarried herself, she saw that marriage was a woman's best option: but only if that marriage (and that woman) came up to her inordinately high standards.

The demands which Austen makes of her heroines are high indeed. It has long been recognized that her female protagonists fall into two groups: the flawed ones (Marianne Dashwood, Catherine Morland, Elizabeth Bennet, Emma Woodhouse), who make mistakes and learn from them; and the 'good' ones (Elinor Dashwood, Fanny Price, Anne Elliot), who are the moral arbiters of those around them. Such a polarization is only useful, however, if we recognize that even the most flawed of Austen's central characters has intelligence, strength of character, a willingness to learn once mistakes are acknowledged, and a capacity for moral development that far exceeds that possessed by any of the secondary female characters. Marianne has abilities 'in many respects, quite equal to Elinor's': all she lacks is prudence (Austen, 1974: vol. i, 6). Catherine, though 'ignorant and uninformed' (Austen, 1974: vol. v, 18), is open, honest and sincere. Elizabeth is warm-hearted, and, apart from her one blind spot, 'prejudice', highly intelligent and perceptive. Emma, clever, independent and powerful, has only to learn to judge human nature compassionately and not to use her superior intelligence to manipulate those around her.

The lessons these young women have to learn are intensely painful: agitation, shame, mortification, grief, self-blame – even near death, in the case of Marianne – are all necessary in order for them to fulfil their potential of fully developed 'sense' and rationality, and to receive their reward. But all is not plain sailing for Elinor, Fanny and Anne either. Indeed, the trials of being the only person possessed of a clear moral vision in a society composed of everything from well-meaning blunderers to downright villains are arguably even greater. Elinor, who *feels* as deeply as her sister, is forced by circumstances to conceal 'emotion and distress beyond anything she had ever felt before' (Austen, 1974: vol. i, 135). The silent suffering Anne has borne for more than seven years is intensified almost beyond her capacity to endure it when Wentworth reappears on the scene. As for Fanny Price, on the surface the weakest, and the most socially disadvantaged, of all Austen's female protagonists, she finds herself in the position of being the only person in Mansfield Park capable of seeing things as they really are. Fanny's extreme physical delicacy and timidity has made her unpopular with many readers and critics.[12] Arguably, however, she has been given these qualities precisely in order to highlight the extraordinary inner strength of will that her many tests necessitate. As one after another her patrons and mentors prove to have feet of clay, Fanny is increasingly forced to rely on her own inner resources and to speak up, at great cost to herself, for what she believes in. Her reward is not only the love and respect accorded to her by the powerful but misguided patriarch Sir Thomas Bertram but also, of course, her marriage of 'affection and comfort' with Edmund (Austen, 1974: vol. iii, 473).

Mansfield Park in many ways serves as an exemplar for the value system that Austen endorses in all of her works. Wealth and patriarchal power are subjected to a remorseless critique, sexual desire is shown to be dangerously misleading. Men, seemingly dominant, are shown the folly of their ways by apparently fragile and helpless women, who prove to have the power where it really counts – in the mind. Mistrustful of the aristocracy, and largely ignoring the lower classes, Austen fixes her vision firmly on the middle classes. She offers a vision of qualified optimism for women who are capable of living up to her stringent demands. Develop the inner self, never let up for an instant, and you may be lucky enough to find a partner with whom to participate in a marriage of equals, in which esteem, understanding, and rational love replace the usual, but equally dangerous, polarities of romantic fantasy and financial greed. Such a marriage of soundly moral minds is, she suggests, the only viable foundation for a workable bourgeois society. In this she resembles Mary Wollstonecraft far more than may appear at first glance. As a recent, and most perceptive, critic of Austen's fictions has written, 'Austen may slacken the desperate tempos employed by her more strenuously politicized contemporaries, but she shares their artistic strategies and their commitment to uncovering the ideological underpinnings of cultural myths' (Johnson, 1988: 27).

The most important female novelist of the last part of the Romantic period is one who appears as different from Jane Austen as could possibly be. The daughter of William Godwin and Mary Wollstonecraft, Mary Shelley (1797–1851) began writing her first, and most celebrated, novel *Frankenstein, or The Modern Prometheus* (1818) when she was 18 years old. The work, frequently adapted and much misread, has become a modern classic and has achieved the status of 'international cultural myth' (Blumberg, 1993: 1). There can be few people anywhere in the world who are unaware of the story of Victor Frankenstein's creation of a huge being of terrifying appearance and supernatural strength out of materials collected from dissecting rooms and charnel houses, and of the devastating train of events, eventually destroying all that he holds dear and resulting in his own death, that his subsequent rejection of the creature brings in its wake.

Since Ellen Moers's important reading, in 1969, of the novel's motif as 'revulsion against newborn life, and the drama of guilt, dread, and flight surrounding birth and its consequences' (Moers, 1977: 93), feminist critics have had much to say about *Frankenstein*. Many have agreed with Moers that Victor Frankenstein's failure to parent the creature he has fathered is central to the work, and connections have been made with its author's own 'buried feelings of parental abandonment' (Mellor, 1988a: 46). But the work clearly has intellectual and political ramifications as well as psychological ones, as recent critics have convincingly argued.[13]

The most interesting 'political' reading of the novel rests on what appears to be its assertion that domesticity can and should be the ground of political harmony. Perhaps few twentieth-century readers would recognize the novel from Shelley's description of it, in the Preface to the first edition, as 'an exhibition of the amiableness of domestic affection, and the excellence of universal virtue' (Shelley, 1969: 14). If these things are exhibited in *Frankenstein*, we may feel that it is only by default. But although there is much in the novel that appears to strain against this interpretation, there seems little doubt that it does represent its author's purpose, if we are to take seriously (as there seems little reason not to do) Frankenstein's 'moralising' digression as he recounts his story to Walton:

> A human being in perfection ought always to preserve a calm and peaceful mind, and never to allow passion or a transitory desire to disturb his tranquillity. . . . If the study to which you apply yourself has a tendency to weaken your affections, and to destroy

your taste for those simple pleasures in which no alloy can possibly mix, then that study is certainly unlawful, that is to say, not befitting the human mind. If this rule were always observed; if no man allowed any pursuit whatsoever to interfere with the tranquillity of his domestic affections, Greece had not been enslaved; Caesar would have spared his country; America would have been discovered more gradually; and the empires of Mexico and Peru had not been destroyed. (Shelley, 1969: 55–6)

If it is indeed this philosophy which underpins the dramatic 'science fiction' of the plot, then the novel, so radically different in its themes and concerns from the vast majority of women's texts of the Romantic period, can be seen to have more in common with them than at first appears.

In its call for 'the domestic affections' as the ground for political action, *Frankenstein* recalls the political gradualism that Shelley's mother, Mary Wollstonecraft, recommended in her later works: 'Revolution in states should be gradual . . .' (Wollstonecraft, 1989: vol. vi, 346). For this reason, it is easy to agree with Jane Blumberg, who has seen Shelley's fiction as driven by 'a fundamental intellectual conflict with the men in her life' (Blumberg, 1993: 6). Percy Shelley, in particular, was still immersed in optimistic revolutionary ideology despite the fact that such views had long become outdated.

Shelley may have wished that the family unit could be the ground of world harmony, but she does not appear to have been even remotely optimistic that this could be so in reality. This seems to be confirmed by her second full-length novel, *Valperga* (1823) and her third, *The Last Man*, published in 1826, which have only recently been read as important successors to *Frankenstein*. Both works are undoubtedly extremely pessimistic. *Valperga* shows two women, the educated and independent Euthanasia and the innocent, spiritual Beatrice, destroyed by the supremely ambitious and egotistical male tyrant Castruccio. *The Last Man* depicts a political state which is apparently ideal, tranquil and happy – and which is clearly derived from the democratic idealism of Shelley's father and of her husband – and then shows how that state and its people are remorselessly annihilated by a terrifying plague which leaves only one survivor. Whether we see this as 'the first fictional example of nihilism' (Mellor, 1988a: 169) or find in it a 'glimmer of hope' (Blumberg, 1993: 154), there is little doubt that Shelley was subjecting the sphere of human relations to a remorseless critique almost unparalleled in the history of fiction.

The feminist polemics which were expressed in so much of the prose of the 1790s, both fictional and non-fictional, are much less frequently found in the women's poetry of the period. This is not because women were not writing and publishing poetry at this time. By the last decade of the eighteenth century there were a number of successful and respected female poets, but by and large they appear to have been indifferent, or even hostile, to the feminist radicalism of the day. Anna Seward (1742–1809), who had started publishing in the 1770s and was recognized as an important member of the literary establishment by the last decade of the century, was heavily critical of the work of most of her female contemporaries (Lonsdale, 1989: 313). Anna Laetitia Barbauld (1743–1825), a successful essayist and literary critic, had no sympathy for the feminism which emerged so vociferously in the 1790s. Highly educated herself, she opposed female education, believed there was 'no bond of union among literary women' and deplored Wollstonecraft's *Rights of Woman* (Lonsdale, 1989: 300). She wrote a good deal of serious, didactic poetry, and had considerable success with her *Epistle to William Wilberforce* (1791), one of several attacks on the slave trade by women poets at this time.[14] Barbauld does not make explicit links between the condition of women and that of slaves, as Wollstonecraft was to do in her *Rights of Woman* the following year, but her depiction of the pitiful condition of the slaves, whose 'Dumb sullen looks of woe announce despair/And angry eyes through dusky features glare' (82–3) shows considerable sympathy for the oppressed.

More appealing, for the twentieth-century reader at least, is the witty verse she wrote in the 1790s for the *Monthly Magazine*, much of which celebrates the 'quotidian values' which, as Stuart Curran has recently pointed out, have been 'largely submerged from our comprehension of Romanticism' (Curran, 1988: 190). Her 'Washing Day', for example, invokes the 'domestic Muse' to help her to 'sing the dreaded Washing-Day' in a manner which at least acknowledges that married life may be tediously far from ideal (Barbauld's own marriage, like that of so many of the female writers of the period, was an extremely unhappy and difficult one):

> Ye who beneath the yoke of wedlock bend
> With bowed soul, full well ye ken the day
> Which week, smooth sliding after week, brings on
> Too soon . . .
>
> (3, 8–12)

The poem slides effortlessly through vivid description to childhood memory, only to end on a note of self-deprecation ('Earth, air, and sky, and ocean, hath its bubbles, / And verse is one of them – this most of all' (85–6)) which is entirely consistent with Barbauld's declared view that in becoming an author she had 'stepped out of the bounds of female reserve' (Lonsdale, 1989: 300).

The best seller of all the women poets of this decade was the highly reactionary Hannah More (1745–1833), who refused to read Wollstonecraft's *Rights of Woman* (she is supposed to have said 'Rights of women! We shall be hearing of the Rights of Children next!' (Shattock, 1994: 304)). Her collection in verse, *Cheap Repository Tracts* (1795–8), directed towards reform and addressed directly to the poor, sold two million copies in its first year of publication (not to the poor themselves, of course – the book was bought by the middle classes for distribution to their less fortunate neighbours). Despite her conservative, reforming agenda, the fact that More's poems are written in the deliberately simple language and verse forms she deemed suitable for the working classes (the real language of men?) gives them a lively, democratic readableness and perhaps explains why she admired Wordsworth's *Lyrical Ballads* when they were published a few years later. But her declared views are very different from those of Wordsworth, who shows considerable sympathy for the plight of marginalized female outcasts.[15] More, who argued in her *Strictures on Female Education* (1799) that women who had wandered from the path of morality should be ostracized by society, has little time for fallen women in her poetry either. In 'The Gin Shop; or, A Peep into Prison', for example, she urges that a wise social benefactor will reserve his charity for 'the deserving poor', and that he 'withhold his gift' from such as:

> that shivering female there,
> Who plies her woeful trade!
> 'Tis ten to one you'll find that Gin
> That hopeless wretch has made.
>
> (8, 12–16)

Very different in style, subject matter, and political content is the work of More's onetime protégée Ann Yearsley (1752–1806). Discovered and patronized in the 1780s by More, Yearsley enjoyed some popularity for a decade or so. She soon quarrelled with More, whom she felt, with some justification, was high-handedly attempting to control her life and her finances, but she continued to write and publish her poetry, producing her last important volume, *The Rural Lyre*, in 1796.

Although Yearsley has been described as 'not, by and large, a poet of lasting claims' (Curran, 1988: 197), her sometimes harsh and frequently obscure poetry is often illuminated by flashes of imaginative brilliance and glimpses of sublimity which have no parallel in the work of any other woman poet of the era. But though Yearsley writes that she has known what it is to experience being 'awaked/. . . to ecstasy untaught,/To all the transport the rapt sense can bear' by the beauties and sublimity of nature, she expresses also her overwhelming sense of inadequacy, as 'all expired, for want of powers to speak' ('On Mrs Montagu', 1785: 61–4). Her poetry of the 1790s indicates that her anger has taken a more specifically feminist angle ('Estrang'd from tyrant man/I'll keep my liberty!' ('The Indifferent Shepherdess to Colin', 1796: 31–2)). In 'Remonstrance in the Platonic Shade, Flourishing on an Height' (1796), she seems to attribute her difficulties and the 'feeble sounds' which 'give not my soul's rich meaning' specifically to her gender. She has 'climbed a height/So frightful', attained 'with wretchedness this summit', sustained only by her own stubbornness of soul. Other, weaker, women have fallen by the wayside: vision has been granted to her only by virtue of her 'rough, laborious' spirit. But her vision, though 'sublime' in its scope and grandeur, is one of the ruin of empires and the death of kings – patriarchal power, she seems to suggest, will crumble as the earth returns to a more primitive and enduring natural state:

> I see the bleating lamb trot o'er the turf
> That covers long-descended kingdoms: hear
> The tiger roar, where tyrants scourged mankind;
> On roofs of buried palaces remark
> The mole rearing her fabric; learn the hymn
> Sweet Philomel sings to the warrior's shade –
> Far o'er the plain, beneath the midnight moon.
>
> (56–62)

Of all the women poets of the 1790s, Yearsley – marginalized both by her gender and by her social class – has perhaps the most polemically feminist voice.[16] But the work of a few of her female contemporaries also demonstrates a clear dissatisfaction with the role of women in society.

If Yearsley's marginalization was doubled by her working-class origins, Mary Robinson's was so by reasons of morality. Like many of the women poets of this period, Robinson (1758–1800) started writing early. Her first collection, *Poems* (1775), was published when she was 16, by which time she had been married for a year and had spent several months living in a debtors' prison with her profligate husband and infant daughter. *Captivity: A Poem; and Celadon and Lydia: A Tale* followed two years later, after which Robinson virtually abandoned writing for over ten years, during which she became a successful actress at Drury Lane. She was persuaded to become the mistress of the Prince of Wales (later George IV) at this time; but the scandal which followed her demands for fulfilment of his unpaid bond of £20,000 when the relationship finished put an end to her acting career and ensured that she was never again accepted into 'respectable' society. By 1788 she had returned to poetry, and her *Poems* (1791) had an impressive list of 600 subscribers. Like many women poets at this time, she was forced to turn to more lucrative prose writing, producing a total of seven novels between 1792 and 1799, but she continued to publish poetry throughout the decade both in single editions and in collections. She was also a regular contributor of poetry to the *Morning Post*, through which she became friends with Coleridge. Her last volume of poetry, *Lyrical Tales*, appeared a few months before her death in 1800 at the age of 42. Her daughter edited her *Memoirs* (4 vols, 1801) and her 3-volume *Poetical Works* (1806).

Although Robinson was always possessed of an almost faultless ear for rhythms and an admirable willingness to experiment with poetic form, her early poetry is conventional to the point of affectation, as she came fully to recognize. By the 1790s, she had found a stronger and more interesting voice. She eulogized Coleridge in 'To the Poet Coleridge' (1800), a poem which both echoes and rewrites 'Kubla Khan', and wrote her own versions of the newly invented 'lyrical ballad'. Her (fairly rare) self-revelatory poetry shows her to be a poet capable of expressing passion in a manner which makes her sound rather like a feminist Byron. Her 'Stanzas. Written between Dover and Calais, in July, 1792', for example, describes her personal anguish when her lover, Colonel Banestre Tarleton, tried to end their ten-year relationship:

> Proud has been my fatal passion!
>   Proud my injured heart shall be!
> While each thought and inclination
>   Proves that heart was formed for thee!
>
> Not one sigh shall tell my story;
>   Not one tear my cheek shall stain!
> Silent grief shall be my glory,
>   Grief that stoops not to complain!
>
> Let the bosom, prone to ranging,
>   Still, by ranging, seek a cure!
> Mine disdains the thought of changing,
>   Proudly destined to endure!
>
> (21–32)

Some of her best poetry of this decade, during which she became a member of Godwin and Wollstonecraft's circle, frames social satire in an experimental technique of 'poetic montage' which has been admired as 'realistic genre-painting . . . years ahead of its time' (Curran, 1988: 190, 192).

Her 'January, 1795', 'Stanzas' (1797), 'The Birthday' and 'Winkfield Plain' (both written in 1800) play confidently with an impressive variety of metres and verse-forms, juxtaposing wealth and poverty, success and failure, merit and dishonesty to produce a breathtakingly broad and wholly realistic vision of a corrupt society at odds with itself throughout every level. In 'Stanzas', for example, although the poem is not directly feminist, Robinson manages to suggest marginalization by positioning herself as a liberal humanitarian, sickened by the injustices of a conservative patriarchal culture.

> While the court breeds the sycophant, trained to
>   ensnare;
> While the prisons re-echo the groans of Despair;
> While the State deals out taxes, the Army dismay;
> While the rich are upheld, and the poor doomed to pay;
> Humanity saddens with pity to see
> The scale of injustice, and trembles like me!
>
> (31–6)

Another woman poet whose career was largely precipitated by virtue of her unsatisfactory personal life was Charlotte Smith (1749–1806). Married at 15 to a feckless and extravagant husband, the mother of twelve children, nine of whom survived childhood, Smith was rapidly forced into the position of breadwinner for the family. She had showed an early talent for poetry, which she put to use in her *Elegiac Sonnets and Other Essays* (1784). The volume was immediately successful, a second edition was called for, and Smith won an enduring reputation as a poet. As well as the ten editions of *Elegiac Sonnets* which appeared between 1784 and 1800, she also published a long and complex blank-verse poem, *The Emigrants*, in 1793. After what her epitaph described as 'a life of great and various sufferings' (quoted Smith, 1993: xxvi), she died in 1806. Her *Beachy Head; With Other Poems* was published posthumously in 1807.

Nearly twenty years after her death, Wordsworth described Smith as a poet 'to whom English verse is under greater obligations than are likely to be either acknowledged or remembered' (quoted Smith, 1993: xiii). Certainly in the best of her sonnets and shorter poems, Smith manages to combine an intense, personal note of melancholy with keen and sensitive observation of the natural world which would, presumably, have appealed to Wordsworth. Whether she is empathizing with society's outcasts or hinting mysteriously at her own sorrows, her poems convey a pervasive sense of solitary, isolated sensibility which is undoubtedly reminiscent of elements in the work of later Romantic poets. But it is perhaps in her longer blank-verse pieces, *The Emigrants* and the posthumous *Beachy Head*, that her most free and direct writing is to be found.

The Emigrants was written in 1792 against a background of revolutionary violence in France which threatened to undermine the cause of liberty in which Smith believed so passionately. Set on the Kentish shoreline, the poem depicts its author wandering 'with step/Mournful and slow, along the wave-worn cliff' (Book II, 3–4) and encountering a group of French exiles who have been thrown on the English coast 'like shipwreck'd sufferers' as a result of France's 'wild disastrous Anarchy' (Book I, 10, 11). Throughout the poem, the public, political cause of the French victims of the Terror slides into Smith's personal account of the injustices she has endured at the hands of the British legal system to give a powerful representation of the tyranny of establishments and the plight of the outcast.

Both *The Emigrants* and *Beachy Head*, which was left unfinished at Smith's death, contain a combination of natural observation, childhood memories, personal meditation and political reflection which points forward irresistibly to Wordsworth's *Prelude* and perhaps accounts for his sense of the great obligations later poets have owed to her. But writing as a woman, and as a mother, Smith has a perspective which is lacking from the work of her male contemporaries. Wordsworth's memories of his soul's 'fair seed-time' on the banks of the Derwent are looked back on with gratitude for their formative influence. Smith's recollections, in *The Emigrants*, of 'hours of simple joy' beside the Arun serve only to remind her how little she then dreamed of her future of 'never-ending toil, / [Of] terror and [of] tears' (Book II, 332, 350–1). The poem's concluding image of its author wearily struggling on:

> With feeble hands and cold desponding heart
> To save my children from the o'erwhelming wrongs,
> That have for ten long years been heaped on me! –
> The fearful spectres of chicane and fraud . . .
> Pursuing my faint steps . . .
>
> (Book II, 352–5, 356)

is a powerful one, and seems to typify the sense of marginalization which women writers in all genres were expressing at this time.

By the early 1800s, all the women poets of the generation that had enjoyed so much success during the last decade of the eighteenth century had fallen silent. Robinson died in 1800, as did both Smith and Yearsley in 1806 and Seward in 1809. More and Barbauld survived (Barbauld until 1825, More until 1833), but both had turned almost exclusively to prose writing, as had another successful poet of the 1780s and 1790s, Helen Maria Williams. Joanna Baillie, whose *Poems; Wherein it is Attempted to Describe Certain Views of Nature and of Rustic Manners* (published anonymously in 1790) shows her to be a poet of considerable skill and great potential, was discouraged by the volume's lack of success and turned her attention to drama.

Given the degree of public acclaim these women poets enjoyed during the final decade of the eighteenth century, it is a curious fact that not one of them found a place in the emerging literary canon. A number of factors seem to have contributed to this. As Roger Lonsdale has pointed out, not only were their dates such that they missed being included in the two most influential, 'canonizing', multi-volume editions of English poetry edited by Anderson (1792–5) and Chalmers (1801) – which did not include living poets – but also the 'relentlessly masculine' definitions of a poet given by Wordsworth in his Preface to *Lyrical Ballads* (1800) mitigated against the possibility of women being recognized as having any major achievements in this genre (Lonsdale, 1989: xl–xliii). In addition, the post-revolutionary, conservative, anti-feminist backlash that followed the death of Wollstonecraft meant that this group of women writers was doubly suspect, on the grounds of their association with radical politics as well as of their gender.

Although new talents began to emerge as the nineteenth century progressed, it is difficult to find any interesting new voices among the women poets of the first decade of the century. Mary Tighe, born in Dublin in 1772, had her *Psyche; or The Legend of Love* privately printed in 1805, but the work, which was highly successful and influenced a number of poets including Keats, was not published until 1811, by which time its author had died of consumption aged only 38. The most enduringly popular poet to emerge at this time, and one of the few whose works have been reprinted in the twentieth century, was the Methodist Jane Taylor (1783–1824). Taylor, who is best remembered as the author of 'Twinkle twinkle little star', was almost exclusively a writer of moral works for children. Her most admired collection, *Essays in Rhyme on Morals and Manners* (1816), is framed as didacticism. But, as Stuart Curran has recently argued, the best poems in the volume are not only highly successful and entertaining in themselves but also, through their blend of social satire, quotidian detail, and moral argument, provide an important link between Augustan satire and the Victorian 'social' novels of Dickens and Hardy (Curran, 1988: 192–4, 203–5).

By the early 1820s, the picture had changed once more. Two important and popular female poets, Laetitia Landon and Felicia Hemans, emerged at this time and quickly came almost to dominate the field of poetic production until their (early) deaths in the 1830s.

Largely forgotten today, or remembered only as the poet of the much-parodied 'Casabianca' ('The boy stood on the burning deck . . .'), Felicia Hemans (1793–1835) was almost as popular in her own day as her most successful male contemporary Lord Byron. Precociously talented – her first volume, *Poems* (1808) was published when she was 15 – she produced a total of nineteen volumes of poetry, a new collection almost every year, until her death, from heart disease and tuberculosis, at the age of 41. Her earnings from poetry, drama, and contributions to annuals, were substantial, so that she was well able to pay for the upbringing and education of her five sons after the permanent departure of her husband during her final pregnancy. After her death, her work remained in print throughout the nineteenth century and, it has been said, 'arguably formed the poetic taste of the Victorian period' (Clarke, 1990: 32).

Hemans was viewed in her day as the supreme poet of the domestic sphere. The many eulogies of her writings by contemporary commentators concentrated on the 'feminine' qualities of her writing, and her poetry was seen as an embodiment of the woman herself, idealized as 'essentially womanly – fervent, trustful, unquestioning' (Chorley, 1836: vol. i, 139).

There is some irony in the fact that Hemans undoubtedly constructed herself through her work as the ideal of domestic womanhood, eschewing the public sphere in favour of private satisfactions, as in 'Woman and Fame', for example:

> Thou hast a charmed cup, O Fame!
>   A draught that mantles high,
> And seems to lift this earthly frame
>   Above mortality.
> Away! to me – a woman – bring
> Sweet waters from affection's spring.
>
> (1–6)

while in her own life she tirelessly pursued public success, leaving the day-to-day business of everyday life largely in the hands of her mother, with whom she lived after her husband's departure. It would be unfair to Hemans to suggest that her celebration of the home, the hearth, and the domestic affections was hypocritical. But careful reading of her poetry suggests that she was profoundly ambivalent about the domestic ideology she appears to endorse. Her 'Evening Prayer at a Girls' School', for example, depicts a woman's lot in life in grim terms as one of 'silent tears' and 'patient smiles', an existence in which affection becomes a 'wasted shower', poured on 'broken reeds', and the making of idols to worship only 'to find them clay' (25–30).

Hemans's most interesting volume, and the one into which 'she . . . put her heart and individual feelings more than in anything else she had written' (Hughes, 1839: vol. i, 136), was her *Records of Woman with Other Poems* (1828). The poems in the volume idealize noble women of the past, both real and invented. Hemans never spoke openly, in public at least, of the failure of her marriage, but it seems likely that her feelings about it are transmuted into the poetry of *Records of Woman*. Poem after poem shows heroic female devotion leading to self-sacrifice and, frequently, to death. Men are either absent, faithless, dying or dead, often through violence (it has rightly been said that *Records of Woman* 'is awash with blood' (Clarke, 1990: 79)). Eudora, 'The Bride of the Greek Isle', sees her husband murdered by pirates at their wedding feast; the heroine of 'Edith, A Tale of the Woods' sits 'pale and silent on the bloody ground' covered with her dead husband's blood; 'Imelda' finds her lover dead in the woods, stabbed by her brothers; 'Gertrude' sits by, helpless, as her husband slowly dies, strapped to the wheel. Women suffer endlessly, but they also endure, sacrificing themselves for love.

Hemans's ambivalent feelings about the conflict women face if they engage in public endeavours is demonstrated in several poems. In 'Joan of Arc, in Rheims', Joan longs to return to the idyllic domestic peace and happiness of her childhood, but realizes at the end of the poem that she cannot do so. She has gained 'too much of fame', and as a result 'the paradise of home' must be sacrificed: public success and private contentment cannot, it seems, coexist.

This message is expressed even more forcefully in the most interesting poem in the volume, 'Properzia Rossi'. Based on the true history of Rossi, a sculptor, musician and poet in Renaissance Bologna, the poem is in the form of a dramatic monologue. Famous and celebrated, possessed of a passionate creativity, Rossi suffers and eventually dies as a result of her unrequited love for a Roman knight. Her inner conflict exemplifies what, Hemans suggests, is the inescapable problem faced by female artists: how to be true to the demands of one's creativity without losing the rewards of womanliness. Rossi, in Hemans's poem, fails in both areas. She is aware of her own creative genius, and celebrates it with passion, while simultaneously recognizing its uselessness as far as human relations are concerned:

> It comes! the power
> Within me born flows back – my fruitless dower
> That could not win me love. Yet once again
> I greet it proudly, with its rushing train
> Of glorious images: they throng – they press –
> A sudden joy lights up my loneliness –
> I shall not perish all!
>
> (25–31)

But Rossi acknowledges that her art has suffered from her loneliness and isolation. However splendid her vision, her achievement is blocked by solitude and the pain of unrequited love. She goes to her death in the poem, seeing it as a release from pain and conflict, and leaving her art as a legacy to the man who, ironically, has never appreciated it.

As Anne Mellor has recently pointed out, Hemans's contemporaries were aware of her 'obsession with suffering and death', and possibly her very popularity was the result of a general recognition of the fact that the domestic felicity she appeared to be espousing in her works 'was an ideology now in danger of permanent collapse under the . . . pressure of an increasingly industrialized, materialistic, competitive society' (Mellor, 1993: 142–3).

Laetitia Elizabeth Landon (L.E.L.) (1802–38) enjoyed considerable material success as a poet. Her annual income from poetry was estimated by her editor as £250 minimum, and her total earnings at about £2,585. Certainly she earned enough to support herself and her mother (in separate houses) and additionally to pay for her brother's university education and to buy him a clerical living (Jerdan, 1852–4: vol. ii, 256). To do so, however, involved her in considerable struggle: she was frequently unwell and exhausted from the effort involved in producing enough poetry, as well as prose contributions to various annuals, to support herself and her family.

A Victorian editor of her work wrote, with some justification, that '[t]he strain of nearly all her poems is warm and passionate: love, devoted, self-sacrificing, absorbing and unsatisfied, being her favourite theme' (Bethune, 1848: 275). Landon's self-construction as an icon of female beauty, both personally (through the many portraits which were painted of her) and poetically has led to the accusation that she supports 'an *essentialist* definition of the woman as the *one who loves*' (Mellor, 1993: 114, author's italics). But Landon, like Hemans, whom she greatly admired, also shows a consciousness of the price, for a woman, of artistic endeavour, as her 'Stanzas on the

Death of Mrs Hemans' demonstrates. Perhaps the poem is as much autobiography as elegy:

> Ah! dearly purchased is the gift,
>   The gift of song like thine;
> A fated doom is her's who stands
>   The priestess of the shrine.
> The crowd – they only see the crown,
>   They only hear the hymn;
> They mark not that the cheek is pale,
>   And that the eye is dim.
>
> Wound to a pitch too exquisite,
>   The soul's fine chords are wrung;
> With misery and melody
>   They are too highly strung.
> The heart is made too sensitive
>   Life's daily pain to bear;
> It beats in music, but it beats
>   Beneath a deep despair.
>
> It never meets the love it paints,
>   The love for which it pines . . .
>
> (49–66)

The price of an acute sensibility seems to be sickness, despair and death – art may succeed, but the female artist will suffer, not least because her over-developed imagination will conjure up a love too fine and too ideal to be met with in the real world.

Angela Leighton has argued persuasively for Landon's 'late imaginative development' (Leighton, 1992: 64). The poem just quoted is an example of the scepticism which becomes more evident in her later work. Self-honesty, regret for a life of emotional hollowness, and a sense of wasted gifts are all increasingly evident in the poetry of her final years:

> Oh, what a waste of feeling and of thought
> Have been the imprints on my roll of life!
> What worthless hours! to what use have I turned
> The golden gifts which are my hope and pride!
> My power of song, unto how base a use
> Has it been put!
>
> ('Gifts Misused', 1–6)

It is difficult to see any way in which the position of women, either as authors or as members of society, had improved by the end of the Romantic period. Wollstonecraft's pioneering efforts in both fiction and non-fiction in the 1790s, while clearly possessing a powerfully inspirational value both for her contemporaries and for many women who came later, only served to antagonize the establishment and to drive feminist polemics underground. That unsatisfactory figure, domestic woman, transmuted in the Victorian period into the 'Angel in the House', had been born in the poetry of Hemans and Landon, and arguments for the domestic as a template for political harmony had appeared as early as 1818 in *Frankenstein*. Women writers were, if anything, more ambivalent about literary fame at the end of the period than they had been at the beginning. Ambivalent or not, however, a number of female authors had achieved undoubted success during the period, a fact which helped to pave the way for their successors in the Victorian period.

Notes

1. Mellor, 1993: Introduction, 1–11 for a discussion of 'male' and 'female' Romanticism.
2. Baillie's 'Introductory Discourse' is discussed in Carhart, 1923, where it is argued that some of her ideas anticipate those of the Preface to Wordsworth's *Lyrical Ballads* (1800). Watkins, 1993 devotes a chapter to her *De Montfort*.
3. For a discussion of this process, see Kelly, 1993: *passim*.
4. See, for example, Hester Chapone, *Letters on the Improvement of the Mind* (2 vols, 1773), Hannah More, *Essays on Various Subjects, Principally Designed For Young Ladies* (1777) and, most influential on Wollstonecraft, Catharine Macaulay, *Letters on Education* (1790).
5. At the beginning of the French Revolution the term Jacobin was applied to members of a French political club founded in 1789 who supported principles of absolute equality and democracy. Within a few years the term was transferred to anyone who supported these principles, while conservatives were referred to as anti-Jacobins.
6. Dorothy Wordsworth has not been particularly well served by recent criticism. There is only one book-length critical study devoted to her work, Levin, 1987. See also Alexander (1988) and (1989); Homans (1980); James Holt McGavran Jr, 'Dorothy Wordsworth's Journals – Putting Herself Down' in Benstock, 1988: 230–53; and Mellor, 1993: 154–68.
7. See Moers's chapter 'Female Gothic' in *Literary Women*, 1977: 90–110.
8. See Doody, 1988: 385–8.
9. The a-historical approach to Austen is typified by that of F.R. Leavis, who elected Austen to membership of *The Great Tradition* (1948).
10. Among the supporters of the 'conservative' view of Jane Austen are Monaghan, 1981 and Poovey, 1984. Critics who view her as a 'radical' feminist include Kirkham, 1983a and 1983b and Evans, 1987. Those who see her as a 'moderate' feminist include Johnson, 1988 and Sulloway, 1989.
11. But see Kirkham, 1983a and b for an argument that Austen was directly influenced by Wollstonecraft's *Rights of Woman*.
12. Among the most extreme attacks on Fanny Price are those of Lionel Trilling, '*Mansfield Park*', Kingsley Amis, 'What Became of Jane Austen' (both reprinted in Southam, 1976: 216–35 and 243–6) and Nina Auerbach, 'Jane Austen's Dangerous Charm: Feeling as one ought about Fanny Price' in Todd, 1983: 201–21.
13. See, for example, Blumberg, 1993; Clemit, 1993; Mellor, 1988a.
14. Among other poems on slavery were Hannah More's 'Slavery: A Poem' (1788), Amelia Opie's 'A Negro Boy's Tale' (1795), Helen Maria Williams's 'A Poem on the Bill' (1788) and Ann Yearsley's 'On the Inhumanity of the Slave Trade' (1788). See Ferguson, 1992 for a discussion of these and other relevant works.
15. See, for example, Margaret in *The Ruined Cottage* (1797), and the 'Female Vagrant', 'Mad Mother', 'Forsaken Indian Woman', and Martha Ray in 'The Thorn' (all in the first edition of *Lyrical Ballads*, 1798).
16. But see Landry (1990) for a discussion of the contradictions and 'bourgeoisification' of Yearsley.

Bibliography

Primary materials

Austen, Jane (1969), *The Letters*, R.W. Chapman (ed.), London, New York, Toronto: Oxford University Press.

Austen, Jane (1974), *The Novels*, R.W. Chapman (ed.), 5 vols, London, New York, Toronto: Oxford University Press.

Baillie, Joanna (1798–1812), *A Series of Plays in which it is attempted to Delineate the Stronger Passions of the Mind*, 3 vols, London: T. Cadell and W. Davies.

Burney, Fanny (1991) [1814], *The Wanderer*, Margaret Anne Doody, Robert L. Mack and Peter Sabor (eds), Oxford and New York: Oxford University Press.

Edgeworth, Maria (1993) [1801], *Belinda*, Eilean Ni Chuilleanain (ed.), London: J.M. Dent.

Ferrier, Susan (1986) [1818], *Marriage*, Herbert Foltinek (ed.), Oxford and New York: Oxford University Press.

Hays, Mary (1799), *The Victim of Prejudice*, 2 vols, London.

Hays, Mary (1987) [1796], *Memoirs of Emma Courtney*, London: Pandora Press.

Hemans, Felicia (1887), *Poetical Works*, Edinburgh and London: William Blackwood and Sons.

Landon, Laetitia E. (1873), *Poetical Works*, William B. Scott (ed.), London.

Opie, Amelia (1986) [1804], *Adeline Mowbray*, London: Pandora Press.

Radcliffe, Ann (1980) [1794], *The Mysteries of Udolpho*, London, New York, Toronto: Oxford University Press.

Radcliffe, Ann (1991) [1797], *The Italian*, Oxford, London, New York, Toronto: Oxford University Press.

Robinson, Mary (1800), *Lyrical Tales*, London: T.N. Longman and O. Rose.

Robinson, Mary (1806), *Poetical Works*, M.E. Robinson (ed.), 3 vols, London: R. Phillips.

Shelley, Mary (1823), *Valperga*, London: G. & W.B. Whittaker.

Shelley, Mary (1969) [1818], *Frankenstein or The Modern Prometheus*, M.K. Joseph (ed.), London, New York, Toronto: Oxford University Press.

Shelley, Mary (1994) [1826], *The Last Man*, M.D. Paley (ed.), Oxford: Oxford University Press.

Smith, Charlotte (1993), *The Complete Poems*, Stuart Curran (ed.), Oxford and New York: Oxford University Press.

Wollstonecraft, Mary (1989), *Works*, Marilyn Butler and Janet M. Todd (eds), 7 vols, London: Pickering and Chatto.

Wordsworth, Dorothy (1992), *The Journals*, Pamela Woof (ed.), Oxford: Oxford University Press.

Yearsley, Ann (1785), *Poems on Several Occasions*, London: T. Cadell.

Yearsley, Ann (1796), *The Rural Lyre*, London: G.G. and J. Robinson.

Secondary materials

Alexander, Meena (1988), 'Dorothy Wordsworth: The Grounds of Writing', *Women's Studies*, 14, 195–210.

Alexander, Meena (1989), *Women in Romanticism: Mary Wollstonecraft, Dorothy Wordsworth, and Mary Shelley*, Towota, N.J.: Barnes & Noble.

Alston, Robin (1990), *A Checklist of Women Writers 1801–1900*, London: British Library.

Ashfield, Anthony (ed.) (1995), *Romantic Women Poets 1770–1838: An Anthology*, Manchester and New York: Manchester University Press.

Benstock, Shari (ed.) (1988), *The Private Self – Theory and Practice of Women's Autobiographical Writings*, Chapel Hill: University of North Carolina Press.

Bethune, George W. (1848), *The Female Poets: With Biographical and Critical Notes*, Philadelphia, Pa.: Lindsay and Blakiston.

Brown, Julia Prewitt (1979), *Jane Austen's Novels: Social Change and Literary Form*, Cambridge, Mass.: Harvard University Press.

Blumberg, Jane (1993), *Mary Shelley's Early Novels: 'This Child of Imagination and Misery'*, Basingstoke and London: Macmillan.

Butler, Marilyn (1987) [1975], *Jane Austen and the War of Ideas*, Oxford: Clarendon Press.

Carhart, Margaret (1923), *The Life and Work of Joanna Baillie*, Yale: Yale University Press, repr. Archon Books, 1970.

Chorley, H.F. (1836), *Memorials of Mrs Hemans*, 2 vols, London: Saunders and Otley.

Clarke, Norma (1990), *Ambitious Heights: Writing, Friendship, Love: The Jewsbury Sisters, Felicia Hemans, and Jane Welsh Carlyle*, London and New York: Routledge.

Clemit, Pamela (1993), *The Godwinian Novel: The Rational Fictions of Godwin, Brockden Brown, and Mary Shelley*, Oxford: Clarendon Press.

Cullinan, Mary (1984), *Susan Ferrier*, Boston: Twayne Publishers.

Curran, Stuart (1988), 'Romantic Poetry: The I Altered' in *Romanticism and Feminism*, Anne K. Mellor (ed.), Bloomington: Indiana University Press.

Doody, Margaret (1988), *Frances Burney: The Life in the Works*, Cambridge: Cambridge University Press.

Evans, Mary (1987), *Jane Austen and the State*, London: Tavistock.

Ferguson, Moira (1992), *Subject to Others: British Women Writers and Colonial Slavery 1670–1834*, London and New York: Routledge.

Gallagher, Catherine (1994), *Vanishing Acts of Women Writers in the Market Place 1670–1820*, Oxford: Clarendon Press.

Holmes, Richard (ed.) (1987), Mary Wollstonecraft, *A Short Residence in Sweden, Norway and Denmark* and William Godwin, *Memoirs of the Author of the Rights of Woman*, Harmondsworth: Penguin.

Homans, Margaret (1980), *Women Writers and Poetic Identity*, Princeton, N.J.: Princeton University Press.

Homans, Margaret (1986), *Bearing the Word: Language and Female Experience in Nineteenth-Century Women's Writing*, Chicago: Chicago University Press.

Howells, Coral Ann (1978), *Love, Mystery and Misery: Feeling in Gothic Fiction*, London: Athlone Press.

Howells, Coral Ann (1989), 'The Pleasure of the Woman's Text: Ann Radcliffe's Subtle Transgressions' in *Gothic Fictions: Prohibition/Transgression*, Kenneth W. Graham (ed.), New York: AMS Press, pp. 151–62.

Hughes, Harriet (1839), *The Works of Mrs Hemans; with a Memoir of Her Life by Her Sister*, 7 vols, Edinburgh: William Blackwood & Sons; London: Thomas Cadell.

Jackson, J.R. de J. (1993), *Romantic Poetry by Women: A Bibliography 1770–1835*, Oxford: Clarendon Press.

Jerdan, William (1852–4), *The Autobiography of William Jerdan*, 4 vols, London: Hall, Vertue.

Johnson, Claudia L. (1988), *Jane Austen: Women, Politics and the Novel*, Chicago: University of Chicago Press.

Jump, Harriet Devine (1994), *Mary Wollstonecraft: Writer*, Hemel Hempstead: Harvester Wheatsheaf.

Kelly, Gary (1976), *The English Jacobin Novel 1780–1805*, Oxford: Clarendon Press.

Kelly, Gary (1989), *English Fiction of the Romantic Period 1789–1830*, London and New York: Longman.

Kelly, Gary (1991), *Revolutionary Feminism: The Mind and Career of Mary Wollstonecraft*, Basingstoke: Macmillan.

Kelly, Gary (1993), *Women, Writing, and Revolution 1790–1827*, Oxford: Clarendon Press.

Kirkham, Margaret (1983a), *Jane Austen: Feminism and Fiction*, Hemel Hempstead: Harvester Wheatsheaf.

Kirkham, Margaret (1983b), 'Feminist Irony and the Priceless Heroine of *Mansfield Park*' in *Jane Austen: New Perspectives*, Janet Todd (ed.), *Women and Literature*, vol. 3 n.s., London and New York: Holmes and Meier.

Landry, Donna (1990), *Muses of Resistance: Labouring Class Women's Poetry in Britain 1739–1796*, Cambridge, New York, Port Chester, Melbourne, Sydney: Cambridge University Press.

Leighton, Angela (1992), *Victorian Women Poets: Writing Against the Heart*, Hemel Hempstead: Harvester Wheatsheaf.

Levin, Susan (1987), *Dorothy Wordsworth and Romanticism*, New Brunswick: Rutgers University Press.

Lonsdale, Roger (ed.) (1989), *Eighteenth Century Women Poets: An Oxford Anthology*, Oxford: Oxford University Press.

Mellor, Anne K. (1988a), *Mary Shelley: Her Life, Her Fiction, Her Monsters*, London and New York: Routledge.

Mellor, Anne K. (ed.) (1988b), *Romanticism and Feminism*, Bloomington: Indiana University Press.

Mellor, Anne K. (1993), *Romanticism and Gender*, London and New York: Routledge.

Miles, Robert (1995), *Ann Radcliffe: The Great Enchantress*, Manchester: Manchester University Press.

Moers, Ellen (1977), *Literary Women*, Garden City, N.Y.: Anchor Books.

Monaghan, David (ed.) (1981), *Jane Austen in a Social Context*, New York: Barnes and Noble.

Paxton, Nancy L. (1976), 'Subversive Feminism: A Reassessment of Susan Ferrier's *Marriage*', *Women & Literature* IV, 18–29.

Poovey, Mary (1984), *The Proper Lady and the Woman Writer: Ideology as Style in the Works of Mary Wollstonecraft, Jane Austen and Dorothy Wordsworth*, Chicago and London: University of Chicago Press.

Punter, David (1980), *The Literature of Terror: A History of Gothic Fiction from 1795 to the Present Day*, London and New York: Longman.

Ross, Marlon B. (1989), *The Contours of Masculine Desire: Romanticism and the Rise of Women's Poetry*, London and New York: Oxford University Press.

Shattock, Joanne (1994), *The Oxford Guide to British Women Writers*, Oxford and New York: Oxford University Press.

Shiner, Carol (1994), *Revisioning Romanticism: British Women Writers 1776–1837*, Philadelphia: University of Pennsylvania Press.

Southam, B.C. (ed.) (1976), *Jane Austen: 'Sense and Sensibility', 'Pride and Prejudice' and 'Mansfield Park': A Casebook*, London: Macmillan.

Spencer, Jane (1986), *The Rise of the Woman Novelist: From Aphra Behn to Jane Austen*, Oxford: Basil Blackwell.

Sulloway, Alison (1989), *Jane Austen and the Province of Womanhood*, Philadelphia: University of Pennsylvania Press.

Todd, Janet M. (1986), *Sensibility: An Introduction*, London: Methuen.

Todd, Janet M. (1989), *The Sign of Angelica: Women, Writing and Fiction, 1660–1800*, New York: Columbia University Press.

Todd, Janet M. (ed.) (1983), *Jane Austen: New Perspectives, Women and Literature*, vol. 3 n.s., London and New York: Holmes and Meier.

Tompkins, J.M.S. (1969) [1932], *The Popular Novel in England 1770–1800*, London: Methuen.

Trinder, Peter (1984), *Mrs Hemans*, Cardiff: University of Wales Press.

Turner, Cheryl (1992), *Living by the Pen: Women Writers in the Eighteenth Century*, London and New York: Routledge.

Watkins, Donald P. (1993), *A Materialist Critique of English Romantic Drama*, Gainsville: University of Florida Press.

Yaeger, Patricia (1989), 'Towards a Female Sublime' in *Gender and Theory: Dialogues on Feminist Criticism*, Linda Kauffman (ed.), Oxford: Basil Blackwell, pp. 191–212.

6

A woman's business: women and writing, 1830–80

Lyn Pykett

The extreme activity of mind which showed itself in the later eighteenth century among women . . . was founded on the solid fact that women could make money by writing. Money dignifies what is frivolous if unpaid for. It might still be well to sneer at 'blue stockings with an itch for scribbling', but it could not be denied that they could put money in their purses. Thus, towards the end of the eighteenth century a change came about which, if I were rewriting history, I should . . . think of greater importance than the Crusades or the Wars of the Roses. The middle-class woman began to write. For if *Pride and Prejudice* matters, and *Middlemarch* and *Villette* and *Wuthering Heights* matter, then it matters . . . that women generally, and not merely the lonely aristocrat shut up in her country house among her folios and her flatterers, took to writing. (Virginia Woolf, 1992 [1929]: 84)

This chapter aims to explore some important aspects of that most significant of phenomena in Virginia Woolf's revisionary feminist cultural history: the advent of the professional woman writer, the woman who self-consciously thought of herself as a writer, and who wittingly (if sometimes very tentatively) entered a public domain of cultural production through publication for payment. I have elected to address the topic of 'women and writing' in the mid-nineteenth century, rather than what I take to be the more contentious subject of 'women's writing' because I want to focus on the literary work and works of women in relation to both the material conditions and ideological contexts of literary production at a specific moment in history rather than a trans-historical concept of female or feminine literature or writing. Indeed, I shall argue that it is precisely the idea of women's writing or 'female literature' – an historically specific construction of femininity or womanliness and of the 'proper' relations between women, the feminine and writing, which masquerades as a universal truth – which generated the complex network of permissions and constraints which nineteenth-century women had to negotiate both in producing literary texts and in the texts they produced.

Most students of women's writing in the Victorian period have by now registered their horror or incredulity at the stern advice offered to Charlotte Brontë, then a young literary aspirant, by the Poet Laureate Robert Southey: 'Literature cannot be the business of a woman's life, and it ought not to be' (Wise and Symington, 1933:

vol. I, 155). In the latter half of the twentieth century, historians of publishing and feminist literary historians have documented in detail what Virginia Woolf asserted so forcefully in *A Room of One's Own* (1929) that, on the contrary, literature was very much the business of the lives of a considerable number of middle-class women in the nineteenth century.[1] Indeed, the reader of nineteenth-century periodicals might easily form the impression that in Victorian England the domain of letters (or at least the low-lying terrain of the literary marketplace) was in danger of being overrun by an army of inkstained women. For example, in 1847 George Henry Lewes, the eclectic man of letters who was later to become the common-law husband of George Eliot (and hence consort to the queen of the high Victorian novel), bemoaned the fact that the profession of letters which ought properly to be 'a Macedonian phalanx, chosen, compact and irresistible', was unfortunately being invaded by 'women, children and ill-trained troops' (Lewes, 1847: 285). A few years later in his mockingly ironic and nervously condescending 'Gentle Hint to Writing Women', in which he claimed that his 'idea of a perfect woman is one who can write but won't', Lewes noted that the 'group of female authors is becoming every year more multitudinous and more successful' (Lewes, 1850: 189). The 'Lady novelists' were chiefly responsible for swelling the ranks of these multitudes of female authors, and the reasons for their increase were the subject of endless speculation. 'There are vast numbers of lady novelists', wrote W.R. Greg in 1859, 'for much the same reason that there are vast numbers of sempstresses. Thousands of women have nothing to do, and yet are under the necessity of doing something' (Greg, 1859: 144–67). In fact, rumours of female dominance were (as they usually are) greatly exaggerated, and most of the available figures suggest that about one in five writers in the nineteenth century were women (see Altick (1957); Cross (1985); Sutherland (1976) and (1995); and Lovell (1987)).

Nigel Cross, reviewing a range of evidence on literary participation rates in the nineteenth century in his fascinating if rather depressingly titled chapter on 'The Female Drudge' in *The Common Writer*, suggests that there were about 4,000 women writing in Britain in the nineteenth century, and that they constituted approximately 20 per cent of the entire literary corps. Taking only those women writers listed in the *Cambridge Bibliography of English Literature*, Cross notes that they were mainly engaged in what one might call imaginative literature: one-third of them were predominantly or exclusively novelists, half were children's writers and a mere 14 per cent were poets. Only 3 per cent of nineteenth-century women writers produced works of philosophy, history and economics (Cross, 1985: 167). The figures for male writers reveal a significantly different pattern of literary production: one-quarter were poets, 14 per cent novelists, 14 per cent critics and essayists, 11 per cent wrote children's fiction, 8 per cent wrote philosophy, and the rest produced historical, theological and other miscellaneous prose writings.

The career pattern of the woman writer also tended to be different from that of her male counterpart. There is general agreement that women began writing for a living at a different age and stage of life from men. However, the evidence (which mostly relates to fiction publishing) is complex and disputed. According to Nigel Cross (1985), Terry Lovell (1987) and Elaine Showalter (1978a), women novelists tended to begin publishing later than men and took longer to establish a critical reputation. John Sutherland (1995), on the other hand, argues that the average age at which men began publishing fiction was 36, whereas for women it was 33. Most commentators are agreed that women novelists enjoyed or endured a longer writing career than men; Sutherland gives 29.9 years as the average length of the male writer's career, and 35.2 years as the woman's (1995: 155). Middle-class women often took to writing – producing poetry, stories, or essays for the popular Annuals (illustrated miscellanies usually produced around Christmas time), the growing number of periodicals, and the lucrative market for novels – as one of the few means at their disposal of resolving a financial crisis in the family, usually caused by a sick, indolent, dead, or disappearing father or husband. Middle-class male writers, on the other hand, quite often combined a career as a writer of books with the pursuit of another profession (and source of income) in the law, medicine, the universities, or journalism. During the period covered by this chapter journalism (almost exclusively for weekly, fortnightly, monthly or quarterly journals rather than daily newspapers) was the only one of these careers open to women.

I would make two observations about these facts and figures. First, they suggest that the frequently heard lament of male (and some female) writers throughout the nineteenth century that the literary marketplace was being swamped by women, and that male writers were being outnumbered by women writers, was simply not true. Nevertheless, what that lament signified is extremely important; it is a point on which I have written at length elsewhere (Pykett, 1992), and to which I return below. Second, as the figures reproduced above suggest, and as numerous publishing and social histories confirm, women writers had a different relationship to writing, to the institutions of publishing, and to the literary marketplace from men. Women tended to be associated with a particular and limited range of genres and modes of writing, and even with particular publishers. They did not have access to the same social and professional networks as their male counterparts: women, as Cross puts it, 'wrote discreetly to each other courtesy of the General Post Office while their male colleagues enjoyed the privileged freedom of the Garrick Club' (Cross, 1985: 165; see also Swindells, 1986). While acknowledging the force of this latter generalization in conveying something of the differences and inequalities in the situation of the female and the male writer I would note that the conditions in which women wrote varied quite significantly depending on the precise point at which we touch down in the period under discussion. It is also worth pointing out that some women writers did succeed in gaining entry if not to the Garrick, then to the unofficial clubs of the writing profession.

Here I am thinking particularly of the role of women as regular contributors to the periodical press, of the involvement of a number of women in the running of both 'heavyweight' journals and more middlebrow literary magazines, and of the influence exerted by others in their work as reviewers (particularly of fiction) or as publishers' readers. In 1979 Walter Houghton identified about 14 per cent of writers in monthly and quarterly magazines as women, but acknowledged that this was probably a rather conservative figure given the practice of anonymous and pseudonymous authorship in the periodical press (1979: xvi). George Eliot, for example, who began her writing career as a translator of German theological works, was a reviewer for periodicals before she was a novelist, and in the early 1850s was assistant editor of John Chapman's radical *Westminster Review*. Harriet Martineau, a formidable Victorian woman of letters, who diffused much useful knowledge through her publication of such unappetizingly titled works as *Illustrations of Political Economy* (1832–4) and *Illustrations of Taxation* (1834), contributed regularly to a number of periodicals, including Dickens's *Household Words*, the *Westminster Review*, and the *Edinburgh Review*. She also wrote regularly for the *Daily News* between 1852 and 1856. Mary Howitt, who published some 110 works ranging from fiction for both children and adults, through works of popular history, to translations of the Swedish novelist Frederika Bremer, founded and edited (with her husband William Howitt) the shortlived *Howitt's Journal* which published some of Elizabeth Gaskell's early fiction (1847–8). Geraldine Jewsbury, the author of children's fiction as well as novels such as *Zoe* (1845) and *The Half Sisters* (1848), both of which shocked their first readers with their religious and sexual unorthodoxy, exerted a considerable influence on male and female writers and readers of fiction through her extensive work as a reviewer of fiction for the *Athenaeum* (1849–80), and as a reader of fiction for the publisher William Bentley from 1858 to 1880 (see Fahnestock, 1973). Margaret Oliphant exerted a similar influence at *Blackwood's*, where she produced a constant stream of reviews from 1860 until her death in 1897. Eliza Lynn Linton, another woman whose writing career extended well into the 1890s, was the first woman to be paid as a journalist on a daily paper, and was on the staff of the *Morning Chronicle* from 1848 to 1851. She was also a regular (anonymous) contributor to the influential *Saturday Review* (from 1866) where she generated a great deal of controversy with a series of essays, beginning with the notorious 'The Girl of the Period' (1868), attacking modern emancipated women. At the height of the boom in new magazines for fiction in the 1860s the best-selling novelists Mary Elizabeth Braddon and Ellen (Mrs Henry) Wood were both successful editors and/or owners: Braddon ran *Belgravia* (1866–76) and the *Belgravia Annual* (1867–76) for her partner (subsequently her husband) William Maxwell, and Wood bought the *Argosy* from Alexander Strahan in 1867 and ran it in direct competition with *Belgravia*.

Women, then, were very active in a range of professional writing activities in the Victorian period, even if less numerous and dominant than some contemporary commentators (both male and female) claimed. On the whole, however, the women writers of the nineteenth century have fared less well in the literary survival stakes than have their male contemporaries, for reasons which several literary historians have explored (see Lovell (1987); Cross (1985); Showalter (1978a); and Pykett (1992)). Women novelists have, hitherto, enjoyed a firmer footing in the literary canon than have female poets, although until feminist-inspired attempts to redraw the map of nineteenth-century fiction 'women's territory [was] usually depicted as a desert bounded by . . . the Brontë cliffs [and] the Eliot range' (Showalter, 1978a: vii). Women have figured hardly at all in the pantheon of essayists, historians and critics, although the efforts of feminist literary historians and their impact on publishing practices since the 1970s have succeeded in bringing some of this work back into view, however fleetingly.

The novel was indisputably the literary form most widely and successfully practised by women in the Victorian period. If one includes those writers who wrote for children, about 80 per cent of all professional women writers in the nineteenth century wrote fiction. John Sutherland's *Companion to Victorian Fiction* (which, of course, extends beyond the 1880 cut-off point for this chapter) contains entries for 878 novelists, of whom 312 are women. The average lifetime production of these women 'breaks down' (as no doubt many of them did under the strain of constant literary production) to 21 titles as compared with 17.6 titles for male novelists. In virtually every decade in the period covered by this chapter, and certainly from the late 1840s onwards, both male and female commentators on the literary scene regularly pronounced that (for good or ill) this was 'the age of female novelists' (Oliphant, 1855: 555). It is certainly true that there were a great number of women novelists publishing between 1830 and 1880. Several of them, and not always those that appear on today's school and university syllabuses, enjoyed notable critical success. Several succeeded in generating considerable sums of money for their publishers, if not always for themselves, by producing best sellers. However, it is also the case that, as Nigel Cross has noted, 'no sooner had fiction writing become the most profitable form of literary activity, in the 1840s, than men began to outnumber women in the fiction publisher's lists' (Cross, 1985: 186). Despite this statistic the novel continued to be perceived as a 'feminine' form throughout the period covered by this chapter.

Throughout its history there has been a close connection between the novel and women, and, more complexly, between fiction and a culturally constructed idea of the feminine. From its emergence in the eighteenth century (see Chapter 4), and throughout the period discussed in this chapter the form and subject matter of fiction, the means by which it was produced and distributed, and the social and critical debates it generated were complexly but inextricably interconnected with women's establishment of themselves as professional writers, with the growth of a female reading public, and with ideas (or a contestation of ideas) about femininity. As several recent literary historians have argued, the development of the novel in the eighteenth century not only permitted the entry of women into the writing profession, but it was also associated with a feminization of literature and culture; a process by which literature became increasingly defined 'as a special category supposedly outside the political arena, with an influence on the world as indirect as women's was supposed to be' (Spencer, 1986: xi). This feminization of literature was much commented upon by nineteenth-century critics. For example, Alfred Austin in 1869, surveying developments in fiction since the death of Walter Scott, described Anthony Trollope, that quintessential Victorian man of letters, as a 'feminine novelist, writing for women in a womanly spirit and from a woman's point of view' (Austin, 1869: 464).

Fiction continued to be perceived as a feminized form, and the fiction market as disproportionately engrossed by women (as both producers and consumers) throughout the nineteenth century. Numerous commentators on the literary scene argued that the new and rapidly developing form of the novel was the literary medium most suited to women's relatively limited education, and to the particular kind of training which women received for and by life. The views of this male reviewer in the *Edinburgh Review* in 1830 are typical:

> There are some things which women do better than men; and of these, perhaps, novel-writing is one. *Naturally* endowed with greater delicacy of taste and feeling, with a moral sense not blunted and debased by those contaminations to which men are exposed, leading lives rather of observation than of action, with leisure to attend to the minutiae of conduct, and more subtle developments of character, they are peculiarly qualified for the task of exhibiting faithfully and pleasingly the various phases of domestic life, and those varieties which chequer the surface of society. (Lister, 1830: 459, emphasis added)

The novel was deemed to be a form which was both produced by and reproduced a 'natural' but limited range of 'feminine' qualities. It was also seen as a form of literary production particularly compatible with the material conditions in which women lived and worked. In the nineteenth century, as Virginia Woolf observed when she was pressing the woman writer's claims to a room of her own, 'if a woman wrote, she would have to write in the common sitting-room' (1992: 86), where she was expected to be constantly available to meet the demands of social and domestic duties. Elizabeth Gaskell, for example, wrote in the dining room of her Manchester home, its four doors open so that she could supervise activities in the rest of the house. The prodigiously prolific novelist and essayist Margaret Oliphant recorded in her autobiography that she had never had a study, but had always written in 'the little 2nd drawing room where all the (feminine) life of the house goes on' (quoted in Showalter, 1978a: 85). However, this pattern was by no means universal in the latter half of the nineteenth century. Eliza Lynn Linton lived and worked alone in London both before and after her unsuccessful marriage. George Eliot lodged in the rather irregular household of the publisher John Chapman when she was assistant editor of the *Westminster Review*, and subsequently set up home with George Henry Lewes, who was inconveniently married to someone else. Partly as a result of the social ostracism resulting from this illicit liaison George Eliot, rather unusually, enjoyed something of the sequestered writing conditions of the established male novelist.

As Virginia Woolf intimated in *A Room of One's Own*, the common sitting-room was not simply the *physical location* in which much women's writing occurred in the nineteenth century, but it was also, so to speak, an *intellectual formation*. It was, by common consent, what *made women into novelists* (rather than poets or historians); it made women into novelists of a particular kind, and was thus also instrumental in shaping the dominant forms and preoccupations of nineteenth-century fiction:

> all the literary training that a woman had in the early nineteenth century was training in the observation of character, in the analysis of emotion. Her sensibility had been educated for centuries by the influences of the common sitting-room. People's feelings were impressed upon her; personal relations were always before her eyes. Therefore, when the middle-class woman took to writing, she *naturally* wrote novels. (1992: 87, emphasis added)

For Woolf, writing in the early twentieth century, there may have been a certain inevitability about the female writer's gravitation towards the novel form, but it was anything but 'natural'; women's involvement in the production of novels was over-determined by their cultural conditioning and economic position. However, as my earlier quotation from the *Edinburgh Review* indicates, contemporary commentators on women's penchant for fiction writing tended to fudge the distinction between 'culture' and 'nature'. George Henry Lewes, who often sought to advise women writers on how they might best use what he saw as their particular nature and experience, is a case in point:

> Woman by her greater affectionateness, her greater range and depth of emotional experience, is well fitted to give expression to the emotional facts of life, and demands a place in literature corresponding with that which she occupies in society. . . . The domestic experience which forms the bulk of woman's knowledge finds an appropriate form in novels; while the very nature of fiction calls for that predominance of Sentiment which we have already attributed to the feminine mind. Love is the staple of fiction, for it 'forms the story of a woman's life.' The joys and sorrows of affection, the incidents of domestic life, assume typical forms in the novel. Hence we may be prepared to find women succeeding better in *finesse* of detail, in pathos and sentiment, while men generally succeed better in the construction of plots and the delineation of character. (1852: 133)

Here, Lewes slips almost imperceptibly from representing 'woman' as *naturally* endowed with 'greater affectionateness' than men, to attributing her greater emotional range and depth to the particular circumstances of women's 'domestic experience'. Lewes's enumeration, even celebration, of the particular qualities of 'female literature' is an example of the nineteenth-century critical double standard which judged writing by women according to different criteria from those applied to writing in general (i.e. by men). It also provides us with a classic example of one of the many double binds which the woman writer in the nineteenth century had to negotiate: women are assigned to a special but ultimately circumscribed realm of the emotions and an aesthetic of the detail; plot, character, abstraction, reflection and matters of great public import, Lewes and others intimated, are best left to male writers (or 'masculine writing'). As Christiane Rochefort has put it, 'A man's book is a book. A woman's book is a woman's book' (1981: 183).

By what means did the fiction of the woman writer find its way from the common sitting-room in which it was written to the common sitting-room or, increasingly, from the late 1840s, the railway carriage, in which it was read? At the beginning of this period the standard form of publication for middle-class fiction was the expensive three-volume or 'three-decker'-format which sold at half a guinea per volume (or 31s. 6d. per novel). Such pricing obviously placed the purchase of novels beyond the reach of all but the affluent, and by 1830 the practice of book borrowing (or hiring), which had developed in the second half of the eighteenth century, had become firmly established. During the early Victorian years the production and distribution of fiction remained closely connected to the prevalence of the borrowing habit and the dominance of the circulating libraries: small print runs of a large number of titles and high unit costs were the norm (see Sutherland (1976); Lovell (1987); and Cross (1985)). From the 1840s one library dominated the field: Mudie's Select Library, established in 1842 by the bookseller and stationer Charles Edward Mudie (see Griest, 1970). Mudie's chief competitor was W.H. Smith and Son, who opened their first railway bookstall in 1848, went on to build up a monopoly in this sector of the market, and began operating a circulating library from the bookstalls in 1860. The circulating libraries, and the men who ran them, exerted extraordinary commercial and financial power on publishers and authors. As the major purchasers of new fiction they were also able to exercise both direct and indirect aesthetic policing and censorship: authors and publishers were acutely aware that their novels had to meet with the approval of Mr Mudie or Mr Smith if they were to succeed commercially. Towards the end of the period covered by this chapter, as novelists sought to extend the scope of fiction and to make greater claims for the novel as an art form, they began to come into increasing conflict with the screening policies of the libraries and the supposedly delicate tastes of the 'young girls and widows of sedentary habits' (Moore, 1976: 28) who used them.

Despite the dominance of the three-decker and the circulating libraries, from the 1830s onwards fiction was produced and distributed in an increasing range of formats, and at increasingly accessible prices. This was, above all, the great age of the serialized novel. After Dickens's enormous success with *Pickwick Papers* (1836–7) numerous mid-Victorian novels were published serially in twelve or twenty monthly parts, at one shilling for each 32-page number. Dickens was also associated with the beginning of the serialization of novels in magazines in the 1830s, as the first editor of the successful illustrated monthly, *Bentley's Miscellany* (1837). The shilling monthly magazine became the first place of publication for more and more fiction following the successful launch of *Macmillan's Magazine* in 1859 and the *Cornhill* in 1860, whose first issue (under Thackeray's editorship) sold 110,000 copies. As I indicated earlier several of the magazines which were set up in the 1860s were edited and sometimes even owned by women. Women were also active contributors to the penny and sixpenny weekly magazines which burgeoned in the 1850s and 1860s. During this period more and more readers were also introduced to novel-buying through cheap one-volume reprints. The six-shilling Standard Novel was pioneered by Henry Colburn and Richard Bentley during their brief period of partnership at the beginning of the 1830s. In 1846 at the height of the vogue for the 'domestic novel' the Belfast publisher Simms and McIntyre began the 'Parlour Novelist' series with the publication of fourteen popular one-volume novels at two shillings each. A year later this became the 'Parlour Library', offering new and reprinted one-volume novels at one shilling or one shilling and sixpence depending on the binding, and in 1848 Routledge launched its one-shilling reprint series, the 'Railway Library'.

The novel was, in short, a very popular and saleable commodity in the mid-Victorian period. It was – to use the current jargon – a major part of the Victorian entertainment industry. The reasons for the growth in the novel-reading habit have been well documented: it was one of the results of commercial and manufacturing growth (particularly in overseas markets), which produced an expanded and largely town-dwelling middle class with surplus income, aspirations towards education and genteel accomplishments, and an increased leisure time in which to pursue them (especially in the case of women and young people). This increased demand for new titles, fed by the proliferation of outlets for fiction to which I have referred, fostered the careers of a number of women writers, some of whom had serious literary aspirations, and others who were content (or forced by circumstances) to produce potboilers.

What kinds of fiction did Victorian women writers produce? At the beginning of the period women writers made a notable contribution to the 'silver-fork' novel, or novel of fashionable high life, which flourished from the mid-1820s to the mid-1840s. The genre was derided as a *'mind-and-millinery* species' of fiction by George Eliot in an essay in which she prepared the ground for her own realistic regional novels by distancing herself from 'Silly Novels by Lady Novelists', and from their female authors who were dismissed as meretricious propagators of 'vacillating syntax and improbable incident':

> Belgravia and 'baronial halls' are their primary truths, and they have no idea of feeling interest in any man who is not at least a great landed proprietor, if not a prime minister. . . . [T]hey write in elegant boudoirs, with violet-coloured ink and a ruby pen . . . and their intellect seems to have the peculiar impartiality of reproducing both what they *have* seen and heard, and what they have *not* seen and heard, with equal unfaithfulness. (1992: 298)

'Silver-fork' fiction traded on the middle-class reader's fascination with the fashions and passions of Regency high life. Bulwer Lytton's *Pelham* (1828) was, perhaps, the single most successful novel in this genre, but the 'undisputed leader' (Sutherland, 1988: 254) of the silver-fork novel was Mrs Gore, one of the most prolific novelists of the nineteenth century, who produced about seventy novels between 1824 and 1862. Praised by her contemporaries as a well-bred and amusing woman of the world who 'excels in the portraiture of the upper section of the middle class, just at that point of contact with the aristocracy' (R.H. Horne quoted in Sutherland, 1988: 254), Catherine Gore produced a series of novels in the 1830s dealing with social mobility, and the anxieties created by the changing social climate after the first Reform Bill. In the 1840s and 1850s Gore's fiction dwelt increasingly on money and social class, and the precariousness of both (issues which were also prominent in the sensation fiction of the 1860s). Today Gore is perhaps best known through Thackeray's parody of her work in 'Lords and Liveries' in his *Punch's Prize Novelists* (1847), but at her best – in novels such as *Mrs Armytage, Or Female Domination* (1836), *Cecil, Or the Adventures of a Coxcomb* (1841), or *The Banker's Wife, Or Court and City* (1843) – she writes as racily, and observes contemporary society as sharply as Thackeray himself in his own fashionable fiction. Like Thackeray's *Vanity Fair*, Gore's novels were designed to unmask the hypocrisy of the fashionable world and to expose social pretension, the follies of social climbing, and the iniquities of the marriage market.

If the silver-fork novel represented the doings of 'Society', that is to say a largely metropolitan world of the aristocracy and upper middle classes, another 'women's genre' of the early decades of this period represented a modern urban, industrial society of workers and bosses (masters and men). From the late 1830s a fiction of social protest developed which named, defined, and addressed the problems of the urban industrial age, and intervened in contemporary debates about what constituted a society and about the nature of the interrelationships and mutual obligations of the different strata of society. Social protest fiction, as Joseph Kestner has observed, was 'a literary form much practiced by women . . . [who] identified with the disenfranchised working classes and sought to influence legislative reform through social protest narratives that depicted conditions requiring improvement' (Kestner, 1985: 3). At least since the early eighteenth century, the cultural sphere has been an important area of intervention for women. In the early Victorian period an interventionist form of cultural production was one way in which unenfranchised women were able to participate in public debates on social and political issues, and engage in the political reform process. Many of the social problem novels by women were based on detailed research in Parliamentary Blue Books and other social reports, and were associated with specific campaigns to improve the conditions of urban life or reform the factory system. The reforming impulse of much of this fiction was religious; women of an evangelical persuasion, and female members of dissenting churches (particularly the Unitarian movement) were particularly active as writers of this strongly didactic genre.

Many of these novels did not survive the specific social conditions and campaigns in which they were produced. Few now read Frances Elizabeth Trollope's *Michael Armstrong, the Factory Boy* (1840), a shocking novel on the exploitation of child labour, and, in effect, a political tract in favour of the Ten Hours Bill for which Lord Ashley and other social reformers were campaigning at the time when it was written. Another factory novel, Charlotte Elizabeth Tonna's *Helen Fleetwood Tale Of The Factories* (1841) – which was widely discussed in its own day, but dismissed by a more recent critic as having 'no merit whatever beyond its good intentions' (Colby, 1974: 175) – opposed the factory system from a Christian perspective which viewed industrialism as inherently corrupting and destructive.

Among the earliest examples of this industrial social-problem fiction were the *Illustrations of Political Economy*, a series of exemplary social fables written by the Unitarian writer Harriet Martineau, and published in monthly parts between 1832 and 1834. Like many of the so-called 'Condition of England' novels of the 1840s and 1850s (by men as well as women), Martineau's short novel, *A Manchester Strike* (the ninth of her *Illustrations of Political Economy*), deals with a workers' campaign against their masters, including a strike, to force an improvement in wages. This novel's mixing of different narrative conventions and its narrative and ideological contradictions are typical of its genre. On the one hand the tale is a deterministic narrative designed to illustrate the inexorable laws of political economy: that strikes cannot permanently raise the level of wages because these are determined by market forces outside the control of either masters or men. The story of the strike is thus a story whose ending is already written: it is doomed to failure. However, as in so many other social-protest novels of the thirties, forties and fifties, other narratives begin to emerge from the gaps in this deterministic narrative. One of these emergent narratives is a narrative of failed communications which is articulated in the narrator's rhetorical interventions: 'when will masters and men work cheerfully together for their common good, respect instead of proscribing each other, and be equally proud to have such men as Wentworth [a sympathetic capitalist] and William Allen [the strike leader] of their membership?' (Martineau, 1834: 133). In another of these emergent narratives the suffering worker-victim has a potentially heroic role as agent.

Both of these emergent narratives and also their problematic relationship with the deterministic narrative of political economy were later reworked by Elizabeth Gaskell in *Mary Barton* (1848) and *North and South* (1854–5). Published in the year of revolutions in Europe and haunted by the spectre of Chartism in Britain, *Mary Barton* focuses minutely and graphically on the fluctuating conditions of working-class life in good economic times and bad, and on the gulf between the lives of the masters and the men (underlined by repeated reference to the parable of Dives and Lazarus). *North and South* is also a novel of sharp contrasts and social divisions, but whereas in *Mary Barton* the main actors are the working-class characters (John Barton, the mill worker and later trade union activist and Chartist, his sempstress daughter, Mary, and her noble working-class lover, Jem), in the later novel the focus of attention and narrative agency have shifted back to the gentry and the masters (Margaret Hale, the genteel clergyman's daughter who has been precipitately transplanted to the industrial North, and John Thornton, the self-made and self-educated mill-owner, whose cross-class marriage is used, as is often the case in the fiction of this period, to figure social reconciliation). *North and South* was conceived, in part, as an answer to the criticism that the earlier novel, in its attempt to portray 'the romance in the lives of some of those who elbowed me daily in the busy streets' (Author's Preface to *Mary Barton*), had taken sides with the workers and failed to understand the masters' position. However, although there is indeed a shift in emphasis between the two novels, there is also a considerable continuity in their preoccupations and in their modes of representation. Despite their different emphases both novels represent the working class in similar ways; both, by turns, demonize, and infantilize the men or hands. Discontented or dissident working men and the working class in its mass or mob form are persistently represented as rebellious children, beasts of prey, or monsters. Examples of this can be found in the riot scene in Chapter 22 of *North and South* ('A Blow and its Consequences'), in which Thornton (urged on by Margaret to face his striking workers 'like a man') confronts a howling mob, 'gaunt as wolves, and mad for prey', and in this narratorial gloss from Chapter 15 of *Mary Barton*:

> The actions of the uneducated seem to me typified in those of Frankenstein, that monster of many human qualities ungifted with a soul, a knowledge of the difference between good and evil.
>
> The people rise up to life; they irritate us, they terrify us, and we become their enemies. Then in the sorrowful moment of our triumphant power, their eyes gaze on with a mute reproach. Why have we made them what they are; a powerful monster, yet without the inner means of peace and happiness?

The narratorial rhetoric and the plot of each of these novels ultimately work towards the taming and domestication or feminization of the Frankenstein monster of the working class. Both novels are 'fictions of resolution' (David, 1981) in which melodramatic and romance plots and a Christian rhetoric of reconciliation are used to resolve structural and political problems in the 'public sphere' by means of the domestic and emotional values of the 'private sphere'. Gaskell's rhetoric of resolution is articulated through the mediating role of her heroines, whose 'womanly nature' and domestic experience make them effective agents in a familial model of social reform in which masters and men (and Gaskell's readers) are required to recognize their common brotherhood. The rhetoric of reconciliation is also articulated through a self-consciously feminine narrative mode of address, which focuses minutely on the details of domestic interiors and elevates the interiority of the feelings over political economy, of whose complexities the narrator disarmingly denies all knowledge.

Gaskell's 'industrial novels' developed further the focus of the earlier women writers of social narratives on the daily domestic life of the working-class family. Ordinary domestic life, usually of the middle classes, was the subject of the other dominant genre of the early decades of the Victorian period – the domestic novel, the novel of closely observed, ordinary, everyday life. Harriet Martineau's *Deerbrook* (1839) is perhaps the prototypical domestic novel of this period. Set in the 'rather pretty' village of Deerbrook, Martineau's novel tells the tale of two sisters, who are, like so many of the female protagonists of Victorian fiction by women, orphans.[2] *Deerbrook* focuses on the problematic marriage of one, and the convoluted progress towards marriage of the other. The narrative form and the preoccupations of this chronicle of the commonplace trials and tribulations of living, loving, working and struggling in a small, gossip-ridden, provincial community are reworked by numerous later writers, including Elizabeth Gaskell in *Cranford* (1851–3) and *Wives and Daughters* (1865), Margaret Oliphant in her seven-volume 'Chronicles of Carlingford' (beginning with *Salem Chapel* in 1863) and most notably in George Eliot's closely observed studies of the 'stealthy convergence of human lots' in *Adam Bede* (1859), *The Mill on the Floss* (1860) and *Middlemarch* (1871–2).

The domestic novel, as Charlotte Brontë intimated in her Preface to *Shirley* (1849), was 'real, cool, and solid . . . unromantic as Monday morning'. Its main topics, according to contemporary male critics such as Alfred Austin, were 'the sentimental love of youths and maidens, of coy widows and clumsy middle-aged men, beginning in flirtation and ending in marriage . . . pretty, pious, half-comical domestic love – love within the bounds of social law' (Austin, 1869: 467); or, as a twentieth-century literary historian has put it, 'its subjects [were] . . . courtship, marriage, children, earning a living, adjusting to reality, learning to conform to the conventions of established society and to live within it tranquilly, if not always happily' (Colby, 1974: 4).

In fact, the domestic was less a genre than a mode of representation. By the 1840s 'domestic realism', or the minute observation of the surfaces of ordinary life, had become, perhaps, the dominant mode of representation in fiction by both men and women. The Victorian novelists themselves were among the first to draw attention to this aspect of domestic fiction, and to compare their own methods and *mis en scène* with those of realist genre painting. Perhaps the most famous example of this is found in Chapter 17 of *Adam Bede* ('In which the Story Pauses a Little'). Here George Eliot's narrator claims to aspire 'to give no more than a faithful account of men and things as they have mirrored themselves in my mind', and celebrates the 'rare, precious quality of truthfulness . . . [found] in many Dutch paintings, which lofty-minded people despise':

> I find a delicious source of sympathy in these faithful pictures of a monotonous homely existence . . . I turn without shrinking from cloud-borne angels, from prophets, sibyls, and heroic warriors, to an old woman bending over her flower-pot, or eating her solitary dinner . . .

Reviewing the rise of realism from a mid-century perspective, Robert Buchanan saw it as inextricably connected to the rise of the female novelist. Unlike Virginia Woolf, Buchanan presents an entirely unironic view of the intellectual (or, more accurately, aesthetic and affective) formation produced in and by the common sitting-room:

> Realism has served at least one admirable purpose – that of bringing women prominently before the public as book writers. The lady-novelists are the most truthful of all aesthetic photographers. . . . Disciplined in a school of suffering, closely observant of detail, and painfully dependent on the caprice of the male sex, they essay to paint in works of art the everyday emotions of commonplace or unimaginative women, and the domestic experience of sensible daughters, wives and mothers. (Buchanan, 1862: 134–5)

The domestic was not simply a matter of the subjects and settings of fiction, nor merely of its representational mode. As the work of George Eliot so graphically demonstrates, domestic realism was also an ethos or ideology; it was bourgeois and anti-romantic, it *celebrated* (rather than merely recorded) the domestic and familial, and it reinforced the Christian and 'feminine' 'imperatives of duty, submission of the individual will, self-sacrifice, and endurance', and 'compromise co-operation and common sense' (Colby, 1974: 212). Women and, more generally, a particular construction of the feminine, occupied a role of central importance in the ethos of domestic fiction, whatever the sex of the author. However, as Inga-Stina Ewbank noted in her proto-feminist study of the Brontës, in fiction written by women 'the central preoccupation' was,

> with the woman as an influence on others within her domestic and social circle. It was in this preoccupation that the typical woman novelist of the 1840s found her proper sphere: in using the novel to demonstrate (by assumption rather than exploration of standards of womanliness) *woman's* proper sphere. (1966: 41)

Since the mid-1960s Victorian ideas of womanliness, and the corpus of the domestic novel (and of its revisionary forms) have all been subjected to intense scrutiny from a variety of perspectives by feminist critics and literary historians. The fiction of Emily and Charlotte Brontë has been a particular focus of attention. Ewbank's study was, perhaps, the first to attempt to locate the fiction of the Brontës in the context of contemporary ideas about the feminine and about women's familial and social roles, and the ways in which these ideas shaped women's writing. Ewbank demonstrated how the Brontës were constrained by the ideology of 'woman's proper sphere' and, at the same time, empowered by their resistance of the restrictions of the dominant definitions of womanliness and women's writing. The novels of all three Brontë sisters reproduced but also revised and/or subverted the codes of domestic fiction.

As I have suggested elsewhere (Pykett, 1989: 71–85) some of the apparent oddities of Emily Brontë's *Wuthering Heights* (1847) – which led F.R. Leavis to exclude it from his own 'great tradition' of the novel in 1948 – look decidedly less odd (though no less disturbing) when it is relocated in the context of women's fictional practice and the gendered discourse of and about fiction in the early nineteenth century. *Wuthering Heights* is a heady brew of competing fictional traditions and genres: it mixes legend, folk tale and ballad, with the Romantic tale of evil possession and a Romantic view of childhood and of Nature. Most significantly, for my purposes, it combines the Domestic with the Gothic in a vivid dramatization of the discontents of civilization and a fierce critique of genteel femininity. In *Wuthering Heights* the Domestic is frequently the site of the Gothic: the home is a place of imprisonment rather than shelter, and is the locus of terror and the uncanny. The bleak and stormy moorland, the inhospitable Heights, the pampered enclosure of Thrushcross Grange under the Lintons, Heathcliff the hero-villain who combines the roles of demonic Gothic villain and Romantic outcast/rebel, all variously signify pre- or anti social natural energies and the restrictions of the social/domestic. The repressions and oppression involved in learning to be, and then living as a woman are dramatized in the history (and after-history) of Cathy, and in the first two phases of the history of her daughter Catherine. In the case of Cathy, the wild rebellious child of nature, femininity is represented as a state into which she falls (almost literally) when she is confined to a sofa at Thrushcross Grange following an injury to her foot incurred on a youthful escapade with her double, Heathcliff. Cathy is both seduced and betrayed (and ultimately stifled to death) by the version of genteel femininity into which she is educated at this period. Catherine's history reverses her mother's, since she falls from genteel femininity at the Grange into a wild, rebellious, slatternly incarceration at the Heights. In fact, Catherine's early life is no less a form of imprisonment than is her period under Heathcliff's tyrannical rule at the Heights. She merely exchanges a 'soft' form of imprisonment, in which her life is confined to the limits of her father's estate and his conventional notions of appropriate feminine behaviour, for a harsher regime in which she unlearns her womanly role and remakes herself through her spirited resistance to Heathcliff's oppressive masculinity. The refashioned Catherine turns out to be a prototypical Victorian heroine, who saves her man (her cousin Hareton Earnshaw) by reclaiming him from a brutalized masculinity, and by educating and civilizing and joining with him in a companionate marriage of equals. It was a pattern that was repeated in the novels of countless women writers of the nineteenth century (and no doubt, occasionally, in life). What makes Brontë's novel distinctive and disturbing is its insistence on the continuing presence of Heathcliff and Cathy whose wandering spirits serve to remind us of what has been lost and gained in the movement to the idealized version of the modern family which her novel charts.

Charlotte Brontë's *Jane Eyre* (1847) and *Villette* (1853) also combine Domestic and Gothic elements in what Gilbert and Gubar describe as their 'distinctively female story of enclosure and escape' (1979: 314). Haunted rooms in gentry houses or respectable Belgian schools, the English country house as Bluebeard's castle complete with a madwoman in the attic are among the Gothic effects employed as Charlotte Brontë psychologizes, moralizes, domesticates and modernizes Gothic. *Jane Eyre* and *Villette* are also *bildungsromane*, or novels of development which chart their heroines' differing paths from isolated and alienated childhood (in the case of Jane Eyre) or youth (Lucy Snowe) to a more socially integrated and purposive maturity: marriage and motherhood in Jane Eyre's case, an independent life as the owner of a flourishing school for Lucy Snowe, the heroine of *Villette*. Like most of Charlotte Brontë's heroines (indeed like many other heroines of nineteenth-century novels) Jane and Lucy are orphans. This device allows Brontë to emphasize the economic and emotional vulnerability that derives from women's status as 'relative creatures' (i.e. legally, economically and experientially defined through their familial relations as daughters, wives and mothers). Paradoxically, orphanhood is an opportunity as well as a problem: it is the means of representing female characters who are freed from the full rigours of normative feminine social conditioning and of projecting them into situations in which they are able to demonstrate their independence, spirit and resourcefulness. Brontë uses her orphaned first-person narrators, Jane Eyre and Lucy Snowe, to offer a defamiliarizing perspective on the confinements of ordinary domestic life and on a range of socially sanctioned versions of femininity. The first person narrative voice of these isolated, alienated women is also one of the means by which Brontë focuses on feminine interiority – on the social and emotional aspirations, ambitions, conflicts and frustrations of her female protagonists – which is, perhaps, the main subject of these novels.

Yet another perspective on the restrictions of the feminine and the domestic – this time in realist mode – is offered in George Eliot's *The Mill on the Floss* (1860) and *Middlemarch* (1871–2). Like Cathy Earnshaw and Jane Eyre, Eliot's heroine Maggie Tulliver is formed and deformed by that conventional femininity against which she rebels. Maggie has romantic (even Romantic) longings: she yearns for freedom, learning, music, poetry. Disenchanted with books in which 'the blond-haired women carry away all the happiness', Maggie wants stories 'where the dark woman triumphs' (V, ch. 4). However, the story that George Eliot creates for her is one in which the triumph of the blonde woman (Maggie's cousin Lucy) is repeated, and Maggie is defeated by the 'oppressive narrowness' of both the feminine ideal and 'A Variation of Protestantism unknown to Bossuet' (IV, ch. 1). Torn by the conflicting 'temptations' of renunciation and submission on the one hand, and giving herself up to dreams of romantic fulfilment on the other, Maggie is ultimately destroyed by her inability to adapt to a world in which 'since the days of Hecuba and of Hector' the women have stood 'inside the gates . . . watching the world's combat from afar, filling their long empty days with memories and fear; outside the men, in fierce struggle with things divine and human' (V, ch. 2). It is one of the merits of George Eliot's novel that she offers a deeply felt critique of the consequences of this gendered division of labour for both men and women.

Dorothea Brooke, the heroine of *Middlemarch* also wants to be a combatant, but George Eliot's narrative requires her to learn that they also serve who only stand and wait. Dorothea's history foregrounds the question 'what can a woman do?', rather than Freud's later question, 'What does a woman want?', but in the end, like the novels of Charlotte Brontë, it fuses the two, attempting to reconcile ambition and desire, action and fantasy. Dorothea is an idealist, who yearns for 'some lofty conception of the world which might frankly include the parish of Tipton and her own rule of conduct there' (I, ch. 1). Eliot's plot requires Dorothea to adjust her lofty conception to the stark realities of a woman's life in the parish of Tipton in the early nineteenth century. Whereas Maggie Tulliver's (like Hardy's Jude the Obscure's) is a tragedy of unfulfilled aims in which she is destroyed by her inability to perform this adaptation, Dorothea is redeemed by becoming increasingly practised in the 'feminine' values of sympathy and self-submission (also well-illustrated in Mary Garth and Mrs Bulstrode), and, like the Wordsworthian poet, spreading relationship and love. In *Middlemarch* George Eliot moves beyond the circumscribed territory of 'female literature' (as defined by George Henry Lewes). She does so in two ways: first by attempting a social panorama (or 'natural history') of provincial life which engages with the important intellectual and political issues of its day and also investigates the nature of the process of history; second, by offering that 'difference of view' which Virginia Woolf found in writing by women:

> It is probable . . . that in both life and art the values of a woman are not the values of a man. Thus, when a woman comes to write a novel, she will find that she is perpetually wishing to alter the established values – to make serious what appears insignificant to a man, and trivial what to him is important. And for that she will be criticized; for a critic of the opposite sex will be genuinely puzzled and surprised by an attempt to alter the current scale of values, and will see in it not merely a difference of view, but a view that is weak, or trivial, or sentimental, because it is different from his own. (1966–7: II, 146)

In their realism and didacticism, their advocacy of self-abnegation, altruism and the doctrine of sympathy Eliot's novels appropriated those values which Victorian society increasingly defined as womanly and attributed to women, but they also invested those concepts and values with full ethical force, and insisted on their centrality and on the necessity that they should become diffused throughout society. It was a high risk strategy, and Eliot's fiction does not always avoid simply reproducing the dominant view of the 'incalculably diffusive' (*Middlemarch*, Finale) effects of indirect feminine influence in the domestic sphere.

As Judith Lowder Newton has argued, George Eliot's novels, like those of the Brontë sisters, 'both support and resist ideologies which have tied middle-class women to the relative powerlessness of their lot and which have prevented them from having a true knowledge of their situation' (1985: 11). The fiction of Eliot and the Brontës has also been used by Sandra Gilbert and Susan Gubar to illustrate the tortuous complexities of the woman writer's ambivalent relationship to dominant (i.e. patriarchal) values and the dominant (i.e. masculine) tradition of literature. In *The Madwoman in the Attic* (1979) Gilbert and Gubar argue that writing by women in the nineteenth century was produced by an 'anxiety of influence' in relation to the dominant male tradition. Women writers are depicted as endlessly revising the writings of their literary fore*fathers*: *Wuthering Heights*, for example, is said to be haunted by 'Milton's bogey' as it rewrites *Paradise Lost*, and *Jane Eyre* rewrites Bunyan's *Pilgrim's Progress* with a female hero. In the course of revising the dominant tradition, Gilbert and Gubar suggest, women writers also subverted it by the force of their covert resistance or their concealed or unconscious anger. In Gilbert and Gubar's influential account the most important text of women's writing is its subtext. Certainly they offer a fascinating account of the way in which women's anger about their lot and their critique of social injustice is displaced and figured in their plotting and modes of representation. In their account of Bertha Rochester, the madwoman in the attic of Thornfield Hall, as Jane Eyre's 'truest and darkest double' (1979: 360), who actually does what Jane wants to do, they remind us, as does so much feminist criticism of the last thirty years, that women writers often work by indirection. However, it is equally important that, in our preoccupation with strategies of indirection, we do not lose sight of the courage of the directness of some of the writing by women in the nineteenth century. Charlotte Brontë did not simply engage in a covert critique which submerges a subversive anger, she actually gave her heroine a proto-feminist speech to address to the reader:

> Women are supposed to be very calm generally: but women feel just as men feel; they need exercise for their faculties, and a field for their efforts as much as their brothers do; they suffer from too rigid a restraint, too absolute a stagnation, precisely as men would suffer; and it is narrow-minded in their more privileged fellow-creatures to say that they ought to confine themselves to making puddings and knitting stockings. . . . It is thoughtless to condemn them, or laugh at them, if they seek to do more or learn more than custom has pronounced necessary for their sex. (*Jane Eyre* I, ch. 12)

Over twenty years later the narrator of *Middlemarch* offered a similarly direct and fierce indictment of her society's treatment of women in the Finale:

> Certainly those determining acts of her [Dorothea's] life were not ideally beautiful. They were the mixed result of young and noble impulse struggling under prosaic conditions. Among the many remarks passed on her mistakes, it was never said in the neighbourhood of Middlemarch that such mistakes could not have happened if the society into which she was born had not smiled on propositions of marriage from a sickly man to a girl less than half his own age – on modes of education which make a woman's knowledge another name for motley ignorance – on rules of conduct which are in flat contradiction with its own loudly asserted beliefs. While this is the social air which we breathe, there will be collisions such as those in Dorothea's life, where great feelings will take the aspect of error, and great faith the aspect of illusion.

Both authors paid for such directness with the ferocity of the criticism which it attracted from reviewers. Charlotte Brontë had to cope with personal attacks, such as Matthew Arnold's claim (he was writing of *Villette*) that 'her mind contained nothing but hunger, rebellion and rage' (Russell, 1896: I, 34). George Eliot's (proto-) feminist critique was so roundly condemned by reviewers of the first edition of *Middlemarch* that it was dropped from subsequent editions.

If critics such as Gilbert and Gubar have represented mid-Victorian women writers' revisions of domestic fiction as a form of resistance to, or a psycho-social symptom of, a male-dominated culture, some materialist-feminist critics have been concerned to examine the ideological work performed by women's writing *within* that male-dominated culture. Both Judith Lowder Newton (quoted above) and Nancy Armstrong (1987), for example, examine the domestic novel as an instrument of female power, the means by which women became complicit in their own subjection and played a central role in securing bourgeois hegemony in the mid-nineteenth century. In Armstrong's account (which is perhaps rather tendentious, and should be read sceptically) the domestic novel's emphasis on love and marriage, on the emotional and psychological (in short, on desire and subjectivity), played a crucial part in a cultural move by which the political was relegated to the margins. In the domestic novel from the 1840s onwards, Armstrong has argued, desire, 'instead of constituting a form of resistance, . . . became a strategy for dealing with the problem posed by the machine, the problem of political resistance' (Armstrong, 1987: 163).

The dominance of the domestic novel in realist mode was challenged in the 1860s by the sensation phenomenon. From the early 1860s reviewers of fiction began to note (or, in most cases, fulminate against) the advent of what they described as an entirely new genre of fiction, the sensation novel. Wilkie Collins is perhaps the best-known of the sensation novelists, at least to modern readers, but in the 1860s sensationalism was most closely associated with women writers and readers. Mary Elizabeth Braddon's *Lady Audley's Secret* (1862) and Ellen Wood's *East Lynne* (1861) were two of the most successful of the sensation novels (indeed they were two of the best-selling novels of the entire nineteenth century). Rhoda Broughton and 'Ouida' (Mary Louise de la Ramée) were also included among the ranks of the sensationalists whose novels were:

> devoted to Harrowing the Mind, making the Flesh Creep . . . Giving Shocks to the Nervous System, Destroying Conventional Moralities, and generally Unfitting the Public for the Prosaic Avocations of Life. (quoted in Tillotson, 1969: xiii)

Otherwise described as crime novels, 'fast' novels, bigamy novels or novels of adultery, sensation novels were, above all, novels of modern life:

> Proximity is, indeed, one great element of sensation. It is necessary to be near a mine to be blown up by its explosion; and a tale which aims at electrifying the nerves of the reader is never thoroughly effective unless the scene be laid in our own days and among the people we are in the habit of meeting. (quoted in Hughes, 1980: 18)

These exciting and disturbing novels of modern life were remarkable for their devious and dangerous villains, or more usually villainess/heroines, and for their extraordinarily complicated plots usually involving suspense, concealment, disguise and duplicity, fraud, forgery (often of a will or occasionally of a marriage certificate), deception, illegal imprisonment (usually of a young woman), blackmail, bigamy, and even murder or attempted murder. As far as their form was concerned sensation novels were something of a generic hybrid, mixing realism and melodrama, the journalistic with the fantastic, and the domestic with the exotic.

Contemporary commentators saw the sensation novel as displacing the domestic novel from its position of dominance in the literary marketplace, and they habitually defined the new genre against the conventions of domestic fiction. Margaret Oliphant, who was by no means an advocate of the sensation novel, nevertheless saw it as offering some of those narrative satisfactions which the domestic novel did not (or possibly could not) provide:

> it is a fact that the well-known old stories of readers sitting up all night over a novel had begun to grow faint in the public recollection. Domestic histories, however virtuous and charming, do not often attain that result – nor, indeed, would an occurrence so irregular and destructive of all domestic proprieties be at all a fitting homage to the virtuous chronicles which have lately furnished the larger part of our light literature. (Oliphant, 1862: 565)

In fact, as some of my comments above might indicate, the sensation novel was also domestic. Sensation novels were, as Tania Modleski has observed of Gothic novels, ' "domestic" novels too, concerned with the often displaced relationships among family members, and with driving home to women the importance of coping with enforced confinement and the paranoid fear it generates' (Modleski, 1984: 20). Like its domestic counterpart, the sensation novel focused minutely on the domestic space of the marital home. The home and the family, the goals and objects of desire of the heroine of the domestic novel – 'the shelter, not only from all injury, but from all terror, doubt and division' (Ruskin, 1865: 91) – were transformed in the sensation novel into sites of deception, violence, crime and division. The narrative dynamics of sensation novels are driven by family relationships and the secret skeletons in familial cupboards. Indeed, Elaine Showalter has argued that 'the power of Victorian sensation derives . . . from its exposure of secrecy as the fundamental and enabling condition of middle-class life' (1978b: 104).

In practice the various fictional genres which I have attempted to sketch in were habitually mixed together in varying proportions. Certainly the women novelists who were both successful in their own day and continue to have a readership today all combined a variety of modes and genres. The Brontë sisters combined the Gothic and domestic (usually in the way suggested in my earlier quotation from Modleski), and often anticipated the preoccupations and techniques of the sensation novel (Anne Brontë's narrative of a secretive, unhappily married woman, *The Tenant of Wildfell Hall* (1848) is particularly interesting in this last respect). Elizabeth Gaskell combined social protest, religious didacticism, and domestic realism with some elements of the melodramatic mode favoured by the sensationalists. Melodrama is in fact an important common denominator in the writing of the period. The melodramatic mode, or 'the melodramatic imagination', as Peter Brooks has put it in an influential book on the subject, is one of the characteristic nineteenth-century modes of representation. Produced by, and symptomatic of, profound and rapid social dislocation, it signifies a nostalgia for a lost social order and a morally legible universe. As well as functioning as a 'cultural touchstone', nineteenth-century melodrama also functioned as a 'psychological touchstone' for the poor, the powerless and 'those who felt themselves to be "helpless and unfriended" ' (Vicinus, 1981: 128). As Martha Vicinus has shown, domestic melodrama with its characteristic deployment of motifs of rebellion, confinement, suffering and self-sacrifice, had a particular resonance for women writers and readers since it addressed the social and emotional contradictions and tensions of women's lives.

Even George Eliot, whose self-conscious attempts to transform the novel into an aestheticized ethical instrument have earned her recognition for her role in the process by which the novel was transformed into 'literature', also learned lessons from those genre-blending and bending popular lady novelists whom she affected to despise. *Felix Holt the Radical* (1866), published in the middle of the sensation decade, is a 'Condition of England' novel whose plot is complicated by the intricacies of the law and originates in the secrets of an adulterous woman, Mrs Transome. As I have argued elsewhere, Mrs Transome's secret 'functions in the same way as the secrets of the sensation novel: a cross-class, illicit liaison undermines the upper classes, puts them in the power of their social inferiors, and disrupts the stability and continuity of the family and its property' (Pykett, 1994: 70). Even *Middlemarch*, the epitome of high-Victorian moral seriousness, which, according to Henry James, 'set a limit to the old-fashioned Victorian novel' (Carroll, 1981: 359), has some of the elements of the sensation novel: marital intrigue, the hint of adultery, a character with a criminal past whose current life of rigid respectability is built on a lie (Bulstrode, the banker). These elements are, if anything, even more pronounced in Eliot's final novel *Daniel Deronda* (1876) with (as Barbara Hardy has noted) its 'lost fathers and unknown mothers', 'melodramatic confrontations', 'mysterious past passions', irregular liaisons and illegitimate children and other skeletons in the cupboard (Hardy, 1966: 27). However, perhaps George Eliot's most important link with the women's sensation novel lies in her preoccupation with marriage, not as the goal of narrative and a device of closure, but as a source of narrative and a problematic subject for investigation. In this respect both the sensationalists and George Eliot anticipated one of the major subjects of fiction in the latter part of the nineteenth century: the marriage problem.

The women's sensation novel is a good example of an area of women's literary activity which has not simply been reviewed, but rather which has been brought back into view in the latter half of the twentieth century by the scrutiny of feminist literary and cultural historians. Another area of Victorian women's writing which has been restored to critical visibility by feminist scholarship is women's poetry. In a letter of 1845 Elizabeth Barrett Browning bemoaned the absence of literary models for the woman who aspired to be a poet: 'England has had many learned women . . . and yet where are the poetesses? . . . I look everywhere for grandmothers and see none' (Kenyon, 1897: vol. 1, 230–2). The conventional wisdom of literary history has, on the whole, appeared to concur with Barrett Browning's judgement, and has tended to overlook writers such as Jean Ingelow, whose *Collected Poems* (1863) went through twenty-three editions by 1880. Of the large number of women poets successfully publishing poetry in the Victorian period Barrett Browning herself, Charlotte and

Emily Brontë, and Christina Rossetti were the only ones who retained their critical visibility, at least before late twentieth-century feminism began to remap the terrain of the literary tradition, and it is arguable that some of the interest in their poetry was related to an interest in their eccentricity or the unusual circumstances of their lives.

Only very recently has the work of Barrett Browning, the Brontës and Rossetti been reviewed in the context of a significant contemporaneous body of poetry by women. Recent books by Angela Leighton and Isobel Armstrong have shown that not only did Elizabeth Barrett Browning have a number of poetic grandmothers, but that she also had numerous sisters and daughters. Angela Leighton has gone so far as to suggest that 'to be a woman poet in the nineteenth century, much more than to be a woman novelist, was to belong to an electively separate female tradition' (1992: 123). Both Leighton and Armstrong see Victorian women's poetry as beginning in the two decades preceding Victoria's accession, in 'the post-Romantic decades of the 1820s and 1830s' when 'the woman poet as a self-professed, rather than just self-supporting writer' appears virtually for the first time (Leighton, 1992: 2). Certainly the 1820s and 1830s were crucial in shaping the network of permissions and constraints in which the woman poet wrote. As in the case of the novel, women's poetry in the Victorian period was held to occupy a particular 'sphere of influence', and to work 'inside defined moral and religious conventions' (Armstrong, 1993: 321). Elizabeth Barrett Browning made Romney Leigh the mouthpiece for this conventional view of women's poetic abilities in *Aurora Leigh*, her epic poem about the making of the woman poet; and she also made him pay a terrible price for the limitations of his vision, by constructing a narrative in which he is blinded:

> Women as you are,
> Mere women, personal and passionate,
> You give us doting mothers, and perfect wives,
> Sublime Madonnas, and enduring saints!
> We get no Christ from you, – and verily
> We shall get no poet, in my mind.
>   (*Aurora Leigh*, II, 220–5)

This view of women's poetry as 'personal and passionate' in fact 'helped to make women's poetry and the "poetess" . . . respected in the nineteenth century as they have never been since' (Armstrong, 1993: 321). This was simultaneously enabling and constraining: it encouraged women to produce poetry, but it also produced a limiting 'myth of what being a woman poet means' (Leighton, 1992: 2).

The women poets of the Victorian period inherited an affective, expressive aesthetic from self-mythologizing post-Romantic 'poetesses' such as Felicia Hemans (memorialized by Wordsworth in his 1835 'Extempore Effusion upon the Death of James Hogg', as a 'holy Spirit, / Sweet as the spring, as ocean deep;'), and L.E.L. (Letitia Elizabeth Landon), the title of whose first collection – *The Improvisatrice* – indicates something of the 'natural', effusive quality of her popular and influential early work. To Victorian readers women's poetry, as represented by Hemans and L.E.L., was, as Leighton argues, a form of writing from the heart. It was both within and against this cult of sensibility that Victorian women's poetry defined itself, focusing on the forms and conditions of feminine subjectivity, women's relationship to language, and their social and sexual desires. It is of some considerable interest that a significant number of the more successful women poets who sought to enter a literary field characterized by a 'dissociation of sensibility from the affairs of the world' (Leighton, 1992: 3) were themselves associated with, and often actively engaged in, a wide range of social reform movements, and, more especially, in movements and campaigns on behalf of women. Like a number of her less well-remembered contemporaries Elizabeth Barrett Browning wrote political poems ('of factories and of slaves'), most notably 'The Cry of the Children', published in *Blackwood's* (1843) and 'The Runaway Slave at Pilgrim's Point' published in the Boston anti-slavery journal, *The Liberty Belle* (1848). Adelaide Procter was an active member of the Langham Place Group of feminists and became the leading poet of the group's organ the *Englishwoman's Journal* (founded in 1858). Like so many women poets Procter published her earliest work in an illustrated annual, *Heath's Book of Beauty* (1843), but she soon found a place in reform-minded miscellanies such as *Household Words* and *All the Year Round*. In volumes such as *Legends and Lyrics* (1858) Procter published narrative and lyric poems written in a bold, direct style on such matters of social and political concern as the conditions of the poor, and the feelings and socio-cultural situation of women, the oppressed and the dispossessed.

Augusta Webster, who published three volumes of poems between 1866 and 1870 (including the interestingly titled *A Woman Sold and Other Poems*, 1867) was also a notable contributor to debates on the Woman Question, and produced a series of essays in the *Examiner* in the 1870s on the suffrage issue and the situation of married women. Webster, who also wrote for the theatre, was a successful exponent of the dramatic monologue. Most accounts of the development of the dramatic monologue in the nineteenth century focus on the work of male poets such as Alfred Tennyson and Robert Browning, but women writers such as Webster also played an extremely important part in shaping it. Webster's *Portraits* (1870), for example, comprised thirteen dramatic monologues with both male and female speakers, including a prostitute – 'A Castaway' (Leighton and Reynolds, 1995: 433–48). Several of Webster's monologues were concerned with women's issues, particularly the marriage question and the position of the single or surplus woman.

Dora Greenwell, some of whose later poems (like those of her friend Christina Rossetti) are better known as hymns, also produced a number of poems on social and political subjects (the Lancashire cotton famine and the American Civil War, for example). Greenwell also wrote for a variety of journals on a range of social problems. One of her most interesting essays is 'Our Single Women', a plea for educational and employment opportunities for women, published in the *North British Review* in 1862. As well as being a social critique this essay was also an interesting intervention in contemporary debates about women's poetry. Greenwell linked the expressiveness of Victorian women's poetry to the social- and self-suppression from which Victorian femininity was constructed:

It is surely singular that woman, bound, as she is, no less by the laws of society than by the immutable instincts of her nature, to a certain suppression of all that relates to personal feeling, should attain, in print, to the fearless, uncompromising sincerity she misses in real life; so that in the poem, above all in the novel . . . a living soul, a living voice so sad, so truthful, so earnest, that we have felt as if some intimate secret were at once communicated and withheld, – an Open Secret, free to all who could find its key – the secret of a woman's heart, with all its needs, its struggles, and its aspirations. (Greenwell, 1866: 3–4)

Concealment, secrecy, the unlocking of secrets, the struggles of the heart and struggles with or against the heart – these were the tensions from which Victorian women's poetry emerged. Its common figures (from Emily Brontë onwards) were imprisonment, entrapment, slavery, escape, exile, displacement and journeying – as Isobel Armstrong puts it, 'across and between cultural boundaries' (1993: 325). The intensities of the dramatic lyric were often used by women poets as a vehicle for exploring and articulating the interdependent problems of the damming up or over-flow of feeling. Victorian women poets also exploited the complex possibilities offered by the dramatic lyric and dramatic monologue for masking and self-concealment, and also for role playing and the projection of alternative selves.

In this age of the novel women poets also turned to narrative: two of the best-known poems by women writers – Barrett Browning's *Aurora Leigh* (1857) and Christina Rossetti's *Goblin Market* (1862) – are long narrative poems. Barrett Browning described *Aurora Leigh* as a 'sort of novel-poem . . . running into the midst of our conventions, and rushing into drawing rooms and the like "where angels fear to tread"; and so, meeting face to face and without mask the Humanity of the age and speaking the truth of it out plainly' (Kintner, 1969: I, 31). The subject matter of *Aurora Leigh* is self-consciously modern; it turns its fierce and frank gaze on the issues of female self-realization and self-definition, the material and psychological predica-ment of the woman with an artistic vocation, the sexual politics and economics of marriage, the fallen woman as victim, the plight of the working class. But, above all *Aurora Leigh* is a poem about the growth of the female poet's mind, and one which ultimately distances itself from the expressive aesthetic; Aurora rejects the poetical and picturesque in an effort to represent her own 'live and throbbing age' (V, 203), and ultimately produces a book that is 'separate from [her]self' (VIII, 606).

At first sight nothing could be more different from Barrett Browning's modern epic than Christina Rossetti's odd and disturbing fairy tale *Goblin Market*. However, Rossetti's poem returns to several of the issues explored by its predecessor: relations between women, the interrelationship of sexual politics and economics, and the fallen woman. Using the rhymes and rhythms of a tale for children *Goblin Market* relates the story of two sisters, one of whom, Laura, succumbs to the lure of goblin fruit-sellers. Lacking money Laura obeys the goblins' injunction to 'Buy from us with a golden curl' of her hair, and then wastes away, sick with desire for more of the goblins' fruit. The fallen Laura is saved by her resourceful sister, Lizzie, who seeks out the goblins, this time equipped with a silver coin (which interestingly she does not have to use in the end). Lizzie returns covered with the juice of the fruit (with which she is smeared during the goblins' assault on her), which Laura sucks from her and is thus revived. *Goblin Market* has been variously read as an innocuous nursery tale for children, a moral or religious allegory, a social critique, and, latterly, as a sexual fantasy with lesbian connotations. Like some of Rossetti's more conventionally religious poetry, *Goblin Market* is disturbing and sometimes violent; it is also impossible to pin down. It is tempting to see it as a glorious wish-fulfilment fantasy for the woman writer. As Angela Leighton has argued:

> [It] gives women money, fruit, pleasure, children and, above all, a laughter at the heart which defies all the morally punitive connections between them. It gives them the aesthetic playfulness, the freedom of art for art's sake, which had seemed to be reserved for men. (1992: 140)

The complex relationships between money, pleasure, the family, women's self-realization, art and work which are addressed, both directly and indirectly, in *Aurora Leigh* and *Goblin Market* form the subject or subtext of much writing by women in the period covered by this chapter; they became increasingly important and pressing preoccupations in women's writing towards the end of the century.

Notes

1. It is, of course, important to remember that in this period, for both men and women, professional authorship was almost exclusively the preserve of the middle class.
2. For an interesting discussion of the female orphan in Victorian fiction, see Adrienne Rich (1980).

Bibliography

Alston, R.C. (1990), *A Checklist of Women Writers 1801–1900. Fiction, Verse, Drama*, London: British Library.

Altick, R.D. (1957), *The English Common Reader*, Chicago and London: University of Chicago Press.

Altick, R.D. (1962), 'The Sociology of Authorship: The Social Origins, Education and Occupations of 1,100 British Writers, 1800–1935', *Bulletin of the New York Public Library* 66, 389–404.

Armstrong, I. (1993), *Victorian Poetry: Poetry, Poetics and Politics*, London: Routledge.

Armstrong, N. (1987), *Desire and Domestic Fiction*, New York: Oxford University Press.

Auerbach, N. (1978), *Communities of Women: an Idea in Fiction*, Cambridge, Mass.: Harvard University Press.

Austin, A. (1869), 'The Poetry of the Period: Mr. Swinburne', *Temple Bar* 26, 457–74.

Basche, F. (1974), *Relative Creatures: Victorian Women in Society and the Novel, 1837–1867*, trans. Anthony Rudolf, London: Allen Lane.

Beer, G. (1986), *George Eliot*, Hemel Hempstead: Harvester Wheatsheaf.

Boumelha, P. (1990), *Charlotte Brontë*, London: Macmillan.

Brady, K. (1992), *George Eliot*, London: Macmillan.

Brooks, P. (1976), *The Melodramatic Imagination*, New Haven: Yale University Press.

Buchanan, R. (1862), 'Society's Looking-glass', *Temple Bar* 6, 129–37.

Carroll, D. (ed.) (1981), *George Eliot, The Critical Heritage*, London: Routledge and Kegan Paul.

Colby, V. (1974), *Yesterday's Women: Domestic Realism in the English Novel*, Princeton: Princeton University Press.

Corbett, M.J. (1992), *Representing Femininity: Middle-Class Subjectivity and Victorian Women's Autobiographies*, Oxford: Oxford University Press.

Cross, N. (1985), *The Common Writer: Life in Nineteenth-Century Grub Street*, Cambridge: Cambridge University Press.

David, D. (1981), *Fictions of Resolution in Three Victorian Novels: 'North and South', 'Our Mutual Friend' and 'Daniel Deronda'*, London: Macmillan.

David, D. (1987), *Intellectual Women and Victorian Patriarchy: Harriet Martineau, Elizabeth Barrett Browning, George Eliot*, London: Macmillan.

Davies, S. (1988), *Emily Brontë*, Hemel Hempstead: Harvester Wheatsheaf.

Davies, S. (1994), *Emily Brontë, Heretic*, London: Women's Press.

Eliot, G. (1992) [1856], 'Silly Novels by Lady Novelists' in *George Eliot: Selected Critical Writings*, Rosemary Ashton (ed.), Oxford: Oxford University Press.

Ewbank, I.-S. (1966), *Their Proper Sphere: A Study of the Brontë Sisters as Early Victorian Female Novelists*, London: Edward Arnold.

Fahnestock, J.R. (1973), 'Geraldine Jewsbury: The Power of the Publisher's Reader', *Nineteenth Century Fiction* 28, 253–72.

Figes, E. (1982), *Sex and Subterfuge: Women Novelists to 1850*, London: Macmillan.

Flint, K. (1993), *The Woman Reader, 1837–1914*, Oxford: Oxford University Press.

Gallagher, C. (1985), *The Industrial Reformation of English Fiction*, Chicago: University of Chicago Press.

Gilbert, S. and S. Gubar (1979), *The Madwoman in the Attic: The Woman Writer and the Nineteenth Century Literary Imagination*, New Haven: Yale University Press.

Greenwell, D. (1866) [1862], 'Our Single Women' in *Essays*, London and New York: A. Strahan.

Greg, W.R. (1859), 'False Morality of Lady Novelists', *National Review* 7, 144–67.

Griest, G. (1970), *Mudies' Circulating Library and the Victorian Novel*, Bloomington: Indiana University Press.

Hardy, B. (1966), Introduction to Penguin edition of *Daniel Deronda*, Harmondsworth: Penguin.

Helsinger, E.K. et al. (1983), *The Woman Question: Society and Literature in Britain and America, 1837–1883*, 3 vols, Manchester: Manchester University Press.

Homans, M. (1981), *Women Writers and Poetic Identity, Dorothy Wordsworth, Emily Brontë and Emily Dickinson*, Princeton: Princeton University Press.

Homans, M. (1986), *Bearing the Word: Language and Women's Experience in Nineteenth Century Women's Writing*, London and Chicago: Chicago University Press.

Houghton, W. (1979), *Wellesley Index to Victorian Periodicals*, 4 vols, vol. II, Toronto: University of Toronto Press; London: Routledge.

Hughes, W. (1980), *The Maniac in the Cellar; The Sensation Novel of the 1860s*, Princeton: Princeton University Press.

Kenyon, F.G. (ed.) (1897), *The Letters of Elizabeth Barrett Browning*, 2 vols, London: Smith Elder.

Kestner, J. (1985), *Protest and Reform: The British Social Narrative by Women, 1827–1867*, London: Methuen.

Kintner, E. (1969), *The Letters of Robert Browning and Elizabeth Barrett, 1845–1846*, 2 vols, Cambridge, Mass.: Harvard University Press.

Leavis, F.R. (1948), *The Great Tradition*, London: Chatto and Windus.

Leighton, A. (1986), *Elizabeth Barrett Browning*, Hemel Hempstead: Harvester Wheatsheaf.

Leighton, A. (1992), *Victorian Women Poets: Writing Against the Heart*, Hemel Hempstead: Harvester Wheatsheaf.

Leighton, A. and M. Reynolds (eds) (1995), *Victorian Women Poets: An Anthology*, Oxford: Blackwell.

Lewes, G.H. (1847), 'The Condition of Authors in England, Germany and France', *Fraser's* XXXV, 285–95.

Lewes, G.H. (1850), 'A Gentle Hint to Writing Women', *Leader* I, 929–30.

Lewes, G.H. (1852), 'The Lady Novelists', *Westminster Review* 58, 129–41.

Lister, T.H. (1830), 'Mrs Gore's *Women as they Are; or the Manners of the Day*', *Edinburgh Review* 51, 444–62.

Lovell, T. (1987), *Consuming Fiction*, London: Verso.

Mitchell, S. (1981), *The Fallen Angel: Chastity, Class and Women's Reading, 1835–1880*, Bowling Green, Ohio: Bowling University Popular Press.

Modleski, T. (1984), *Loving With a Vengeance: Mass-produced Fantasies for Women*, London: Methuen.

Moore, G. (1976) [1884], 'A New Censorship of Literature' in *Literature at Nurse, or Circulating Morals: A Polemic on Victorian Censorship*, P. Coustillas (ed.), Hemel Hempstead: Harvester Wheatsheaf.

Nestor, P. (1985), *Female Friendships and Communities, Charlotte Brontë, George Eliot, Elizabeth Gaskell*, Oxford: Oxford University Press.

Nestor, P. (1987), *Charlotte Brontë*, London: Macmillan.

Newton, J.L. (1985), *Women, Power and Subversion: Social Strategies in British Fiction, 1778–1860*, London: Methuen.

Oliphant, M. (1855), 'Modern Novelists – Great and Small', *Blackwood's* LXXVII, 554–68.

Oliphant, M. (1862), 'Sensation Novels', *Blackwood's* 91, 564–84.

Poovey, M. (1988), *Uneven Developments: The Ideological Work of Gender in Mid-Victorian England*, Chicago: University of Chicago Press.

Pykett, L. (1989), *Emily Brontë*, London: Macmillan.

Pykett, L. (1992), *The 'Improper' Feminine: The Women's Sensation Novel and the New Woman Writing*, London: Routledge.

Pykett, L. (1994), *The Sensation Novel from 'The Woman in White' to 'The Moonstone'*, London: Northcote House.

Rich, A. (1980), *On Lies Secrets and Silence: Selected Prose, 1966–1978*, London: Virago.

Rochefort, C. (1981), 'Are Women Writers Still Monsters?' in *New French Feminisms*, E. Marks and I. de Courtivron (eds), Hemel Hempstead: Harvester Wheatsheaf.

Ruskin, J. (1865), 'Of Queen's Gardens' in *Sesame and Lilies*, London: Smith, Elder.

Russell, W.E. (ed.) (1896), *The Letters of Matthew Arnold*, London: Macmillan.

Sanders, V. (1989), *The Private Lives of Victorian Women: Autobiography in Nineteenth-Century England*, Hemel Hempstead: Harvester Wheatsheaf.

Showalter, E. (1978a), *A Literature of their Own*, London: Virago.

Showalter, E. (1978b), 'Family Secrets and Domestic Subversion: Rebellion in the Novels of the Eighteen-sixties' in *The Victorian Family: Structure and Stresses*, A. Wohl (ed.), London: Croom Helm.

Spencer, J. (1986), *The Rise of the Woman Novelist*, Oxford: Blackwell.

Spencer, J. (1993), *Elizabeth Gaskell*, London: Macmillan.

Stoneman, P. (1987), *Elizabeth Gaskell*, Hemel Hempstead: Harvester Wheatsheaf.

Sutherland, J.A. (1976), *Victorian Novelists and Publishers*, London: Athlone.

Sutherland, J.A. (1988), *The Longman Companion to Victorian Fiction*, London: Longman.

Sutherland, J.A. (1995), *Victorian Fiction: Writers, Publishers Readers*, London: Macmillan.

Swindells, J. (1986), *Victorian Writing and Working Women: The Other Side of Silence*, Oxford: Polity.

Tillotson, K. (1956), *Novels of the Eighteen-Forties*, Oxford: Oxford University Press.

Tillotson, K. (1969), 'The Lighter Reading of the Eighteen-sixties', introduction to Riverside edition of Wilkie Collins, *The Woman in White*, Boston, Mass.: Norton.

Trodd, A. (1989), *Domestic Crime in the Victorian Novel*, London: Macmillan.

Vicinus, M. (1981), ' "Helpless and Unfriended": Nineteenth-century Domestic Melodrama', *New Literary History* 13, 127–43.

Wise, T.J. and J.A. Symington (1933), *The Brontës: Their Lives, Friendships and Correspondence*, 4 vols, Oxford: Shakespeare Head.

Wolff, R.L. (1981–6), *Nineteenth-Century Fiction: A Bibliographical Catalogue*, 5 vols, New York: Garland.

Woolf, V. (1966–7), *Collected Essays*, Leonard Woolf (ed.), London: Hogarth Press.

Woolf, V. (1992) [1929], *A Room of One's Own and Three Guineas*, ed. and intro. Morag Schiach, Oxford: Oxford University Press.

Primary texts

Since some of the less well-known books are out of print and there are so many different editions of the better-known works I have given the date of first publication. Further details of the careers of the writers listed below can be found in Joanne Shattock, *The Oxford Guide to British Women Writers* (Oxford: Oxford University Press, 1993). Because of the diversity of editions available, references have been made to chapters, not pages.

Banks, I. (Mrs Linnaeus Banks)	*The Manchester Man* (1876)
Braddon, M.E.	*Lady Audley's Secret* (1862)
Braddon, M.E.	*Aurora Floyd* (1863)
Brontë, A., C. and E.	*Poems* [by Currer, Ellis and Acton Bell] (1846)
Brontë, A.	*Agnes Grey* (1847)
Brontë, A.	*The Tenant of Wildfell Hall* (1848)
Brontë, C.	*Jane Eyre* (1847)
Brontë, C.	*Shirley* (1849)
Brontë, C.	*Villette* (1853)
Brontë, C.	*The Professor* (1857)
Brontë, E.	*Wuthering Heights* (1847)
Broughton, R.	*Cometh Up As A Flower* (1867)
Broughton, R.	*Not Wisely But Too Well* (1867)
Browning, E. Barrett	*Poems* (1844)
Browning, E. Barrett	*Poems* (1850)
Browning, E. Barrett	*Casa Guidi Windows* (1851)
Browning, E. Barrett	*Aurora Leigh* (1857)
Browning, E. Barrett	*Last Poems* (1862)
Craik, D.M.	*The Ogilvies* (1850)
Craik, D.M.	*John Halifax Gentleman* (1856)
Eliot, G.	*Scenes of Clerical Life* (1858)
Eliot, G.	*Adam Bede* (1859)
Eliot, G.	'The Lifted Veil' (1859)
Eliot, G.	*The Mill on the Floss* (1860)
Eliot, G.	*Silas Marner* (1861)
Eliot, G.	*Romola* (1863)
Eliot, G.	*Felix Holt the Radical* (1866)
Eliot, G.	'The Spanish Gypsy' (1868)
Eliot, G.	'Armgart' (1871)
Eliot, G.	*Middlemarch: A Story of Provincial Life* (1871–2)
Eliot, G.	*Daniel Deronda* (1876)
Gaskell, E.	*Mary Barton* (1848)
Gaskell, E.	*Cranford* (1851–3)
Gaskell, E.	*Ruth* (1853)
Gaskell, E.	*North and South* (1854–5)
Gaskell, E.	*The Life of Charlotte Brontë* (1857)

Gaskell, E.	*Wives and Daughters* (1865)
Gore, C.	*The Hamiltons* (1834)
Gore, C.	*Mrs Armytage; or Female Domination* (1836)
Gore, C.	*Cecil; or the Adventures of a Coxcomb* (1841)
Gore, C.	*The Banker's Wife* (1843)
Greenwell, D.	*Poems* (1861 and 1867)
Greenwell, D.	*Songs of Salvation* (1867)
Greenwell, D.	*Carmina Crucis* (1869)
Greenwell, D.	*The Soul's Legend* (1873)
Greenwell, D.	*Camera Obscura* (1876)
Howitt, M.	*Wood Leighton* (1836)
Howitt, M.	*The Children's Year* (1847)
Ingelow, J.	*Poems* (1863)
Ingelow, J.	*The Story of Doom and Other Poems* (1867)
Jewsbury, G.	*Zoe* (1845)
Jewsbury, G.	*The Half Sisters* (1848)
Linton, E.L.	*Azeth the Egyptian* (1846)
Linton, E.L.	*Sowing the Wind* (1867)
Martineau, H.	*Illustrations of Political Economy* (1832–4)
Martineau, H.	*A Manchester Strike* (1834)
Martineau, H.	*Deerbrook* (1839)
Oliphant, M.	*The Rector* and *The Doctor's Family* (1862)
Oliphant, M.	*Salem Chapel* (1863)
Oliphant, M.	*Miss Marjoribanks* (1866)
'Ouida' (Marie Louise de la Ramée)	*Held in Bondage* (1863)
'Ouida'	*Under Two Flags* (1867)
'Ouida'	*Folle Farine* (1871)
Procter, A.	*Legends and Lyrics* (1858)
Procter, A. (ed.)	*The Victoria Regia* (1861)
Procter, A.	*A Chaplet of Verses* (1862)
Ritchie, A.	*The Story of Elizabeth* (1863)
Ritchie, A.	*The Village on the Green* (1867)
Ritchie, A.	*Old Kensington* (1873)
Rossetti, C.	*Goblin Market and Other Poems* (1862)
Rossetti, C.	*The Prince's Progress and Other Poems* (1866)
Sewell, E.M.	*Amy Herbert* (1844)
Sewell, E.M.	*The Experience of Life* (1853)
Tonna, C.E.	*Helen Fleetwood: Tale of the Factories* (1841)
Tonna, C.E.	*The Wrongs of Women* (1843–4)
Trollope, F.	*The Vicar of Wrexhill* (1837)
Trollope, F.	*Widow Barnaby* (1839)
Trollope, F.	*Michael Armstrong, the Factory Boy* (1840)
Webster, A.	*Blanche Lisle and Other Poems* (1860)
Webster, A.	*Lilian Gray* [a poem] (1864)
Webster, A.	*Lesley's Guardians* [a novel] (1864)
Webster, A.	*Dramatic Studies* (1866)
Webster, A.	*A Woman Sold and Other Poems* (1867)
Wood, E. (Mrs Henry Wood)	*East Lynne* (1861)
Wood, E.	*The Shadow of Ashlydyat* (1863)
Wood, E.	*Lord Oakburn's Daughters* (1864)

7

Out of the attic . . .: women and writing at the fin de siècle

Viv Gardner

Not only did the nineteenth-century woman writer have to inhabit ancestral mansions (or cottages) owned and built by men, she was also constricted and restricted by the Palaces of Art and the Houses of Fiction male writers authored. (Gilbert and Gubar, *The Madwoman in the Attic*, 1979: xi)

She left her bedroom, and walked through the other rooms on the same floor . . .; then she went up to the next floor where the servants slept. Above that again there was an attic used as a box room, and she went there too. . . . At the farther end, opposite the door, there was a pile of packing-cases and travelling trunks. . . . On the other side of the pile it was almost dark. She could see something, however, as she stood up, which looked like a mark on the whitewash, and on running her hand over it she discovered it to be a narrow door flush with the wall. There was no handle or latch to it, but there was a key which had rusted in the keyhole and was not to be turned. The door was not locked, however, and Beth pushed it open, and found herself in a charming little room with a fireplace at one end of it, and opposite, at the other end, a large bow window. . . . Beth dropped on to one of the dusty chairs, and looked round. Everything about her was curiously familiar, and her first impression was that she had been there before. On the other hand, she could hardly believe in the reality of what she saw, she thought she must be dreaming, for here was exactly what she had been pining for most in the whole wide world of late, a secret spot, sacred to herself, where she could be safe from intrusion. (Sarah Grand, *The Beth Book*, 1980: 346–7)

The attic is a recurrent feature in women's writing about women writing at the *fin de siècle*, both as a literal and metaphorical space. For the American Charlotte Perkins Gilman, the attic was a place in which the woman writer in *The Yellow Wallpaper* (1892) is confined and goes mad. For Mary Cholmondeley's heroine, Hester Gresley 'the little attic room' was a place of creative suffering where 'the cold of winter and the heat of summer had each struck in turn and in vain at the indomitable perseverance of the writer' (Cholmondeley, 1985: 261). But for the heroine of *The Beth Book* the attic offers not confinement and suffering but the freedom in which to create: it is the first stage in her emancipation. In her 'secret spot' Beth Caldwell is able to escape from her unhappy marriage and begins to earn money by her embroideries, and to write. Forty-one years before Virginia Woolf gave her paper on women and writing to Girton and Newnham colleges in 1928, Sarah Grand's semi-autobiographical heroine made the discovery that in order to create 'a woman must have money and a room of her own' (Woolf, 1945: 6). The journey that she makes from the bedroom to the attic, then from another attic in London, to the platform where her radical speech on 'The Desecration of Marriage' inspires her all-female audience, serves not only as a metaphor for Sarah Grand's own creative trajectory but for that of the generality of women writers in the period from 1880 to 1910. Whilst there is a great danger in following this narrative too literally – the sense of closure, the 'happy ending', is of course illusory – it does offer us a frame within which to consider the history of women's writing in a period that has been dismissed by many critics as merely 'transitional'.

Raymond Williams in the 1950s expressed the dominant view in describing the period 1880–1914 as 'a kind of interregnum', an era between 'the masters' [*sic*] producing 'a working out . . . of unfinished lines; a tentative redirection' and work which 'requires notice but suggests brevity' (1958: 161–2). More recent studies – particularly those engaged in feminist revisions of literary history – have seen the period between the death of George Eliot and the First World War as an immensely fertile one in which the grand narrative of Victorianism was challenged and 'many of the concepts and conflicts around issues of "race", class and gender which inform contemporary cultural criticism' originated (Ledger and MacCracken, 1995: 3).[1] Central to the disruption of Victorian norms in this volatile and insecure period was the part played by women in articulating, through both their work and their lives, contemporary arguments around sex, marriage and gender. Women writers both reflected and contributed to what the Victorians and Edwardians called 'The Woman Question'.

The woman question

The social and political context for women had changed perceptibly by the 1880s through educational, occupational and legislative advances. The work of Emily Davies and her associates in opening up educational opportunities for, largely middle-class, women – deliciously sentimentally represented in L.T. Meade's *A Sweet Girl Graduate* (1891) – meant that by the end of the century women's place in higher education was an accepted, if peripheral, one. As Martha Vicinus points out, 'improved educational standards, combined with new opportunities made possible by the telephone, telegraph, and typewriter, meant that the more venturesome members of the middle class could find jobs that were both respectable and clean' (1980: xvii). Ella Hepworth Dixon charts the progress of one such educated middle-class girl, Mary Erle, in *The Story of a Modern Woman* (1894). Forced to find work in journalism when her father dies and she fails in her chosen vocation, fine art, Mary's initial romantic belief that work would 'probably save some of us from the madhouse' (Dixon, 1990: 56) is soon altered when she encounters the realities of writing to live. The chapter 'In Grub Street' describes a clubby, male world of journalism where writers are two a penny, women treated with coarseness or indifference and a fiction writer ends up producing society articles – 'something smart, you know, and just a wee bit malicious' (114) – for *The Fan*. Nor was work always a matter of choice, for many women it was a matter of necessity. The demographic shifts of the 1880s and 1890s left Britain with a superfluity of single women, the 'odd women' of George Gissing's novel.[2] The change in women's position was, therefore, not unequivocally positive. Vicinus continues,

> Better education meant, in theory, financial independence and wider career choices, but as with similar legal reforms, women found that the end results of their education were often less than the promise . . . the struggles of women were most successful when they chimed with larger social and economic needs, and least successful when they clashed with a specific power base or dominant attitudes. (1980: xvii)

As we shall see, and as Mary Erle learned, women's access to the male-dominated publishing industries was determined largely by economic rather than philanthropic or political considerations. When women writers appeared to be encroaching too far into male territory, men tended to redraw the boundaries. And the reality for most women writers was that few earned enough money to achieve independence from a male breadwinner. One of the most important legal advances for those women who did earn sufficient from writing was the Married Women's Property Act of 1882 which gave women the legal right to their own property, and hence earnings, after marriage. It was the success of *Ideala: A Study from Life* in 1888 and the fact of the Married Women's Property Act that made it practicable for Sarah Grand to leave her husband and to survive on her own.

Whilst the prevailing ideology throughout this period continued to be that of 'separate spheres', public and male, private and female, the 1890s saw significant challenges to that ethos. Through forums such as the Men and Women's Club,[3] Emily Massingberd's all-female Pioneer Club, founded in 1892, and the pages of the national press, relationships between the sexes in both private and public domains were debated. At every stage women's writing participates in and advances contemporary radical thought. Once the women writers had found 'their attic' in the 1880s and 1890s they produced significant changes in the cultural representations of their own sex and challenged the constructs of what Gertrude Stein called 'patriarchal poetry' (Gilbert and Gubar, 1979: xi). Many of the women writers found a 'platform' through their writing, some literally through feminist campaigns like the fight against the Contagious Diseases Acts[4] and the suffrage movement, some through their fiction, plays and poems, and in the expanding magazine industry. As Judith Gardiner points out:

> the explosion in magazine and periodical publishing aimed at women [in the 1890s], *The Englishwoman's Review, The Freewoman*, the *Girl's Own Paper, Women's World* and the later political periodicals, *The Suffragette, Votes for Women* and *The Common Cause*, provided new outlets for women's writing; and the burgeoning of fiction magazines – including *The Yellow Book* (with female assistant editor, Ella D'Arcy) – gave women writers new opportunities to perfect the genre of the short story. (1993: 6)

By 1910 there had been significant changes in the circumstances under which women wrote. Many women had found a confidence, a voice, that enabled them to move out of the attic and to choose their creative space.

Women writers' position on feminist issues, however, was not uniformly supportive, nor did they hold a single position on individual issues such as marriage, motherhood and the suffrage. It would be misleading to represent all women's writing in the period as 'feminist'. Much of the writing that women engaged in was 'bread and butter' work, romance, children's fiction, regular journalism. It is possible, however, to map the intersections between the feminist movement and women's writing through the most notorious and self-consciously transgressive writing of the period. In doing so this chapter will not represent the totality of women's writing in the period. In concentrating on the 'radical' rather than the conservative, on work for adults rather than that written for children, on fiction, plays and poetry rather than journalism, travel books, biography and autobiography, inevitably there will be significant omissions.

Finding the attic door

The struggle for the material circumstances in which to write continued to be the prime concern for women authors at the end of the nineteenth century. Residual, but substantial, hostility to women engaging in intellectual activity manifested itself in the medical discourse of the day. Over-stimulation of the female brain was thought to lead to all manner of debilitating illnesses from stunted growth to insanity.[5] Sir James Crichton-Browne, an eminent member of the medical establishment, described meeting a group of college girls at a station, many of whom 'had a stooping gait and withered appearance, shrunk shanks, and spectacles on the nose' (Rubinstein, 1986: 6). This in his view confirmed the debilitating effect of academic education on the female as brain activity diverted the blood from its 'natural' nurturing sphere, the womb. The 'cure' for many female maladies attributed to over-excitement, was its opposite, rest. In Charlotte Perkins Gilman's semi-autobiographical novel, *The Yellow Wallpaper*, the nameless narrator is taken by her husband to a house in the country to recover from an undefined nervous illness following the birth of her child and is forbidden to write. All stimulation removed – social, emotional and intellectual – confined to an attic nursery with barred windows to sleep, the woman begins to write, but overwhelmed by her predicament she also begins to disintegrate. She sees other women crawling behind the yellow wallpaper of the attic, struggling to get free. Finally she finds freedom in madness. She gets 'out at last . . . in spite of [her husband]' and has 'pulled off most of the paper, so you can't put me back' (Gilman, 1981: 36).[6]

If women succeeded in negotiating the medical obstacles to intellectual activity, there remained more subtle barriers that defined women's drive to creative expression as indicative of psychological or emotional inadequacy, for, as Catherine J. Hamilton opined in 1892, 'Happy women, whose hearts are satisfied and full, have no need of utterance' (Showalter, 1982: 85).

Within the 'separate spheres' ideology there was a general acceptance that if women *needed* to create, their natural *métier* was the novel, or perhaps poetry. The association of women with the domestic and romantic novel served to reinscribe the notion of women's rightful place as in the home, replicating women's experience in their writing. The interiority of much poetry also reinforced the belief in the primacy of privacy and emotion in women's lives. Gale Tuchman, through a study of the archives of the publisher Macmillan, estimates that from mid-century to 1880 most novelists were probably women, though this gender balance was to change by 1910 (Tuchman and Fortin, 1989: 7). However, the volume and popularity of women's fiction among its, predominantly female, readers also told against the writers, as the female audience was considered the less intellectually demanding. Women's very success worked against them. With the collapse of the three-decker novel in the 1880s and 1890s and the rapid expansion in publication of fiction in cheap, single editions – a process that had started in play publication as early as the 1820s[7] – the perceived gap between popular works and 'high art' increased. Women's contribution to the market in popular and accessible fiction, for both adults and children, served to exacerbate the problems of the status of women's writing. According to Tuchman's analysis of the period 1880–99 'men of letters, including critics, redefined the nature of a good novel and the great author. They preferred a new form of realism that they associated with "manly" literature' (Tuchman and Fortin, 1989: 8). Realism, the exposure of the mechanics of the world, as opposed to 'romance' or 'entertainment', became the measure of great literature, a view reiterated continually as a product of the dominance of male critics in the literary journals. Resistance to the 'realities' of women's lives exposed by the New Women writers of the 1890s shows how extensively gender bias was at work among the literary critics. Further evidence of the opposition to women's incursions into the literary profession came with the setting up of the Society of Authors in 1884. A collective venture by writers to protect their members' interests with publishers and theatre managers, the Society sought to introduce more effective copyright controls and to promote writing as a profession. Women were excluded from membership. In this antagonistic climate Sarah Grand's claim for her writer-heroine that she was 'a woman of genius'[8] – to many a contradiction in terms – was at the very least a gauntlet thrown down.

There were other, practical, problems faced by women writers. Finding the right publisher was crucial, particularly in the case of subject matter judged too transgressive for the established houses. Sarah Grand's experience over the publication of the novel which made her name, *The Heavenly Twins* (1893), is an example. She quotes one publisher who, in rejecting the novel, wrote:

> All delicately-minded women must feel themselves aggrieved, if not insulted by the prominence which is given to the physical side of marriage [in your novel]. . . . Even if I had not the reputation of my House to go by in the case of *The Heavenly Twins*, I could not, and would not dare to place this work in the way of ladies, who compose so large a proportion of the novel-reading public. (Kersley, 1983: 70)

After a three-year search for a publisher, the book was eventually published by William Heinemann who had set up his own publishing house in 1890 and was in Grand's words 'in touch with the spirit of the day, if ever a man was' (Kersley, 1983: 71). Even Olive Schreiner's publisher, Chapman & Hall, had shown some nervousness when publishing *The Story of an African Farm* (1883) and suggested that her heroine, Lyndall, should marry the father of her child, otherwise 'Smith's, the railway booksellers, would not put it on their stalls' (Schreiner, 1971: 12). Schreiner declined the suggestion and the book and its author were an immediate success. George Egerton found a publisher for her 'decadent' short stories, *Keynotes*, in a man similarly 'in touch with the times', John Lane, originator of the notorious *Yellow Book*.

If the relationship between women novelists and poets and publishers was problematic, that between women dramatists and theatre managers was more so. Actress, dramatist and novelist, Elizabeth Inchbald had written in 1807:

> The Novelist [by comparison] is a free agent. He lives in a land of liberty, whilst the Dramatic Writer exists but under a despotic government. Passing over the subjection in which the author of plays is held by the Lord Chamberlain's office [the Censor responsible for enforcing the 1737 Licensing Act], and the degree of dependence which he has on his actors – he is the very slave of the audience. He must have their tastes and prejudices in view, not to correct, but to humour them . . . the will of such critics is law, and execution instantly follows judgement. (Donkin, 1995: 5)

To which 'despotic' cabinet she might have added the theatre manager. Access to the relatively closed world of the theatre was difficult for an outsider, the relationships between dramatist and manager or actor-manager were generally negotiated directly, not from the drawing room or attic. Writing for the stage requires experience of the stage. Middle-class women were not expected to go to the theatre unless chaperoned, and were certainly not expected to take part in the Green Room socializing that nurtured so many male dramatists' relationships with theatre managements.[9] Women were excluded from membership of the precursor of the Society of Authors, the Dramatic Authors' Society, except as 'honorary members',[10] limiting access not only to theatre managers, but to publishers. Once inside the theatre, women dramatists were particularly vulnerable in a relationship where power was so unequally distributed and the manager, according to Ellen Donkin, combined the roles of 'chaperone and mentor' (1995: 25) as well as paymaster.

It is not surprising then that the women who did write for the stage in the early part of the century were often members of theatrical families with experience of and access to theatre like Hannah and Sophia Lee, daughters of an actor-manager and an actress, and Eliza Planché, wife of dramatist J.R. Planché. Some of the 520 women known to have written for the stage from the late eighteenth century to 1900 began writing after taking up a career as a performer.[11] Mary Braddon, for example, left home at the age of 20 to become an actress and whilst she abruptly left the stage three years later in 1860 to write, continued to write plays as well as her notorious sensation novels.[12] Some women dramatists were educated and well-placed 'women of letters' like Catherine Gore, best known for her 'silver-fork' novels mid-century, but also winner of Ben Webster's 1843 competition for a modern comedy with her play, *Quid Pro Quo*. However, given the difficulties that women experienced in the theatre, it is also not surprising that when women in the 1890s turned to playwriting they often did so under the auspices of one of the avant-garde theatres that were predisposed to radical agendas, or in the 1900s, to those theatres run by feminist managers like Lena Ashwell and Annie Horniman.

It has traditionally been argued that one of the other problems that women had to confront as novelists, as well as dramatists, was the question of their 'reputation'. The use of male pseudonyms by female authors has been seen to be a sign of this. In reality, however, in mid-century more men wrote under female pseudonyms than the reverse, and the number of women using men's names was relatively small, though more common among writers of 'advanced' works (Tuchman and Fortin, 1989: 53–4). Looking at individual cases the strategy of the pseudonym is clearly more complex than a simply defensive one. Mrs Frances McFall, having left her husband after an unhappy nineteen-year marriage to an army surgeon who disapproved of her views and her writing, changed her name to Sarah Grand 'in order to save him [David McFall] the annoyance' (Kersley, 1983: 65), thus distancing herself from her husband but not her sex. But Mary Chavelita Dunne adopted the first two names of her husband, George Egerton Clairmonte, possibly because, if 'Miss de Maupassant' (1895), a satirical short story by Elizabeth Robins, is to be believed, John Lane, initially at least, was one of those publishers who, though 'desperate to secure . . . [material to satisfy] the raging taste for sensationalism in fiction' and was unable 'to accept the fact that a woman [could] write what the publishers were hungry for' (Gates, 1994: 87). And 'It never once dawned on [Egerton's first editor, T.P. Gill] that the author of those virile sketches was not one of [his] own sex' (Miller, 1994: 29). In the theatre, Cicely Hamilton records in her autobiography, *Life Errant* (1935), how in 1906 she was advised by the producer of her first, 'somewhat gruesome one-act play' to conceal her gender until after the notices were out as 'plays which were known to be written by women were apt to get a bad press'. She goes on to say that she would:

> not go so far as to assert that Otto Stuart was correct in his assumption that the women playwrights of the early nineteen-hundreds could not hope for fair play from the critics of that epoch; but certain it is that the two or three critics who discovered that C. Hamilton stood for a woman were the one or two critics who dealt out hard measure to her playlet. (1935: 60)

Yet another argument for pseudonymity was given by the co-authors, Katharine Bradley and Edith Cooper, writing as 'Michael Field'.[13] In a letter to Robert Browning in 1884 explaining that the use of a male pseudonym allowed them to say 'the many things [that] the world would otherwise not tolerate from a woman's lips', Bradley went on:

> the report of lady authorship will dwarf and enfeeble our work at every turn. . . . We must be free as dramatists to work out in the open air of nature – exposed to her vicissitudes, witnessing her terrors: we cannot be stifled in drawing room conventionalities. (Leighton, 1992: 202)

This strategy is echoed by Elizabeth Robins in her novel *George Mandeville's Husband* (1894) in which the author-heroine chooses to adopt a male name:

She would not consent, however, to be criticised by the narrow standards applied in these evil days to women's work. She was assured she had a powerful and original mind – she would not allow the soft veil of her sex to hide her merit from the public eye. She would call herself 'George Mandeville': George out of a sense of kinship with Madame Dudevant [George Sand] and Marian Evans [George Eliot]; Mandeville, because, by some obscure process of reasoning, she had come to consider herself allied to a noble English family of that name. . . . Yes, she would be George Mandeville henceforth!

(Gates, 1994: 56)

Robins published this novel under the gender *non*-specific name of C.E. Raimond and offers us another even more complex example of the use of concealment. In the world of theatre, by the 1890s, reputation had become a key issue. But while a steady rise in the acceptability of the legitimate theatre was discernible – marked most clearly by the knighting of Henry Irving in 1895 – it did not protect women from disrepute by association with some, if not all areas of theatre, and women writers as well as actors were protective of their reputation. Elizabeth Robins and Lady Florence Bell chose not to put their names to their play *Alan's Wife* when it was performed by the Independent Theatre Society in 1893, though Robins played the central role, probably because they realized the play's sympathetic examination of a woman who kills her deformed baby was bound to cause controversy. In the two previous years Lady Bell, a wealthy woman of some standing, had had plays performed under her own name, while Robins had made her name when she had played Hedda Gabler in the British première of Ibsen's play in 1891, so it was clearly not association with theatre *per se* that mattered to the two women. Perhaps they were wary of the dangers inherent in two women arguing the case for infanticide – the assumption being that women only write what they know[14] – while it is possible that Robins did not wish the notoriety attached to her Ibsen performances to prejudice reception of the play or her earning ability as a mainstream actress to be affected by taking responsibility for such a 'hopeless, heartless, odious' piece, as *Alan's Wife* was described by critic A.B. Walkley (*Speaker*, 6 May 1893, p. 512). Whatever the reasons for their decision, Bell and Robins were clearly not alone among women writers in manipulating the space between private self and public name in an attempt to control the reception of their work. This negotiation became even more crucial as the 1880s and 1890s progressed and feminist issues began to take centre stage and women writers found themselves, willingly or unwillingly, associated with the burgeoning women's movement.

Out of the attic

'Don't you wish you were a woman, Waldo?'

'No,' he answered readily. She laughed.

'I thought not. Even you are too worldly-wise for that. I never met a man who did. . . . It is delightful to be a woman; but every man thanks the Lord devoutly that he isn't one.'

(Schreiner, 1971: 186–7)

The 1890s saw the emergence of what came to be known as the New Woman novel, though the roots of the phenomenon lie in the realist novels that were written in the decade following the death of George Eliot in 1880. What Elaine Showalter has categorized as the 'feminine' novels of the mid-century, were gradually superceded by the 'feminist' realist novels of the late 1880s and 1890s. Showalter writes that 'whereas the feminine novelists had expressed female cultural values obliquely and proclaimed anti-feminism publicly, the feminist novelists had a highly developed sense of belonging to a sisterhood of women writers' (Showalter, 1982: 182). Women began to explore women's experience and expose patriarchal issues, not in coded form, as in the sensation novels of Mary Braddon, but directly. A new realistic genre emerged where women – and men – spoke about the troubled relationships between women and men, about the problematics of marriage from a woman's point of view, about sexual experience and sexual rights, about motherhood. The debates of the Men and Women's Club and the Pioneer Club were rehearsed time and time again in the novels, plays and journalism that women wrote in the 1890s. The writings were generically classed as 'New Woman'. The term became common currency in 1894,[15] the *annus mirabilis* of the New Woman, when scarcely a *Punch* magazine could be opened without the severe features and rational dress of the New Woman being depicted, and the popular dramatist Sydney Grundy's play *The New Woman*, with four of the 'species' in it, ran for two months at the Comedy Theatre. Gail Cunningham in one of the first books on the New Woman heroine, identifies the fictional New Woman as middle-class, educated and independent, one who prioritizes career over marriage, feels free to choose her sexual partner, is in conflict with social convention as a matter of principle – eccentricity or flamboyance is not enough – and stands outside any recognizable movement or organization. She was identifiable, says Cunningham, by her short hair, frank language, rational dress, bicycle, latchkey and cigarette (1978: 10–11).

It is significant that the four New Women in Grundy's play were all writers, and writers of 'advanced' books, for writing was perceived to be the *sine qua non* of the proselytizing New Woman. In an exchange between the neglected husband of one of the New Women and his military friend, these 'Frankensteins' are anatomized:

Colonel: [*Picking up a book.*] 'Man, the Betrayer – a study of the Sexes – by Enid Bethune.'

Sylvester: O I know her. She comes to our house.

Colonel: And has any man betrayed her?

Sylvester: Never. Not likely to.

Colonel: That's what's the matter, perhaps?

Sylvester: Her theory is, that boys ought to be girls, and young men ought to be maids. That's how she would equalise the sexes.

Colonel: Pshaw! [*Takes up another book.*] 'Ye Foolish Virgins! A Remonstrance – by Victoria Vivash.'

Sylvester: Another soul! She's also for equality. Her theory is that girls should be boys, and maids should be young men. Goes in for latchkeys and that sort of thing.

Colonel: Bah! [*Takes up a third book*.] 'Naked and Unashamed – A Few Plain Facts and Figures – by Mary Bevan, M.D.' Who on earth's she?

Sylvester: One of the plain figures. She comes to our house too. (Grundy, 1894: 8–9)

The title of his wife's book is 'Aspirations after an Higher Morality'. Grundy's satirical depiction of the women writers can be found replicated in many different forms. New Women writers in the popular imagination were seen to be eternal spinsters – or transgressive wives – obsessed with, and confused about, gender whether they are writing fiction, polemic, scientific tracts or philosophy. Serious depictions of the New Woman in the period by men tended to be similarly problematic. If sympathetically characterized, they were almost always neurotic and fated to either literal suicide (Grant Allen's Herminia Barton in *The Woman Who Did* (1895), and Constance Denham in John Todhunter's play, *The Black Cat* (1893) both prefigure Eleanor Marx's suicide by prussic acid), or metaphorical suicide (Sue Bridehead in Hardy's *Jude the Obscure* (1895) returns to her loveless marriage, Agnes Ebbsmith in Pinero's *The Notorious Mrs Ebbsmith* (1895) exiles herself to a remote Yorkshire rectory), or the emotional desert of spinsterhood (Gissing's aptly named Rhoda Nunn in *The Odd Women* (1893), G.B. Shaw's Vivie Warren in *Mrs Warren's Profession* (1898)). Agnes Ebbsmith – and by inference her author – sees her failure to live up to her ideals as evidence that 'My sex has found me out' (Pinero, 1895: 156). Jill Davis attributes this ambiguous response to the New Woman on the male writers' part to 'the negotiation in progressive men in this period between conscious desires, which led them to support women's emancipation, and the unconscious fears of that as a threat to masculine gender identity' (Gardner and Rutherford, 1992: 25). Women writing New Women, do not minimize the problems and challenges facing their protagonists, but they rarely show their heroines as inherently weak and neurotic. Physical and mental illness is usually shown as the result of social pressure or individual oppression rather than female weakness, as in *The Yellow Wallpaper*, or *Red Pottage* where Hester Gresley's breakdown follows the destruction of her novel by her clergyman brother.

The central concern of all the New Woman fiction was female autonomy, whether in the matter of marriage, sexuality, motherhood or work. 'New Woman writing consistently problematized, deconstructed, demystified, or rethought "womanliness"' writes Lyn Pykett, and continues:

The New Woman writers . . . rethought the plots of domestic realism, particularly the marriage plot. Marriage the destination of the mainstream Victorian novel, and the resolution of all its (and supposedly the heroine's) problems, became, in the New Woman novel, both the origin of narrative and the source of the heroine's problems. (1995: 57)

One of the earliest novels to do this was *The Story of an African Farm*, considered by many to be the Ur-New Woman novel. Written by a South African, Olive Schreiner, and published under the pseudonym Ralph Iron in 1883, the novel found a ready audience in Britain. The originality of the novel's revolt can be found in its explicit articulation in the words and actions of its heroine, Lyndall, of the repressive socialization of Victorian womanhood, and in Lyndall's rejection of the role that has been determined for her.

'Look at this little chin of mine, with a dimple in it. It is but a small part of my person; but though I have the knowledge of all things under the sun, and the wisdom to use it, and the deep loving heart of an angel, it would not stead me through life like this little chin. I can win money with it, I can win love; I can win power with it, I can win fame. What would knowledge help me? The less a woman has in her head the lighter she is for climbing. . . . They begin to shape us for our cursed end when we are tiny things in shoes and socks. We sit with our little feet drawn up under us in the window, and look at the boys in their happy play. We want to go. Then a loving hand is laid on us: "Little one, you cannot go," they say, "your face will burn, and your nice white dress will spoil." . . . Afterwards we go and thread blue beads and make a string for our necks; and we go and stand before the glass. . . . Then the curse begins to act on us. It finishes its work when we are grown women, who no more look out wistfully at a more healthy life; we are contented. . . . In some of us the shaping to our end has been completed. The parts we are not to use have been quite atrophied, and have even dropped off. . . . A little bitterness, a little longing, when we are young, a little futile searching for work, a little striving for room for the exercise of our powers, – and then we go with the drove. A woman must march with her regiment. In the end she must be trodden down or go with it; and if she is wise she goes.' (Schreiner, 1971: 188–9)

Lyndall chooses not to 'go with the drove', but seeks an independent life away from the farm on the veldt and her two conventional suitors. She dies a protracted death, following the birth and death of her illegitimate daughter, child of an unnamed lover. But she does not die with a sense of sin – Lyndall is no Isabel Vane – but a lack of fulfilment. In rejecting her lover's offer of marriage she says, 'I am not afraid of the world – I will fight the world. One day – perhaps it may be far off – I shall find what I have wanted all my life; something nobler, stronger than I, before which I can kneel down . . .' (279). Though the ending is superficially the conventional closure of the Victorian narrative where the Magdalen dies and the passive 'angel in the house', Em, marries one of the abandoned suitors, the power of Lyndall's critique of Victorian gender hegemony remains with the reader.[16] And whilst Lyndall's aspirations remain vague, her frustration and her vision of a different future for women and men, when 'each woman's life is filled with earnest, independent labour, then love will come to her . . . not sought for but found. Then, but not now . . .' (195), is too strong to be entirely dissipated by the final chapters.

The radicalism of Schreiner's novel is not confined to the construction of her heroine, but the narrative strategy she employs enables Lyndall's voice to speak '"beyond the ending" even if she [Lyndall] cannot write or live beyond it' (Ardis, 1990: 68). In her Preface to the second edition of the book Schreiner elaborates on her narrative methodology, contrasting her own where 'nothing can be prophesied [and] men appear, act and re-act with each other, and pass away', with the 'stage method [where] we know with an immutable certainty that at the right crises each one will reappear and act his part, and when the curtain falls, all will stand before it bowing'. In eschewing the 'sense of satisfaction . . . of completeness' (Schreiner, 1971: 27) to be got from the conventional narrative structure and what D.H. Lawrence was to call 'the old stable ego of the character',[17] Schreiner resists both narrative and thematic closure and the presence of a hidden, omniscient narrator, thus prefiguring some of the characteristics of the modernist novel.

In many ways though, Olive Schreiner's protagonist is atypical among the New Women heroines. While they normally share Lyndall's view of the Victorian construction of womanhood and marriage, they rarely follow her path into 'free union'. The critiques of marriage and relationships between the sexes found in the novels of Sarah Grand, Mona Caird, Emma Frances Brooke, Ménie Muriel Dowie and other women writers are every bit as passionate as Schreiner's, but they are predicated upon a belief in the women's agency for good and a recognition of the practicalities of sex relationships. 'Free unions' and illegitimate births meant social ostracism; for the majority of women economic dependence and inadequate contraception meant that marriage remained the most common reality. Divorce was still too exclusive and too costly, in financial and social terms, to be an option for most women, so marriage reform as a means of social transformation rather than divorce[18] or 'free love' is the subtext to most New Woman novels.

In a number of novels 'free union' is offered to the heroine, usually when one or other of the parties is still married. As Vincent Hemming argues with Mary Erle in *The Story of a Modern Woman*: 'Other women – great women – have been strong enough, single-hearted enough, to do that much for the men they loved. Dear heart, think of the years we might spend together' (Dixon, 1990: 254). But these women did not want to be 'great women', just to live their unexceptional lives on their own terms. Mary's response is that she cannot do it:

> 'I can't, I can't – not even for you! It is not that I mind what people would say – that's nothing. It isn't that I don't love you. I-I- why, I have always loved you. But it's the other woman, your wife. I can't, I won't, deliberately injure another woman. Think how she would suffer! Oh the torture of women's lives – the helplessness, the impotence, the emptiness!' (254–5)

Robert Maitland, saddled with an unsympathetic, invalid wife, and Alexandra Hope in the Findlater sisters' *Crossriggs* (1908), share a similarly thwarted love and again it is the woman who, with the plea 'Don't – oh don't. . . . You'll never forgive yourself, nor will I; won't you help me, dearest?' frustrates their moment of passion and then agonizes as to 'why were no easier places hers, a less high moral attitude, on a lower level?' (Findlater, 1986: 330–1). Alexandra is no prig but her control of her feelings is part of her larger sense of moral duty which has led her to assume responsibility for her unworldly father and her widowed sister and five nieces and nephews. She does not, however, martyr herself by accepting any offer of marriage. The economic imperative of her family's situation does not lead her to sacrifice herself in a relationship where she does not love or respect. She chooses work – as a public reader – over marriage. Alex is contrasted in the book with her sister, Matilda, who having married early has been left widowed with five children and without the resources, personal or economic, to cope and who marries one of Alex's rejected lovers in order to do 'what she thinks is best for herself and her children, and [to make] a good man happy' (352). The decision is not seen as a negative but a realistic one for a woman temperamentally inclined and raised to be dependent.

The New Woman novels and short stories constantly problematize the assumptions underlying marriage in the nineteenth century, but in doing so they do not offer a single, simple analysis of either cause or solution. Like *Crossriggs* they explore a wide range of marital situations and sexual relationships, often through the contrast of real or symbolic sisters. This strategy enabled the writers to explore opposed female ideologies such as those represented by the 'angel in the house' and the New Woman: Matilda and Alexandra Hope, Evadne Frayling and Edith Beale in *The Heavenly Twins* (1893), Margaret Essex and Gallia in Ménie Muriel Dowie's *Gallia* (1895). It enabled them to contrast the paths of New Women inside and outside marriage, for example, sisters Hadria and Algitha Temperley and their friend Valeria Du Prel in Mona Caird's *The Daughters of Danaus* (1894), Lucretia Bampfylde and Kitty Manners in Isabella O. Ford's *On the Threshold* (1895), or the differing experience of women making their way in the world, such as wealthy Rachel West and impoverished writer Hester Gresley in *Red Pottage* (1899) or rich philanthropist Alison Ives and Mary Erle in *The Story of a Modern Woman* (1894). Mrs Oliphant's classification of this group of novelists as 'the Anti-Marriage League', in a *Blackwood's* article in 1896 (Oliphant, 1896: 135–49), is misleading as most of the writers were not anti-marriage *per se*, but against marriage as it was experienced at that time. At root marriage was seen as – in Cicely Hamilton's phrase – 'a trade' which women's economic vulnerability forced them into. Hamilton writes:

> How to eat, how to maintain existence, is the problem that has confronted woman, as well as man, since the ages dawned for her. Other needs and desires may come later; but the first call of life is a means of supporting it. To support life it is necessary to have access to the fruits of the earth, either directly . . . or indirectly . . . [Man], even when direct access to the earth has been denied to him, has usually been granted some measure of choice as to the manner in which he would pay for the necessities the earth produced for him – that is to say he was permitted to select the trade by which he earned his livelihood. From woman, who has always been far more completely excluded from direct access to the necessities of life, who has often been barred, both by law and custom, from the possession of property, one form of payment was demanded, and one only. It was demanded that she should enkindle and satisfy the desire of the male, who would thereupon admit her to such share of the property he possessed or earned as should seem good to him. In other words she exchanged, by the ordinary process of barter, possession of her person for the means of existence. (1981: 26–7)

Many of the heroines of New Woman fictions enter marriage against their own wishes or desires. Viola Sedley in Mona Caird's *The Wing of Azrael* (1889) is forced, in a classic melodrama scenario, to marry her handsome but cruel neighbour in order to save her sick parents from having to leave their home. Beth Caldwell in *The Beth Book* succumbs to the pressure exerted by her mother to marry the elderly doctor, Dan Maclure. Listening to her mother's sobs she berates herself:

What should she do? Her unhappy mother – heartbroken, indeed. What a life hers was – a life of hard privation, of suffering most patiently borne, of the utmost self-denial for her children's sake, of loss, of loneliness, of bitter disappointment! First her husband taken, then her dearest child; her ungrateful boys not over-kind to her; and now this last blow dealt her by Beth, just when the prospect of getting her well married was bringing a gleam of happiness into her mother's life. (Grand, 1980: 336)

Her mother in turn sees marriage to the successful doctor as a way for Beth to escape the cycle of debt that had 'crushed' her own marriage – and because it will mean 'one less mouth to feed' (337). The opening act of Cicely Hamilton's play *Diana of Dobson's* (1908) shows how the trade of marriage is not confined to daughters of the middle and upper middle classes. For the shop girls in Dobson's department store marriage offers the only escape from 'the delectable atmosphere of Dobson's'. Diana Massingberd predicts that her life will consist of crawling 'round similar establishments, cringing to be taken on at the same starvation salary – then settl[ing] down in the same stuffy dormitory, with the same mean rules to obey – [serving] the same intelligent customers – and bolt[ing her] dinner off the same tough meat in the same gloomy dining-room with the same mustard-coloured paper on the walls' (Hamilton, 1991: 40) if she does not follow her colleague Kitty's example.

The pressures to marry were not only economic but tied up with women's own expectations and desires for emotional fulfilment through love and motherhood. As Mrs Caldwell tells Beth, '*I* know girls! They all want to be married, and they all pretend they don't. Why when I was a girl I thought of nothing else' (Grand, 1980: 335). In Sarah Grand's *The Heavenly Twins* (1893), Edith Beale, who has been brought up in complete ignorance of life to fall in love with a 'Lord' and 'Master' who will 'keep her pure', sees her destiny to reform her future husband, Sir Mosley Menteith:

'Edith has accepted him because she loves him and that is enough,' said Mrs Beale . . .
   'If he is *bad* I will make him good; if he is lost, I will save him!'
   'Spoken like a true woman, dearest!' her mother said . . .

Even her friend and critic, the New Woman, Evadne, recognizes the emotional imperative:

'I know how you feel,' she said to Edith drearily, 'You glow and are glad from morning till night. You have a great yearning here,' she clasped her hands to her breast . . . He is your last thought at night, your first in the morning. Even when he is away from you, you do not feel separated from him as you do from other people, for a sense of his presence remains with you, and you flatter yourself that your spirits mingle when your bodies are apart. You think too, that the source of all this ecstasy is holy because it is pleasurable; you imagine it will last for ever.' (Grand, 1893: 234–5)

The consequence of Victorian women's ignorance is exposed when Edith discovers shortly after her marriage to Menteith that he is 'not the repentant erring sinner she imagined him' (288) and that he has infected her and her child with syphilis. The consequence of her 'training' in female passivity prevents her from acting when 'the natural instinct of her womanhood impelled her to war with him'. As she has 'been robbed of all means of self-defence by the teaching which insisted that her only duty as a wife consisted in silent submission to her husband's will' she finally succumbs to the 'shadow of an awful form of insanity' (280). Female submissiveness also led to what George Egerton was to describe in one short story as 'a legal prostitution, a nightly degradation, a hateful yoke under which they [married women] age, mere bearers of children conceived in duty, not love' (Egerton, 1983: 155). In Egerton's story the blame lies with women themselves who collude in the perpetuation of ignorance. Florence, three years married, confronts her mother with:

> Man is what we have made him, his very faults are of our making. No wife is bound to set aside the demands of her individual soul for the sake of individual obedience. . . . I say it is your fault, because you reared me a fool, ignorant of everything I ought to have known, everything that concerned me and the life I was bound to lead as a wife; my physical needs, my coming passion, the very meaning of my sex, my wifehood and motherhood to follow. (155–7)

Florence's solution is to leave her husband as does Beth Caldwell. The New Woman writers offered few solutions *within* marriage. The argument seems to be that gender relations as then constituted rendered marriage an intolerable and potentially destructive condition for women. George Egerton's stories in the volumes *Keynotes* (1893) and *Discords* (1894) are both frank in their treatment of female desire and depressing in their reiteration of the impossibilities of the female condition. If the struggle for autonomy within marriage was doomed to failure small wonder that a significant number of young, middle-class women are shown to reject marriage. Lucretia Bampfylde in Isabella Ford's *On the Threshold* (1895) writes to her newly wed friend, Kitty, that she intends to pursue her music career rather than marry, for 'the idea of marriage does not attract or interest [her] very much; women's lives are so cut up when they marry. And after all, is it worth it?' (Ford, 1895: 201), she asks.

There are instances of the New Woman asserting her right to choose her sexual partner, but they are rare. Gallia, eponymous heroine of Ménie Muriel Dowie's novel, ultimately selects her husband rationally and eugenically. Having fallen in love with the neurotic aesthete, Dark Essex, who proves indifferent to her, she marries Mark Gurdon who she sees as 'keen and gamey and lifey' (Dowie, 1895: 215). Interestingly, several instances of choice involve women turning their back on their own class. In Bell and Robins's play *Alan's Wife* (1893) based on a short story by Swedish writer Elin Ameen, the educated heroine, Jean, answers her mother's chiding about her preferences for Alan Creke over the bookish curate, with,

> We can't all marry scholars, Mother dear – some of us prefer marrying men. Ah to be happy – to be alive! (Bell and Robins, 1991: 11–12)

The vigour of their love is evidenced in Jean's pregnancy and the openness with which it is celebrated. In Emma Frances Brooke's *A Superfluous Woman* (1894), Jessamine Halliday recalls her sexual feelings for the 'noble peasant' Colin Macgillvray who has rescued her from a rutting stag. 'As bare to feeling as any pagan girl,' she imagines that 'his rude forceful pressure returned again upon her slender figure with an alluring yet terrifying sweetness' (Brooke, 1893: 143). She is prepared to give herself to Colin, but he refuses unless they marry. In Githa Sowerby's play, *Rutherford and Son* (1912), Janet, the daughter of the tyrannical mill owner, John Rutherford, defies him and forms a liaison with his foreman, Martin, 'a good-looking man of the best type of working man' (Sowerby, 1991: 153). Doomed as the relationship is by Martin's subservience to Rutherford, it is the start of Janet's emancipation from her father. Such alliances across class boundaries – that according to Linda Dowling in her essay on the New Woman and the Decadent (Dowling, 1978) were almost as much feared as those between the New Woman and the aesthete – are not common. The failure of middle-class men in marriage did not automatically drive their wives into the arms of the artisan class.

However, while some New Woman novels argued superior female purity in the face of male animalism, many depicted female desire in a direct, uncoded way, but it was rarely shown as unproblematic nor separated from the social conditions that rendered sexual relations unequal. Ann Ardis argues that when a New Woman like Mary Erle chooses celibacy it is 'because celibacy is the only way she can possess her "self" in a culture that conceives of a sexual relationship as a man's "possession" of a woman' (1990: 110).

In the face of Victor Hemmings's proposal that she goes to France with him as his mistress, Mary Erle feels

> drawn, in spite of herself, by the mysterious, inexorable bond of the flesh. Youth, the will to live, the imperious demands of human passion for one moment were to have their way . . . as he held her two wrists like a vice . . . then slowly, with a long shudder, she was conscious that his arms were enfolding her. It was good to rest there . . . (Dixon, 1990: 250)

But she chooses not to betray herself or her fellow woman, his wife. In a number of the novels the strength of feeling and commitment between women outweighs that between any man and woman. However, it is in the poetry of the writers, Katherine Bradley and Edith Cooper – 'Michael Field' – that the era's most explicit erotic exchange between women can be found.

> Her hand the thigh's tense surface leaves,
> Falling inward. Not even sleep
> Dare invalidate the deep,
> Universal pleasure sex
> Must unto itself annex –
> Even the stillest sleep; at peace,
>   More profound with rest's increase,
> She enjoys the good
> Of delicious womanhood.
>   (Field, 1892: 101–2)

The most notorious eroticist among the women writers of the 1890s was undoubtedly George Egerton. Many of her short stories in *Keynotes* and *Discords* centre on women's, often troubled, erotic lives. In 'A Cross Line' the heroine fantasizes as she lies on the riverbank that she is dancing voluptuously in the open air before an audience of hundreds ending with 'One quivering, gleaming, daring bound, and she stands with outstretched arms and passion-filled eyes, poised on one slender foot, asking for a supreme note to finish her dream of motion' (Egerton, 1983: 20). While she waits for the fisherman who is not her 'monotonous' husband, she muses on men's failure to understand women, believing that

> They have all overlooked the eternal wilderness, the untamed primitive savage tempera-
> ment that lurks in the mildest, best woman. Deep in through the ages of convention this
> primeval trait burns, an untameable quality that may be concealed but is never eradi-
> cated by culture – the keynote of women's witchcraft and woman's strength. (22)

But as the woman herself acknowledges to her would-be lover, she shares the 'crown-ing disability of [her] sex' – the capacity for affection – 'though [she] chafe[s] under it'. Without that, she avers, women 'would master the world (28). At the end of the story the woman, pregnant, chooses to remain with her husband, transferring her sensuality to the coming child.

The erotic and romantic focus in women's lives often shifts to motherhood during this period. Ann Ardis again argues that the women writers' heroines often 'discover their "true nature" as mothers . . . [but] eroticize maternity in a way that would have been completely incompatible with the Victorian code of womanliness' (1990: 93). She cites Iota's 1894 novel, *A Yellow Aster*, as typical of one section of New Woman writing in its presentation of the transformational nature of motherhood. In *A Yellow Aster*, the heroine Gwen Waring marries a man she does not love and bears his child. Only when the child falls ill does 'the latent truth in her own nature' come out and she becomes a 'beautiful sexual mother-woman' in love with her husband as well as her child (Iota, 1894: 172). This essentialist argument about motherhood found in Egerton and Iota, can be found elsewhere among women's novels in the 1890s, notably Lucas Cleeve's [Adeline Kingscote] *The Woman Who Wouldn't* (1895) and Eliza Lynn Linton's *The New Woman in Haste and Leisure* (1895). Polemicists like Mona Caird argued against this 'natural' conception of motherhood without denying maternal responsibility for the raising of children. In her essay, 'A Defence of the "Wild Women"' she writes that:

> we shall never have really good mothers, until women cease to make motherhood the
> central idea of their existence. The woman who has no interest larger than the affairs
> of her children is not a fit person to train them . . . it is to be hoped that women will
> come to regard motherhood with new eyes; that the force of their artificially fostered
> impulses will become less violent . . . [for] all the inferences of phrases such as
> 'Nature intends', 'Nature desires' [are false.] She intends and desires nothing – she is
> an abject slave. *Man* intends, *Man* desires, and 'Nature' in the course of centuries,
> learns to obey. (1897: 173)

Among the female poets, Alice Meynell wrote, according to Angela Leighton, 'almost the first, serious adult poems, by any poet, about biological motherhood' (1992: 257). 'The Modern Mother' (1900) explores the realities of the complex mutual needs of mother and child.

> Unhoped, unsought!
> A little tenderness, this mother thought
> The utmost of her meed.
> She looked for gratitude; content indeed
> With thus much that her nine years' love had
>   bought.
>
> (Leighton and Reynolds, 1995: 521)

Like sexuality, motherhood was valorized in much New Women fiction, but like marriage it was also seen as problematic, particularly while 'sex-antagonism' still existed.

The New Woman writers, though still too often effaced or dismissed as 'minor' in considerations of the literature of the period, indisputably effected 'an important shift in the relationship of the idea and the ideal of marriage to the form of the novel' (Miller, 1994: 45). In doing so they also changed the way women writers were perceived. They exploited and subverted the novel form traditionally associated with the woman writer, the romance, and embraced the new social realism in order to expose the evils generated by Victorian attitudes towards sex and marriage. The rhetoric of Evadne's evocation of love in *The Heavenly Twins* quoted above could have come from the pen of Mrs Humphry Ward, but, like the melodramatic narrative of Caird's *The Wing of Azrael*, it is put to a radically different purpose. There is, though, a continuing tension in the New Woman fiction between the authors' attempts to implicate society in their heroines' often tragic lives, and the traditional narratives of female martyrdom and failure.

Onto the platform

In 1890 Lady Florence Dixie published a novel, *Gloriana; Or the Revolution of 1900*, in which her heroine at the age of 12 tells her mother that she wants 'all women to rise as one' to emancipate themselves and thereby men too. By disguising herself as a boy and going to Eton and then Oxford, she eventually becomes Prime Minister and sets about establishing an equal society in a Utopia of full employment, green parks and food for all.[19] While Utopian visions, particularly woman-centred ones, are uncommon among women novelists before the 1900s (Jane Hume Clapperton's *Margaret Dunmore; or, A Socialist Home* (1888) and Gertrude Dix's *The Image Breakers* (1900) are rare exceptions, as is Ethel Voynich's 1897 novel, *The Gadfly* which draws a sympathetic portrait of revolutionary idealism in the Italian Risorgimento[20]), it is possible to perceive a muted subliminal optimism. Underlying the isolation of the heroines of the 1880s and 1890s was the recognition of a genuine, albeit unstructured and often invisible, community of women, sometimes literally, sometimes metaphorically, a sisterhood. Mary Erle believes that 'All we modern women mean to help each other now' (Dixon, 1990: 255) and Beth Caldwell finds her salvation among a group of sympathetic women dedicated to 'feminist' causes. The heroine of Elizabeth Robins's *Votes for Women* (1907), Vida Levering, describes her path from isolation to communal action in the last act of the play:

the time has come when a woman may look about her, and say, 'What general significance has my secret pain? Does it "join on" to anything?' And I find it does. I'm no
longer merely a woman who has stumbled on the way. I'm one who has got up bruised
and bleeding, wiped the dust from her hands and the tears from her face, and said to
herself not merely, 'Here's one luckless woman! but – here is a stone of stumbling to
many. Let's see if it can't be moved out of other women's way.' And she calls people to
come and help. No mortal man, let alone a woman, *by herself*, can move that rock of
offence. But (*With a sudden sombre flame of enthusiasm*.) if many help . . . the thing can be
done. (Robins, 1985: 87)

A concern with specific single issues emanating from the feminist causes of the day
emerges in a large number of the earlier novels. *The Heavenly Twins* is concerned not
only with the problem of venereal disease and female ignorance, but the double
standard. Evadne, on discovering that she has married a 'vice-worn' man elects to
'sacrifice the man instead of the woman' and to live with her husband but refuse to
consummate the marriage rather than risk the hereditary consequences of vice. Central to Beth Caldwell's revolt against her husband in *The Beth Book* is the discovery
that he runs a Lock Hospital for the examination and treatment of alleged prostitutes
under the Contagious Diseases Acts. Georgina Weldon's semi-autobiographical play,
Not Alone (1886), in which Weldon appeared as her own heroine Hester Stanhope,
deals with an attempt by Hester's husband to have her incarcerated in a mental
asylum for her unconventional behaviour. Elizabeth Robins treats infanticide in
Alan's Wife (1893), incestuous marriage and genetics in *The Open Question* (1899),
female homelessness and abortion in *Votes for Women/The Convert* (1907), the 'white
slave trade' in *Where Are You Going To . . .?* (1913). In 'Gone Under' George
Egerton tells a story of youthful seduction and the effects of abortion. Edith Lyt-
telton's three-act drama, *Warp and Woof* (1904) treats the issue of female sweated
labour, Cicely Hamilton's *Diana of Dobson's* (1908) that of female shop workers. The
novels, short stories, poems, plays and journalism became the platform for many
women to articulate current political campaigns. All this found a particular focus in
the newly energized franchise movement of the 1900s. Like Gloriana in 1890 and
Vida Levering in 1907, many women saw the enfranchisement of women as the 'root
of all future social reform, which means progress, comfort, and happiness for the
toiling millions' (Dixie, 1890: 182).

Just as it would be wrong to characterize all women's writing in the 1880s and
1890s as 'New Woman', it would be wrong to characterize all women's writing in the
Edwardian era as suffragist. However, the suffrage movement did produce a new
strand of writing, not simply in terms of narrative content, but also strategy. Women
writers wielded their pens in the propaganda war surrounding the suffrage movement, forming the Women Writers' Suffrage League in June, 1908, in the belief that
'A body of writers working for a common cause cannot fail to influence public
opinion' (Showalter, 1982: 219). Opportunities were opened up for writers of prose,
poetry and drama by the inauguration of the various suffrage journals (the Women's
Social and Political Union's *Votes for Women* and *The Suffragette*, the NUWSS's *The
Common Cause*, the Women's Freedom League's *The Women's Franchise* and *The*

Vote, the East London Federation's *The Women's Dreadnought*) and suffrage presses. The United Suffragists published Evelyn Sharp's *Rebel Women* (1909) and the Women's Freedom League Gertrude Colmore's short story collection, *Mr Jones and the Governess* (1913). The Women's Press produced mainly non-fiction and the Actresses' Franchise League, plays. And as Glenda Norquay points out in the Introduction to her anthology of material from the suffrage movement, *Voices and Votes* (1995) commercial publishers were prepared to handle pro-suffrage novels where it could be marketed as popular romantic fiction, as in the case of *Outlawed* (1908) by Charlotte Despard and Mabel Collins, and Adrienne Mollwo's *A Fair Suffragette* (1909), or where the author's reputation could guarantee sales (Norquay, 1995: 3–5).

Much of the fiction, poetry and drama produced for 'the Cause' in the period up to 1910 was unashamedly propagandist. This can be seen most clearly in the plays produced by the Actresses' Franchise League which were written for performance at the meetings and rallies organized by the various suffrage societies. Necessarily short and direct, they range in style from the broadly comic (Mrs Harlow Phibbs's monologue *The Mothers' Meeting* and L.S. Phibbs's *Jim's Leg*, Evelyn Glover's *A Chat with Mrs Chicky*) to naturalistic sketches (Gertrude Jennings's *A Woman's Influence*, Evelyn Glover's *Mrs Appleyard's Awakening*), and allegorical pageants (Vera Wentworth's *The Allegory*, Cicely Hamilton's *A Pageant of Great Women*).[21] Some of the plays were more substantial. Cicely Hamilton and Christopher St John's one-act comedy, *How the Vote was Won* (1909), and Elizabeth Robins's three-act drama, *Votes for Women* (1907), both received West End performances and positive critical responses as contributions to the 'Theatre of Ideas'. Nor were the plays produced by the AFL confined to franchise scenarios. The intersection between feminist and suffragist positions can be seen clearly in Inez Bensusan's *The Apple*, which deals with sexual harassment at work and the unequal treatment of sons and daughters, and *Before Sunrise* by Bessie Hatton, which deals with the old tensions between marriage, motherhood and work.

The drama produced by the AFL was often written by non-dramatists, and similarly the poetry produced for 'the Cause' often came from the pen of women better known for their suffrage activities, like Emily Wilding Davison with her militaristic poem 'L'Envoi', or the sixteen imprisoned contributors to *Holloway Jingles* (Norquay, 1995: 172–8). But established poets, like Eva Gore-Booth and Alice Meynell, also wrote in support of the movement. Gore-Booth's 'Women's Rights' expresses the difference between the world of men and the future promised by the women's movement:

> . . .
>
> But where men in office sit
> Winter holds the human wit.
>
> In the dark and dreary town
> Summer's green is trampled down.
>
> Frozen, frozen everywhere
> Are the springs of thought and prayer.
>
> Rise with us and let us go
> To where the living waters flow.

> Oh, whatever men may say
> Ours is the wide and open way.
>
> . . .
>
> Men have got their towers and walls
> We have cliffs and waterfalls.
>
> Oh, whatever men may do
> Ours is the gold air and the blue.
>
> Men have got their pomp and pride –
> All the green world is on our side.
>
> (Gardiner, 1993: 228–9)

The most enduring literary relics of the suffrage movement are the novels and memoirs. The experience of the campaign, particularly the militant campaign, provided the women with material for both fiction and non-fiction. Books like Elizabeth Robins's *The Convert* (1907) – an adaptation of her play, *Votes for Women* – and Gertrude Colmore's *Suffragette Sally* (1911), are based on experience and observation. Since they were both produced during the campaign itself they offer unique, if partial, testimony of the lived-reality of the movement, particularly the moment of conversion and the effect of its charismatic leaders. These leaders, the Pankhursts, Pethick-Lawrences, and Constance Lytton all produced their accounts of the period of political activity after the event. Some, like Christabel Pankhurst's *Unshackled* (1959), are disappointingly dull compared with the vigour of her reputation and her notorious polemic against male sexuality and venereal disease, 'The Great Scourge and How to End It' (1913). Some, like Annie Kenney's *Memories of a Militant* (1924), are personal and engaging. The campaign also produced its anti-suffrage journalism and fiction, notably Mrs Humphry Ward's *Delia Blanchflower* (1914), written at the height of the militant campaign and containing a damning portrait of the fanatic in Gertrude Marvell, who exploits the eponymous heroine's love for her in order to draw her into the militant campaign.

Elaine Showalter writes that on balance, 'the suffrage movement was not a happy stimulus to women writers [because] no real manifesto of female literature was produced' (1982: 236). This may be so. Some of the suffrage writings are limited as 'high art' since the first concern of the work was political and celebratory rather than aesthetic but as such they are as successful as any other examples of twentieth-century political literature. However, even these 'agit-prop' pieces stand as important historical documents and represent a period of intense social and political engagement in women's writing which was not, nor could be, sustained beyond the movement but form an important stage in the advance of women's writing and women as writers.

Conclusion

The years between 1880 and 1910 may not have produced any easily accepted major, canonical, female writers. Successful commercial writers like Sarah Grand, the dramatist Madeline Lucette Ryley – who provoked a jealous jibe from Shaw when her play *Jedbury Junior* was published in an *édition de luxe* priced at eighteen pence rather than the usual sixpence – and the children's writer, E. Nesbit, are discounted in orthodox literary histories. But these decades did produce significant changes in the representation of women, and foregrounded the problems of women and writing. Fiction, drama, poetry and journalism were all used to interrogate and destabilize notions of femaleness, sexuality and gender in both popular and 'highbrow' literature. Dominated by the 'New Woman' writers, whether they were exploiting traditional fiction forms or negotiating new authorial strategies, female writers of the *fin de siècle* were breaking new ground.

In 1910 May Sinclair published her novel, *The Creators*. In it the five protagonists are writers but three of them are women, something unthinkable thirty years earlier. The old tensions are still there, the choices between marriage, children, household management and creativity, and Sinclair, like her New Woman predecessors, eschews the easy happy ending. But the heroine, Jane Holland, does not leave her husband, does not go mad, does not die, but struggles on:

> She had so many balls to keep going. There was her novel; and there was Brodrick, and the baby, and Brodrick's family, and her own friends. She couldn't drop one of them. . . . But now she was beginning to feel the trembling of the perfect balance. It was as if, in that marvelous adjustment of relations, she had arrived at the pitch where perfection topples over. She moved with tense nerves on the edge of peril. (Sinclair, 1910: 342)

Her image of herself as the juggling tight-rope walker is at least up in the air – and not in the attic.

Notes

1. See also: Showalter, 1991; Pykett, 1995.
2. In the novel Rhoda Nunn expounds upon the situation to Monica Madden, 'But do you know that there are half a million more women than men in this happy country of ours. . . . So many *odd* women – no making a pair with them. The pessimists call them useless, lost, futile lives. I, naturally – being one of them myself – take another view. I look upon them as a great reserve' (Gissing, 1980: 37).
3. For a full consideration of the debates in the Men and Women's Club and other forums where sexuality was discussed in the period 1885–1914, see Bland (1995). David Rubinstein wrote of the Pioneer Club: 'From its inception the club was intended as a home for women of advanced views. . . . Members were expected to hew a path through the jungle of prejudice and outdated ideas, guided by their own convictions and uninhibited by the constraints of convention. If any single institution could claim to be the home of the new woman it was the Pioneer Club' (Rubinstein, 1986: 222).
4. Finally repealed in 1886.
5. See Dally, 1991: 92–6.
6. Elizabeth Robins's novel, *A Dark Lantern* (1905) also deals with the effects of the fashionable rest-cure for 'neurotic' women.
7. See: Stephens (1992), Chapter 5 'Booksellers and dramatic publishing'. Stephens argues that the proliferation of cheap 'acting' editions 'reinforced the widely recognized divorce

between the stage and literature, which set the nineteenth-century drama apart from all previous centuries since Shakespeare's time' (p. 117).

8. *The Beth Book* is subtitled: 'Being a Study of the Life of Elizabeth Caldwell Maclure, A Woman of Genius'.

9. See: Donkin (1995) for a study of the relationships between seven eighteenth-century women dramatists and their theatre managers, much of which can be applied to similar relationships throughout the nineteenth century. See also Stephens (1992) on the rise of playwriting as a reputable profession, who incidentally illustrates the invisibility of women dramatists in the nineteenth century, and in twentieth-century histories of the nineteenth-century stage.

10. It may be significant that in my limited research into the Dramatic Authors' Society list, I have found that the female honorary members are often related to prominent members of the Society as either daughters or wives.

11. I am grateful to Susan Croft and Kate Newey for access to the unpublished material and figures relating to women dramatists in the early nineteenth century which I have used in this section of the chapter.

12. Interestingly, Braddon's plays were published by her common-law husband, John Maxwell, thus obviating the need to negotiate in the male world of dramatic publishing.

13. According to Lillian Faderman 'Field' had been Edith Cooper's nickname from childhood, and 'Michael' Katherine Bradley's from before the two women's literary collaboration (Faderman, 1985: 209).

14. Robins may have been particularly sensitive to publicity having already suffered intrusive speculation about her private life following the suicide of her actor-husband in 1886.

15. For the disputed genealogy of the New Woman see: Ardis (1990), Chapter 1 'Preliminaries: Naming the New Woman', pp. 10–28.

16. Schreiner's subversion of gender is not confined to the heroine. Gregory, one of Lyndall's suitors, is described as 'a true woman – one born for the sphere that some women have to fill without being born for it. How happy he would be sewing frills into his little girls' frocks . . .' (197) and it is Gregory who is employed to nurse Lyndall on her deathbed.

17. In a letter to Edward Garnett, dated 5 June 1914, Lawrence warned that the reader 'mustn't look into my novel for the old stable ego of the character' (Lawrence, 1981: 183).

18. Pykett (1995) cites Arnold Bennett's *Whom God has Joined* (1906) as 'one of the first British novels to focus exclusively on the issue of divorce' (Pykett, 1995: 65).

19. See Bland, 1995: 209–11 and Ardis, 1990: 119–22.

20. Isabel Meredith's (pseudonym of Helen and Olivia Rossetti, daughters of William Michael Rossetti) *A Girl Among the Anarchists* (1903) provides a satirical portrait of London's anarchist community of the 1890s, but whilst not 'anti' can hardly be categorized as 'Utopian'.

21. For these and other examples see: Gardner (1985) and Spender and Hayman (1985).

Bibliography

Primary materials

Allen, Grant (1995) [1895], *The Woman Who Did*, Oxford: Oxford University Press.

Bell, Florence and Elizabeth Robins (1991) [1893], *Alan's Wife* in *New Woman Plays*, L. Fitzsimmons and V. Gardner (eds), London: Methuen.

Caird, Mona (1889), *The Wing of Azrael*, London: Trubner & Co.

Caird, Mona (1894), *The Daughters of Danaus*, London: Bliss, Sands & Foster.

Caird, Mona (1897), *The Morality of Marriage*, London: George Redway.

Cholmondeley, Mary (1985) [1899], *Red Pottage*, London: Virago.

Clapperton, Jane Hume (1888), *Margaret Dunmore; or, A Socialist Home*, London: Swan Sonnenschein, Lowry & Co.

Colmore, Gertrude (1984) [1911], *Suffragette Sally*, reprinted as *Suffragettes: A Story of Three Women*, London: Pandora Press.

Dix, Gertrude (1900), *The Image Breakers*, London: William Heinemann.

Dixie, Lady Florence (1890), *Gloriana; Or, The Revolution of 1900*, London: Henry & Co.

Dixon, Ella Hepworth (1990) [1894], *The Story of a Modern Woman*, London: Merlin Radical Fiction.

Dowie, Ménie Muriel (1895), *Gallia*, London: Methuen.

Egerton, George (1983) [1893 & 1894], *Keynotes and Discords*, London: Virago.

Field, Michael (1892), *Sight and Song*, London: Lane & Matthews.

Findlater, Jane and Mary (1986) [1908], *Crossriggs*, London: Virago.

Fitzsimmons, Linda and Viv Gardner (eds) (1991), *New Woman Plays*, London: Methuen.

Ford, Isabella O. (1895), *On the Threshold*, London: Edward Arnold.

Gardiner, Juliet (ed.) (1993), *Women's Voices 1880–1918: The New Woman*, London: Collins and Brown.

Gardner, Viv (ed.) (1985), *Sketches from the Actresses' Franchise League*, Nottingham: Nottingham Drama Texts.

Gilman, Charlotte Perkins (1981) [1892], *The Yellow Wallpaper*, London: Virago.

Gissing, George (1980) [1893], *The Odd Women*, London: Virago.

Grand, Sarah (1893), *The Heavenly Twins*, London: William Heinemann.

Grand, Sarah (1980) [1897], *The Beth Book*, London: Virago.

Grundy, Sydney (1894), *The New Woman*, London: The Chiswick Press.

Hamilton, Cicely (1935), *Life Errant*, London: J.M. Dent & Sons.

Hamilton, Cicely (1981) [1909], *Marriage as a Trade*, London: The Woman's Press.

Hamilton, Cicely (1991) [1908], *Diana of Dobson's* in *New Woman Plays*, L. Fitzsimmons and V. Gardner (eds), London: Methuen.

Iota (K.M. Caffynn) (1894), *A Yellow Aster*, London: Hutchinson.

Kenealy, Arabella (1990) [1899], *A Semi-Detached Marriage*, London: Virago.

Meade, L.T. (1891), *A Sweet Girl Graduate*, London: Cassell & Co.

Meredith, Isabel (1992) [1903], *A Girl among the Anarchists*, Lincoln and London: University of Nebraska Press.

Norquay, Glenda (1995), *Voices and Votes: A Literary Anthology of the Women's Suffrage Campaign*, Manchester: Manchester University Press.

Oliphant, Margaret (1896), 'The Anti-marriage League', *Blackwood's* 159, 135–49.

Pinero, Arthur Wing (1895), *The Notorious Mrs Ebbsmith*, London: Heinemann.

Robins, Elizabeth (1894), *George Mandeville's Husband*, London: William Heinemann.

Robins, Elizabeth (1980) [1907], *The Convert*, London: The Women's Press.

Robins, Elizabeth (1985) [1907], *Votes for Women* in *How the Vote Was Won and Other Suffragette Plays*, D. Spender and C. Hayman (eds), London: Methuen.

Schreiner, Olive (1971) [1883], *The Story of an African Farm*, Harmondsworth: Penguin Classics.

Sharp, Evelyn (1910), *Rebel Women*, London.

Showalter, Elaine (ed.) (1993), *Daughters of Decadence: Women Writers of the* Fin de Siècle, London: Virago.

Sinclair, May (1910), *The Creators*, New York: Century.

Smith, Joan (ed.) (1992), *Femmes de Siècle. Stories from the 90s: Women Writing at the End of Two Centuries*, London: Chatto & Windus.

Sowerby, Githa (1991) [1912], *Rutherford and Son* in *New Woman Plays*, L. Fitzsimmons and V. Gardner (eds), London: Methuen.

Spender, Dale and Carole Hayman (eds) (1985), *How the Vote Was Won and Other Suffragette Plays*, London: Methuen.

Stead, W.T. (1894), 'The Novel of the Modern Woman', *Review of Reviews* 10, 64–74.

Voynich, Ethel (1897), *The Gadfly*, London: William Heinemann.

Ward, Mary Augusta (Mrs Humphry) (1914), *Delia Blanchflower*, London: Ward, Lock.

Weldon, Georgina and George Lander (1886), *Not Alone,* London: C.W. Mayo.

Secondary materials

Ardis, Ann L. (1990), *New Woman, New Novels*, New Brunswick and London: Rutgers University Press.

Bland, Lucy (1995), *Banishing the Beast: English Feminism & Sexual Morality 1885–1914*, Harmondsworth: Penguin.

Cunningham, Gail (1978), *The New Woman and the Victorian Novel*, London: Macmillan.

Dally, Ann (1991), *Women under the Knife*, London: Hutchinson Radius.

Davis, Jill (1992), 'The New Woman and the New Life' in *The New Woman and Her Sisters*, V. Gardner and S. Rutherford (eds), London: Methuen.

Donkin, Ellen (1995), *Getting into the Act: Women Playwrights in London 1776–1829*, London: Routledge.

Dowling, Linda (1978), 'The Decadent and the New Woman in the 1890s' in *Nineteenth Century Fiction* 33 (1978–9).

Eliot, Simon (1995), 'Some Trends in British Publishing, 1800–1919' in *Literature in the Market Place: Nineteenth-Century British Publishing & Reading Practices*, John O. Jordan and Robert L. Patten (eds), Cambridge: Cambridge University Press.

Faderman, Lillian (1985), *Surpassing the Love of Men*, London: The Women's Press.

Gardner, Viv and Rutherford, Susan (eds) (1992), *The New Woman and Her Sisters: Feminism and Theatre 1850–1914*, Hemel Hempstead: Simon and Schuster.

Gates, Joanne E. (1994), *Elizabeth Robins: Actress, Novelist, Feminist*, Tuscaloosa and London: University of Alabama Press.

Gilbert, Sandra M. and Susan Gubar (1979), *The Madwoman in the Attic*, New Haven and London: Yale University Press.

Kent, Susan Kingsley (1987), *Sex and Suffrage in Britain 1860–1914*, London: Routledge.

Kersley, Gillian (1983), *Darling Madame: Sarah Grand & Devoted Friend*, London: Virago.

Lawrence, D.H. (1981), *Letters of D.H. Lawrence, Vol. 2*, George S. Zysank and James T. Boullen (eds), Cambridge: Cambridge University Press.

Ledger, Sally and Scott MacCracken (1995), *Culture and Politics at the* Fin de Siècle, Cambridge: Cambridge University Press.

Leighton, Angela (1992), *Women Poets: Writing Against the Heart*, Hemel Hempstead: Harvester Wheatsheaf.

Leighton, Angela and Margaret Reynolds (eds) (1995), *Victorian Women Poets: An Anthology*, Oxford: Blackwell.

Miller, Jane Eldridge (1994), *Rebel Women: Feminism, Modernism and the Edwardian Novel*, London: Virago.

Pykett, Lyn (1992), *The Improper Feminine: The Women's Sensation Novel and the New Woman Writing*, London: Routledge.

Pykett, Lyn (1995), *Engendering Fictions: The English Novel in the Early Twentieth Century*, London: Edward Arnold.

Rubinstein, David (1986), *Before the Suffragettes*, Hemel Hempstead: Harvester Wheatsheaf.

Showalter, Elaine (1982) [1977], *A Literature of Their Own*, London: Virago.

Showalter, Elaine (1991), *Sexual Anarchy: Gender and Culture at the* Fin de Siècle, London: Bloomsbury Publishing.

Stephens, John Russell (1992), *The Profession of the Playwright: British Theatre 1800–1900*, Cambridge: Cambridge University Press.

Stowell, Sheila (1992), *A Stage of Their Own: Feminist Playwrights of the Suffrage Era*, Manchester: Manchester University Press.

Tuchman, Gale with Nina E. Fortin (1989), *Edging Women Out: Victorian Novelists, Publishers and Social Change*, London: Routledge.

Vicinus, Martha (1980), *A Widening Sphere: Changing Roles of Victorian Women*, London: Methuen.

Walkley, A.B. (1893), Review of *Alan's Wife*, *Speaker*, 6 May, p. 512.

Williams, Raymond (1958), *Culture and Society*, London: The Hogarth Press.

Woolf, Virginia (1945) [1929], *A Room of One's Own*, Harmondsworth: Penguin Books.

Woolf, Virginia (1979) [1929], 'Women and Fiction' in Virginia Woolf, *Women and Writing*, London: The Women's Press.

8

Looking within: women's writing in the modernist period, 1910–40

Clare Hanson

Definitions and redefinitions

The particular contours of women's writing in the modernist period have become obscured for two main reasons. The first is the spectacular success of a small group of male artists and critics (among them Ford Madox Ford, T.E. Hulme, Ezra Pound and T.S. Eliot) in publicizing and promoting their version of modernism in the early twentieth century. Their success meant that a particular kind of modernism became accepted as the most important and significant art of its time. T.S. Eliot was a key figure in this process: his doctrines of impersonality and of the objective correlative were extremely influential in the period when modernism became institutionalized and codified in the 1920s and 1930s. The fact that Eliot's rhetoric went on to inspire aspects of New Critical theory ensured the continuing dominance of a formalist view of modernism within the academy: the influence of the New Critics is thus the second major reason for the marginalizing of the work of women modernists. What Pound and Eliot had created, the New Critics (re)instated, providing a hegemonic model of modernism which largely excluded the work of women. It was only with the rise of feminist criticism in the 1980s that this view of the period was challenged. Feminist critics began to argue that the Eliotean interpretive model in fact creates a very limited sense of the writing produced in this period. They have suggested that our understanding of modernism needs to be expanded to represent the difference of view of women writers, the difference of their experimentation with form and content. They have also argued for the importance of recognizing work from this period which falls outside the category of modernism and which may have been written in explicit opposition to it. This chapter will concentrate on the 'difference' of work by women which has clearly 'modernist' characteristics (self-reflexiveness, ambiguity, fragmentation of form and so on), but will also consider writing by women which moves in a different direction.

Feminist criticism has foregrounded the fact that definitions are always political. In the modernist period, the argument over, in Bourdieu's words, 'what deserves to be represented and the right way to represent it' was won by a group of male, middle-class writers who advocated an art which would avoid the personal, the emotional and the mundane (Bourdieu, 1986: 154–5). For decades, these artists' belief that this art conveyed a 'transcendent' reality was echoed by mainstream male critics and scholars. Feminist critics have challenged this claim, arguing that an art which passed as 'transcendent' was always in fact deeply embedded in particular social and ideological systems in which gender was a key element. In their monumental, three-volume study of women's writing in the modernist period, *No Man's Land: The Place of the Woman Writer in the Twentieth Century*, Sandra Gilbert and Susan Gubar have thus argued that literary modernism actually arose as a reaction to the 'woman question' and in response to the increasing numbers of women entering the literary market-place. They suggest that a major motive for modernism, with its exclusions and discriminations, was 'a reaction-formation' against the rise of literary women (Gilbert and Gubar, 1988: 156). While Gilbert and Gubar's work has been criticized recently for its lack of theoretical rigour (no *theory* of sex/gender is offered to support their analyses, for example), their account usefully highlights the way in which gender inflected supposedly 'aesthetic' debates in the modernist period.

The connection between gender and aesthetics in this period has been taken up by other feminist critics, for example Suzanne Clark, who in *Sentimental Modernism: Women Writers and the Revolution of the Word* (1991) analyzes the ways in which American modernism, in particular, defined itself against a 'sentimental' tradition associated with women. Bridget Elliott and Jo-Ann Wallace's study *Women Artists and Writers: Modernist (Im)positionings* (1994) similarly explores the way in which four key terms (the avant-garde, professionalism, genius and economic disinterestedness) have circulated and been manipulated in discourses about modernism up to the present day. They argue that such discourses have had a disciplinary function, making some meanings available to us and others not, surrounding us with some images and texts while others have simply dropped out of sight. So, as they point out, 'Picasso's *Les Demoiselles d'Avignon* is reproduced in countless coffee-table and text books, Romaine Brooks's *Peter (A Young Girl)* is not; Joyce's *Ulysses* is reprinted, re-edited, re-authorized, Natalie Barney's poems are unread' (15). What these critics share, then, is the view that hegemonic modernism (modernism as it has been con-structed by male artists and critics), far from being 'impersonal', has frequently carried strongly masculinist meanings. If modernism is gendered in the masculine (not simply in the sense that standard textbooks on the period still routinely concen-trate on male authors, but also in a deeper ideological sense) why should this be so?

Contexts

The gendering of modernism can be explained on one level in terms of women's restricted access to publication. As Richard Altick has shown, the proportion of women writers to men remained fairly constant throughout the period 1800–1935. Surprisingly, despite women's increased access to higher education, there was no significant increase in the overall percentage of women writers between 1900 and 1935, the figure rising only from 21.4% to 22.0% (Altick, 1962: 392). In the early twentieth century, women still did not have access to the same social and professional networks as their male counterparts. Control of prestigious literary and cultural journals remained in the hands of male editors, with the occasional woman as assistant editor (Beatrice Hastings, for example, was an assistant editor of A.R. Orage's influential *New Age*). Only one major periodical was edited by a woman, *The Freewoman* (later *The New Freewoman*, then *The Egoist*), and it is significant that this was financed by the independently wealthy Harriet Shaw Weaver. A similar pattern can be seen in book publication. In the modernist period, 'serious' women writers found publication extremely difficult, and in many cases it was only possible through access to an independent income. Writers like Woolf and Katherine Mansfield were able to set up their own presses and thus to disregard a hostile publishing climate. Others like Dorothy Richardson were able to go on writing only due to the intervention of a female patron ('Bryher', the writer and heiress Winifred Ellerman).

In part, then, modernism was gendered as masculine simply because, as ever, the overwhelming majority of writers in this period were men. However, as Gilbert and Gubar indicate, there was also a more subtle reaction to the threat posed by women in this period. As we have seen in the previous chapter, the period from 1880 to 1920 was one of instability and extreme anxiety over gender roles and privileges. It was a period of increased opportunity for many women. Women entered higher education in increasing numbers after the establishment of the first women's colleges at Girton and Newnham in the 1870s. By 1914, there were 11,000 full-time students at universities and university colleges in England and Wales, of whom 2,900 were women (McWilliams-Tulberg, 1977: 293). More professions were open to women: in 1908, for example, the medical and dental professions were opened to women. Particularly significant areas of expansion were in nursing and in clerical work. Both these areas offered respectable employment for unmarried women who would otherwise have had to be provided for by a male relative. Between 1891 and 1911 the number of women in clerical jobs rose from 19,000 to 125,000, and by 1914 a quarter of all clerks were women (Jackson, 1991: 124). The middle-class woman was thus moving out of the private sphere to which she had been restricted in the Victorian period, a 'voyage out' which is reflected in much modernist women's writing. Dorothy Richardson's long novel *Pilgrimage*, for example, vividly evokes the feelings of mingled terror and exhilaration which accompany the heroine's leaving home first for the 'pseudo work' of being a governess (still in the private sphere), then to become a clerical worker living on her own in London. During the First World War, women moved further into the public sphere, entering what had previously been masculine occupations, such as engineering and transport, although these occupations reverted to men once the war was over.[1]

This literal opening up of the space surrounding middle-class women was accompanied by a radical questioning of traditional gender roles. Women had been campaigning for the vote and for civic rights since the 1860s, but in the years immediately before the First World War the suffrage movement became increasingly militant as the Women's Social and Political Union resorted to controversial tactics of harassment and disruption. Cate Haste has argued that the government's response of imprisoning and force-feeding suffragettes stimulated in turn 'a more acute awareness of the constraints on women's freedom in all areas' (Haste, 1994: 18). So in the years just before the war younger women, in particular, began to stress not just the need for constitutional reform but also for much greater personal and sexual emancipation for women. While older feminists had argued for a single moral standard of sexual restraint, younger feminists began to defend women's right to enjoy their sexuality on similar terms to men. The publication of the work of Edward Carpenter and Havelock Ellis encouraged this emphasis on understanding and acknowledging the sexual self, as did the work of Freud, which first became available in translation in 1909. Freud's work, in particular, became the basis for a new sexual ethic which stressed the need for fulfilment for both sexes.

In this period women thus entered the workforce in increasing numbers, creating a new and highly visible class of independent women. They campaigned with eventual success for political and legal rights and for personal and sexual emancipation. Their success inevitably meant that gender roles became a site of anxiety, anxiety which seems to have been projected onto the particular construction of the high art/low art dichotomy in this period. It is as though, fearing the incursion of women into the realm of art, male writers and critics sought to intensify the exclusiveness and the 'masculinity' of art, foregrounding such qualities as authority and autonomy. 'High' art could thus become coded as masculine, while women writers (who have traditionally been important as producers of popular fiction) could be associated with and directed towards the expanding mass markets. So, as one commentator has put it, 'political, psychological, and aesthetic discourse around the turn of the century consistently and obsessively genders mass culture and the masses as feminine, while high culture . . . clearly remains the privileged realm of male activities' (Huyssen, 1986: 47).

Modernist art thus maintained its avant-garde position by defining itself against mass culture and by implication against the feminine. This created particular problems for the woman writer, some of which are explored in an early story by Katherine Mansfield, 'The Tiredness of Rosabel' (1908). This story concerns the daydreams and romantic fantasies of an overworked shop assistant, and is particularly interesting because it represents an early, defining moment in which Mansfield aligns herself both with 'high' art and with mass culture. At the beginning of the story, we are placed at a critical distance from popular romance. Coming home on the bus, the central character Rosabel watches another girl reading a popular novel, with distaste. She criticizes the way in which the girl is 'mouthing the words in a way that Rosabel detested, licking her first finger and thumb each time that she turned the page' (Mansfield, 1984: 17). Popular romance is thus connected with vulgarity and the body and is apparently condemned. As the story continues, pointed contrasts are made between the romantic daydream Rosabel falls into and the pinched and impoverished realities of her life. Romance is thus shown to be dangerous because it 'covers over' the real (economic and sexual) causes of Rosabel's oppression. Yet as we are drawn into the texture of Rosabel's dream we find that it powerfully affirms the value of the life of the female body, and indeed celebrates it. Rosabel's dreamworld offers her light, warmth, colour and sexual pleasure:

Harry took her home, and came in with her for just one moment. The fire was out in the drawing room but the sleepy maid waited for her in her boudoir. She took off her cloak, dismissed the servant, and went over to the fireplace, and stood peeling off her gloves; the firelight shone on her hair. Harry came across the room and caught her in his arms: 'Rosabel, Rosabel, Rosabel!' . . . (20, ellipsis Mansfield's)

Mansfield's text thus discloses the way in which popular romance, while denying some needs, speaks powerfully to other female needs, pleasures and desires. The text points in two directions and dramatizes the dilemma Mansfield finds herself in as a woman writer in this period. On the one hand she is pulled towards a high art which is critical both of romance and of femininity: she is thus pulled towards a 'masculine' writing position and the opportunities offered by it. On the other hand to adopt such a position means, necessarily, that her 'femininity' must be denied. This is not to suggest that femininity is in any sense essential, but to stress the pressure which was (and is) created by the psychic constructions of femininity. At this early point in her career Mansfield is caught up in what seems to be a mutually exclusive opposition between masculine and feminine positions. As we shall see, one of the achievements of Mansfield and other women modernists is to push at this limit and attempt to deconstruct this opposition.

In the sections which follow, gender, subjectivity and other key issues raised by modernist women writers will be explored in more detail. The discussion will refer mainly to texts which are readily available, in part because of the simple practical difficulties of obtaining books by lesser-known writers, which tend to go in and out of print. (May Sinclair's novel *Life and Death of Harriett Frean*, for example, is at the time of writing, frustratingly, out of print.) However, the decision to focus on a relatively small number of writers has also been influenced by the fact that modernist women's writing is often perceived to be 'difficult'. Like modernist writing by men, such writing is occupied with the finer shades of consciousness and is often fragmentary and elliptical in form. As such, it makes particular demands on the reader. In the sections which follow I have opted for fairly detailed discussion of key texts in the hope of making these more accessible.

'Which of my many . . . hundreds of selves?': subjectivity and gender identity

In a journal entry of 1920, Katherine Mansfield vividly articulates her sense of being caught between two opposing views of individual identity. On the one hand is the 'modern' understanding of the self as multiple and fragmented, on the other the Symbolist or Romantic belief in an essential and unified self:

True to oneself! which self? Which of my many – well, really, that's what it looks like coming to – hundreds of selves? For what with complexes and repressions and reactions and vibrations and reflections, there are moments when I feel I am nothing but the small clerk of some hotel without a proprietor, who has all his work cut out to enter the names and hand the keys to the wilful guests.

Nevertheless, there are signs that we are intent as never before on trying to puzzle out, to live by, our own particular self. *Der Mensch muss frei sein* – free, disentangled, single. Is it not possible that the rage for confession, autobiography, especially for memories of earliest childhood, is explained by our persistent yet mysterious belief in a self which is continuous and permanent; which, untouched by all we acquire and all we shed, pushes a green spear through the dead leaves and through the mould, thrusts a scaled bud through years of darkness until, one day, the light discovers it and shakes the flower free and – we are alive – we are flowering for our moment upon the earth? This is the moment which, after all, we live for – the moment of direct feeling when we are most ourselves and least personal. (Mansfield, 1977: 173)

This is a telling passage in which we see Mansfield torn between the attractions of a decentred modern subjectivity and nostalgia for a coherent and unified self. In the terms of the imagery, she is drawn to the attractive freedoms of the hotel without a proprietor, but also to the security offered by the traditional, organic image of the flower. The multiple self is linked with the modern, the urban, and with sexual freedom: the unified self with the past, the natural and the chaste. Interestingly, the language of psychoanalysis/the unconscious is used to evoke multiple subjectivity, which is also imaged through domestic space (the hotel rooms). Rather confusingly, however, the unconscious also seems to be connected with the singular self, which is imaged in contrasting terms of depth ('which . . . pushes a green spear through the dead leaves').

This passage enacts a tension between old and new conceptions of the self which appears in the work of many other women writers of this period. In Dorothy Richardson's thirteen-volume novel-sequence *Pilgrimage*, for example, the imagery of domestic space is used, as by Mansfield, to suggest the multiplicity of the self. Each of the various rooms and houses occupied by the heroine of *Pilgrimage* reflects and produces a different kind and level of consciousness. The plain room Miriam occupies in the second volume, *Backwater*, for example, with its three Bibles, coarse cloths and cheap mirror, reflects and creates a reduced and subdued feminine consciousness, overburdened by restrictive social codes and religious ideology. Conversely, the room which she occupies at the beginning of the fourth volume, *The Tunnel*, an attic room full of space and light with windows opening onto the London skyline, reflects and creates a more adventurous and voyaging 'masculine' self, uninhibited in its exploration of contentious issues in religion and theology, now reading Darwin's *The Voyage of the Beagle*. In general in *Pilgrimage*, the multiplicity of the central consciousness (the name Miriam can translate of course into myriad–I–ams) is not just accepted but is enthusiastically welcomed. Richardson, like Mansfield, is residually attracted to the idea of a coherent self, and on occasion she suggests its existence through the superimposition of one level of reality over another. In such 'moments of being', past and present meet and overlap and consciousness is heightened. However, a sense of the heterogeneity of consciousness is as strong or stronger, and is welcomed precisely because it opens up the promise of freedom for Miriam, the possibility of living many lives.

This acceptance of heterogeneity is in marked contrast to the response of male writers, who tend to figure multiplicity in terms of fragmentation, breakdown and loss. A major reason for this difference lies in the fact that a belief in subjectivity as multiple holds out the promise of escape from limiting or oppressive social and cultural roles. On the level of conscious life there is the prospect of the performance of multiple roles and identities, while the rich space of the unconscious opens up the possibility of multiple psychic *identifications*. The freedom which this offers is particularly welcome, of course, in relation to the constraints of gender identity, constraints which were the central preoccupation of many women modernists. Reacting against the Victorian stereotype described by Woolf as the 'Angel in the House' – 'She excelled in the difficult arts of family life. She sacrificed herself daily' (Woolf, 1993: 102) – these writers sought to redefine woman's role, experimenting almost obsessively with new 'stories' about femininity. For some, the focus on gender involved the search for a truer, more authentic female identity which (it was thought) had been obscured by centuries of male cultural dominance. Dorothy Richardson, for example, frequently uses metaphors of surface and depth to suggest a 'truer', more essential female identity. In an essay entitled 'Women and the Future' she describes the ideal 'womanly woman' in the following terms:

> For the womanly woman lives, all her life, in the deep current of eternity, an individual, self-centered. Because she is one with life, past, present, and future are together in her, unbroken. Because she thinks flowingly, with her feelings, she is relatively indifferent to the fashions of men . . .. It is man's incomplete individuality that leaves him at the mercy of that subtle form of despair which is called ambition . . .. Only a complete self, carrying all its goods in its own hands, can go out, perfectly, to others, move freely in any direction. (Richardson, 1990: 413)

In the choice of metaphors as well as in the sentiments expressed, Richardson here seems to anticipate French feminist ideas of sexual difference and *écriture féminine*. Indeed, her novel *Pilgrimage*, with its *roman fleuve* technique, its refusal of plot and formal closure and its resistance to conventional forms of punctuation, can be seen as an early attempt at 'writing the feminine', with the benefits and difficulties which that entails. On the one hand, Richardson's unremitting attention to Miriam Henderson's consciousness combined with her refusal to code that consciousness in conventional narrative terms makes for a novel which is genuinely innovative, unsettling the reader and destroying habitual points of reference. The centre of gravity shifts as we read, and an alternative, feminine perspective comes into view. Richardson's achievement in thus disclosing a difference of view and of values should not be underestimated. On the other hand, of course, the apparent privileging of an essential femininity can be said to simply reverse rather than undermine the terms of the binary opposition between the masculine and the feminine.

Richardson, however, is not simply or unproblematically 'essentialist': her writing is richer and more complex than this. As Jean Radford has suggested, Richardson often represents femininity in terms of a masquerade, in Joan Riviere's sense of the term (Radford, 1991: 72). As Riviere describes it, femininity is a matter of

performance only: 'The reader may now ask . . . where I draw the line between
genuine womanliness and the masquerade. My suggestion is not, however, that there
is any such difference; whether radical or superficial, they are the same thing'
(Riviere, 1986: 38). Richardson uses the similarly performative metaphor of piano-
playing to suggest the ways in which Miriam takes up different gender identifications.
In the third book of *Pilgrimage*, *Honeycomb*, she takes up a 'masculine' position as she
plays to her mother/plays the role of the son her mother never had:

> Nothing could happen as long as she could keep on playing like that . . .. She had a clear
> conviction of manhood . . .. This time it was welcome. It served. She asserted it, sadly
> feeling it mould the lines of her face. (Richardson, 1979: I, 471)

Later, we see Miriam taking up a 'feminine' position when she plays to a conventional
male admirer, Mr Tremayne, inspiring him to 'adoration' of her gracious and feminine bearing. This mobility, this crossing over from one side to the other, is marked
in *Pilgrimage*, thus suggesting, of course, that gender identity is not essential but
constructed and permutable.

Virginia Woolf's work offers an extraordinarily rich and sustained meditation
on questions of gender identity, with an increasing emphasis on the constructed
nature of gender. Her early fiction, however, shows a romantic attachment to a
femininity which is seen as original and essential. In *Jacob's Room* (1922) and *Mrs
Dalloway* (1925), for example, Woolf celebrates what Hélène Cixous might call a
depropriative 'feminine economy' through the figures of Betty Flanders and
Clarissa Dalloway.[2] These 'mother-figures' are associated with an 'economy without reserve' like that evoked by Cixous: they flow, they give, they merge, rather
like Richardson's 'womanly woman'. Femininity is a kind of ideal in these early
texts, a touchstone of value. Relations between women – the blind woman and the
daughter who hears her song in *Jacob's Room*; Clarissa Dalloway and Sally Seton
in *Mrs Dalloway* – are privileged as offering a model for a 'new' form of relation
to the other, a relationship not based on exclusive, oppositional difference. The
most powerful evocation of this idealized relation comes in a famous passage in
which Clarissa Dalloway remembers 'the most exquisite moment' of her whole
life in Sally Seton's kiss:

> Sally stopped; picked a flower; kissed her on the lips. The whole world might have
> turned upside down! The others disappeared; there she was alone with Sally. And she
> felt that she had been given a present, wrapped up, and told just to keep it, not to look at
> it – a diamond, something infinitely precious. (Woolf, 1992b: 45–6)

In *To the Lighthouse* (1927), however, we see how much this apparently 'new' economy depends on and reproduces very old ideas about femininity. In this novel,
Woolf undertakes a patient deconstruction of femininity as represented through the
figure of Mrs Ramsay. In the first part of the novel, Mrs Ramsay is presented as an
icon, bearing the eternal truth of a sacred femininity:

> [Lily] imagined how in the chambers of the mind and heart of the woman who was,
> physically, touching her, were stood, like the treasures in the tombs of kings, tablets

bearing sacred inscriptions, which if one could spell them out would teach one everything, but they would never be offered openly, never made public. (Woolf, 1992c: 70)

It is only after Mrs Ramsay's death that Lily can begin to take apart this idealized
mother-figure, separating the real woman from the fantasies about femininity and
maternity which have become entwined with her image. Lily must relinquish these
fantasies, however, and see femininity for what it is, a construction which takes shape
according to particular social and historical pressures. This is the 'vision' which Lily
has at the end of *To the Lighthouse*, and it is this vision or realization which inspires
Orlando (1928), the novel which follows it.

Orlando is the story of a noble lord who lives for four hundred years and who
changes sex half-way through the novel. It is a dazzling text of contradictions, dealing
in paradoxes and refusing either/or formulations. Restlessly, the novel unsettles
binary oppositions – the boundary between fact and fiction, for example, is de-
stabilized as Woolf includes in the first edition of the novel pictures of the 'real life'
Vita Sackville-West posing as the fictional Orlando. Sexual difference is just one
among many differences which are thrown into the air. 'Orlando' (the supposedly
singular character) 'is' both a man and a woman: Woolf stresses the fact that his/her
identity remains the same, despite the change of sex: 'The change of sex, though it
altered their future, did nothing whatever to alter their identity' (Woolf, 1992d: 133).
The novel thus forces us to think the impossible, to conceive of a person who is
neither man nor woman but both. The novel challenges us to think beyond gender, as
Orlando does when he first sees the Russian princess Sasha:

> He beheld, coming from the pavilion of the Muscovite Embassy, a figure, which,
> whether boy's or woman's, for the loose tunic and trousers of the Russian fashion served
> to disguise the sex, filled him with the highest curiosity. The person, whatever the name
> or sex, was about middle height, very slenderly fashioned, and dressed entirely in oyster-
> coloured velvet, trimmed with some unfamiliar greenish-coloured fur. But these details
> were obscured by the extraordinary seductiveness which issued from the whole person.
> (Woolf, 1992d: 35–6)

The imaginative work of *Orlando* thus takes us towards the understanding that, as
Julia Kristeva has put it, 'the very dichotomy man/woman as an opposition between
two rival entities may be understood as belonging to *metaphysics*' (Kristeva, 1989:
214). Woolf's delight in the freedom this prospect offers may be contrasted with
Eliot's trepidation: Orlando is a long way from Eliot's androgynous Tiresias, painfully 'throbbing between two lives' (Eliot, 1972: 35).

History and myth

Orlando offers a convenient starting point for considering other aspects of the challenge to prevailing habits of thought offered by modernist women writers. *Orlando*
rewrites history from one person's point of view, or more accurately, disrupts conventional history, crumpling time up or stretching it out to reflect Orlando's subjective

experience. Woolf comments in the text on the importance of subjective time – 'This extraordinary discrepancy between time on the clock and time in the mind is less known than it should be' – and repeatedly fast-forwards historical time in order to pause for a single, key moment in which 'the seconds began to round and fill until it seemed as if they would never fall' (Woolf, 1992d: 95). The fact that four hundred years of history is encompassed in a single life-span intensifies the sense this text conveys of privileging 'time in the mind' over the time of history. A similar process is at work in *A Room of One's Own* (1929), in which Woolf again retells history (this time, literary history) from the point of view of an oppressed woman. Here, chronology is still more seriously disrupted because the unifying figure Judith Shakespeare is presented both as already dead ('buried at some cross-roads . . . outside the Elephant and Castle') and as yet unborn ('Drawing her life from the lives of the unknown . . . she will be born') (Woolf, 1992e: 62, 149). In her last novel, *Between the Acts* (1941), Woolf again subverts conventional historical narrative. Here, hundreds of years of history are squeezed into Miss La Trobe's scrambled and fragmentary pageant, in which all sorts of conventional histories seem to come unstuck. Miss La Trobe rewrites patriarchal myths, creating, for example, a revisionist 'Moses' story in which a baby girl is substituted for the boy in the rush basket. As the colonel in the audience points out, she also offers a history 'without the Army', and refuses to end her pageant with the traditional Empire Day 'Grand Ensemble, round the Union Jack' (Woolf, 1992f: 141). She thus calls into question the validity of those historical narratives which elide the experience of, for example, women or the colonized.

The play which Woolf makes with time and history in so many of her texts does more than simply call into question the truth of dominant historical narratives: it also suggests a desire to challenge the very basis of the socio-symbolic order, that is, the order of language and culture as we know it. Again, Julia Kristeva has described this desire for '*insertion* into history' combined with a 'radical *refusal*' of the limitations imposed by linear time as the time of project and history (Kristeva, 1989: 197–8). Woolf's utopian project is the opening up of history to its other, the recognition of the oppressed and the repressed of history. This approach is shared by other women modernists, among them the poet H.D. (Hilda Doolittle). H.D.'s earliest poems, the ones with which she became famous as 'H.D. Imagiste', wind back to the origins of history and evoke an empty space before language and culture. In them, H.D. plays with the possibility of other ways of being and of reconfigurations of meaning:

> The Pool
>
> Are you alive?
> I touch you.
> You quiver like a sea-fish.
> I cover you with my net.
> What are you – banded one?
>> (H.D., 1983: 56)

As a 'borderline' figure, an American living in Europe, H.D. is not concerned with the specifics of American or European history, but focuses in a more general way on the coercive force of history and myth. Throughout her career, H.D. engaged in a critique of the Greek myths which have been central to Western philosophy and to the Western imagination. The relatively early poem 'Helen' (from *Heliodora*, 1924) is an example of her deconstructive technique:

Helen

All Greece hates
the still eyes in the white face,
the lustre as of olives
where she stands,
and the white hands.

All Greece reviles
the wan face when she smiles,
hating it deeper still
when it grows wan and white,
remembering past enchantments
and past ills.

Greece sees unmoved,
God's daughter, born of love,
the beauty of cool feet
and slenderest knees,
could love indeed the maid,
only if she were laid,
white ash amid funereal cypresses. (1983: 154–5)

As Susan Friedman has pointed out, although the main character is silent, the poem shows the processes of masculine myth-making which have surrounded the iconic central figure (Friedman, 1981: 232–6). Helen of Troy is the archetype of woman as object of desire, and H.D.'s poem suggests the ambivalence of such (male) desire in which adoration can quickly turn to hatred and repudiation. Helen can speak only obliquely through the poem, as man's desired and feared 'other', but the poem invites us to reconsider the way in which she has been culturally 'framed' as fatal woman. H.D.'s project of giving a voice to the muted woman and of symbolizing her desire culminates, perhaps, in the long poem *Helen in Egypt* (1961). In this poem H.D. returns to the figure of Helen of Troy and to the task of articulating her subjectivity. The poem is an inward epic in which Helen journeys to discover herself, but finds that the wholeness and integration which she seeks is a chimera. Instead, she discovers herself to be fissured and multiple: as Rachel Blau DuPlessis has suggested, H.D.'s Helen can be read as a subject-in-process, forever unravelling and reconstituting her 'self' (DuPlessis, 1986: 110).

In the modernist period, writers such as Eliot and Joyce turned to myth and history in order to find a means of restructuring both social order and individual identity. In a famous discussion of *Ulysses*, Eliot explained this process in the following terms:

In using the myth, in manipulating a continuous parallel between contemporaneity and antiquity, Mr Joyce is pursuing a method which others must pursue after him. . . . It is simply a way of controlling, of ordering, of giving a shape and a significance to the immense panorama of futility and anarchy which is contemporary history. (Eliot, 1975: 177)

By contrast, women writers such as H.D., Woolf and Richardson challenged the use of history and myth to 'control and order' life. They offered revisionist myths and histories to contest those of patriarchy, and strove to realize meanings 'outside' history. To suggest that women writers (of any period) will have a different attitude to history, myth and culture from that of men is not to endorse any fixed view of sexual difference but to recognize that there will be an inevitable difference in the degree of men and women's investment in a social structure which favours men. Similarly, to recognize the existence of the desire to step 'outside history' is not to suggest that such a move is actually possible or desirable. What is important is to try to understand the historical determinants of that desire. In this period, the desire to step 'outside history' is clearly bound up in part with the traumatic effects of the First World War. While experimental modernist writers such as Woolf and H.D. did not write about the war as directly as did Rebecca West, for example, in *The Return of the Soldier* (1918), the war none the less shadows much of their work. In *The Return of the Soldier*, as Claire Tylee has argued, West ends up endorsing both the materialist bourgeois values of the central married couple and the war which is to some extent an expression of these values (Tylee, 1990: 145). The need for the soldier to return to the trenches is never really questioned, and at the end of the novel Chris Baldry duly walks once again with 'the soldier's hard tread upon the heel' (West, 1918: 187). In the work of Woolf and H.D., on the contrary, the war and the social system which supported it are found abhorrent. During the war H.D. was married to the writer Richard Aldington, who strongly identified with the code of militaristic masculinity. H.D. on the contrary felt profoundly alienated by the war, which she linked with a miscarriage which she had in 1915. She felt that the war was the result of an over-development of masculine values and a repression of the feminine principle. This led to a 'war-phobia' which she overcame to some extent in *Trilogy*, written during the Second World War. In *Trilogy* H.D. sets the two World Wars in the context of the rise and fall of earlier civilizations, finding emblems not only of death but of rebirth in the ruins of London. She finds, for example, a bomb-damaged may tree, 'half-burnt-out' but blossoming, another 'flowering of the rood'.

Virginia Woolf wrote extensively about the war, in *Jacob's Room*, *Mrs Dalloway*, *To the Lighthouse*, *The Waves* and *The Years*. Woolf also associated war with an over-development of 'masculine' values. She makes this point most forcibly in the 1938 essay *Three Guineas*, in which she links patriarchal oppression with the rise of Fascism, but the point is also made in her novels. In *Jacob's Room*, for example, Woolf underscores the connection between the training young men receive in public schools and universities and the 'discipline' of war:

With equal nonchalance a dozen young men in the prime of life descend with composed faces into the depths of the sea; and there impassively (though with perfect mastery of machinery) suffocate uncomplainingly together. (Woolf, 1992a: 216)

For Woolf, the war was like 'the contagion of the world's slow stain' and she uses a similar image to evoke the war in *To the Lighthouse*:

> There was the silent apparition of an ashen-coloured ship for instance, come, gone; there was a purplish stain upon the bland surface of the sea as if something had boiled and bled, invisibly, beneath. (Woolf, 1992c: 182)

If the desire to move 'outside history' can be linked with the trauma of the First World War, the modernist emphasis on the pre-history of the individual has rather different determinants. The pre-Oedipal comes into modernist women's writing as a desiring space which in many ways overlaps with the 'space outside history' discussed above. In the early poetry of H.D., for example, the landscape of origins suggests both a time before history in the wider social sense (prehistory) and the time before history in the life of the individual (infancy). Women's writing of the period repeatedly turns back to the earliest period of life, as though to articulate a story of origins which would recognize the authority of the mother as well as the father. The 'mother/daughter plot', as Marianne Hirsch calls it, thus becomes a key thematic and structural principle in modernist women's writing.[3] Katherine Mansfield's short story *Prelude* is a good example. The story is structured around a young girl's perception of sexual difference, and Mansfield uses the central image of the aloe to suggest the way in which this perception of difference is culturally organized under the sign of the phallus. The story also contains a 'scene of castration' in which the children watch Pat the handyman decapitate a duck. The scene is full of ambivalence, for the children are both frightened and excited by this scene of primitive violence. The central character, Kezia, screams 'Put head back! Put head back!', wanting to deny the reality of the separation she has seen, and is only distracted from her fear when she suddenly notices that Pat is wearing ear-rings. Through this tiny detail Mansfield suggests the possibility of escape from the seemingly immutable nature of the social and sexual order: if Pat can cross-dress, it might be possible to cut across the barrier of sex/gender difference.

Against the violence of the social order of patriarchy, Mansfield sets the counterweight of a richly imagined alternative world of women. *Prelude* shows us the connections between three generations of women, presided over by Mrs Fairfield who must mother both her adult daughter and her grandchildren. Her daughter Linda cannot imagine life without her: 'She thought her mother looked wonderfully beautiful with her back to the leafy window. There was something comforting in the sight of her that Linda felt she could never do without' (Mansfield, 1984: 238). Mrs Fairfield offers the care and love which make Linda's life with her predatory husband bearable. She creates an alternative world and order to set against Stanley's aggression and sexual demands, so that in her presence even the threatening aloe plant is transformed into an imaginary ship which will carry Linda to freedom: 'As they stood on the steps, the high grassy bank on which the aloe rested rose up like a wave, and the aloe seemed to ride upon it like a ship with the oars lifted' (253). Through the relationship of Linda and Mrs Fairfield, Mansfield suggests the possibility of a different story of origin and identity, one which recognizes maternal as well as paternal law.

Why should this mother/daughter plot emerge at this particular time? Susan Gubar has argued that women writers in the modernist period were able to 'reimagine the maternal' due to practical changes in the organization of women's reproductive lives. The invention, improvement and greater availability of contraception, the lower birth rate and decrease in mother and infant mortality which occurred in the early years of the century made it possible for the first time to think of maternity as a choice rather than as a burden. After the First World War, Marie Stopes and other birth controllers such as Stella Browne were extremely successful in their crusade to publicize and make available artificial methods of birth control. A measure of the huge demand for information can be found in the sales figures for Marie Stopes's pioneering book *Married Love* (1918), which sold over 2,000 copies in the first fortnight, and by the end of 1923 had sold over 400,000 copies. In the early 1920s, the first birth-control clinics in Britain were set up, and by the decade 1931–41, some 60 were in operation (Weeks, 1989: 195). Gubar argues, then, that feminists could begin to valorize maternity, precisely because it was no longer experienced as 'a biological imperative' (Gubar, 1983: 25). Significantly, however, as Marianne Hirsch has pointed out, women writers of the modernist period 'reimagined the maternal' not for themselves, but for the generation of their mothers. Characteristically, they looked back at the mother from the perspective of the daughter, and focused particularly on an imagined early period of closeness to maternal creativity. We can see this in *Prelude* in the scene when Linda and Mrs Fairfield stand by the aloe at night. Linda speaks to her mother 'with the special voice that women use at night to each other as though they speak in their sleep or from some hollow cave' (Mansfield, 1984: 253–4): the imagery of sleep and of the womb suggests the recovery of a relationship from the earliest phase of life. This retrospective longing for fusion with the mother might be related to the gap which had actually opened up between two generations. The tremendous expansion of opportunity for women due to increased educational opportunities and more efficient birth control meant that the younger generation was in many respects cut off from the experience and traditions of the previous one. The idealization of mother–daughter relations in the writing of this period can be seen as having a compensatory function, enabling writers imaginatively to unite with an earlier generation.

Street haunting: modernist women and urbanization

It is impossible to separate modernist consciousness from the experience of urbanization. During the nineteenth century, Britain like other European countries became a predominantly industrial and urban society. The rapid growth of the cities created new patterns of work and leisure and offered new possibilities of identity and affiliation on the one hand, on the other alienation and isolation. The modern city came to be seen as, in Elizabeth Wilson's words, 'a crucible of intense and unnerving contrasts':

The hero, or less often the heroine, of urban literature was lured by the astonishing wealth and opportunity, threatened by the crushing poverty and despair of city life. Escape and entrapment, success and disaster offered heightened, exaggerated scenarios of personal triumph or loss of identity. (Wilson, 1991: 6)

As Wilson's comment suggests, the new experience of city life was at first seen very much from the male point of view. Baudelaire celebrated the kaleidoscope of modern urban life from the point of view of the *flâneur* (the stroller or the dandy), who located a new kind of beauty in the streets and factories of the metropolis. As Janet Wolff has pointed out in her essay 'The Invisible *Flâneuse*', the dandy was necessarily male: respectable women in the late nineteenth century did not have the freedom of the streets (Wolff, 1990: 41). Originally, for Baudelaire, the isolation and lack of connection of city life were the conditions of a new and lively perception: the city offered a new kind of pleasure, a new enlargement of identity. As we move on into the twentieth century, however, the city is represented by male writers in increasingly negative and threatening terms (James Joyce being a notable exception in this respect). For T.S. Eliot, in particular, the breakdown of traditional forms and beliefs and the indifference and struggle of modern life is inextricably linked with the emergence of an urban wasteland:

> Unreal city,
> Under the brown fog of a winter dawn,
> A crowd flowed over London Bridge, so many,
> I had not thought death had undone so many.
> Sighs, short and infrequent, were exhaled,
> And each man fixed his eyes before his feet.
>   (Eliot, 1972: 29)

By contrast, a drive towards freedom and an optimistic orientation to the future are expressed through the representation of the city in texts by women. Elizabeth Wilson has suggested that this may be because urban life is itself based on the struggle between 'routinised order and pleasurable anarchy', terms which can be related to the male–female dichotomy:

> Perhaps the 'disorder' of urban life does not so much disturb women. If this is so, it may be because they have not internalised as rigidly as men a need for over-rationalistic control and authoritarian order. The socialisation of women renders them less dependent on duality and opposition; instead of setting nature against the city, they find nature *in* the city. For them, that invisible city . . . is an Aladdin's cave of riches. (Wilson, 1991: 8)

For women in the early twentieth century the space of the city offered possibilities of knowledge and discovery, as they took possession of the public sphere which had been denied to them in the nineteenth century. The very anonymity of the city, and the transient and fleeting nature of human contact within it, made possible for the strolling spectator a new range of imaginative life, a potentially endless 'sampling' of other lives and identities. Indeed, the kaleidoscopic spectacle of city life offers an uncannily apt metaphor for that sense of the multiplicity of the self which has been discussed earlier as characteristic of the modernist period. Wilson suggests that Freud 'produced a theory of human subjectivity that was itself essentially urban' (1991: 86), and the relationship between the topography of the city and the topography of the modern self is a close and suggestive one. Did the changing contexts and suggestions of city life in part *create* that sense of the self as plural and mobile, able to be 'read' differently in different situations, which we see as quintessentially modern?

Virginia Woolf's 1927 essay 'Street Haunting: A London Adventure' takes up some of these questions in what is virtually a manifesto for the now-visible *flâneuse*. The essay, which describes a walk across London on the pretext of buying a pencil, articulates a modern, even a postmodern sensibility. It begins with desire, the desire to lose oneself in the anonymity of the city streets, and to roam half across London:

> We are no longer quite ourselves. As we step out of the house on a fine evening between four and six, we shed the self our friends know us by and become part of that vast republican army of anonymous trampers, whose society is so agreeable after the solitude of one's own room. (Woolf, 1993: 70)

Released from the burden of the self, consciousness becomes purely visual, the self being 'an enormous eye' which has the 'strange property' that it rests only on beauty, like a butterfly seeking colour and basking in warmth. The eye, then, follows the pleasure principle and looks only at surfaces, aestheticizing urban experience in a thoroughly postmodern way. Passing, glimpsing, from the suggestions of figures and houses, the mind also builds up in imagination different scenes and lives. The narrator pauses on the 'absurdity' of the fact that she is both walking to the Strand on a winter evening and standing on a balcony, wearing pearls in June, but then asserts the 'streaked' and 'variegated' nature of the self:

> Is the true self this which stands on the pavement in January, or that which bends over the balcony in June? Am I here, or am I there? Or is the true self neither this nor that, neither here nor there, but something so varied and wandering that it is only when we give the rein to its wishes and let it take its way unimpeded that we are indeed ourselves? (76)

Woolf finds the idea that each of us has within him/herself the potential to live many lives enormously liberating. In her later work, she builds on this insight, indicating that we could transform our relations with others if we could connect the 'strangeness' which seems to be expressed in them with the strangeness which is repressed within us. Or as the Rev. G.W. Streatfield puts it in *Between the Acts* (written in the first months of the Second World War), 'we act different parts; but are the same' (Woolf, 1992f: 173).

In 'Street Haunting' Woolf celebrates the new perceptions of modern urban life but also registers the 'unnerving' nature of the contrasts found within it. The essay is disrupted quite early on by a description of a dwarf, who calls into being an atmosphere which 'seemed actually to create the humped, the twisted, the deformed'. The narrator then notices a hunger-bitten Jew, an old woman abandoned on the step of a public building, and goes on to foreground the strangeness of the contrast between the lives of rich and poor:

> Often enough these derelicts choose to lie not a stone's throw from theatres, within hearing of barrel organs, almost, as night draws on, within touch of the sequined cloaks and bright legs of diners and dancers. They lie close to those shop windows where commerce offers to a world of old women laid on doorsteps . . . sofas which are supported by the gilt necks of proud swans. (Woolf, 1993: 74–5)

The physical proximity of doorstep and sofa only serves to underline the economic distance between the lives of the derelicts and of the bourgeoisie.

The unsettling contrasts of city life were, of course, registered by writers other than Woolf. Dorothy Richardson, who wrote more intensively about the city than any other female modernist, is particularly interesting in this respect. For Richardson's heroine in *Pilgrimage*, London offers immense opportunities for knowledge and self-discovery. The space of the city, for ever opening onto new vistas and bringing new images and sounds, mirrors and creates Miriam's expanding consciousness throughout the novel. At one point London is described as 'a mighty lover', and Miriam exults specifically in the freedom which it brings, as she is 'liberated . . . to the whole range of her being' (Richardson, 1979: III, 272). Yet Richardson makes it clear that this freedom is absolutely contingent on Miriam's £1 a week, coming from her clerical work. Her work guarantees her independence and her respectability: without it, Miriam might be forced to take the other option open to a woman in the city, prostitution. At various points in the novel, Miriam becomes aware of the existence of this other kind of *flâneuse*. In *Interim*, when she is out walking at night, she becomes aware of shadowy figures with 'a foreign walk, steadily slow and wavy and expressive'. She turns towards the safety of the station, with the thought 'A murder might happen here' (II, 409–10). She is aware of having come too close to the danger attendant on her state as an unprotected woman, and only regains her peace of mind and sense of self when she sees a post office ahead. The post office is significant because it represents exactly the world of respectable clerking which gives Miriam her living and her security. Entering its 'warm yellow gaslight', Miriam is soothed by its atmosphere and by the way in which it reproduces 'a steady quiet workaday feeling; late at night' (II, 410).

Richardson celebrates the city in *Pilgrimage* (as Woolf does in *Mrs Dalloway* and in *The Years*) creating a sense of multiplicity of meaning constantly building up and overwhelming Miriam with its richness. Yet there is a clear recognition of the financial underpinning of Miriam's modern consciousness. A similar recognition of the economic determinants of women's subjectivity is apparent in the fiction of Jean Rhys, a writer who, like Katherine Mansfield, was doubly marginalized as a woman and as a colonial. In her fiction of the 1920s and 1930s, Rhys paints a picture of woman's alienation in the modern metropolis. As Coral Howells has suggested, her fiction offers a critique of male modernist representations of the city. If texts by male modernists tend to circle around issues of domination and control, Rhys's texts 'circle around issues of marginality and resistance, reflecting a sense of heterogeneity within the subject' (Howells, 1991: 100). These qualities are evident in Rhys's first published story, 'Vienne', which appeared in 1924. The story evokes urban life in a series of 'snapshots', the city being represented metonymically by a series of interiors in which women must sell themselves. The narrator (a woman) appraises other women in terms of their success in appealing to the male gaze. The story opens with a dancer 'typed' in terms of a painting and also described as half-bestial:

> The little dancer at the Parisien with a Kirchner girl's legs and a little faun's face.
> She was so exquisite that girl that it clutched at one, gave one pain that anything so lovely could ever grow old, or die, or do ugly things. (Rhys, 1987: 188)

In this early story, as throughout her fiction, Rhys presents her female heroes with only two options for survival: marriage or prostitution. This severely limited view of the opportunities open to women is mirrored in the restricted nature of the city space which is open to them. Intriguingly, Ford Madox Ford, Rhys's patron, editor and lover, wanted her to 'introduce some sort of topography' into these early stories, to enable the reader to get (his) bearings (Rhys, 1987: 139). Rhys's response was to delete still more detail, which suggests her determination to close down all escape routes for her female characters. They remain trapped in interiors in which they perform or masquerade, barred because of their economic dependence on men from the wider thoroughfares celebrated by Richardson and Woolf.

'O sister my sister': sexuality

Modernist writing by women questions not just conventional ideas about gender but also the heterosexist assumptions which often accompany these. Sexuality is foregrounded as an issue in many modernist texts by women, to a far greater extent than is the case in modernist writing by men. As Gillian Hanscombe and Virginia Smyers have pointed out, many modernist women writers lived outside the structures of conventional heterosexual marriage.[4] Most notable perhaps was the group of writers and artists associated with Natalie Barney's lesbian salon in Paris in the 1920s – a group which included Djuna Barnes, Radclyffe Hall and Romaine Brooks. However, even among those writers who married and led apparently conventional lives, such as Woolf, Mansfield, H.D. and Richardson, a striking pattern recurs of emotional, sexual or practical dependence not on a husband but on another woman.[5] Living outside the structures of what Adrienne Rich has called 'compulsory heterosexuality', it is not surprising that these writers produced a strong critique of such heterosexuality in their work (Rich, 1987). The most famous text to foreground the question of sexuality is Radclyffe Hall's *The Well of Loneliness* (1928), which was successfully prosecuted for obscenity in November 1928. *The Well of Loneliness* is not a modernist text in the usual sense. It is formally unadventurous and the language is often turgid: Virginia Woolf thought it a 'meritorious dull book' (Woolf, 1980: 193). None the less it is significant in its challenge to hegemony, in its attempt to publicly identify and to make claims for a 'deviant' sexuality.

The Well of Loneliness defines homosexuality in terms of nature, not nurture, and can productively be read alongside a modernist text which does exactly the opposite, H.D.'s *Her*, also written in 1927 but not published until 1981 (in the United States). The characterization of Stephen Gordon, the central figure in Hall's novel, shows the influence on the writer of the theories of Havelock Ellis and of Richard von Krafft-Ebing (the latter is specifically referred to in the text). Following these theorists, Hall conceives of her lesbian hero as the victim of biology. Stephen is an 'invert', marked from earliest childhood by strongly masculine physical and mental characteristics. She is neither man nor woman, but inhabits a 'no-man's land' in between the two (Hall, 1991: 271). Hall also uses the term 'freak' for Stephen, and appears to follow Krafft-Ebing's view that the 'true invert' (represented by Stephen) will wish to pair with a 'womanly woman' (represented by her lover Mary Llewellyn) who is only lesbian by persuasion. The 'true invert' is thus a kind of degenerate who corrupts the 'womanly woman', preventing her from fulfilling her true destiny in marriage. In the sacrificial plot of *The Well of Loneliness*, Stephen finally gives Mary up because she feels she is denying Mary the 'normal' happiness which could be hers.

The Well of Loneliness has been viewed negatively by many recent critics. It has been argued that one of the problems with the novel is that through the 'masculine' and 'feminine' characterization of Stephen and Mary the polarities of conventional gender ideology are reinforced rather than undermined. Masculinity is indeed privileged in this 'lesbian' text, as Jane Rule has pointed out:

> Though inept and feminine men are criticized, though some are seen to abuse the power they have, their right to that power is never questioned . . .. Male domination is intolerable to [Stephen] only when she can't assert it for herself. Women are inferior. Loving relationships must be between superior and inferior persons. (1975: 60)

It is largely true that conventional gender ideology is not challenged but endorsed by Hall, whose lesbian identification does not lead to any politicized critique of the institutions of patriarchy or heterosexuality. She fails in the novel to link the persecution Stephen undergoes with wider structures of coercion in a society premised on inequality between men and women and on compulsory heterosexuality. Yet it can also be argued that Hall's novel represents the beginning of an alternative discourse whereby a transgressive identity could begin to 'speak itself'. At the very end of the novel, for example, Stephen/Hall pleads for the 'right to existence' for inverts like herself:

> They possessed her. Her barren womb became fruitful – it ached with its fearful and sterile burden. It ached with the fierce yet helpless children who would clamour in vain for their right to salvation . . .
> 'God,' she gasped, 'we believe; we have told You we believe . . .. We have not denied You, then rise up and defend us. Acknowledge us, oh God, before the whole world. Give us also the right to our existence! (Hall, 1991: 446–7)

Jonathan Dollimore has described the ways in which a 'deviant' social group becomes politically resistant through a series of negotiated stages, and has argued that Hall's text represents a stage which he terms transformation through (mis)appropriation

(Dollimore, 1986: 182). In other words, Hall does not denounce dominant ideology (which could be counter-productive), but speaks on behalf of the oppressed group through the very terms and categories which have produced and marginalized it. Despite its conservative ideology and rhetoric of sacrifice and denial, *The Well of Loneliness* thus demands acknowledgement and affirms the right to exist of the 'invert'.

H.D.'s *Her* is far more radical in terms of its exploration of sexuality and of its form. The novel draws on events in H.D.'s own life, and represents in coded form her early engagement to Ezra Pound (who appears in the novel as George Lowndes) and the love affair with Frances Gregg (Fayne Rabb) which disrupted this engagement. Whereas in *The Well of Loneliness* the 'love triangle' between two women and a man is resolved in favour of the heterosexual couple, in *Her* it is the relation between the two women which is reinstated at the close of the novel. In exploring the theme of same-sex love, H.D. draws on the work of Havelock Ellis and of Freud, but the scope and the radical nature of her insight bring her much closer to recent French feminist thinking about sexuality. As recent commentators have pointed out, there is a particularly close parallel with the philosophy of Luce Irigaray.[6] The radical content of *Her* is matched by its radical, experimental form. The text is elliptical and poetic, deploying cinematic techniques of montage and close-up to follow the movements of thought and consciousness.

The dominant narrative of sexuality at the time when *Her* was written (1927) was that of Freud. H.D. had been interested in Freud since 1911, and remained engaged with his work throughout her life. In his early model of the development of 'normal' femininity, Freud posited an original 'psychic bisexuality', which was channelled into 'normal' heterosexuality via the Oedipus complex and the fear of castration. As countless feminist critics have pointed out, this is a very masculinist view of the construction of sexuality, which in many ways replicates the masculinist power structures of the period. However, by the time Freud came to write his 1931 essay 'Female Sexuality', he had modified his view of the centrality of the phallus in the construction of female sexuality, and noted instead the importance of the girl's early relationship with her mother. This insight has proved richly suggestive for later feminist thinkers. Luce Irigaray, in particular, has suggested that the early relation between mother and daughter holds the potential for nothing less than a reordering of the symbolic. At present the mother is not symbolized except as mother-object (lack). If she were to be symbolized as a subject for herself, the way would be open for the articulation of a subject-to-subject relation between mother and daughter. This subject-to-subject relation would be outside the phallic law, and would represent a new kind of 'intersubjectivity', a form of relation to the other not based on oppositional differences.

In *Her* H.D. anticipates many aspects of Irigaray's thought. The heroine, Her Gart, is torn between identification with the symbolic order (represented by the poet George Lowndes) and the attractions of what Rachel Blau DuPlessis calls 'Otherness', i.e. 'feminine' experience not recognized by the symbolic, as in maternal/sororal mirroring. H.D.'s text struggles to articulate the difference of this experience, employing particular linguistic strategies to point to that which lies outside the symbolic. In one key scene, for example, the experience of maternity is suggested through the concentric structure of the text itself (a storm is recalled within a storm); through the accentuated rhythmicality of Eugenia's speech as she tells of Her's birth, and through the lustrous, overlapping visual images of Her, Her's mother, and the black servant Mandy who acted as midwife when Her was born. The three women come together in the following description of Mandy, whose links with earlier, pre-patriarchal civilizations suggest a strongly maternal genealogy:

> I can't say Mandy looks like Etruscan bronze dredged from the mid-Ionian with colour flashing against her polished bronze . . . I won't say Mandy is like a bronze giving out iridescence like a flying fish, there is a blue-green iridescence across the copper polish and her face is fixed like a bronze face, her eyes are set in like agates in a Mena-period Egyptian effigy. (H.D., 1984: 88)

The relationship between Her and Fayne Rabb is also one of intersubjectivity, a relation involving both sameness and difference. Repeatedly the text suggests that authentic female identity can only be found in relation with other women. The male gaze distorts and diminishes the self (as George's gaze diminishes Hermione), whereas the female gaze holds out the possibility of a different kind of mutual identification. This sororal absorption and identification is suggested partly through the mirroring and doubling patterns of syntax linking Her and Fayne ('Her bent forward, face bent towards Her') and partly through striking imagery:

> George had said 'Oh rot, what rot is this you're talking' when for a moment she had realized her head – the bit here, the bit there, the way it fitted bit to bit – was two convex mirrors placed back to back. The two convex mirrors placed back to back became one mirror . . . as Fayne Rabb entered. (138)

Significantly, H.D. places this new form of identification/relation in the context of reproduction and creativity outside the narrative of heterosexuality:

> I know her. Her. I am Her. She is Her. Knowing her, I know Her. She is some amplification of myself like amoeba giving birth, by breaking off, to amoeba. I am a sort of mother, a sort of sister to Her. (158)

H.D.'s exploration of same-sex love, unlike that of Radclyffe Hall, does not involve the reproduction of society's investment in a privileged masculinity. Her's love for Fayne Rabb is 'woman identified' and she loves Fayne precisely as 'a sort of mother, a sort of sister', as the allusions to Swinburne's poem 'Itylus', which run through the novel, suggest – 'O sister my sister O singing swallow, the world's division divideth us'. However, as Susan Stanford Friedman has pointed out, this refrain also foreshadows the difficulties and prejudice which Fayne and Her must face in their 'unconventional love' (Friedman, 1981: 43). H.D.'s awareness of contemporary homophobia must have been a factor in her decision not to publish the novel in 1927. None the less, although *Her* cannot be read as a public intervention in the debate about sexuality at this time, it helps us to 'read between the lines' not just of H.D.'s published poetry and prose, but also that of other female modernist writers who explore sexuality in a coded way.

'The flowering of the self': autobiography

Autobiography is a hybrid form, mixing the forms of fiction, history, diary and private letter. It blurs the boundaries between genres, and also blurs the boundary between public and private writing. Autobiography was the dominant mode for modernist women writers, who often wrote across genre boundaries in their attempt to inscribe a new form of subjectivity. There is perhaps a link between the emergence of psychoanalysis and the 'autobiographical turn' taken by women's writing in this period. For Freud, the neurotic was someone who could not tell their own story, and the task of analysis (the 'talking cure') was to enable them to construct that story, to create both narrative and self in language. Modern theorists would argue that this is what happens in autobiography: the autobiographer does not remember but *creates* the past and (the illusion of) a coherent self. As Linda Anderson puts it, 'The autobiographer can never write the "image-double" of his life; instead in referring to himself he creates himself at every moment afresh within the text' (Anderson, 1986: 59). The connection between psychoanalysis and autobiographical writing in this period is by no means necessarily a causal one, but the parallel suggests the contemporary sense of the interdependence of language, memory and identity.

Virginia Woolf's comments on her most autobiographical novel, *To the Lighthouse*, illustrate some of these points. She stressed the hybrid character of this fiction *cum* memoir, which constituted a form for which there was as yet no name – 'I have an idea that I will invent a new name for my books to supplant "novel". A new —— by Virginia Woolf. But what? Elegy?' (Woolf, 1980: 34). She also used the terms of psychoanalysis to describe what she had achieved in this text – 'I suppose that I did for myself what psychoanalysts do for their patients. I expressed some very long felt and deeply felt emotion. And in expressing it I explained it and then laid it to rest' (Woolf, 1989: 90). Above all, her novel conveys the contemporary sense of the self as limitless. Inner space offers infinite possibility:

> And to everybody there was always this sense of unlimited resources, she supposed; one after another, she, Lily, Augustus Carmichael, must feel our apparitions, the things you know us by, are simply childish. Beneath it is all dark, it is all spreading, it is unfathomably deep . . . (Woolf, 1992c: 85)

Woolf's whole *oeuvre* can be thought of as an autobiographical project, stretching across (and stretching) the forms of fiction, letters, diaries and memoir, culminating in the 1939 memoir 'A Sketch of the Past' written under the influence of Freud (Woolf, 1989: 72–173). H.D.'s work can similarly be seen as a transgressive form of autobiography, written across genre divisions and blurring the boundaries between forms. H.D. subverted genres from within, unsettling conventional modes of self-inscription. In her poetry, for example, she moved from what she calls, in *Her*, the 'pepigrammatic' form of her early lyrics to the production of long, freely associative poems which borrow widely from other genres. Her three early novels *Paint it To-day* (written 1921), *Asphodel* (written 1921–2) and *Her* (written 1927) represent a different and more intense form of autobiographical inscription. As the same story is repeated in each of these novels, H.D. creates a series of 'screen memories' which allow her to articulate each time a slightly different aspect of a plural and transgressive self. None of these novels was published in H.D.'s lifetime, and it is probable that she never intended them for immediate publication. Like much autobiographical writing, they thus have a curious and ambivalent status. They both were and were not intended for publication: they inscribe a decentred self for an audience which is absent or virtual.

H.D.'s *Tribute to Freud* (written in 1944, first published 1954) applies a Freudian technique to the experience of being analyzed by Freud: it remembers remembering. H.D. was analyzed by Freud in 1933 and 1934, and *Tribute to Freud* is composed of a reconstruction of the analysis written by H.D. in 1944, together with transcriptions from her notebooks from 1933. *Tribute to Freud* makes explicit the link between Freudian hermeneutics and the direction taken by much autobiographical writing in this period. The text enacts or embodies Freud's conception of the self as a palimpsest (or mystic writing pad) on which all experience leaves its trace. H.D. describes the way in which she 'tunnels' or 'mines' in the sessions with Freud, creating a tissue of memories which constitute not the self but a self, a self which exists for the duration of speech or writing. The text is layered, as H.D. remembers remembering and reflects on reflection. It is also circular in structure: H.D. insists that the second part of the text (in terms of written sequence) is both the continuation of and prelude to the first part. Paradoxically, this circular quality reinforces our sense of the endlessness of the self, of the extent and depth of subjectivity.

Tribute to Freud has the ambivalent status of H.D.'s earlier *romans-à-clef* in that a considerable part of the text was not originally intended for publication. There is thus a split in H.D.'s work between the 'official' autobiography of *Trilogy* and *Helen in Egypt* and the more fluid and radical counter-texts such as *Her* and *Tribute to Freud*. This is a repeated pattern among modernist women writers. For example, Dorothy Richardson's *Pilgrimage* represents the most intense and sustained autobiographical work of this period: it seems to represent everything there is to know about Miriam/Richardson's developing consciousness, leaving nothing out. And yet the recent publication of Richardson's letters has made visible another counter-text, in which the emphases in the life-story of Miriam/Richardson are very differently placed (Richardson, 1995). Thus, even in a period in which women writers consciously seek to realize the self in writing, a kind of displacement seems to take place. Public autobiography still has its necessary supplement in writing which is poised more ambivalently between public and private worlds.

This can be seen very clearly in the work of Katherine Mansfield. The autobiographical nature of much of her writing has often been commented on: indeed, this has been seen by earlier critics as a limiting feature of her work. The 'Burnell' sequence of stories, which is traditionally seen as the high point of her writing achievement, is set in the New Zealand of her childhood, and revolves around the consciousness of a young

girl who has many of the characteristics of the young Katherine Mansfield. These inter-
linked stories thus inscribe an autobiographical self which corresponds to the unified
self invoked in the quotation earlier in this chapter, a self which is 'continuous and
permanent'. The stories chart the growth and development of this self: in *Prelude* Kezia
is confronted with the riddle of sexual difference; in 'At the Bay' she becomes aware of
the inescapability of death; in 'The Doll's House' she encounters the rigidity of class
and gender boundaries. To a considerable degree (as the title *Prelude* suggests), the
Burnell stories chart the growth of a (girl) poet's mind within the framework of
relatively conventional assumptions about the self. However, this group of stories does
not constitute by any means the larger part of Mansfield's work. In numerous other
stories she explored the self as multiple, shifting, discontinuous. More significantly
from the point of view of autobiography, she also constructed a fictional 'self' in her
letters and journals which comes far closer to the view also proposed in the earlier
quotation, of the self as a 'hotel without a proprietor'.

Mansfield's letters and journals constitute an enormous body of writing. This
writing was in a sense 'under erasure' because of its ambiguous positioning on the
public/private axis, although like H.D. in her 'alternative autobiography', Mansfield
wrote both letters and journal with half an eye to publication. The understanding of
the self expressed particularly in her letters and journals is an understanding of the
self as a series of masks. This view derived partly from early enthusiasm for Symbolist
poetry and prose, and especially from Wilde, with his view that the self must be
created like a work of art. As she made her way in the London literary world,
Mansfield continued to experiment with a variety of different roles, partly as a
defensive strategy. In her later life, conducting her friendships largely by letter, she
adopted a different persona for each correspondent, so that for Virginia Woolf, for
example, she was firm, professional and direct, while for her friend the translator S.S.
Koteliansky she played the part of the enigmatic *femme fatale*. She not only played
these parts, but underscored the performative nature of the self. In a 1917 letter to
Murry, for example, she warned him, 'don't lower your mask until you have another
mask prepared beneath – as terrible as you like – but a mask' (Mansfield, 1977: 81).
The implication is that underneath such masks there may be nothing but a void.

In accordance with this sombre view, Mansfield on more than one occasion staged
in writing a kind of dissolution of the self. In a remarkable letter to Murry, for
example, she recounts a dream in which she goes to the theatre to see a Restoration
play (presumably a Restoration comedy). Performance, specifically sexual performance, is expected, but suddenly the actors begin to falter and drift off the stage, and a
black iron curtain is lowered. The crowd move silently out into Piccadilly Circus, to
discover that '*our* earth had come to an end':

> I looked up. The sky was ashy-green; six livid quarters swam in it. A very fine soft ash
> began to fall. The crowd parted. A cart drawn by two small black horses appeared.
> Inside there were Salvation Army women doling tracts out of huge marked boxes. They
> gave me one! 'Are you corrupted?'
>   It got very dark and quiet and the ash fell faster. Nobody moved. (Mansfield, 1977:
> 196–7)

Sexual guilt is clearly inscribed in this dream, in which Piccadilly's Eros has been blacked out and replaced by the Salvation Army women with their funereal cart. The unnatural and perverse is also hinted at in the moon with six quarters, and this links the dream with one that follows about Oscar Wilde. None the less, the most striking aspect of the dream is its representation of the death of the performative subject, reduced to ashes, silence and stasis. Mansfield's autobiographical counter-text is highly unusual in that it stresses the emptiness rather than the plenitude of the space 'behind' the surface self.

Writing otherwise: against the modernist grain

There were also, of course, many women writers of the period who resisted the drift of modernism and who found themselves unable to endorse its fundamental assumptions. Such writers distrusted the characteristic modernist emphasis on the isolated individual consciousness, and were unhappy with the break with realistic representation which resulted from this emphasis on subjectivity. Such writers – Sylvia Townsend Warner, Rebecca West and Winifred Holtby among them – can be aligned with Lukács in his celebrated critique of modernism in *The Meaning of Contemporary Realism* (1963). Lukács attacked what he felt was the solipsism and decadence of modernist writing, which concentrated only on the immediacy of subjective experience and failed to penetrate to the deeper social forces which created 'reality'. In her 1932 study of the work of Virginia Woolf (the first critical work on Woolf), the novelist and socialist Winifred Holtby made much the same points about Woolf's work. She argued that Woolf lacked 'the immense detailed knowledge of the material circumstances of life mastered by Thackeray or Arnold Bennett'. Despite Holtby's admiration for Woolf's writing, she thus felt that it remained in some ways limited:

> She will remain – it seems possible – shut off from intimate contact with Hilda Thomas of Putney and Edgar J. Watkiss, who lays lead piping among the bowels of Bond Street. She may catch a fleeting vision of their world. Moggridge may sit for a moment opposite Minnie Marsh at Eastbourne; Mrs McNab may decide that she could do no harm in picking the Ramsays' flowers – and, indeed, these glimpses of insight into the minds of Mrs MacNab and Minnie Marsh may be among her surest, her most successful flashes of intuition. But they are glimpses only. (Holtby, 1969: 201)

There were, then, a number of writers who felt uneasy with the apparent solipsism of modernist art, its apparent neglect of a common social reality. In the 1930s, in particular, there was thus a movement back to more conventional realist forms as a means of representing shared and contingent experience.

Sylvia Townsend Warner is one of the most interesting of these writers. Her work is little known at present despite the fact that she was an extremely prolific writer of poetry, novels, essays and stories. She was a well-known and respected literary figure in the 1930s and 1940s. Interest in her work subsequently declined, to revive to some extent in the 1970s with the advent of the second wave of feminism. Warner's poetry is striking: fine, spare and musical. Jane Marcus has suggested that it was its very musicality which prevented its being claimed as part of the modernist enterprise (Marcus, 1990: 532). Following accepted and established forms, Warner none the less offers in her poetry a radical critique of conventional social and sexual ideology. Her work can interestingly be compared with that of H.D., a contemporary who, as we have seen, favours ellipsis and obliquity in her attempt to represent woman as the repressed other of culture (in the poems of *Sea Garden* and *Heliodora*, for example). Warner, using a more conventional form, none the less offers a devastating critique of the construction of 'family life' in poems such as 'Cottage Mantleshelf' (Warner, 1990: 546–47). This First World War poem uses the image of the pairs of objects on a cottage mantelpiece (vases, fans, china dogs) to suggest the all-pervasiveness of heterosexual ideology. Among these paired objects is the photograph of a young man killed in the war, a 'nancy boy' disowned by time and by the relatives who simply gesture to his memory by keeping the photograph. With economy and subtlety Warner's poem points to the irony of the fact that this boy should have given his life for nothing better than the reproduction of 'family values'.

Warner became a Communist in the 1930s, and the poems which she published in *Left Review* in this period offer a more direct political message (Warner, 1989: 363–6). 'Red Front' is a poem in the form of a ballade which constitutes a direct call for action in the Spanish Civil War. Despite the fact that it was actually read as a declamation in Battersea and Whitechapel in 1935 and 1936, the poem is remarkable for its restraint and control of tone. It takes a long view of European history, and is resonant with references to the French Revolution, the uprising of 1848 and other earlier struggles for democratic rights. 'In this Midwinter', written in the same period, shows a similar sobriety and mistrust of heroic rhetoric. Against such rhetoric Warner affirms her commitment to the ordinary and her sense of responsibility for all human beings, for every 'co-heir of earth'.

Warner's poetry is wide-ranging in thematic and formal terms, and the same is true of her fiction. Her novels have settings ranging from the fourteenth century to the present-day, and they vary considerably in form and tone. In general, her fiction tends towards the mode of fantastic realism, appropriately enough for a utopian reformer. *Lolly Willowes* (1926) is a good example, the story of a middle-class spinster, one of the thousands who are described in the following terms in the novel: 'all over England, all over Europe, women living and growing old, as common as blackberries, and as unregarded' (Warner, 1928: 234). Lolly Willowes, however, leaves the house of her brother and sister-in-law, moves to the village of Great Mop and becomes a witch. Her transformation can be interpreted in a number of ways. Some readers see the witch figure as a means of suggesting a lesbian identity, so that the novel becomes a kind of 'coming out' novel. Alternatively, the witch can be seen as representing all those characteristics which women have had to repress in the past – their wit, anger and aggression. In Lolly Willowes's own words, which anticipate Woolf's famous phrase, being a witch offers one 'a life of one's own, not an existence doled out to you by others' (239).

This search for 'a life of one's own' is the key to much of Warner's writing. It is the key to *Summer Will Show*, a novel of historical realism published in 1936 but set in

1848. This novel combines the unsentimental political realism and the utopian political impulse evident in the Spanish Civil War poems of the same period. The plot is remarkable enough. An English landowning gentlewoman, Sophia Willoughby, bereft of her husband and children, seeks a 'life of her own', wondering what she can do 'to appease her desire to leave a mark' (Warner, 1987: 53). She follows her faithless husband to Paris and there seeks out and falls in love with her husband's mistress, a story-teller, visionary and revolutionary. She eventually joins Minna on the barricades in the 1848 uprising. The novel is intensely political in its foregrounding of issues of sexuality and class but never proselytizing. As Terry Castle has pointed out, the novel deftly displaces the structure of feeling which, according to Eve Kosofsky Sedgwick, dominates English literature, the homosocial triangle in which a woman is the object of exchange between two men (Castle, 1992: 139–40). In *Summer Will Show*, this triangle is displaced, and a man becomes an object of exchange between two women. In keeping with the lightness of touch which characterizes her work, Warner presents this displacement in almost comic terms, as Sophia's husband bursts in to find his wife and his mistress 'absorbed' not in him, but in each other:

> 'Well, Minna, well Sophia.'
>   Frederick, arriving during the afternoon, seemed instantly felled into taking it for granted that his wife and his mistress should be seated together on the pink sofa, knit into this fathomless intimacy, and turning from it to entertain him with an identical patient politeness. (Warner, 1987: 157)

At the end of the text, Sophia is similarly 'absorbed' in reading the *Communist Manifesto* – alone, her future and prospects entirely uncertain. The blending at the end of the novel of the real historical text (the *Manifesto* is quoted at some length) and the fictional character's thoughts point to Warner's understanding of art and the imagination as an integral and necessary part of political struggle.

Superficially, Elizabeth Bowen could not be more different from Sylvia Townsend Warner. While Warner was a feminist and Communist, Bowen disdained both feminism and politics and remained attached to her privileged Irish land-owning background. Yet there is a parallel in Bowen's concern with social structures rather than with the isolated consciousness of her central figures. Her work is representative of a general shift in emphasis in the 1930s. While modernist writers such as Richardson and Woolf were primarily occupied with 'the space within', later writers such as Warner, Bowen and Lehmann were more concerned with the constraints on feeling imposed by external social structures and realities. And while Bowen and Lehmann did not espouse feminism publicly, this does not mean that their texts are devoid of interest for the feminist critic.[7]

Bowen's fiction is akin to that of Warner in offering a radical critique of heterosexual romance and marriage, in other words of the 'family plot' being offered to women in the post-war period, when they were being directed back into the domestic sphere. Her novels borrow from the forms of popular romance in order to offer a critique of it: allusions to film and romantic fiction are frequent. In *The House in Paris*, for example (published in 1935), the hero, Max, is represented in terms of a screen lover, offering an exaggerated impersonation of masculinity. The radical suggestion is that masculinity, like femininity, might be a form of masquerade:

> She thought, young girls like the excess of any quality. Without knowing, they want to suffer, to suffer they must exaggerate; they like to have loud chords struck on them. Loving art better than life they need men to be actors; only an actor moves them, with his telling smile, undomestic, out of touch with the everyday which they dread. (Bowen, 1946: 99)

Despite his glamorous appearance, Max is unstable and eventually commits suicide. He has been too much under the influence of the elderly Madame Fisher who, bedridden in the house in Paris, represents the dead-end of the domestic plot. This pattern of unstable and unconvincing masculinity appears in other novels by Bowen, for example *The Death of the Heart* (1938). In this novel it is Eddie, 'the brilliant child of an obscure home' (Bowen, 1972: 75) who fails to play his part in the romance plot scripted by Portia, the central character. Eddie's uncertainty over the script of masculinity is clearly linked to wider social changes and uncertainties. After leaving Oxford, Eddie has had to make his own way in the world and as this is the 1930s, he lives in constant fear of losing his job. Major Brutt, the other male character to whom Portia turns in her distress, is actually unemployed. Returning from the First World War he has found no place in a dislocated and disturbed society: the heroic code of masculinity with which he was brought up is entirely inappropriate in a post-war, post-imperial culture.

Bowen's texts thus dramatize a sense of masculinity in crisis, no longer underwritten by clear public roles and automatic employment. In parallel with this her fiction dramatizes a refusal to mother, a refusal to engage in, to borrow Nancy Chodorow's phrase, 'the reproduction of mothering' (Chodorow, 1978). Both *The House in Paris* and *The Death of the Heart* have absent mothers. *The House in Paris* is structured around the absence of Karen and her refusal to meet Leopold, the child she has not seen since his infancy. Interestingly, Karen's place is taken at the end of the novel by her husband Ray, Leopold's step-father. It is he who is the 'good enough mother' in a cross-gender role reversal. In *The Death of the Heart* the strain is intensified because there are (at least) two absent mothers. Portia's mother is dead and she has never really recovered from her loss, while Anna, Portia's step-sister, who should take over the role of mother, refuses to do so. Anna obdurately refuses to take part in the reproduction of femininity via identification with the maternal role. At the end of the novel, rather as in *The House in Paris*, the lost child is reclaimed by a substitute figure, here the servant Matchett.

In Bowen's fiction, the loss of a secure code of masculinity leads to a dissolution of identity which is expressed in terms of suicide or breakdown (male suicide or breakdown is frequent in the fiction of Rosamond Lehmann, too). But if the role of mother as it has been constituted by society no longer exists, if women refuse this role, what are the implications for *feminine* identity? This is a question which Bowen's texts cannot answer. They offer no positive blueprints for the future but rather a sense of makeshift accommodation to contingent circumstances, in this being representative of the literature following immediately after modernism. Indeed, it could be argued that in this respect realist fiction of the 1930s offers both a response and a resistance to some of the tendencies of women's writing in the modernist period. If the modernist women tended to concentrate on individual subjectivity largely detached from its social and material context, women's writing of the 1930s turns our attention firmly back to the contingent, to the material and social constraints on women's lives.

Notes

1. This point is made in Tylee, 1990: 250.
2. See Shiach, 1991: 21–2 for a helpful account of Cixous's 'feminine economy'.
3. See Hirsch, 1989, Part II, Chapter 3, for a discussion of the 'mother/daughter plot' in modernist texts by women.
4. See Hanscombe and Smyers, 1987, Chapter 1 for a discussion of the lifestyle of many modernist women writers.
5. Virginia Woolf, while married to Leonard, depended on the love of her sister Vanessa Bell and Vita Sackville-West; Katherine Mansfield, while married to John Middleton Murry, depended still more on the devotion of her companion Ida Baker ('L.M.'); H.D. was twice married but formed her closest relationship with the writer Winifred Ellerman ('Bryher'); Richardson, while married to Alan Odle, maintained a lifelong relationship with Veronica Leslie-Jones.
6. See, especially, Buck, 1991 for a reading of H.D.'s work in the light of recent French feminist theory.
7. For good studies of these writers see Lassner, 1990; Simons, 1992.

Bibliography

Primary materials
Bowen, Elizabeth (1946) [1935], *The House in Paris*, London: Penguin.
Bowen, Elizabeth (1972) [1938], *The Death of the Heart*, London: Jonathan Cape.
Eliot, T.S. (1972) [this selection 1940], *The Waste Land and Other Poems*, London: Faber.
Eliot, T.S. (1975), '*Ulysses*, Order, and Myth' in *Selected Prose of T.S. Eliot*, Frank Kermode (ed.), London: Faber.
Hall, Radclyffe (1991) [1928], *The Well of Loneliness*, London: Virago.
H.D. (1973) [1944, 1945, 1946], *Trilogy*, Cheadle Hulme: Carcanet Press.
H.D. (1983) *Collected Poems 1912–44*, Louis L. Martz (ed.), New York: New Directions.
H.D. (1984), *Her*, London: Virago Press.
H.D. (1985) [1961], *Helen in Egypt*, Manchester: Carcanet Press.
H.D. (1985) [1954] *Tribute to Freud*, Manchester: Carcanet Press.
Holtby, Winifred (1988a) [1923], *Anderby Wold*, London: Virago.
Holtby, Winifred (1988b) [1936], *South Riding*, London: Virago.
Lehmann, Rosamond (1981) [1932], *Invitation to the Waltz*, London: Virago.
Lehmann, Rosamond (1972) [1936], *The Weather in the Streets*, Harmondsworth: Penguin.
Lehmann, Rosamond (1982) [1944], *The Ballad and the Source*, London: Virago.
Mansfield, Katherine (1977), *Letters and Journals*, C.K. Stead (ed.), Harmondsworth: Penguin.
Mansfield, Katherine (1984), *The Stories of Katherine Mansfield: Definitive Edition*, Anthony Alpers (ed.), Auckland: Oxford University Press.
Rhys, Jean (1971) [1930], *After Leaving Mr Mackenzie*, Harmondsworth: Penguin.
Rhys, Jean (1969) [1934], *Voyage in the Dark*, Harmondsworth: Penguin.

Rhys, Jean (1969) [1939], *Good Morning, Midnight*, Harmondsworth: Penguin.
Rhys, Jean (1987) [1968], *Tigers Are Better-Looking, with a selection from The Left Bank*, Harmondsworth: Penguin.
Richardson, Dorothy (1979), *Pilgrimage*, 4 vols, London: Virago.
Richardson, Dorothy (1990), 'Women and the Future' in *The Gender of Modernism*, Bonnie Kime Scott (ed.), Bloomington and Indianapolis: Indiana University Press.
Richardson, Dorothy (1995), *Windows on Modernism: Selected Letters*, Gloria G. Fromm (ed.), Athens and London: University of Georgia Press.
Sinclair, May (1980a) [1922], *Life and Death of Harriett Frean*, London: Virago.
Sinclair, May (1980b) [1919], *Mary Olivier: A Life*, London: Virago.
Smith, Stevie (1980) [1936], *Novel on Yellow Paper*, London: Virago.
Smith, Stevie (1979) [1949], *The Holiday*, London: Virago.
Warner, Sylvia Townsend (1928) [1926], *Lolly Willowes*, London: Chatto and Windus.
Warner, Sylvia Townsend (1985), *Selected Poems*, Claire Harman (ed.), Manchester: Carcanet Press.
Warner, Sylvia Townsend (1987) [1936], *Summer Will Show*, London: Virago.
Warner, Sylvia Townsend (1989), 'Red Front' and 'In this Midwinter', repr. in Barbara Brothers, 'Writing Against the Grain: Sylvia Townsend Warner and the Spanish Civil War' in *Women's Writing in Exile*, Mary Lynn Broe and Angela Ingram (eds), Chapel Hill and London: University of North Carolina Press.
Warner, Sylvia Townsend (1990), 'Cottage Mantleshelf', repr. in *The Gender of Modernism*, Bonnie Kime Scott (ed.), Bloomington and Indianapolis: Indiana University Press.
West, Rebecca (undated edn) [1918], *The Return of the Soldier*, London: The Queensway Press.
West, Rebecca (1980) [1922], *The Judge*, London: Virago.
Woolf, Virginia (1980) *The Diary of Virginia Woolf, Vol. 3, 1925–30*, Anne Olivier Bell and Andrew McNeillie (eds), London: Hogarth Press.
Woolf, Virginia (1989), *Moments of Being: Unpublished Autobiographical Writings*, Joanne Schulkind (ed.), second edition, London: Grafton.
Virginia Woolf (1992a) [1922], *Jacob's Room*, Oxford: Oxford University Press (World's Classics).
Virginia Woolf (1992b) [1925], *Mrs Dalloway*, Oxford: Oxford University Press (World's Classics).
Virginia Woolf (1992c) [1927], *To the Lighthouse*, Oxford: Oxford University Press (World's Classics).
Virginia Woolf (1992d) [1928], *Orlando*, Oxford: Oxford University Press (World's Classics).
Virginia Woolf (1992e) [1929, 1938], *A Room of One's Own, Three Guineas*, Oxford: Oxford University Press (World's Classics).
Virginia Woolf (1992f) [1941], *Between the Acts*, Oxford: Oxford University Press (World's Classics).
Virginia Woolf (1993), *The Crowded Dance of Modern Life*, Rachel Bowlby (ed.), Harmondsworth: Penguin.

Secondary materials

Altick, R. (1962), 'The Sociology of Authorship: The Social Origins, Education, and Occupations of 1,100 British Women Writers, 1800–1935', *Bulletin of the New York Public Library* 66, 389–404.
Anderson, Linda (1986), 'At the Threshold of the Self: Women and Autobiography' in *Women's Writing: A Challenge to Theory*, Moira Monteith (ed.), Hemel Hempstead: Harvester Wheatsheaf.
Benstock, Shari (1987), *Women of the Left Bank: Paris 1900–1940*, London: Virago.
Bourdieu, Pierre (1986), 'The Production of Belief: Contribution to an Economy of Symbolic Goods', trans. Richard Nice in *Media, Culture and Society: A Critical Reader*, Richard Collins et al. (eds), London: Sage Publications. Quoted in Elliott and Wallace (1994): 1.

Buck, Claire (1991), *H.D. and Freud: Bisexuality and a Feminine Discourse*, New York: Harvester Wheatsheaf.

Castle, Terry (1992), 'Sylvia Townsend Warner and the Counterplot of Lesbian Fiction' in *Sexual Sameness: Textual Differences in Lesbian and Gay Writing*, Joseph Bristow (ed.), London: Routledge.

Chodorow, Nancy (1978), *The Reproduction of Mothering: Psychoanalysis and the Sociology of Gender*, Berkeley: University of California Press.

Clark, Suzanne (1991), *Sentimental Modernism: Women Writers and the Revolution of the Word*, Bloomington: Indiana University Press.

Dollimore, Jonathan (1986), 'The Dominant and the Deviant: A Violent Dialectic', *Critical Quarterly* 28, 179–92.

DuPlessis, Rachel Blau (1986), *H.D.: The Career of That Struggle*, Hemel Hempstead: Harvester Wheatsheaf.

Elliott, Bridget and Jo-Ann Wallace (1994), *Women Artists and Writers: Modernist (Im)positionings*, London: Routledge.

Freud, Sigmund (1987), 'Female Sexuality' in *The Pelican Freud, Vol. 7, On Sexuality*, Angela Richards (ed.), London: Penguin.

Friedman, Susan Stanford (1981), *Psyche Reborn: The Emergence of H.D.*, Bloomington: Indiana University Press.

Fulbrook, Kate (1986), *Katherine Mansfield*, Hemel Hempstead: Harvester Wheatsheaf.

Fulbrook, Kate (1990), *Free Women: Ethics and Aesthetics in Twentieth-Century Women's Fiction*, Hemel Hempstead: Harvester Wheatsheaf.

Gilbert, Sandra M. and Susan Gubar (1988), *No Man's Land: The Place of the Woman Writer in the Twentieth Century. Vol. 1, The War of the Words*, New Haven: Yale University Press.

Gilbert, Sandra M. and Susan Gubar (1989), *No Man's Land: The Place of the Woman Writer in the Twentieth Century. Vol. 2, Sexchanges*, New Haven: Yale University Press.

Gilbert, Sandra M. and Susan Gubar (1994), *No Man's Land: The Place of the Woman Writer in the Twentieth Century. Vol. 3, Letters from the Front*, New Haven: Yale University Press.

Gubar, Susan (1983), 'The Birth of the Artist as Heroine: (Re)production, the *Kunstlerroman* Tradition, and the Fiction of Katherine Mansfield' in *The Representation of Women in Fiction*, Carolyn G. Heilbrun and Margaret R. Higonnet (eds), Baltimore and London: Johns Hopkins University Press.

Hanscombe, Gillian and Virginia L. Smyers (1987), *Writing for Their Lives: The Modernist Women 1910–1940*, London: The Women's Press.

Hanson, Clare (1994), *Virginia Woolf*, Basingstoke: Macmillan.

Haste, Cate (1994) [1992], *Rules of Desire: Sex in Britain World War 1 to the Present*, London: Pimlico.

Hirsch, Marianne (1989), *The Mother/Daughter Plot: Narrative, Psychoanalysis, Feminism*, Bloomington and Indianapolis: Indiana University Press.

Holtby, Winifred (1969) [1932], *Virginia Woolf*, Philadelphia: The Folcroft Press Inc.

Howells, Coral Ann (1991), *Jean Rhys*, Hemel Hempstead: Harvester Wheatsheaf.

Huyssen, Andreas (1986), *After the Great Divide: Modernism, Mass Culture, Post-Modernism*, Bloomington and Indianapolis: Indiana University Press.

Jackson, Alan A. (1991), *The Middle Classes 1900–1950*, Nairn, Scotland: David St John Thomas Publisher.

Joannou, Maroula (1995), *Ladies, Please Don't Smash These Windows: Women's Writing, Feminist Consciousness and Social Change, 1918–38*, Oxford: Berg.

Kristeva, Julia (1989), 'Women's Time' in *The Feminist Reader: Essays in Gender and the Politics of Literary Criticism*, Catherine Belsey and Jane Moore (eds), London: Macmillan.

Lassner, Phyllis (1990), *Elizabeth Bowen*, London: Macmillan.

Lukács, Georg (1963), *The Meaning of Contemporary Realism*, trans. John and Necke Maunder, London: Merlin.

Marcus, Jane (1990), 'Sylvia Townsend Warner' in *The Gender of Modernism*, Bonnie Kime Scott (ed.), Bloomington and Indianapolis: Indiana University Press.

McWilliams-Tulberg, Rita (1977), 'Women and Degrees at Cambridge University, 1862–1897' in *A Widening Sphere: Changing Roles of Victorian Women*, Martha Vicinus (ed.), Bloomington and London: Indiana University Press.

Ouditt, Sharon (1993), *Fighting Forces, Writing Women: Identity and Ideology in the First World War*, London: Routledge.

Radford, Jean (1991), *Dorothy Richardson*, Hemel Hempstead: Harvester Wheatsheaf.

Rich, Adrienne (1987), 'Compulsory Heterosexuality and Lesbian Existence' in *Blood, Bread and Poetry: Selected Prose 1979–1985*, London: Virago Press.

Riviere, Joan (1986), 'Womanliness as Masquerade' in *Formations of Fantasy*, Victor Burgin, James Donald and Cora Kaplan (eds), London: Methuen.

Rule, Jane (1975), *Lesbian Images*, New York: Davies.

Scott, Bonnie Kime (ed.) (1990), *The Gender of Modernism: A Critical Anthology*, Bloomington and Indianapolis: Indiana University Press.

Shiach, Morag (1991), *Hélène Cixous: A Politics of Writing*, London: Routledge.

Simons, Judy (1992), *Rosamond Lehmann*, Basingstoke: Macmillan.

Tylee, Claire M. (1990), *The Great War and Women's Consciousness*, Basingstoke: Macmillan.

Watts, Carol (1995), *Dorothy Richardson*, Plymouth: Northcote House.

Weeks, Jeffrey (1989) [1981], *Sex, Politics and Society: The Regulation of Sexuality Since 1800*, Harlow: Longman.

Wilson, Elizabeth (1991), *The Sphinx in the City*, London: Virago.

Wolff, Janet (1990), *Feminine Sentences: Essays on Women and Culture*, Cambridge: Polity Press.

9

'Writing as re-vision': women's writing in Britain, 1945 to the present day

Diana Wallace

The richly diverse landscape of contemporary women's writing is still in the process of formation. This is not, therefore, a definitive mapping of that landscape but a preliminary surveying of some of its main features. While much feminist criticism has focused on the valuable task of recovering and reassessing earlier women's writing, particularly that of the nineteenth century, Paulina Palmer points out that

> What feminist critics . . . have failed to do is investigate those very texts which relate most closely to the rebirth of feminism in the late 1960s – novels and short stories which re-work and popularize the concepts and theories which the Women's Movement has produced. (1989: 2)

This can be connected to a general tendency throughout literary criticism, where the move towards theory has revolutionized approaches to older texts but withdrawn academic interest from contemporary literature (Waugh, 1995: 40). For women's writing there is a real danger that without such critical attention contemporary texts will, like those of earlier writers, disappear from the literary landscape and, once again, a process of recovery will have to be undertaken. As Lorna Sage writes: 'Major writers need re-readers, a chorus of commentary, argument and exegesis, if they are to occupy their proper space in the canon' (1992: 36). At a stage when we are still too close to make out clearly which are 'major' and which 'minor' writers (problematic terms for women in any case) such a 'chorus' is critical.

'Re-reading' is an activity which goes on not just in criticism but within the literary texts themselves. A key strategy in twentieth-century women's literature has been a rewriting of earlier texts: novels, plays, poems, fairy-tales, myths, legends and the Bible. This is, to borrow Adrienne Rich's term, 'writing as re-vision'. 'Re-vision', Rich argues, or 'the act of looking back, of seeing with fresh eyes, of entering an old text from a new critical direction' is 'for women more than a chapter in cultural history: it is an act of survival' (1980: 35). It is both a search for self-knowledge and identity, and a refusal of the cultural myths which allow women only male-defined identities. The task of transgressive 're-vision', Liz Yorke argues, is central to the contemporary women's poetry. This process 'involves both the reworking of old histories, old mythologies, old stories – as well as the fabrication or making of new living myths which draw both from the past and project forward into the future' (Yorke, 1991: 14). The 'retrieval of women's experience in history through the re-visionary telling of women's stories' (5) and 'writing the body' are both subversive strategies in the project of 'constructing *a new symbolic which would re-organize the social socio-symbolic systems of patriarchy*' (3, original emphasis).

The 're-imagining' of women's buried history in contemporary fiction, Linda Anderson suggests, has involved a re-visioning of 'History' itself: 'for women cannot simply be added on to history – expanding the boundaries of historical knowledge empirically – without putting under pressure the conceptual limits that excluded them in the first place' (1990: 130). In fiction the concern to evolve new narrative strategies can be seen most clearly in the rewriting of the romance, a form which has dominated both fiction and women's auto/biography (Heilbrun, 1988). If narrative is 'a version of, or a special expression of, ideology' then romance plots, which traditionally offer women only the closure of marriage or death, 'express attitudes at least towards family, sexuality and gender' (DuPlessis, 1985: x). For novelists in the twentieth century Charlotte Brontë's *Jane Eyre* (1847) has proved a particularly rich touchstone for the strategy of rewriting. Its plot, 'the Cinderella-type heroine, the older man with a mysterious past, and the haunting presence of the hero's first, striking, mad, bad, wife' has become 'a staple of popular romance' (Stoneman, 1996: 4). The critical attention given to the popular romance in the 1980s (Modleski, 1982; Radway, 1984) is anticipated by novelists as diverse as Elizabeth Taylor, Jean Rhys and Margaret Drabble, all of whom use *Jane Eyre* as an inter-text to explore the effects of the romance ideology on women. Each generation 're-visions' in ways which foreground the concerns of their time but by choosing Brontë's text they also locate themselves within a 'female tradition' (Showalter, 1978) or 'maternal genealogy' (Irigaray, 1991) of women writers. However, the need for new strategies for 'writing a woman's life' has been eloquently voiced by Carolyn Heilbrun, who suggests the friendship plot as one possibility.

Real or imagined landscapes – hill country, valleys, caves, gardens, the sea, deserts – are a particularly rich source of metaphors and imagery for women writers. Ellen Moers discusses the importance of the 'female landscape' (1978: 254) as a sexual metaphor in writing, while Maggie Humm has focused on 'borderlands' and the strategies twentieth-century women writers use in crossing literary 'borders' (1991a). The room or house has been another productive image: the restrictions of the red room and the attic in *Jane Eyre*, for example, or Virginia Woolf's empowering 'room of one's own'. The two metaphors – landscape and house/room – are drawn together in Avril Horner and Sue Zlosnick's *Landscapes of Desire* (1990). They explore a specific metaphorical configuration of room, house, land and sea used by early twentieth-century women writers to question the marginality of women by 'querying, *through metaphor*, the fixity of the dominant discourse of their time' (1990: 6). Since its use is always inflected by the contemporary possibilities offered by feminism (8), historical contextualization is imperative. The evocative power of landscape, for instance, has a particular resonance for women from the Diaspora.

The resurgence of feminism in the late 1960s was a defining historical moment which changed and invigorated women's writing. Humm comments that 'Literature is feminism's most visionary terrain' (1991b: 13) and the symbiotic relationship between theory and fiction has been one of feminism's most distinctive features, and one of its greatest strengths. Yet to divide women's writing into 'before feminism' and 'after feminism' obscures the fact that the writers of the 1940s, 1950s and early 1960s often anticipate the concerns of post-1968 writers. Certain texts in the early 1960s – Doris Lessing's *The Golden Notebook* (1962), Jean Rhys's *Wide Sargasso Sea* (1966), Sylvia Plath's *Ariel* (1965) – opened up spaces not just for writers but for feminism itself.

The years between 1945 and the early 1960s are often seen as a 'dead' period, in terms of both feminism and writing. Elizabeth Wilson argues that the post-war years in Britain produced a 'consensus society' (1980: 6) which generated a coercive domestic ideology. The 1953 coronation of Queen Elizabeth II provided an image of woman as both 'equal' (a female monarch whose name recalled her famous predecessor) and yet reassuringly embedded in the family as wife and mother. There was a feeling that the battle for sexual equality had been won but although consumer affluence and birth control sweetened women's lot they did not undermine male dominance (64). Consumerism itself was lauded for giving women equality and the possession of a washing machine or a vacuum cleaner was presented as liberating and also as magically eroding class difference (12–13). This myth is comprehensively confuted by Carolyn Steedman's combination of theory and autobiography in *Landscape for a Good Woman* (1986). Here a Dior New Look coat coveted by Steedman's mother becomes a symbol of the consumer goods and class status desired by those whose lives are 'lived out on the borderlands' (Steedman, 1986: 5). Steedman's mother's refusal to mother, and her attempt to use both her body and her children as 'objects of exchange' (69), mark out both her internalization of and resistance to the ideologies of femininity, romance and domesticity.

Like Steedman's mother, women writers during this period both reflect and contest the dominant ideology. Elizabeth Taylor is a writer in the quiet, domestic interior tradition which runs from Jane Austen to Barbara Pym and Anita Brookner. Her novel *Palladian* (1946) is, Patsy Stoneman suggests, a 'penetrating analysis of the interface between romance and the Gothic' (Stoneman, 1996: 146), reworking elements of *Jane Eyre*, *Wuthering Heights* and *Northanger Abbey*. Cassandra Dashwood becomes governess to Sophy, the daughter of the widowed Marion Vanbrugh, an effete version of the Rochester-figure. Marion's decaying big house is used to figure both the decline of post-war Britain and nostalgia for pre-war Britain:

> the house became a shell only, seeming to foreshadow its own strange future when leaves would come into the hall, great antlered beetles run across the hearths, the spiders let themselves down from the ceilings to loop great pockets of web across corners; plaster would fall, softly, furtively, like snow, birds nest in the chimneys and fungus branch out in thick layers in the rotting wardrobes. (Taylor, 1985: 187)

As a romance reader herself, Cassandra, like Austen's Catherine Morland, knows that she is already inscribed in the romantic plot and has 'a very proper willingness to fall in love, the more despairingly the better, with her employer' (17). The anticipated marriage is not a happy ending. As the newly-married couple enter the house a hen follows them: 'But as the dark shadows of indoors fell coldly across it like a knife, it turned and tottered back into the sunshine' (192). The self-referentiality of the text produces a Gothic 'pattern of uncanny repetition' (Stoneman, 1996: 149), re-enforced by the decaying house, a standard topos in Gothic fiction. Stoneman suggests that 'Taylor's text plays with the categories of romance and Gothic in such a way that what the heroine perceives as romance the reader perceives as Gothic, in which "the enemy" is identified as – romance' (1996: 149). Romance as the 'enemy', as a patriarchally enforced script which both seduces and restricts women, is a recurring motif in twentieth-century women's fiction.

Several novelists more usually associated with the inter-war period in fact produced some of their finest work after the Second World War, among them Rosamond Lehmann, Elizabeth Bowen, Rose Macauley, Rebecca West and Jean Rhys. Their novels anticipate themes which were to become key issues for later writers: the search for the mother, relationships between women, gender identity and madness, and a concern with history – particularly with war and apocalypse. Rose Macauley's *The World My Wilderness* (1950) brings together several of these themes. As the epigraph from T.S. Eliot's *The Waste Land* suggests, the bombed wastelands around St Paul's function as a metaphor for the destruction of civilization in the Second World War. Macauley's novel, however, is also a sustained meditation on the 'waste land' of patriarchal 'civilization' which re-visions Eliot's poem. Exiled from her mother's home in France and sent to her lawyer father in England, 17-year-old Barbary chooses to haunt the bombsites because she cannot function in the 'civilized' world he represents. The bombsites are a 'wild zone' (Showalter, 1986: 262) where those marginalized by society live as 'maquis' (the name given to the French Resistance), 'resisting' the dominant ideology. The ghosts of those who have lived and done business in the city provide a historical dimension to this landscape, suggesting that the patriarchal bastions of commerce and the church have always been unfriendly to the marginal. Where Eliot's poem offers only a faint hope of spiritual healing, Barbary's reconciliation with her mother Helen offers the hope of forgiveness and salvation through the mother–daughter relationship. Helen is a Demeter-like figure who resists and disrupts the patriarchal order. Her final pledge to care for Barbary – 'Whatever other relationships I may have, she will come first' (Macauley, 1983: 247) – validates the pre-oedipal mother–daughter bond. Helen's home in Collioure is a female wilderness, a maternal landscape of colour and warmth.

The strength of female bonds and the influence of the past on the present are also explored in Rosamond Lehmann's *The Echoing Grove* (1953) and Elizabeth Bowen's *The Little Girls* (1964). Lehmann's complex novel uses a classic triangle situation where two sisters are rivals for the same man, husband of one and lover of the other. Opening in the present with the meeting of the sisters, Dinah and Madelaine, some years after Rickie's death, the novel circles back through their memories and then moves to their final reconciliation. It becomes clear that their bond with each other was always the determining factor in the triangle. Rickie was a pawn, or an object of exchange, in their rivalry. Lehmann's novel offers an important corrective to the theory that women's position as objects within exchanges between men, precludes them from taking part in exchanges as equal partners (Irigaray, 1985: 170–91). Here sister bonds, like those of mother and daughter, are primary and enduring. Lehmann also articulates a sense that gender identity in these years was fluid. Dinah speculates:

> I can't help thinking it's particularly difficult to be a woman just at present. One feels so transitional and fluctuating . . . I believe we *are* all in flux – that the difference between our grandmothers and us is far deeper than we realise – much more fundamental than the obvious social economic one. . . . Sometimes I think . . . that a new gender may be evolving – psychically new – a sort of hybrid. Or else it's just beginning to be discovered how much woman there is in man and *vice versa*. (Lehmann, 1953: 311–12)

This concern with gender identity marks Macauley's novel *Towers of Trebizond* (1956), an experiment which predates Jeanette Winterson's *Written on the Body* (1992) by several decades. Whereas in Winterson's text it is only the gender of the narrator which is concealed, Macauley withholds the gender of both lovers until the end of the novel.

Childhood and old age as spaces outside the patriarchally enforced romance plot are an important theme in Bowen's *The Little Girls*, where three school-friends, separated at the outbreak of the war, meet again fifty years later. Jane Rule reads this as a 'lesbian' novel, arguing that in Bowen's novels 'lesbian experience bracket[s] the heterosexual experience of marriage and children' (Rule, 1976: 119). Or as Bowen's Clare puts it: 'Those were the days before love. These are the days after' (Bowen, 1982: 56). The novel ends with the possibility of a closer relationship between Clare and Dinah left open. Like Macauley's, Bowen's novel is concerned with the individual in history. It opens with Dinah gathering together objects to bury as a record of their times. They are 'Clues to reconstruct *us* from. Expressive objects' (15). The 'expressive object' as historical touchstone is a device frequently used in women's writing, particularly poetry, as a 'clue' to reconstruct the unrecorded lives of past women.

The concern with re-imagining women's history is anticipated in the 1950s. Rebecca West's *The Fountain Overflows* (1957) was conceived as part of a trilogy, although the other parts – *This Real Night* (1984) and *Cousin Rosamund* (1985) – were not published until after West's death. The trilogy is an attempt to reconstruct female history around a 'maternal genealogy' which emphasizes sibling bonds. West herself said that it was about 'the difficulty of leading the artist's life' (West, 1984: viii). Her artists, the pianists Rose and her sister Mary, develop within a matriarchal family structure where their talent is nurtured by their mother, and their vocations seen as the crucial part of their identity. As a description of the evolution of a family of women artists (rather than the traditional single heroic male figure) within history West's novel is unparalleled.

Antonia White's semi-autobiographical quartet, begun with *Frost in May* (1933), and continued with *The Lost Traveler* (1950), *The Sugar House* (1952) and *Beyond the Glass* (1954), is also concerned with writing the life of the woman artist. The novels analyze the damage done to a daughter, Clara Batchelor, when her adored father tries to shape her to fit patriarchal society and the Catholic religion to which he has converted. White makes brilliant use of house and mirror metaphors. In *The Sugar House* the tiny, pink-distempered house which the newly-married Clara intended to be a 'symbol of her new-found freedom' (White, 1979a: 142) rapidly closes in on her. Trapped in a marriage with the child-like Archie, who can provide neither financial security nor sexual fulfilment, she comes to see the house as embodying their state: 'she was reminded of the sugar house in which Hansel and Gretal were trapped. Archie and she were trapped too' (212). Although an 'ingenious arrangement of mirrors' convey 'a deceptive sense of space' (139) there is nowhere for her to write. The mirror metaphor is used in the last novel to convey Clara's fragile sense of self and to figure her descent into the 'Looking-Glass Land' (White, 1979b: 233) of madness in a bleak asylum. Her breakdown is triggered by an intense love affair in which her ego boundaries break down until she can not only read Richard's thoughts but his face becomes 'more familiar to her these days than her own' (152). This love with its loss of separate self is itself a kind of 'insanity'. In the asylum she loses her sense of self completely, even seeing herself reflected as a 'fairy horse or stag' (212–13), until she is reborn nine months later into a new life.

The issues of gender identity, madness and suicide have a particular resonance for women poets in the twentieth century who are faced with the example of Sylvia Plath. Undoubtedly the best known of contemporary women poets, Plath's status as mythic figure who 'haunts our culture' (Rose, 1992: 1) has proved problematic. Her poetry, particularly *Ariel* (1965), opened up a new space for women writers, voicing women's alienation and dissatisfaction. But, as Jeni Couzyn testifies, the role model she offers of 'Mad Girl' or woman poet as suicide has proved destructive to other women poets who saw themselves offered a choice between two mutually exclusive options: ' "happiness" (i.e. home, husband and children) or poetry' (Couzyn, 1985: 17), where the latter meant an early suicide.

Among other things, Plath's poetry explores madness or schizophrenia as a response to the imposition of gendered identity, especially the 'feminine mystique' of the 1950s. 'Tulips', with its image of a woman in hospital, is 'a very self-conscious and aware critique of the myths of femininity' (Yorke, 1991: 70), particularly those which require a woman to be passive and submissive. 'The Applicant' is a bitter indictment of an ideology of marriage which constructs man as the subject, woman as the object and therefore for his use:

> You have a hole, it's a poultice.
> You have an eye it's an image.
> My boy, it's your last resort.
> Will you marry it, marry it, marry it.
>   (Couzyn, 1985: 162)

Plath often deals with the return of the repressed (the unconscious/feminine) and with the unspeakable, particularly the myths of women that men find most disturbing. The persona of 'Lady Lazarus' can be read as 'a feminine hysteric/exhibitionist/

sorceress who, in choosing to suffer spectacularly before her voyeuristic audience, stages for the reader a dramatic transformatory passage – from colonised female victim to phoenix-like avenger' (Yorke, 1991: 85):

> Out of the ash
> I rise with my red hair
> And I eat men like air.
> (Plath, 1968: 19)

The most contentious of Plath's poetic strategies has been her use of images of the Holocaust in poems like 'Lady Lazarus' and 'Daddy'. Jacqueline Rose has defended her, arguing that:

> fascism could be described as the historical annexing, or collective seizure, of uncon-
> scious drives . . . . In fascism, the realm of politics reveals itself as massively invested
> with the most private and intimate images of our fantasy life. Plath's writing presents us
> with these images at work . . . (Rose, 1992: 7)

At one level 'Daddy' can be read as the killing of the father as tyrant, offering 'the equation "as father to daughter" so "Nazi to Jew"' (Rose, 1992: 235). Such a reading, however, loses sight of both the specificity of history and the power of fantasy and leaves the troublesome line 'Every woman adores a fascist' (Plath, 1968: 55) unaccounted for. Ultimately, Rose suggests, what 'Daddy' allows us to do is ask whether women might have 'a special relationship to fantasy' and to suggest that 'it is a woman who is most likely to articulate the power – perverse, recalcitrant, persistent – of fantasy as such' (Rose, 1992: 237–8).

Plath's status as pre-eminent woman poet has helped to overshadow the work of her contemporaries. Literary history is, Louise Bernikow writes, 'actually a record of choices' (1979: 3). The traditional canon represents the selections of white men, who restrict women poets to the subjects of love and religion because 'Women's lives bore men. The reality of those lives, especially the embarrassing subject of women's bodies, frightens men' (Bernikow, 1979: 7). Women have been underrepresented in traditional anthologies, so the recent women-only anthologies, although not a new concept, have played an important part in publicizing women's poetry. Given the number of women writing at the moment, looking at a selection of anthologies offers one way of thinking about the variety of women's poetry within the confines of this essay. As the differences between them show, however, these anthologies themselves represent other choices about what women's poetry is or should be.

In *The Bloodaxe Book of Contemporary Women Poets* (1985) edited by Jeni Couzyn, Plath is situated with her near contemporaries, ten other women writers either born in or settled in Britain: Stevie Smith, Kathleen Raine, Fleur Adcock, Anne Stevenson, Elaine Feinstein, Elizabeth Jennings, Jenny Joseph, Denise Levertov, Ruth Fainlight and Couzyn herself. They represent an older generation of women whose work while not necessarily aligned with the feminist movement, takes on new meanings in this context and company. Plath, for instance, who looks starkly aberrant in all-male company, looks less so next to her contemporary Anne Stevenson. Similarly,

Elizabeth Jennings as the only woman associated with the 'Movement' poets is less often situated in relation to women poets. Like Plath, she suffered a mental breakdown and writes movingly about the experience.

Couzyn makes the point that men have disliked women's poetry for its *content* not its style or form (1985: 21) and this collection, from Smith's sophisticated 'doggerel' to Jennings's lyrics, is clear evidence of the technical proficiency of women poets. The re-visionary element which Yorke identifies in Plath is evident in the other poets here. The Muse, traditionally female, is reworked in varying ways. Kathleen Raine's 'bright daimon / Whisperer in my ear / Of springs of water, leaves and songs of birds' (70), is a very different being to Stevie Smith's:

> My Muse sits forlorn
> She wishes she had not been born
> She sits in the cold
> No word she says is ever told
> (Couzyn, 1985: 38)

Different again is Ruth Fainlight's 'The Other' where the muse is 'my forgotten sister- / Her presence my completion and reward' (135). Fainlight's 'Lilith' (141–2) is an excellent example of the reworking of old mythologies which Yorke sees as central to the re-visionary process and one of several poems (Feinstein's 'The Feast of Eurydice' (125–7) and Joseph's 'Persephone' (179–80) are others) which give a new voice to mythic female figures. Lilith, the first companion created for Adam, is banished from Eden because she 'assumed her equality' and replaced by 'Eve, the chattel'. Fainlight's poem exposes the inequalities behind the binaries male/female, good/bad: cast out as Other, 'Lilith's disgrace thus defined / Good and evil'.

The landscapes here, too, are infinitely variable. The internal landscape of Smith's poetry is a strange fairy-tale one, while the 'dark wood' with its 'pale tower', in 'I rode with my darling . . .' (46–7), recalls Robert Browning's 'Childe Roland . . .'. In contrast, Feinstein's 'Coastline' has a geological precision: 'This is the landscape of the Cambrian age: / shale, blue quartz, planes of slate streaked with / iron and lead; soapstone, spars of calcite' (121). Elizabeth Jennings's 'In a Garden' is a meditation on the use of gardens as 'a metaphor for Eden', and the human longing for the prelapsarian: 'I need not have stood long / Mocked by the smell of a mown lawn, and yet / I did. Sickness for Eden was so strong' (107).

The difficulties of relationships between the sexes and the tensions involved in being wife, lover or mother are central to many of these poems. Anne Stevenson's understated 'Generations' reads the imperfectly concealed signs of bitterness in three self-sacrificing mothers: 'Know this mother by the way she says / "darling" with her teeth clenched. / By the fabulous lies she cooks' (192). This poem, Stevenson has noted, was 'probably . . . the seed' (Stevenson, 1979: 168), from which grew her long epistolary poem 'Correspondances: A Family History in Letters' (Stevenson, 1987), which combines newspaper articles and poem-letters to record women's frustrations through the generations of a family. Denise Levertov's 'The Mutes' takes 'Those groans men use / passing a woman on the street / or on the steps of a subway' (Couzyn, 1985: 82) and attempts to translate their possible meanings, as well as understand their effect on a woman. Fleur Adcock's poetry often distils a controlled anger. In 'Instructions to Vampires' she writes 'I would not have you drain / With your sodden lips the flesh that has fed mine'. Instead, she instructs, use 'acid or flame' and 'on the soft globes of his mortal eyes / Etch my name' (207–8). Indeed, what Fainlight calls a 'specifically female anger' (130) is the impetus for several poems in this collection.

Madness as a logical reaction to a patriarchal 'reality' which allows women no autonomous identity, or which defines female sexual desire as 'insanity', is a key theme in two proto-feminist novels of the 1960s: Doris Lessing's *The Golden Notebook* (1962) and Jean Rhys's *Wide Sargasso Sea* (1966). Both use this theme, like Antonia White, to question that 'reality'. Lessing has said that *The Golden Notebook* was written 'as if the attitudes that have been created by the women's liberation movements already existed' (Lessing, 1973: 9). Although Simone de Beauvoir's *The Second Sex* (1949) had been translated into English in 1953, it was not until 1963 that Betty Friedan's attempt to analyze 'the problem without a name' in *The Feminine Mystique* 'exposed the fraud of the fifties and provided the beginnings of a vocabulary for women's liberation' (Coote and Campbell, 1982: 13).

Lessing's *The Golden Notebook* was an important validation of women's experience (despite its controversial privileging of the 'vaginal orgasm'), and opened up the space for the process of 'writing the body' which was a key concern in the 1980s. Lessing herself commented: 'It described many female emotions of aggression, hostility, resentment. It put them into print. Apparently what many women were thinking, feeling, experiencing, came as a great surprise' (Lessing, 1973: 9). Formally, it was a radical departure from Lessing's early realist novels. The fragmented form of the novel dramatizes the impossibility of 'representing' the reality of Anna Wulf's experience. Neither the realist 'Free Women' section, nor the Notebooks which burst open this linear framework can adequately convey that reality. Anna has

> a black notebook, which is to do with Anna Wulf the writer; a red notebook, concerned with politics; a yellow notebook, in which I make stories out of my experience; and a blue notebook which tries to be a diary. (Lessing, 1973: 461–2)

It is this compartmentalization itself which is the problem. In the 'Golden Notebook' Anna experiences a loss of self through her affair with Saul which, like that of Antonia White's Clara, leads to a merging of ego boundaries: they '"break down" into each other' (Lessing, 1973: 7). In a repudiation of the romance plot, the merging Anna and Saul experience is 'a calculated – if crude – parody of the conventional happy ending, in which two become one, and so symbolise the underlying orderliness of social life' (Sage, 1992: 15). Like Macauley, Lessing brings together a concern with the fragmentation of the post-war world (which was then occupying male writers) with a critique of patriarchy. The novel's move away from linear realism can be read not just in terms of the disintegration of pre-war certainties but as looking forward to ideas developed by the French feminists, particularly to Irigaray's ideal of female discourse as disrupting linear progression, as she claims to do in her own *Speculum of the Other Woman* (Irigaray, 1985: 68) and Kristeva's theorization of 'Women's time' (1979) as circular. Anna says of her daughter:

> sometimes I see her as a small baby and I *feel* her inside my belly and I see her as various sizes of small girl, all at the same time . . . . That's how women see things. Everything in a sort of continuous creative stream. (Lessing, 1973: 268)

Similarly Anna's breakdown can be read not just as an engagement with the Laingian notion of psychic breakdown as a means to a new psychic wholeness (Waugh, 1995: 133–4), but in relation to women writers' depiction of madness as a reaction to patriarchal 'reality'.

Perhaps the most radical 're-vision' of the romance plot is Jean Rhys's *Wide Sargasso Sea*, which gives a voice to the first Mrs Rochester. In Rhys's rewriting of *Jane Eyre* the Creole Antoinette Cosway is driven mad by Rochester's rejection of the female sexuality he first initiates and then interprets as a sign of hereditary insanity. While *Jane Eyre* uses the romance plot to dramatize an individual consciousness moving towards fulfilment, Rhys's text lays bare the economic and social structures which underpin that plot, and reveals it as fatal for women. The close intertextual relationship between the two novels is evident in Rhys's reworking of images from *Jane Eyre* – dark and light, fire, stone, colour, mirrors, the moon, dreams, dress. *Wide Sargasso Sea* exemplifies the 'room, house, landscape, sea' configuration (Horner and Zlosnick, 1990: 161–80). Antoinette, accepted by neither white society nor the marginalized blacks she identifies with, is marooned in the seaweed-logged 'Sargasso Sea' between two landscapes. The warm colourful Caribbean landscape is a postlapsarian Eden, from which Antoinette travels to the attic in England 'where I will be cold and not belonging' (Rhys, 1968: 92). Rhys's text anticipates Gilbert and Gubar's influential *The Madwoman in the Attic* (1979), which focuses on the madwoman as the 'Other' of the nineteenth-century heroine and her author, embodying their repressed anger. However, seeing Antoinette as 'Jane's truest and darkest double' (Gilbert and Gubar, 1984: 360) simplifies Rhys's complex understanding of the privileging of the white Jane above Antoinette, who is also doubled by the black Tia. Rhys opens up the issues of race, colonization and 'difference' between women which became key issues in the feminist and postcolonial theory of the 1980s and 1990s.

Wide Sargasso Sea is not so much an example of 'writing beyond the ending' (the writing beyond the closure of the marriage plot which DuPlessis theorizes) but a 'maneuver of encirclement' which 'ruptures' *Jane Eyre* (DuPlessis, 1985: 46). The text is a 'prequel' rather than a 'sequel', dominated by what Frank Kermode has called the 'sense of an ending' (1967). This device is also used by Muriel Spark, whose work is self-consciously metafictional, wittily exposing its own constructedness. Her play with the notion of the author as 'omniscient' god and her use of the 'flash forward' (Lodge, 1971: 126), a device which foregrounds the 'sense of an ending', have their roots in her Catholicism. *The Driver's Seat* (1970) is, among other things, a critique of the romance plot with its pre-determined end. Lise's search for the 'right man' is actually a search for a man who will kill her. Spark's most famous novel *The Prime of Miss Jean Brodie* (1961) is a complex study of the relationship between fantasy (including romance) and Fascism, and their appeal for women, a subject which links her to Plath. *Jane Eyre*, one of Miss Brodie's favourite novels, is an explicit inter-text and Miss Brodie's two lovers, one-armed, married Teddy Lloyd and the singing master Gordon Lowther, double for Mr Rochester and St John Rivers. Miss Brodie's sin, David Lodge suggests, is that, while her pupil Sandy 'uses fictions . . . correctly for "finding things out"' (1971: 141), Miss Brodie insists on them as fixed and unalterable.

Like Spark, Iris Murdoch began writing in the 1950s but is more usually aligned with the 'angry young men' of that decade than within a 'female tradition', partly because of her tendency to use male narrators. She shares with Spark a concern with the metanarratives of religion and philosophy, and with the nature of good and evil. Her *A Severed Head* (1961) is, for instance, like *Jean Brodie*, a study of 'the psychology and myth-making imperatives of power politics and Fascism' (Waugh, 1995: 121). In contrast to feminist theorizations of 'man-made language' (Spender, 1980) Murdoch's fiction is concerned with the attempts of humanity in general to escape from the 'net' of language, explored in her first novel, *Under the Net* (1954). A highly metafictional text, *The Black Prince* (1973) is concerned, like much of her work, with the contingency of experience and the difficulty of representing it in art. With multiple forewords and postscripts, the narrator, Bradley Pearson, repeatedly undermines his own narration, producing an almost Derridean deferral of meaning. Through Bradley, author of three short books in forty years, and his rival, the prolific novelist Arnold Baffin, Murdoch dramatizes one of her own central concerns: the choice between the 'journalistic' novel which is true to the formlessness of life and the 'crystalline' novel which imposes form at the expense of authenticity. Neither, Murdoch suggests in 'Against Dryness: A Polemical Sketch' (1961), is adequate.

It is an exploration of the specificity and significance of female experience, however, which is central to the work of the novelists who began writing in the 1960s, and which anticipates the concept of 'writing the body' in 1980s *écriture féminine*. When Jane Grey in Margaret Drabble's *The Waterfall* (1969) wonders 'What can it have been like, in bed with Mr Knightley?' (1971: 58) she indicates an area of physical female experience about which neither Austen nor Brontë could write directly. It is this area, opened up by Lessing, which is explored by writers like Margaret Drabble, A.S. Byatt, Edna O'Brien and Fay Weldon in their depictions of sex, childbirth and the physical work of caring for small children. Indeed, O'Brien, an Irish woman who moved to England, had several books banned in Ireland because of her explicit treatment of sexuality. The fantasy of romance is demythologized in her treatment of the comic reality of sex in, for instance, *Girl With Green Eyes* (1962), where, after losing her virginity, the protagonist muses:

> It was strange, being part of something so odd, so comic . . . . I thought, so this is it; the secret I dreaded and longed for . . . . All the perfume, and sighs, and purple brassieres,

and curling pins in bed, and gin-and-it, and necklaces had all been for this. (O'Brien, 1964: 149)

O'Brien's reputation and looks have rather overshadowed her writing but her concern with issues of female and Irish identity are shared by other Irish women living in Britain, including Moy McCrory and Maude Casey.

Drabble and Byatt both focus in different ways on motherhood, a central issue in the feminism which was evolving through these years. *The Feminine Mystique* was written, Byatt has remarked, 'for my generation, who had been brainwashed into thinking that a woman's place, whatever her training and talents, was back in the home, bringing up children' (Todd, 1983: 181–95; quoted in Kenyon, 1988, 53). Drabble and Byatt are especially good on the conflicts faced by the middle-class woman graduate who becomes a mother. Byatt's Jenny in *The Virgin in the Garden* (1978), married with a small child, remarks bitterly that 'When I was a student I was fool enough to suppose life opened up once you got out of university. But what I've got is complete closure. No talk, no thought, no hope' (1994: 52). Jenny stands for many young women in the 1960s who found that their hard-won degree opened fewer doors than they anticipated.

Unmarried or separated, Drabble's early protagonists experience maternity as an enriching experience distinct from marriage (the 'romance' of motherhood perhaps) which re-establishes the connections between sexuality and motherhood. In *The Mill-stone* (1965) Rosamond Stacey's only sexual encounter leaves her unmoved. It is only as an unmarried mother that she begins to experience herself in relation to others, while, ironically, pregnancy enhances her intellectual life. In *The Waterfall* Jane Grey, separated from her husband, becomes sexually desiring and desired only as she lies in childbed. Childbirth returns her to a kind of pre-oedipal infancy, enclosed in an overheated, womb-like room, where she is 'mothered' by her cousin's husband James who acts out the male desire for the body of the mother. Both are reborn through sex: 'She was his offspring as he, lying there between her legs, had been hers' (1971: 151). Drabble is frequently seen as a writer of traditional, realist fictions but, like Byatt and Weldon, she uses the devices of metafiction and intertextuality within deceptively 'realist' texts. Her novels draw attention to their own constructedness through intertextual games which link them to their nineteenth-century predecessors. 'Those fictitious heroines, how they haunt me' (1971: 153) reflects Jane Grey, whose name recalls *Jane Eyre*, Jane Austen and the fated nine-day Queen of England, while her love affair with the husband of her cousin Lucy parallels *The Mill on the Floss*. With its alternating first and third person narrations, the novel is concerned, like *The Golden Notebook*, with the inability of the realist novel to convey the 'truth' of women's experience. Yet the first person narration, which in *Jane Eyre* connotes authenticity, is also undermined. The waterfall at Goredale Scar, Jane tells the reader, is 'real, unlike James and me, it exists' (1971: 236). Here Drabble is far closer to Muriel Spark's concern with fiction as 'lies' than she might at first appear.

Similarly, Byatt reworks the realist novel through her use of a dense intertextuality. Where Byatt differs from Iris Murdoch, with whom she has much in common, is in her use of female subjectivity located in the specificity of physical experience. In *The Virgin in the Garden*, the first volume of a projected quartet, Byatt enriches a realist, historical novel inspired by *Middlemarch* with an exploration of Renaissance metaphor and a structuralist understanding of language. The novel's exploration of the iconography of virginity associated with Elizabeth I, portrayed by Frederica in a play within the text, is counterpointed by the messy physicality of Frederica's attempts to lose her own virginity. Like West's trilogy, Byatt's projected quartet offers us a revised, female-centred version of history. The novels focus on two sisters who enact the work *or* marriage choice open to women in the 1950s. In the second of the novels *Still Life* (1985) Stephanie struggles to maintain an intellectual life as a wife and mother, reading Wordsworth as she waits in line at the maternity clinic. The struggle ends with Stephanie's death, electrocuted by a refrigerator, literally killed by the house which traps her. *Still Life* offers a rare subjective account of childbirth which puts the experience on a level with marriage and death as 'a supreme experience which confirms or destroys identity' (Cosslett, 1989: 265), and which revises the birth myth of Wordsworth's 'Ode: Intimations of Immortality' by inserting the physical experience of the woman giving birth.

Stephanie, like the wives discussed by Betty Friedan, is isolated in her struggle to make sense of her dissatisfaction. The Woman's Liberation Movement in the 1960s and 1970s had its roots in small bands of women getting together in what became known as 'consciousness-raising groups' to discuss what Friedan had called 'the problem without a name'. 'Consciousness-raising' was 'what happened when women translated their personal feelings into political awareness' (Coote and Campbell, 1982: 14), hence the slogan 'the personal is political'. This developed into the direct political activism which produced the Equal Pay Acts and the Sex Discrimination Act in the early 1970s. A number of influential theoretical texts provided an increasingly complex vocabulary for the critique of patriarchy over the next decades: Juliet Mitchell's 'Women: The Longest Revolution' (1966), Germaine Greer's *The Female Eunuch* (1970), Kate Millett's *Sexual Politics* (1970), Shulamith Firestone's *The Dialectic of Sex* (1970), and Juliet Mitchell's *Psychoanalysis and Feminism* (1974). The development of a feminist literary criticism was an integral part of this project and Mary Ellmann (1968), Patricia Meyer Spacks (1975), Jane Rule (1975), Ellen Moers (1976) and Elaine Showalter (1977) laid the foundations for a feminist literary criticism and began the project of recovering neglected women writers.

Breaking the silence, naming and exploring female experience and oppression, are the first steps in the process of redefinition or 're-vision' which Liz Yorke argues is central to women's contemporary poetry. The poems in the anthology *One Foot on the Mountain: An Anthology of British Feminist Poetry 1969–1979* (1979) edited by Lilian Mohin are individual acts of 'consciousness-raising' (Mohin, 1979: 1). Much of the poetry is confessional in style, often by women who had never published before, and many poems do not conform to traditional standards of poetic 'excellence', but it also includes early poetry by women like Michèle Roberts, Zoe Fairbairns, Alison Fell, Judith Kazantzis and Michelene Wandor whose work came directly out of the feminist movement. Alison Fell's novel *Every Move You Make* (1984), for instance, is a fictional account of involvement in the radical politics of the 1970s and of the often painful debates and conflicts, between feminism and socialism, women and men, which characterized those years.

What Mohin's anthology as a whole does is to put female experience and subjectivity on the poetic map, and attempt fundamentally to alter our notions of what poetry should be. Challenging the traditional notion that poetry, particularly women's poetry, should not be political, Mohin argues that 'Poetry, with its tradition of concentrated insights, its brevity of form, is an ideal vehicle for the kind of politics we propose' (1979: 1). '. . . we will take language back to the body' writes Deb Symonds (Mohin, 1979: 74) and the physical experience of inhabiting a female body is actively validated as a subject for poetry: Judith Kazantzis writes about abortion, Caroline Halliday about child sexual abuse, Katharyn Gabriella about a D&C, Caroline Gilfillan breaks the taboos around menstruation, while Astra celebrates celibacy. Heterosexuality is redefined and lesbian sexuality reclaimed as Paula Jennings's 'Lesbian' reminds us that 'behind the word lesbian / stinking in men's mouths . . . was always this word / with a soft "l" like in laughter . . .' (Mohin, 1979: 202).

The problematizing of traditional notions of what constitutes 'good' poetry as imposed by patriarchy, including a rejection of standard verse forms, rhythm, rhyme and even punctuation, has been contentious. Carol Rumens in her Introduction to *Making for the Open: The Chatto Book of Post-Feminist Poetry 1964–1984* (1985) suggested that

> The political orientation of much women's publishing . . . has sometimes, particularly
> in the case of poetry, led to the elevation of the message at the expense of the medium.
> Those writers concerned with 'the stern art of poetry' as an end in itself have tended to
> be swamped by the noisy amateurs proclaiming that women, too, have a voice. (Rumens,
> 1985: xv)

Rumens's use of the term 'post-feminist' attracted heated debate and her emphasis on excellence alone as a criterion for judging poetry has been countered by Rebecca O'Rourke who points out that 'Questions of judgment will always be fractured by power lines from the history and culture in which they operate' (O'Rourke, 1990: 279).

Rumens's anthology includes over fifty poets from twenty countries which foregrounds the international influence of writers like Adrienne Rich and Margaret Atwood. It also indicates the regional diversity which has enriched British poetry over recent years by including work by Scottish and Irish women such as Liz Lochead, Elma Mitchell and Kathleen Jamie from Scotland, and Medbh McGuckian from Belfast. Again much of this poetry is clearly engaged in a process of re-visioning and revaluing. U.A. Fanthorpe, whose work opens the collection, excels at creating the voices of the ordinary and the marginalized. Re-imagining the 'Great War' has proved a productive way of thinking about gender for several women writers and Fanthorpe's poem 'The Constant Tin Soldier' (Rumens, 1985: 4–12), deals with the effects of the war on a soldier who afterwards became, not a Great War poet like 'Rupert the Fair and Wilfred the Wise' but a travelling salesman. 'Investing sensibly in job, house, car, / Wife and children, dog and skivvy', he transfers his military skills and language to his private life with devastating effects. The alienation between the sexes which is the product of war is also the subject of Liz Lochead's 'Poppies' (Rumens, 1985: 104–5) where a woman transgresses by breaking the three-minute silence on Armistice day with the sound of her high heels.

The concept of gender difference as biologically based in the body is tackled in Elma Mitchell's 'Thoughts After Ruskin' (Rumens, 1985: 31–2). Women may have reminded Ruskin 'of lilies and roses' but Mitchell reminds us of the messy physicality of their day-to-day lives. While their husbands 'lean across mahogany / And delicately manipulate the market' it is the women who kill mice, evict spiders, clean cupboards, feed children and mop up vomit and afterwards 'somehow find, in mirrors, colours, odours, / their essences of lilies and of roses'. In Medbh McGuckian's poetry the female body and the domestic become a rich source of imagery and metaphor used to weave a complex, challenging and richly allusive poetry, as in the initial image of 'From the Dressing-Room':

> Left to itself, they say, every foetus
> Would turn female, staving in, nature
> Siding then with the enemy that
> Delicately mixes up genders.
>   (Rumens, 1985: 130)

In contrast, comic poetry is rarely treated as 'serious' but, as Wendy Cope's work shows, humour can be a devastating weapon in the task of re-vision. Cope's parodic 'Strugnell's Sonnets', probably achieve as much in the task of demythologizing the icon of the male 'great poet' as several scholarly articles. Strugnell is more interested in wine and women than poetry and is delighted to discover that 'women love a bard, however dire, / And overlook my paunch because I write' (Rumens, 1985: 29).

The project of re-imagining the unheard and silenced women's voices of history and literature has produced poetry which is often both accessible and politically pointed. Carol Ann Duffy (not included in Rumens's anthology) uses the dramatic monologue in 'The World's Wife' to produce a variety of voices from Mrs Aesop's acerbic assessment of her spouse, 'By Christ, he could bore for purgatory' (Duffy, 1994: 141), to Mrs Lazarus's horror at the return of her husband from the grave. An erotic connection between women is explored in her poem 'Warming her Pearls' (Duffy, 1994: 60), which uses the image of a rope of pearls as historical touchstone. Worn by a servant to warm them (this brought out the beauty of the pearls) for her mistress, the pearls signify both their class difference (the servant's labour produces the mistress's beauty) and their complicity.

Feminism provided a theory and a language which many writers found enabling. From the 1980s onwards there has been not only an explosion of feminist literary theory, but a boom in women's publishing, fed partly by the demand for reprints of newly recovered writers, but also by new writing. The establishment of the women's presses began with the launch of Virago in 1973, and others followed, including The Women's Press, Onlywomen, Pandora, Sheba and Honno, often with a commitment to work mainstream publishers would not publish. Ironically, by the early 1980s as the organized feminist movement began to fragment in the face of an anti-feminist backlash, women's publishing had become big business, with many mainstream publishing houses launching women's lists. While 1970s feminism emphasized women's shared experience of oppression, 1980s feminism concentrated on issues of diversity and difference. The publication of *New French Feminisms* (1981), an anthology of translations of the work of French theorists like Hélène Cixous, Julia Kristeva and Luce Irigaray, facilitated the introduction of the influential concept of *écriture féminine* to British writers and critics. Cixous's exhortation to women 'Write your self. Your body must be heard. Only then will the immense resources of the unconscious spring forth' in 'The Laugh of the Medusa' (Marks and de Courtivron, 1981: 250) equated 'writing the body' with experimentation and with subversion. The last two decades have seen an extraordinarily rich and varied output of fiction and poetry by women with the writing of working-class, lesbian, Black and Asian women coming increasingly to the fore.

The novelists of the 1960s and 1970s, Nicci Gerrard has suggested, turned to realist or confessional fiction in order to centralize women's experience and 'tell it like it is' (1989: 111). However, Paulina Palmer has argued that such fiction should be seen within the terms of the theoretical ideas it appropriates and reworks, and suggests the term 'fiction of ideas' (1989: 8). Marilyn French's *The Women's Room* (1977), an influential American realist novel, for instance, bore the claim 'This novel changes lives' on its front cover, highlighting its function as polemic. Palmer points out that 'realist' or 'experimental' techniques are often used for specific issues. While the realist novel is appropriate for exploring social and political issues, experimental techniques are frequently used for exploring issues of the self.

In fact, many of the feminist novels which appear to be 'realist' use experimental techniques. Fay Weldon's novels offer a hard-edged analysis of the intersection of economics and biology in women's oppression. Her abrasive, aphoristic style with its short punchy sentences and use of types rather than rounded characters owes much to her early career as an advertising copywriter, and foregrounds the constructed quality of her texts. In *Down Among the Women* (1971) she uses refrains to provide a commentary which both universalizes the experience of the women characters and implicates the reader in their fate. Nature is the enemy in Weldon's books. It is their biological functions which keep women 'down' in economic terms: 'Down among the women. What a place to be! Yet here we all are by accident of birth, sprouted breasts and bellies, as cyclical of nature as our timekeeper the moon' (1973: 5). Weldon's novels are didactic, consciousness-raising tools which use a black humour to articulate energizing anger.

In the analyses of the complex relationship between sexuality and power within patriarchy, male violence against women, particularly rape, has been a key issue. By destabilizing the division between whore and virgin/mother, Pat Barker makes explicit the connections between male violence and female oppression in *Blow Your House Down* (1984), a novel based on the 'Yorkshire Ripper', Peter Sutcliffe. The working-class women forced into prostitution by poverty, and already vulnerable to domestic violence from husbands or boyfriends and sexual abuse from their clients, are easy prey for the murderer, whose actions are presented as part of a continuum of violence. Barker's gritty realism accommodates a symbolism which comes naturally out of the women's lives. The chicken factory which offers the only other paid work (like prostitution, it is monotonous, physically demanding and badly paid) generates a range of metaphors. The sexual division of labour in the factory – 'Killing's for the men' (1984: 34) – is paralleled with that outside the factory where it is again men who 'kill'. Maggie, a woman attacked by someone who may or may not be the murderer, makes the connection between the murdered prostitutes and chickens: 'The image [of the murdered women's faces] faded and was replaced by a line of chickens waiting to be killed. In each eye the same passive uncomprehending terror' (1984: 156). The anonymous 'Poem for Jacqueline Hill' (the final victim of Peter Sutcliffe) was widely circulated during the winter of 1980/1 (Scott, 1982: 273–8). Like Barker's novel, it refuses the divisions into pure/impure which divide women to make the point that 'It could have been any one of us' (Scott, 1982: 274). The poem becomes both a memorial to the victims and a *'Curse for the Ripper'* (276).

'One is not born, but rather becomes a woman' Simone de Beauvoir famously wrote (1972: 295) and the distinction between 'female' and 'feminine', between biological sex and socially constructed gender, has been vital to feminist theory. Angela Carter is a revisionist *par excellence* and her work, with its magical reworking of myth, folk and fairy-tale, Gothic and film, brilliantly deconstructs the patriarchal myths which construct us as gendered subjects. As she writes: 'Myth deals in false universals, to dull the pain of particular circumstances. In no area is this more true than in that of relations between the sexes' (1979: 5–6). Carter's *The Passion of New Eve* (1977) uses Genesis, the passion of Christ, *The Waste Land*, Blake and Woolf's *Orlando*, to rewrite the gendered body and expose both masculinity and femininity as 'masquerade' (Carter, 1982: 132). Evelyn, a parody of masculinity, is reborn as Eve through plastic surgery carried out by 'Mother' the leader of a band of Amazon-like women. Transformed into a 'Playboy centrefold . . . my own masturbatory fantasy' (1982: 75), Eve has the body of a woman but not, until he has lived as a woman, the mind. He is paralleled by Tristessa, a Garbo-like film star, revealed as a transvestite and thus 'the perfect man's woman! He had made himself the shrine of his own desires, had made of himself the only woman he could have loved!' (1982: 128–9). Sex between Eve and Tristessa involves a complex play of gender where both are male and both female. Like T.S. Eliot's Tiresias, Eve/lyn, despite his experience of both genders, can offer no answers:

> what the nature of masculine and the nature of feminine might be, whether they involve male and female . . . that I do not know. Though I have been both man and woman, still I do not know the answer to these questions. (1982: 149–50)

Eve/lyn's quest takes him through a version of the house/landscape/sea configuration. The apocalyptic desert (recalling Christ's sojourn in the wilderness and Eliot's waste land) incorporates several rooms/houses which figure a series of rebirths: Mother's womb-like caves; the patriarchal Zero's house; and Tristessa's house of mirrors. Emerging through another series of caves in search of the elusive Mother onto a beach, Eve finally puts to sea, rebirthing not only herself but Tristessa's child which she carries in her womb. Carter's destabilization of gender categories here anticipates Judith Butler's *Gender Trouble* (1990).

Michèle Roberts is another writer who has attempted to rewrite the 'grand narratives' of our culture, in her case those of Christianity. *The Wild Girl* (1984) is a brave attempt to use the Gnostic gospels to write a fifth gospel according to Mary Magdalene, and to reinsert a positive validation of both sexuality and women into Christianity through sexual love between Mary and Christ. Using the romance plot to rewrite Christianity is like fighting fire with fire and Roberts's use of heterosexuality to figure a union of binary opposites risks re-enforcing the gender categories Carter destabilizes. Her *Daughters of the House* (1992) is a more successful reworking of the story of Saint Thérèse which explores the power of female relationships and family secrets and uses domestic objects as 'expressive objects' (Bowen, 1982: 15) – touchstones for memory or history.

The concepts of 'sisterhood' and women's community have a central place in feminism and the substantial number of contemporary novels about female friendship can be seen as a direct result of this. While female friendship and community have been an important theme in women's literature from at least the seventeenth century onwards, contemporary novels differ from their predecessors in that they are informed by and engage with feminist concepts. Gillian Hanscombe's *Between Friends* (1982), for instance, articulates the debates around heterosexuality and lesbianism, and uses the epistolary form to allow each woman's voice to be heard. No longer contained within the romance plot, friendship often provides the main interest of the text. Weldon's *Female Friends* (1975) is an ironic illustration of Millett's argument that patriarchy produces in women traits expected in minority groups, including 'group self hatred and rejection, a contempt for both herself and her fellows – the result of that continual, however subtle, reiteration of her inferiority which she eventually accepts as fact' (Millett, 1977: 56). Weldon shows how patriarchal structures function to keep women apart: 'We women, we beggers, we scrubbers and dusters, we do the best we can for us and ours. We are divided amongst ourselves. We have to be, for survival's sake' (1989: 194). Marjorie, Grace and Chloe are bound together only by their shared experience of biological womanhood: they 'bled in unison, punctually and regularly for five days once every four weeks' (1989: 76). Marjorie's conclusion that 'We should interfere more in each other's lives and not just pick up the pieces' (1989: 220) is a plea for an active female solidarity. Doris Lessing's *The Diaries of Jane Somers* (1984) explores a friendship between two very different women – Janna Somers, a magazine editor, and 90-year-old Maudie Fowler. Caring for Maudie transforms Janna's life and the book offers a rare and moving account of the humiliations of being poor, old and female. Friendship between an older and a younger woman is often presented as a way of retrieving women's oral history and Janna transforms Maudie's memories into a romantic novel, a telling comment on the narrative options open for writing women's lives.

While female friendship has existed in the margins of the romance plot for several centuries, lesbianism has been one of the most silenced areas of women's experience.

Maureen Duffy, although contemporary with Drabble and Byatt, stands outside the mainstream, partly because of her class and sexuality, but also because her work crosses genre categories. Her autobiographical first novel *That's How it Was* (1962) is a powerful account of what it means to be marginalized by illegitimate birth, class and gender. Duffy broke new ground in the 1960s with her novel *The Microcosm* (1966), a rare picture of a lesbian underworld centred on a bar called the House of Shades in London which makes intertextual use of the work of Charlotte Charke. In the 1970s publications like *One Foot On the Mountain* helped to open up publishing for lesbian texts. Jeanette Winterson's *Oranges are not the Only Fruit* (1985) reached a mainstream audience, partly because it was made into a television series. Winterson's 'Jeanette' is brought up by an evangelical Christian mother who, when she hears her daughter is in love with another woman, has 'Jeanette' exorcized. The effect of this is to construct 'Jeanette's' feelings as normal and natural and the reactions of other people as abnormal and excessive. Winterson's novel rewrites the male-defined popular romance, positing instead an 'original' concept of Romantic love which can accommodate love between women:

> Romantic love has been diluted into paperback form and has sold thousands and millions of copies. Somewhere it is still in the original, written on tablets of stone. I would cross seas and suffer sunstroke and give away all I have, but not for a man, because they want to be the destroyer and never the destroyed. That is why they are unfit for romantic love. (1985: 170)

In the project of re-vision lesbian writers have played a pioneering role, especially in genre fiction where 'the insertion of Lesbian meanings . . . disrupts the heterosexist codes of desire' (Duncker, 1992: 99).

Genre fiction offers the reader the satisfaction of a certain form and often a predetermined ending. Women have excelled at certain genres, notably the romance and detective fiction, while being largely excluded from science fiction. Feminist genre fiction is 'genre fiction written from a self-consciously feminist perspective, consciously encoding an ideology which is in direct opposition to the dominant gender ideology of Western society, patriarchal ideology' (Cranny-Francis, 1990: 1). The lesbian romance, like the lesbian detective novel, has become a recognized genre. Ellen Galford's *Moll Cutpurse* (1984) is a historical romance centred around the cross-dressing 'Roaring Girl' of Middleton and Dekker's play. Some of the episodes in the novel are based on historical sources, the others, as Galford says, 'may be as close – or closer – to the truth' (1984: 221). Discovering the well-kept secret that 'woman's touch is sweeter' (1984: 59) Moll finds true love with Bridget. Galford's *Moll* may be a romantic romp but it also explicitly re-visions history in order to defy patriarchally imposed stereotypes.

The subversion of genre fiction is not without its problems. The key question is whether the patterning which characterizes genre fiction is innately conservative. Patricia Duncker asks

> Can a romantic novel in which the woman eventually sinks into the tweed-jacketed, fur-lined or taut-leathered breast of the taller, older, richer man be anything other than a

capitulation to the very structures feminist women set out to challenge and subvert – and which for lesbian women constitute nothing less than a complete denial of identity? (1992: 89)

The 1980s answer would appear to be 'No!' While the lesbian romance has blossomed, it has become increasingly difficult for women with any pretensions to be seen as serious writers to write heterosexual romance. Instead, they have focused on a deconstruction of the romance ideologies. Fay Weldon's *The Life and Loves of a She Devil* (1983) and Anita Brookner's *Hotel du Lac* (1984) both focus on women who *write* romance fiction. Weldon's novel engages with both *Jane Eyre* and *Frankenstein*, and 'stages a confrontation between genres – Gothic versus romantic fiction, hate story versus love story – and thus makes novelistic conventions themselves the protagonists' (Sage, 1992: 158). Ruth is the monstrous first wife whose husband leaves her for Mary Fisher, a best-selling romantic novelist, and who reinvents herself through plastic surgery to become Mary's double. *She Devil* exposes the stereotype of femininity enshrined in Mary Fisher's novels where 'little staunch heroines raise tearful eyes to handsome men, and by giving them up, gain them' (Weldon, 1984: 24). In a version of the house/landscape/sea metaphor, Mary Fisher lives in 'a High Tower, on the edge of the sea' (5), a suitably romantic spot. When Ruth moves into the tower she changes not only the landscape but the sea itself, altering the wave direction by shoring up the cliff because 'Nature gets away with far too much. It needs controlling' (240). Although it avoids the essentialism of equating 'Woman' with Nature, the novel is problematic; Ruth's victory is won at the cost of mutilating herself.

Brookner's novel also centres on a building, the aptly named Hotel du Lac, near a 'vast grey lake, spreading like an anaesthetic towards the invisible further shore' (1985: 7), which symbolizes the alienation of the heroine, romance writer Edith Hope. In the tradition of Lehmann and Rhys, Brookner writes about women who 'hope' for love, but despite disappointment, refuse to sacrifice their integrity. Edith refuses a marriage based on rationality, preferring a dignified single life. Nicci Gerrard argues that Brookner articulates a desire for 'security, romantic love and domestic fulfilment' (1989: 110) felt by many women who feel betrayed by a feminism which disregards these emotions. The romance novels Edith writes feed powerful desires and needs which cannot, Brookner implies, simply be dismissed.

The popularity of the feminist detective novel is indicated by the number of publishers' lists devoted specially to the genre. Cora Kaplan has argued that crime fiction is 'an unsuitable genre for a feminist' because traditionally crime fiction has upheld conservative social values, and reproduced 'anxieties about dangerous femininity' (1986: 19). Cordelia Grey in P.D. James's *An Unsuitable Job for a Woman* (1972) was 'one of the first of the new "feminist" detectives' (Shaw and Vanacker, 1991: 96). Like those who follow her – Gillian Slovo's Kate Baeier, Lisa Cody's Anna Lee, Joan Smith's Loretta Lawson – she is more vulnerable than her male counterparts. An outsider by virtue of her sex, the female detective is more likely to operate outside the law – often it is the system itself which is the villain of the story. It would be difficult to find two women more different than Smith's Loretta Lawson, a university lecturer, and O'Rourke's Rats, an unemployed, working-class lesbian. Yet both provide an affirmative answer to Kaplan's question 'Would a feminist novel use a woman detective to find a patriarchal villain?' (1986: 19), and indicate how the feminist detective novel can be used to explore issues of morality and power. In O'Rourke's *Jumping the Cracks* (1987) the villain is a capitalist entrepreneur called 'Cruze Pershing'. The 'real topics' of the novel are 'the scandal of unemployment and inadequate housing, the division between North and South, and the economic decline of urban life' (Palmer, 1991: 13). In Smith's *Why Aren't They Screaming?* (1988), set around a woman's peace camp at a US air base, the villain is a Conservative MP, promoted at the end to the Ministry of Defence. If the system itself is the villain it is indeed more difficult to provide the satisfactorily wrapped-up ending the genre traditionally demanded.

Feminism has a strongly utopian element and science fiction, with its freedom to mingle different discourses and open-endedness, offers special attractions for feminist writers. It makes possible 'the inscription of women as subjects free from the constraints of mundane fiction; and it also offers the possibility of interrogating that very inscription, questioning the basis of gendered subjectivity' (Lefanu, 1988: 9). With this in mind it is notable that, while there is a distinct group of science fiction writers like Gwyneth Jones, Josephine Saxton and Mary Gentle, mainstream writers, among them Doris Lessing, Zoe Fairbairns, Angela Carter, Fay Weldon, Maureen Duffy, have utilized elements of the genre. In Lessing's case the turn from the realism of her early novels to the 'science fiction' of the apocalyptic *Memoirs of a Survivor* (1974) and the *Canopus in Argos* series (1979–) marks her conviction that realism as a form is inadequate to cope with the increasingly fragmented and apocalyptic nature of the world (Gąsiorek, 1995: 92). Science fiction offers another way of writing 'fiction of ideas' as in Zoe Fairbairns's dystopian *Benefits* (1979). By engaging in a specific debate – the 'wages for housework' issue – and pushing it to an extreme in an imagined future, she offers a social critique of the present.

Some of the richest and most innovative writing in Britain over the last decade and a half has come from Black and Asian women. With a richly inventive use of language and images, often drawing on oral traditions, their work challenges the myths and stereotypes of Western patriarchy. Suniti Namjoshi, born in Bombay, is a self-consciously revisionary writer. Her *Feminist Fables* (1981) utilize a subversive brew of fables from India and Aesop, fairy-tales, Greek myths, the Arabian nights and legend and aim, like Carter's stories, to deconstruct the myths of white patriarchy. Certain themes are especially important for Black and Asian writers – the search for identity and history, the geography of 'unbelonging', female community, and 'writing the body' as both locus of oppression and as celebration. Their insistence on the specificity of their experience, that, in Jackie Kay's words, 'we are not all sisters under the same moon' (Burford et al., 1985: 8), problematizes oversimplified notions of 'sisterhood' and 'female experience'.

'Writing a woman's life' has been an important way of asserting an identity and reclaiming a history which has been silenced. The title of Buchi Emecheta's autobiography *Head Above Water* (1986), which tells of her struggle to gain a degree in sociology and publish her novels as a 'second-class citizen' in London, foregrounds the issue of survival: 'my keeping my head above water in this indifferent society' she writes 'is a miracle' (5). Her writing draws on the oral traditions of her Ibo heritage in Nigeria, symbolized by her 'big mother Nwakwaluzo' telling stories 'in her very own compound with her back leaning against the *ukwa* tree' (242). The difference is that Emecheta uses 'a language that belonged to those who once colonised the country of my birth' (242). Her bitterly ironic novel *The Joys of Motherhood* (1979) exposes the undervaluing of mothers in Nigeria and has much in common with Weldon's work.

Joan Riley's *The Unbelonging* (1985) was the first book by a black woman published by a major British feminist press (Wisker, 1993). Like Alice Walker's *The Color Purple* (1983) it confronts the intersection of race, gender and class through an account of father–daughter incest. As a Jamaican girl transposed to British inner-city life by a father she barely knows, Hyacinth, like Rhys's Antoinette, is 'unbelonging', caught between two landscapes. She retreats from the bleak inner-city landscape to her daydreams of the 'secret place' she shared with her friends in Jamaica, a pre-oedipal image of a 'little green cave, the recesses of the bushes laden with long-stemmed hibiscus and yellow trumpet-flowers and humming with insect activity' (Riley, 1985: 9). For Hyacinth, beaten by her father for her bedwetting, 'the body constitutes the site of oppression and becomes the source not of celebration but of permanent anxiety' (Griffin, 1993: 21). The link between sexual power and male violence is made visible by the 'anger bulge' (Riley, 1985: 57) in her father's trousers. Hyacinth's survival is, like Emecheta's, 'a miracle' made possible by her academic achievements.

The poetry collected in the ground-breaking *A Dangerous Knowing: Four Black Women Poets* (Barbara Burford, Gabriella Pearse, Grace Nichols and Jackie Kay) (1985) is an affirmation of women's 'creative fruitfulness' as, in the words of the poem of Burford's which gives the collection its title, 'a bloody, an ancient, / and a dangerous knowing' (Untitled, Burford *et al.*, 1985: 4). Both Jackie Kay and Grace Nichols have produced impressive poem cycles. Nichols's *i is a long memoried woman* (1983) is, like Toni Morrison's *Beloved* (1987), a 're-imagining' of the unrecorded history of women's experience of slavery. Reborn through the Middle Passage into the new world, the Black woman painfully, then triumphantly, forges a new identity and language:

> I have crossed an ocean
> I have lost my tongue
> from the root of the old one
> a new one has sprung
> (Nichols, 1990: 87)

Gabriele Griffin has suggested that Nichols's poem, with its inventive use of layout, punctuation, dialect and African words signalling its location in an oral tradition, is 'in many respects, the perfect example of an *écriture féminine*, of the notion of writing the body' (Griffin, 1993: 33). The female body through its sensuality and fecundity is linked to the natural landscape and becomes a locus of resistance. Issues of identity and origin are also explored in Kay's *The Adoption Papers* (1991), where the story of a black girl's adoption by a white Scottish couple is told through the interwoven voices of the girl, her birth mother and her adoptive mother. Although the girl faces racist attempts to define her – 'I chase his *Sambo Sambo* all the way from the school gate' (1991: 24) – she articulates a strong sense of her own identity rooted in both her adoptive mother's loving care – 'Ma mammy picked me (I wiz the best)' (21) – and her identification as 'Black' like Angela Davis, 'the only female person / I've seen . . . who looks like me' (27).

The use of dialect or another language to foreground questions of cultural identity is a strategy which has also been used by Scottish and Welsh poets. Although she writes in English, Gillian Clarke's use of Welsh words, particularly names, grounds her work in the history, landscape and cultural identity of Wales. In her poem 'Letter From a Far Country' the landscape of memory is 'Hill country, / essentially feminine, / the sea not far off' (Clarke, 1985: 53). It is evoked through interconnections between the landscape, its contours, birds and animals, and domestic objects – sheets, a small black cookery book, homemade jams, jellies and wine which 'preserve' memory as 'Familiar days are stored whole / in bottles' (57). The complex interrelationship of language, power, nationality and gender is explored by another Welsh poet, Gwyneth Lewis in 'Welsh Espionage', where a child is taught English by her father despite her parents' agreement that she should only learn Welsh until she is four:

> Welsh was the mother tongue, English was his.
> He taught her the body by fetishist quiz,
> father and daughter on the bottom stair:
> 'Dy benelin yw *elbow*, dy wallt di yw *hair*,'
> (Rumens, 1990: 90)

Lewis's work is included in *New Women Poets* (1990) edited by Carol Rumens. This anthology, together with two other recent anthologies, *Virago New Poets* (1993) edited by Melanie Silgardo and Janet Beck, and *As Girls Could Boast* (1994) edited by Christina Dunhill, offer a proof of the rich diversity of new women poets writing at the moment.

The approach of the millennium has produced in the fiction of the 1980s and early 1990s not so much a looking forward as a looking back in order to attempt to anticipate in some way the unpredictable future. The theme of apocalypse is projected back into the past in Jane Rogers's *Mr Wroe's Virgins* (1991). Rogers's nineteenth-century Prophet Wroe prophesies the end of the world, knowing that his prophecies are untrue but offering them as 'spiritual comfort, mother's milk for the imagination' (1992: 226) in the face of the 'void' that is death. His prophecies illustrate Kermode's argument that we use narratives, the 'sense of an ending', to impose meaning on a formless experience of life. Both history and myth are attempts to impose 'a plot on time' (Kermode, 1967: 43).

Postmodern accounts of history as contingent, subjective and ultimately a 'form of fabulation' reliant on the narrative strategies which had previously been seen as 'literary' have had 'a clear impact on a good deal of recent fiction' (Gąsiorek, 1995: 149). 'History should be a hammock for swinging and a game for playing, the way cats play. Claw it, chew it, rearrange it and at bedtime it's still a ball of string full of knots' writes Winterson in *Oranges are not the Only Fruit* (1985: 93). Contemporary writers of both sexes have treated history like this and woven their own cat's-cradle patterns out of a mixture of fact and fiction, myth and realism. No longer an immutable 'truth', nor even linear, history is in the words of Penelope Lively's fictional historian Claudia Hampton in *Moon Tiger* (1987) 'kaleidoscopic' (1988: 2), made up of 'composite' voices (5), and 'myriad Claudias' (2) which can be shaken into new patterns. Hence Claudia wants to write 'A history of the world . . . . And in the process, my own. The Life and Times of Claudia H' (Lively, 1988: 1). For women writers, who have been left out of history and denied subjecthood, this re-vision of history is not just a postmodern game but 'an act of survival' (Rich, 1980: 35). To put a woman at the centre of 'History of the World' as Claudia does, to re-imagine Black women's experience of slavery as Grace Nichols does, both press at the limits of our conception of history.

The return to history has, ironically, made it possible for women to write heterosexual romance again but as a form of historical ventriloquism. Both A.S. Byatt and Alison Fell allow the reader to have her romantic cake (satisfying those desires Brookner delineates) and recognize it as a consolatory myth. Byatt's *Possession: A Romance* (1990) has two parallel love stories, one between two Victorian poets, the other between two contemporary academics. Byatt uses pastiche to distance the reader from both romances, offering not only faux Victorian poetry, but a witty commentary on today's 'lit crit' industry (including a parody of a feminist critic's exposition of the female body as landscape metaphor). Both Roland and Maud know that they are postmodern subjects constructed through language and that romance is a fiction – but they do it anyway. As Carter put it:

> our flesh arrives to us out of history, like everything else does. We may believe we fuck
> stripped of social artifice; in bed, we may even feel we touch the bedrock of human
> nature itself. But we are deceived. Flesh is not an irreducible human universal. (Carter,
> 1979: 9)

In *The Pillow Boy of the Lady Onogoro* (1994) Fell explores inequalities of sexual power and freedom in eleventh-century Japan, where the stylization of sex, through gesture, poetry and erotica, foreground its constructedness. Neither Fell's Oyu, a blind stableboy, nor Byatt's Roland, a penniless postgraduate researcher, corresponds to the archetypal romantic hero. They signal a new interest in the concept of masculinity as constructed and in the possibility of alternative masculinities. Pat Barker's powerful *Regeneration* trilogy (1991, 1993, 1995) is based on the work done by Dr W.H.R. Rivers with 'shell-shocked' soldiers during the First World War. The war, Elaine Showalter has noted, 'feminized its conscripts by taking away their sense of control' (1987: 173) and produced in them hysterical symptoms similar to those found in nineteenth-century female hysterics. Meshing fact and fiction, Barker uses this insight to explore a masculinity in crisis, its relationship with class and homosexuality, and the parallels between the position of women and that of the men at the front.

What Liz Yorke calls the project of 'constructing *a new symbolic which would reorganise the social socio-symbolic systems of patriarchy*' (1991: 3, original emphasis), entails not just debunking of old myths but the fabrication of new, empowering ones. In *Nights at the Circus* (1984) Angela Carter offers us a new myth in the bird-woman Fevvers, who manipulates feminine stereotypes and advertises herself with the slogan 'Is she fact or is she fiction' (1984: 7). Set in 1899 and ranging from London to Siberia, *Nights at the Circus* is magic realism with a political purpose as Carter 'provides both an ironic critique of the power underlying and upheld through myths and symbols, and creates and recreates powerful new myths and symbols to enable a theft of power, a flight from patriarchy' (Wisker, 1994: 113). Carter utilizes a Bakhtinian carnivalesque in the subversive, marginal world of the circus and the 'grotesque' body of Fevvers in order to overturn social hierarchies (Gąsiorek, 1995: 126–36). Balanced on the cusp of the new century, the novel is a feminist utopia which melds quest, the picaresque, romance, and female solidarity, and ends with Fevvers's laughter:

> The spiralling tornado of Fevvers' laughter began to twist and shudder across the entire globe, as if a spontaneous response to the giant comedy that endlessly unfolded beneath it, until everything that lived and breathed, everywhere, was laughing. (Carter, 1984: 295)

Fevvers's final words – 'there's nothing like confidence' (1984: 295) – might stand as advice for women writers heading into the next millennium.

I would like to thank the following people for generously sharing their expertise and ideas with me: Marion Shaw, Gill Spraggs, Linden Peach, Deborah Tyler-Bennett, Deirdre O'Byrne and Helen Cory.

Bibliography

Primary materials
Barker, Pat (1984), *Blow Your House Down*, London: Virago.
Barker, Pat (1992) [1991], *Regeneration*, Harmondsworth: Penguin.
Barker, Pat (1994) [1993], *The Eye in the Door*, Harmondsworth: Penguin.
Barker, Pat (1996) [1995], *The Ghost Road*, Harmondsworth: Penguin.
Bernikow, Louise (ed.) (1979) [1974], *The World Split Open: Women Poets 1552–1950*, London: The Women's Press.
Bowen, Elizabeth (1982) [1964], *The Little Girls*, Harmondsworth: Penguin.
Brookner, Anita (1985) [1984], *Hotel du Lac*, London: Triad/Panther.
Burford, Barbara, Gabriella Pearse, Grace Nichols and Jackie Kay (1985), *A Dangerous Knowing: Four Black Women Poets*, London: Sheba.
Byatt, A.S. (1985), *Still Life*, London: Chatto and Windus/Hogarth.
Byatt, A.S. (1991) [1990], *Possession: A Romance*, London: Vintage.
Byatt, A.S. (1994) [1978], *The Virgin in the Garden*, London: Vintage.

Carter, Angela (1979), *The Sadeian Woman: An Exercise in Cultural History*, London: Virago.

Carter, Angela (1982) [1977], *The Passion of New Eve*, London: Virago.

Carter, Angela (1984), *Nights at the Circus*, London: Chatto and Windus/Hogarth.

Clarke, Gillian (1985), *Selected Poems*, Manchester: Carcanet.

Couzyn, Jeni (ed.) (1985), *The Bloodaxe Book of Contemporary Women Poets: Eleven British Writers*, Newcastle upon Tyne: Bloodaxe.

Drabble, Margaret (1968) [1965], *The Millstone*, Harmondsworth: Penguin.

Drabble, Margaret (1971) [1969], *The Waterfall*, Harmondsworth: Penguin.

Duffy, Carol Ann (1994), *Selected Poems*, Harmondsworth: Penguin.

Duffy, Maureen (1966) [1962], *That's How it Was*, London: Panther.

Duffy, Maureen (1967) [1966], *The Microcosm*, London: Panther.

Dunhill, Christina (1994), *As Girls Could Boast*, London: The Oscars Press.

Emecheta, Buchi (1986), *Head Above Water: An Autobiography*, London: Flamingo.

Emecheta, Buchi (1988) [1979], *The Joys of Motherhood*, Oxford: Heinemann.

Fairbairns, Zoe (1979), *Benefits*, London: Virago.

Fell, Alison (1984), *Every Move You Make*, London: Virago.

Fell, Alison (1994), *The Pillow Boy of the Lady Onogoro*, London: Serpent's Tail.

Galford, Ellen (1984), *Moll Cutpurse*, Edinburgh: Stramullion.

Hanscombe, Gillian (1983) [1982], *Between Friends*, London: Sheba.

James, P.D. (1974) [1972], *An Unsuitable Job for a Woman*, London: Sphere.

Kay, Jackie (1991), *The Adoption Papers*, Newcastle upon Tyne: Bloodaxe.

Lehmann, Rosamond (1953), *The Echoing Grove*, London: Collins.

Lessing, Doris (1973) [1962], *The Golden Notebook*, London: Grafton.

Lessing, Doris (1976) [1974], *The Memoirs of a Survivor*, London: Picador.

Lessing, Doris (1985) [1984], *The Diaries of Jane Somers*, Harmondsworth: Penguin.

Lively, Penelope (1988) [1987], *Moon Tiger*, Harmondsworth: Penguin.

Macauley, Rose (1956), *The Towers of Trebizond*, London: Collins.

Macauley, Rose (1983) [1950], *The World My Wilderness*, London: Virago.

Mohin, Lilian (ed.) (1979), *One Foot On the Mountain: An Anthology of British Feminist Poetry 1969–1979*, London: Onlywomen.

Murdoch, Iris (1954), *Under the Net*, London: Chatto and Windus.

Murdoch, Iris (1975) [1973], *The Black Prince*, Harmondsworth: Penguin.

Namjoshi, Suniti (1981), *Feminist Fables*, London: Sheba.

Nichols, Grace (1990) [1983], *i is a long memoried woman*, London: Karnak.

O'Brien, Edna (1964) [1962], *Girl With Green Eyes*, Harmondsworth: Penguin.

O'Rourke, Rebecca (1987), *Jumping the Cracks*, London: Virago.

Plath, Sylvia (1968) [1965], *Ariel*, London: Faber and Faber.

Rhys, Jean (1968) [1966], *Wide Sargasso Sea*, Harmondsworth: Penguin.

Riley, Joan (1985), *The Unbelonging*, London: The Women's Press.

Roberts, Michèle (1985) [1984], *The Wild Girl*, London: Methuen.

Roberts, Michèle (1993) [1992], *Daughters of the House*, London: Virago.

Rogers, Jane (1992) [1991], *Mr Wroe's Virgins*, London: Faber and Faber.

Rumens, Carol (ed.) (1985), *Making for the Open: Post-Feminist Poetry*, London: Chatto and Windus.

Rumens, Carol (ed.) (1990), *New Women Poets*, Newcastle upon Tyne: Bloodaxe.

Scott, Diana (ed.) (1982), *Bread and Roses: Women's Poetry of the Nineteenth and Twentieth Centuries*, London: Virago.

Silgardo, Melanie and Janet Beck (eds) (1993), *Virago New Poets*, London: Virago.

Smith, Joan (1988), *Why Aren't They Screaming?*, London and Boston: Faber and Faber.

Spark, Muriel (1965) [1961], *The Prime of Miss Jean Brodie*, Harmondsworth: Penguin.

Spark, Muriel (1974) [1970], *The Driver's Seat*, Harmondsworth: Penguin.

Stevenson, Anne (1987), *Selected Poems*, Oxford and New York: Oxford University Press.

Taylor, Elizabeth (1985) [1946], *Palladian*, London: Virago.

Weldon, Fay (1973) [1971], *Down Among the Women*, Harmondsworth: Penguin.
Weldon, Fay (1984) [1983], *The Life and Loves of a She Devil*, London: Coronet.
Weldon, Fay (1989) [1975], *Female Friends*, London: Picador.
West, Rebecca (1984) [1957], *The Fountain Overflows*, London: Virago.
West, Rebecca (1987) [1984], *This Real Night*, London: Virago.
West, Rebecca (1988) [1985], *Cousin Rosamund*, London: Virago.
White, Antonia (1978) [1933], *Frost in May*, London: Virago.
White, Antonia (1979a) [1952], *The Sugar House*, London: Virago.
White, Antonia (1979b) [1954], *Beyond the Glass*, London: Virago.
Winterson, Jeanette (1985), *Oranges are not the Only Fruit*, London: Pandora.
Winterson, Jeanette (1992), *Written on the Body*, London: Jonathan Cape.

Secondary materials

Anderson, Linda (1990), 'The Re-Imagining of History in Contemporary Women's Fiction' in *Plotting Change*, Linda Anderson (ed.), London: Edward Arnold.
Beauvoir, Simone de (1972) [1949], *The Second Sex*, trans. H.M. Parshley, Harmondsworth: Penguin.
Bradbury, Malcolm (ed.) (1977), *The Novel Today*, Glasgow: Fontana.
Butler, Judith (1990), *Gender Trouble: Feminism and the Subversion of Identity*, New York and London: Routledge.
Coote, Anna and Beatrix Campbell (1982), *Sweet Freedom: The Struggle for Women's Liberation*, London: Picador.
Cosslett, Tess (1989), 'Childbirth from the Women's Point of View in British Women's Fiction: Enid Bagnold's *The Squire* and A.S. Byatt's *Still Life*', *Tulsa Studies in Women's Literature* 8: 2, 263–86.
Cranny Francis, Anne (1990), *Feminist Fiction: Feminist Uses of Generic Fiction*, Cambridge: Polity.
Duncker, Patricia (1992), *Sisters and Strangers: An Introduction to Contemporary Feminist Fiction*, Oxford and Cambridge, Mass.: Blackwell.
DuPlessis, Rachel Blau (1985), *Writing Beyond the Ending: Narrative Strategies of Twentieth Century Women Writers*, Bloomington: Indiana University Press.
Ellmann, Mary (1979) [1968], *Thinking About Women*, London: Virago.
Firestone, Shulamith (1979) [1970], *The Dialectic of Sex*, London: The Women's Press.
Forsås-Scott, Helena (ed.) (1991), *Textual Liberation: European Feminist Writing in the Twentieth Century*, London and New York: Routledge.
Friedan, Betty (1968) [1963], *The Feminine Mystique*, Harmondsworth: Penguin.
Gąsiorek, Andrzej (1995), *Post-war British Fiction: Realism and After*, London: Edward Arnold.
Gerrard, Nicci (1989), *Into the Mainstream: How Feminism Has Changed Women's Writing*, London: Pandora.
Gilbert, Sandra M. and Susan Gubar (1984) [1979], *The Madwoman in the Attic: The Woman Writer and the Nineteenth Century Imagination*, New Haven and London: Yale University Press.
Greer, Germaine (1971) [1970], *The Female Eunuch*, London: Paladin.
Griffin, Gabriele (1993), '"Writing the Body": Reading Joan Riley, Grace Nichols and Ntozake Shange' in *Black Women's Writing*, Gina Wisker (ed.), Basingstoke and London: Macmillan, pp. 19–42.
Heilbrun, Carolyn (1989) [1988], *Writing a Woman's Life*, London: The Women's Press.
Horner, Avril and Sue Zlosnik (1990), *Landscapes of Desire: Metaphors in Modern Women's Fiction*, Hemel Hempstead: Harvester Wheatsheaf.
Humm, Maggie (1991a), *Border Traffic: Strategies of Contemporary Women Writers*, Manchester and New York: Manchester University Press.
Humm, Maggie (1991b), 'Landscape for a Literary Feminism: British Women Writers 1900 to the Present' in *Textual Liberation: European Feminist Writing in the Twentieth Century*, Helena Forsås-Scott (ed.), London and New York: Routledge, pp. 13–38.

Irigaray, Luce (1985), *This Sex Which is Not One*, trans. Catherine Porter with Carolyn Burke, Ithaca, New York: Cornell University Press.

Irigaray, Luce (1991), 'The Bodily Encounter with the Mother' in *The Irigaray Reader*, Margaret Whitford (ed.), Oxford: Blackwell, pp. 34–46.

Kaplan, Cora (1986), 'An Unsuitable Genre for a Feminist?' in *Women's Review*, 8 (June), 18–19.

Kenyon, Olga (1988), *Women Novelists Today: A Survey of English Writing in the Seventies and Eighties*, Brighton: Harvester.

Kermode, Frank (1967), *The Sense of an Ending*, New York: Oxford University Press.

Kristeva, Julia (1986) [1979], 'Women's Time' in *The Kristeva Reader*, Toril Moi (ed.), Oxford: Blackwell, pp. 187–231.

Lefanu, Sarah (1988), *In the Chinks of the World Machine: Feminism and Science Fiction*, London: The Women's Press.

Lodge, David (1971), *The Novelist at the Crossroads and Other Essays on Fiction and Criticism*, London and New York: Ark.

Marks, Elaine and Isabelle de Courtivron (eds) (1981), *New French Feminisms: An Anthology*, Hemel Hempstead: Harvester Wheatsheaf.

Millett, Kate (1977) [1970], *Sexual Politics*, London: Virago.

Mitchell, Juliet (1975) [1974], *Psychoanalysis and Feminism*, Harmondsworth: Penguin.

Mitchell, Juliet (1984), *Women: The Longest Revolution: Essays on Feminism, Literature and Psychoanalysis*, London: Virago.

Modleski, Tania (1990) [1982], *Loving With a Vengeance: Mass-produced Fantasies for Women*, New York and London: Routledge.

Moers, Ellen (1978) [1976], *Literary Women*, London: The Women's Press.

Murdoch, Iris (1977) [1961], 'Against Dryness' in *The Novel Today*, Malcolm Bradbury (ed.), Glasgow: Fontana, pp. 23–31.

O'Rourke, Rebecca (1990), 'Mediums, Messages and Noisy Amateurs', *Women: A Cultural Review* 1: 3 (Winter), 275–86.

Palmer, Paulina (1989), *Contemporary Women's Fiction: Narrative Practice and Feminist Theory*, Hemel Hempstead: Harvester Wheatsheaf.

Palmer, Paulina (1991), 'The Lesbian Feminist Thriller and Detective Novel' in *What Lesbians Do in Books*, Elaine Hobby and Chris White (eds), London: The Women's Press, pp. 9–27.

Radway, Janice A. (1984), *Reading the Romance*, London: Verso.

Rich, Adrienne (1980) [1979], *On Lies, Secrets and Silence: Selected Prose 1966–1978*, London: Virago.

Rose, Jacqueline (1992) [1991], *The Haunting of Sylvia Plath*, London: Virago.

Rule, Jane (1976) [1975], *Lesbian Images*, New York: Pocket Books.

Sage, Lorna (1992), *Women in the House of Fiction: Post-war Women Novelists*, Basingstoke and London: Macmillan.

Shaw, Marion and Sabine Vanacker (1991), *Reflecting on Miss Marple*, London and New York: Routledge.

Showalter, Elaine (1978) [1977], *A Literature of Their Own; British Women Novelists from Brontë to Lessing*, London: Virago.

Showalter, Elaine (1986), 'Feminist Criticism in the Wilderness' in *The New Feminist Criticism: Essays on Women, Literature and Theory*, Elaine Showalter (ed.), London: Virago, pp. 243–70.

Showalter, Elaine (1987) [1985], *The Female Malady: Women, Madness and English Culture, 1830–1980*, London: Virago.

Spacks, Patricia Meyer (1975), *The Female Imagination*, New York: Alfred Knopf.

Spender, Dale (1980), *Man Made Language*, London: Routledge and Kegan Paul.

Steedman, Carolyn (1986), *Landscape for a Good Woman*, London: Virago.

Stevenson, Anne (1979), 'Writing as a Woman' in *Women Writing and Writing About Women*, Mary Jacobus (ed.), London: Croom Helm; New York: Barnes and Noble.

Stonemen, Patsy (1996), *Brontë Transformations: The Cultural Dissemination of Jane Eyre and Wuthering Heights*, Hemel Hempstead: Prentice Hall/Harvester Wheatsheaf.

Todd, Janet (ed.) (1983), *Women Writers Talking*, New York: Holmes and Meier.

Waugh, Patricia (1988) [1984], *Metafiction: The Theory and Practice of Self-conscious Fiction*, London and New York: Routledge.

Waugh, Patricia (1995), *Harvest of the Sixties: English Literature and its Background 1960–1990*, Oxford and New York: Oxford University Press.

Wilson, Elizabeth (1980), *Only Halfway to Paradise: Women in Postwar Britain 1945–1968*, London and New York: Tavistock.

Wisker, Gina (ed.) (1993), *Black Women's Writing*, Basingstoke and London: Macmillan.

Wisker, Gina (1994), 'Weaving Our Own Web: Demythologising/Remythologising and Magic in the Work of Contemporary Women Writers', in *It's My Party: Reading Twentieth-Century Women's Writing*, Gina Wisker (ed.), London: Pluto, pp. 104–28.

Wisker, Gina (ed.) (1994), *It's My Party: Reading Twentieth-Century Women's Writing*, London: Pluto.

Woolf, Virginia (1977) [1929], *A Room of One's Own*, London: Granada.

Yorke, Liz (1991), *Impertinent Voices: Subversive Strategies in Contemporary Women's Poetry*, London: Routledge.

Index

A Revelation Showed to a Holy Woman, 24–5, 32, 33
abortion, 195, 248
Actresses' Franchise League, 196
Acts of Parliament
  Contagious Diseases Acts, 179, 195
  Equal Pay Acts, 247
  Married Women's Property Act, 179
  Reform Bill, 157
  Sex Discrimination Act, 247
  Ten Hours Bill, 158
Adam, 103–4, 242
Adcock, Fleur, 241
  'Instructions to Vampires', 243
adultery, 114
  novels of, 166
Aesop's fables, 77, 255
Aldington, Richard, 214
All the Year Round, 170
Allen, Grant
  The Woman Who Did, 186
Allen, Hannah, 4
  Satan His Methods and Malice Baffled, 71
American revolution, 122
Amt, Emilie, 9, 14, 15, 16
anarchist community, 199n
Anderson, Linda, 224, 236
'Angel in the House', 144, 187, 189, 209
Angela of Foligno, 19
Anger, Jane
  Jane Anger Her Protection for Women, 59
Anglo-Saxon period, 17, 18
Anne, Queen, 50
Anti-Jacobin Review, 130
'anxiety of influence', 165
apocalypse, 238, 255, 257
Arabian Nights, The, 102

Argosy, 152
'Ariadne'
  She Ventures and He Wins, 102
Armstrong, Isobel, 169
Armstrong, Nancy, 97, 166
Arnold, Matthew, 165
Ascham, Roger, 37
Ashwell, Lena, 183
Asian women writers, 255
Askew, Anne, 39–42, 47, 49, 61
  The First Examinacyon of the worthy Servant of God, Mistresse Anne Askewe, 39–41
  The lattre examinacyon of the worthye servant of God mastres Anne Askew, 39, 41–2
Astell, Mary, 99–100, 101, 108
  A Serious Proposal to the Ladies, 99–100
  Reflections Upon Marriage, 99, 100
Astra, 248
Athenaeum, 152
Atwood, Margaret, 248
Aubin, Penelope, 106
Augustanism, 104
Austen, Jane, 5, 117, 132–4, 145n, 237, 245, 246
  Mansfield Park, 123
  Northanger Abbey, 128, 237
Austin, Alfred, 153, 160
autobiography, 17, 224–7, 236, 237

Baillie, Joanna, 5, 123, 145n
  De Montfort, 123
  Poems, 140
  Series of Plays, 123
  The Family Legend, 123
Baker, Ida (L.M.), 231

Bale, John, 40
Barbauld, Anna Letitia, 96, 114–16, 118, 135–6, 140
  'Corsica', 114–15
  Epistle to William Wilberforce, 136
  'To Dr. Aiken', 114
  'Washing Day', 136
Barker, Jane, 68, 107
  A Patch-Work Screen for the Ladies, 107
  Love Intrigues, 107
  The Lining of the Patchwork Screen, 107
Barker, Pat
  Blow Your House Down, 250–1
  Regeneration Trilogy, 258–9
Barnes, Djuna, 220
Barney, Natalie, 204, 220
Barratt, Alexandra, 9, 10, 11, 16, 18, 22, 23, 24, 25
Barratt Browning, Elizabeth, 3, 168–9, 170
  Aurora Leigh, 169, 171
  'The Cry of the Children', 170
  'The Runaway Slave at Pilgrim's Point', 170
Baudelaire, Charles Pierre, 217
Beaufort, Lady Margaret, 16, 24, 25–6, 32
  The Mirror of Gold to the Sinful Soul, 25–6
Beauvoir, Simone de, 251
  The Second Sex, 243
Behn, Aphra, 5, 66, 67, 68, 76–83, 86, 88n, 94, 101, 102, 104, 106, 118
  Abdelazer, or the Moor's Revenge, 81
  Fables of Aesop, 77
  Love Letters Between a Nobleman and His Sister, 107
  Loveletters to a Gentleman, 77
  Oroonoko, 76, 80, 98
  The Adventure of the Black Lady, 78–9
  The Fair Jilt, 71, 76, 77, 78
  The False Count, 83
  The Feigned Courtesans, 81, 82, 83
  The Forced Marriage, 76
  The History of the Nun, 66, 79–80
  The Lucky Chance, 81, 82
  The Rover, 67, 81–2, 103
  The Widow Ranter, 81, 83
Belgravia, 152
Belgravia Annual, 152
Bell, Lady Florence
  Alan's Wife, 184, 191
Bell, Vanessa, 231n
Bennett, Arnold, 227
  Whom God Has Joined, 199n

Bensusan, Inez
  The Apple, 196
Bentley, Richard, 156
Bentley, Thomas
  The Monument of Matrones, 38
Bentley, William, 152
Bentley's Miscellany, 156
Bernikow, Louise, 241
Bible, the, 40, 47, 48, 60, 69, 70, 72, 235
Biddle, Hester, 67, 86
biography, 5
birth, 247
birth control, *see* contraception
Black women writers, 2, 250, 255–7
Blackwood's, 152, 189
Blake, William, 122, 251
body
  female, 206, 241, 248, 249, 256
  'writing the body', 236, 243, 248, 250, 255, 256
  see also écriture féminine
Boethius, 11
Boffey, Julia, 9, 17
Bowen, Elizabeth, 229–31, 238
  The Death of the Heart, 230
  The House in Paris, 229–30
  The Little Girls, 238, 239
Boyle, Roger, Earl of Orrey, 74
Braddon, Mary Elizabeth, 3, 152, 182, 185, 199n
  Lady Audley's Secret, 166
Bradley, Katherine, *see* Michael Field
Bradstreet, Anne, 73–4, 87n
  'A Letter to My Husband . . .', 73–4
  The Tenth Muse Lately Sprung Up in America, 73
Brews, Margery, 30–31
Bridget of Sweden, 19, 20, 22–3, 25, 27, 32, 33
  Revelations, 22–3
Brontë, Anne
  The Tenant of Wildfell Hall, 167
Brontë, Charlotte, 149, 161–2, 163, 168–9, 245
  Jane Eyre, 6, 163, 165, 236, 237, 244, 245, 246, 254
  Shirley, 160
  Villette, 149, 163, 165
Brontë, Emily, 161, 168–9
  Wuthering Heights, 162, 165, 237
Brontë sisters, 5, 164
Brooke, Emma Frances, 188
  A Superfluous Woman, 191–2

Brookner, Anita, 237
  Hotel du Lac, 254
Brooks, Romaine, 220
  Peter (A Young Girl), 204
Broughton, Rhoda, 166
Browning, Robert, 5, 170
  'Childe Roland to the Dark Tower Came',
    242
Bruto, Gian Michele
  Mirrhor of Modestie, 38
Bryher (Winifred Ellerman), 205, 231n
Buchanan, Robert, 161
Bunyan, John
  Pilgrim's Progress, 165
Burford, Barbara, 256
Burney, Frances, 95, 113, 116–17, 129,
    130
  Cecilia, 116–17
  Evelina, 116, 122
  The Wanderer, 131
Butler, Judith, 2, 252
Butler, Marilyn, 132
Byatt, A. S., 245, 246–7
  Possession, 258
  Still Life, 247
  The Virgin in the Garden, 246, 247
Byron, Lord, 122, 138

Caird, Mona, 188, 193
  'A Defence of the "Wild Woman"', 193
  The Daughters of Danaus, 189
  The Wing of Azrael, 189, 194
Calahorra, Diego Ortunez de, 45
Calle, Richard, 31
Cambridge University, 67
canon, 1, 3, 7, 11, 37, 95, 96, 140–1, 152–3,
    197, 241
Carleton, Dudley, 57
Carleton, Mary, 73, 84, 87n
  The Case of Mary Carleton, 73
Carpenter, Edward, 206
Carter, Angela, 251–2, 255, 258
  Nights at the Circus, 7, 259
  The Passion of New Eve, 251–2
Carter, Elizabeth, 113
Cary, Elizabeth
  Mariam, 48, 51–54
Casey, Maude, 246
Castle, Terry, 229
Catherine of Aragon, 38
Cavendish, Margaret, Duchess of Newcastle,
    67, 83–6, 88n

Assaulted and Pursued Chastity, 85
Nature's Pictures . . ., 85
Philosophical Fancies, 84
Poems and Fancies, 68, 84
'The Hunting of the Hare', 84
The New Blazing World, 85–7
Cavendish, William, Duke of Newcastle, 84
  The Humorous Lovers, 84
celibacy, 192
Centlivre, Susanna, 102–3
  A Bold Stroke for a Wife, 102
  The Busy Body, 102
  The Wonder, 102–3
Chamberlain, John, 57
Chapman, John, 152, 154
Chapman & Hall, 181
Charke, Charlotte, 253
Charles I, 65
Charles II, 65, 76, 83
Chartism, 159
chastity, 128, 130
Cheevers, Sarah
  . . . a short Relation . . ., 70–1
childbirth, 247
children's fiction, 180
Cholmondeley, Mary, 177
  Red Pottage, 177, 186, 189
Christ, Jesus, 41, 48, 49–50, 70, 251, 252
  as 'lover', 73
  as 'mother' 21, 32
Christianity, 109, 252
Chudleigh, Lady Mary, 100
circulating libraries, 155–6
city, the, 216–20
civil war, 65–6
Cixous, Hélène, 96–7, 210, 231n
  'The Laugh of the Medusa', 250
Clapperton, Jane Hume
  Margaret Dunmore, 194
Clare of Assisi, 14, 18, 32
Clark, Suzanne, 204
Clarke, Gillian
  'Letter From a Far Country', 257
class, 51, 97, 116, 178, 191–2, 237, 249,
    253
  aristocracy, 46, 157
  middle classes, 6, 133, 157, 164, 178, 182,
    205
  middle-class women writers, 151
  working classes, 159–60, 253
  working-class women writers, 2, 109,
    111–12, 250

Cleeve, Lucas (Adeline Kingscote)
  The Woman Who Wouldn't, 193
Clemence, 16
clerical work, 205, 219
Clifford, Anne, 51
Clifford, Margaret, Countess of
  Cumberland, 48–9, 50
Clive, Kitty, 103
Cody, Lisa, 254
Colburn, Henry, 156
Coleridge, Samuel Taylor, 116, 122, 138
  'Kubla Khan', 138
Collier, Mary, 109
  The Cry, 112
Collins, An, 86
  Divine Songs and Meditations, 72
Collins, Mabel
  Outlawed, 196
Collins, Wilkie, 166
Colmore, Gertrude
  Mr Jones and the Governess, 196
  Suffragette Sally, 197
colonialism, 97, 244
Common Cause, The, 179
Communist Manifesto, 229
community, 194, 252, 255
'Condition of England' novel, 158, 168
  see also social protest fiction
conduct books, 38, 66
consciousness-raising, 247
contemporary women's writing, Ch. 9
  235–263 *passim*
contraception, 188, 216
conversion narratives, 71
Cooke, Anne, 39
Cooper, Edith, *see* Michael Field
Cope, Wendy
  'Strugnell's Sonnets', 249
Corneille
  Pompée, 75
courtship, 114, 130, 160
Couzyn, Jeni, 240
  The Bloodaxe Book of Women Poets, 241–3
Cowley, Abraham, 74
Cowley, Hannah, 5, 118
  The Belle's Stratagem, 118
Crichton-Browne, Sir James, 180
crime novels
  see detective fiction, sensation
    fiction
Crocker, John Wilson, 131
Cumberland, Duke of, 102

Daily News, 152
D'Arcy, Ella, 179
Davenant, Lady Henrietta Maria ('Dame
  Mary'), 66
Davies, Lady Eleanor, 87n
Davies, Emily, 178
Davis, Angela, 257
Davis, Norman, 30
Davison, Emily Wilding, 196
  'L'Envoi', 196
Davy, Sara, 4
  Heaven Realized, 71
Davys, Mary, 107–8
  *Familiar Letters Betwixt a Gentleman and a
    Lady*, 107–8
death, 68, 226, 227, 236, 247
Defoe, Daniel, 106
Denny, Lord, 57
dental profession, 205
Dering, Edward, 74
Despard, Charlotte
  Outlawed, 196
detective fiction, 253
  lesbian detective novel, 253, 254–5
diaries, 95, 224
Dickens, Charles, 116, 152
  Pickwick Papers, 156
Dillon, Wentworth, Earl of Roscommon, 74
divorce, 188, 199n
Dix, Gertrude
  The Image Breakers, 194
Dixie, Lady Florence
  Gloriana . . ., 194, 195
Dixon, Ella Hepworth
  The Story of a Modern Woman, 178, 188,
    189, 192, 194
Dollimore, Jonathan, 221–2
domestic, the, 145, 160, 163, 167, 249
  domestic fiction, 97 160–1, 162, 166, 167,
    168, 180, 230, 237
  'domestic realism', 160–1, 186
  domesticity, 108, 112, 134
  domestic ideology, 95, 142, 237
Donne, John, 51, 88n
  'The Sun Rising', 75
Dorothea of Montau, 19
Dowie, Méne Muriel, 188
  Gallia, 189, 191
Drabble, Margaret, 236, 245, 246
  The Millstone, 246
  The Waterfall, 245, 246
Drake, Judith, 100

drama, 77–8, 101–13, 123
    closet drama, 52
    comedy, 101, 102
    heroic drama, 101
    tragedy, 101
    see also feminist drama, New Woman
        drama, suffragist drama
Dramatic Authors' Society, 182, 199n
dramatic lyric, 171
dramatic monologue, 170, 171
Duffy, Carol Ann, 249
    'The World's Wife', 249
    'Warming Her Pearls', 249
Duffy, Maureen, 253, 255
    That's How it Was, 253
    The Microcosm, 253
Duncker, Patricia, 253–4
DuPlessis, Rachel Blau, 222, 236, 244

East London Federation, 196
écriture féminine, 96–7, 209, 245, 250, 256
    see also body, writing the
Edgeworth, Maria
    Belinda, 130
Edinburgh Review, 152, 154, 155
education, 16–17, 37–8, 67, 96, 99, 100, 180
    and authorship, 16, 18
    educational literature, 123, 124
    female education, 124, 125, 165, 178–9,
        180, 204, 205, 246
    female learning, 112–13, 180
Egerton, George (Mary Chavelita Dunne),
        182, 192–3, 195
    Keynotes and Discords, 182, 191, 192–3
Egoist, The, 205
eighteenth century, 5, Ch. 4 94–121 *passim*
Eliot, George, 6, 116, 150, 152, 154, 157,
        160, 161, 163–6, 168, 178, 185
    Adam Bede, 160, 161
    Daniel Deronda, 168
    Felix Holt the Radical, 168
    Middlemarch, 6, 160, 163, 164, 165, 166,
        168, 247
    'Silly Novels by Lady Novelists', 157
    The Mill on the Floss, 160, 163, 246
Eliot, T. S., 203, 213–14
    The Waste Land, 238, 251
Elizabeth I, 26, 46, 47, 48, 247
Elizabeth II, 237
Elizabeth of Hungary (Elizabeth of Toess),
        19, 20, 22, 23–4, 32, 33
Elizas Babes, 72–3

Elliott, Bridget, 204
Ellis, Havelock, 206, 221, 222
Ellmann, Mary, 1, 247
Elstob, Elizabeth, 100
Elyot, Thomas, 37
Emecheta, Buchi, 255–6
    Head Above Water, 256
    The Joys of Motherhood, 256
Englishwoman's Journal, The, 170
Englishwoman's Review, The, 179
Enlightenment, the, 96, 97, 122
Ephelia, 68, 74
    Female Poems on Several Occasions, 74
Epictetus, 113
epistolary tradition, 107, 113
Erasmus, 37
eroticism, 192, 193
Etherege, George, 94
    The Man of Mode, 81
Evans, Katharine
    . . . a short Relation . . ., 70–1
Eve, 48, 50, 60, 67, 87n, 242
Ewbank, Inga-Stina, 161
Examiner, The, 106, 170

Facism, 214, 241, 245
Fainlight, Ruth, 241, 242, 243
    'Lilith', 242
    'The Other', 242
Fairbairns, Zoe, 247, 255
    Benefits, 255
fairy-tales, 235, 251, 255
fantasy, 241, 245
Fanthorpe, U. A., 248
    'The Constant Tin Soldier', 248–9
Feinstein, Elaine, 241
    'Coastline', 242
    'The Feast of Eurydice', 242
Fell, Alison, 247–8
    Every Move You Make, 247–8
    The Pillow Boy of the Lady Onogoro, 258
Fell, Margaret, 69
feminine, the, 97, 149, 153, 155, 161, 163,
        209–11, 222, 230, 251, 259
    and mass culture, 206
    'feminine mystique', 240, 246
    'feminine novels', 185
    'writing the feminine', 209, *see also écriture
        féminine*
feminism, 1, 2, 101, 124, 125, 130, 135, 141,
        180, 194–7, 236–7, 246, 249–50, 252,
        254

feminist drama, 196
feminist literary criticism, 1–2, 5, 96, 97,
    203–4, 235, 247
feminist literary history, 96, 168, 178,
    241
feminist movement, 180, 184, 194–7,
    247–8, 250
feminist publishing, 249–50
feminist novels, 185, 194–7, 250
feminist theory, 237, 247, 249–50, 251
femininity, 96, 97, 104, 124, 125, 149, 153,
    154, 155, 161, 162, 163, 170, 207,
    209–11, 237, *see also* womanliness
  ideals of, 62, 66, 99, 163
Ferrier, Susan
  Marriage, 131–2
Field, Michael (Katherine Bradley and Edith
    Cooper), 183, 192, 199n
Field, Sarah, 100
Fielding, Henry, 106, 113, 116
Fielding, Sarah, 96, 112, 113
  Lives of Cleopatra and Octavia, 113
  The Adventures of David Simple, 100, 112,
    113
  The Cry, 112
fin de siècle, 6, Ch7. 177–202 *passim*
Finch, Anne (Countess of Winchilsea), 96,
    98–9, 103–6
  'Adam Posed', 103–4
  'The Introduction', 98–9
  'The Spleen', 104–6
Findlater, Jane and Mary
  Crossriggs, 188–9
Firestone, Shulamith
  The Dialectic of Sex, 247
First World War, 178, 205, 214–15, 228,
    230, 248–9, 258–9
flâneur, 217
flâneuse, 217, 218, 219
force-feeding, 206
Ford, Ford Maddox, 203, 220
Ford, Isabella O.
  On the Threshold, 189, 191
Foucault, Michel, 98
France, 26
France, Marie de, 12, 18, 31, 33
  'Laüstic', 12
Francis of Assisi, 14
Freewoman, The, 179, 205
Fremantle, Bridget, 109
French, 16, 17
French feminism, 209, 222, 244, 250

French, Marilyn
  The Women's Room, 250
French Revolution, 94, 118, 122, 123–4, 131,
    145n, 228
Freud, Sigmund, 164, 206, 224, 225
  'Female Sexuality', 222
Friedan, Betty, 247
  The Feminine Mystique, 243, 246
friendship, 15, 75,107, 111, 252
  friendship plot, 236
  see also relations between women

Gabriella, Katharyn, 248
Galford, Ellen
  Moll Cutpurse, 253
Gaskell, Elizabeth, 152, 154, 159–60, 167
  Cranford, 160
  Mary Barton, 159–60
  North and South, 159–60
  Wives and Daughters, 160
Garnier, Robert, 46
Garrick, David, 103
gender, 2, 96, 97, 178, 186, 198, 203–4, 220,
    221, 226, 236, 249, 255, 256
  and division of labour, 163, 251
  construction, 14, 23, 155, 251
  conventions, 78
  identity, 207–11, 238, 239, 240
  relations, 73, 74, 191
  roles, 125, 155, 205, 206, 221
  socialization, 100
genetics, 195
genre, 59, 68, 123, 167
  boundaries, 224
  'feminine' genres, 95, 122, 123, 157–8,
    180
  genre fiction, 253–5
Gentle, Mary, 255
George II, 108
Gerrard, Nicci, 250, 254
Gilbert, Sandra M., 2, 6, 163, 166
  No Man's Land, 204, 205
  The Madwoman in the Attic, 164, 177, 244
Gilden, Charles, 76
Gilfillan, Caroline, 248
Gill, T. P., 183
Gilman, Charlotte Perkins
  The Yellow Wallpaper, 177, 180, 186
Girl's Own Paper, 179
Girton College, 177, 205
Gissing, George
  The Odd Women, 179, 186, 198n

Glorious Revolution, 66
Glover, Evelyn
   A Chat With Mrs Chick, 196
   Mrs Appleyard's Awakening, 196
God
   divine inspiration, 69, 70
   union with, 72
Godwin, William, 124, 134, 139
   Memoirs of the Author of the Rights of Women, 125
Gore, Catherine, 157
   Cecil, 157
   Mrs Armytage, 157
   Quid Pro Quo, 182
   The Banker's Wife, 157
Gore-Booth, Eva, 196–7
   'Women's Rights', 196–7
Gothic, the, 129, 162, 163, 237, 238, 251, 254
   Gothic novel, 128, 167
Grand, Sarah (Frances McFall), 179, 181, 183, 188, 197–8
   Ideala: A Study from Life, 179
   The Beth Book, 177–8, 189–90, 195, 199n
   The Heavenly Twins, 181, 189, 190–1, 194, 195
Greek, 113
Greenwell, Dora, 170–1
   'Our Single Women', 170–1
Greer, Germaine
   The Female Eunuch, 247
Greg, Frances, 222
Greg, W.R., 150
Griffin, Gabriele, 256
Griffith, Elizabeth, 114
Grundy, Sydney, 185–6
   The New Woman, 185–6
Gubar, Susan, 2, 6, 163, 166, 216
   No Man's Land, 204, 205
   The Madwoman in the Attic, 164, 177, 244
Gwyn, Nell, 83

Hall, Radclyffe, 220–2, 223
   The Well Of Loneliness, 220–2
Halliday, Caroline, 248
Hamilton, Catherine J., 180
Hamilton, Cicely, 183, 189
   A Pageant of Great Women, 196
   Diana of Dobson's, 190, 195
   How the Vote Was Won, 196
   Life Errant, 183
   Marriage as a Trade, 189

Hamilton, Elizabeth
   Letters on Education, 125
   Memoirs of Modern Philosophers, 130
Hanscombe, Gillian
   Between Friends, 252
Hardy, Thomas
   Jude the Obscure, 164, 186
   Tess of the d'Urbervilles, 128
Hastings, Beatrice, 205
Hatton, Bessie
   Before Sunrise, 196
Hays, Mary, 127–8, 130
   Appeal to the Men of Great Britain . . ., 125
   Memoirs of Emma Courtney, 127–8
   The Victim of Prejudice, 128
Haywood, Eliza, 106
   Love in Excess, 106
   Memoirs of a Certain Island, 106
   The Female Spectator, 108
   The History of Miss Betsy Thoughtless, 113
Hazlitt, William, 131
H.D. (Hilda Doolittle), 212–13, 214, 220, 222–5 228, 231n
   Asphodel, 225
   'Helen', 213
   Helen in Egypt, 213, 225
   Heliodora, 228
   Her, 221, 222–3, 224–5
   Paint it Today, 225
   Sea Garden, 228
   'The Pool', 212
   Tribute to Freud, 225
   Trilogy, 214, 225
Heath's Book of Beauty, 170
Heilbrun, Carolyn, 236
Heinemann, William, 181
Helen of Troy, 213
Hemans, Felicia, 123, 141–3, 169
   'Casabianca', 141
   'Evening Prayer at a Girls' School', 142
   Poems, 141
   'Properzia Rossi', 142–3
   Records of Woman . . ., 142
   'Woman and Fame', 142
Henrietta Maria, Queen, 83
Henry VII, 25
Henry VIII, 39
heterosexuality, 220, 248, 252
Hildelith, 16
Hirsch, Marianne, 215, 216

history, 164, 211–16, 224, 235–6, 238, 239,
  255, 257, 257–8
 female view of, 113, 164, 211–12, 235–6,
  239, 247, 249
Holloway Jingles, 196
Holocaust, the, 241
Holtby, Winifred, 227
 South Riding, 6
 Virginia Woolf, 227
homelessness, 195
homosexuality, 221, 259
 see also lesbianism
Horner, Avril, 236, 244
Horniman, Annie, 183
Household Words, 152, 170
Howitt, Mary, 152
Howitt, William, 152
Howitt's Journal, 152
Hoyle, John, 68, 77
Hull, Dame Eleanor, 22, 24, 25, 32, 33
 *Meditations upon the Seven Days of the
  Week*, 25
Hull, Suzanne, 38
Hulme, T.E., 203
Humm, Maggie, 1, 236–7

Ibsen, Henrik
 Hedda Gabler, 184
identity, 186, 207–11, 213, 224, 230, 235,
  239, 255, 256, 257
 female, 1, 2, 13, 48, 66, 85, 98, 207–11,
  223, 235
ideology, 18, 66, 221–2, 228, 236, 253
 female ideologies, 189
 patriarchal ideology, 20, 32, 124, 164, 166,
  221–2, 236, 237, 253
illegitimacy, 188
imperialism, 97
incest, 195, 256
Inchbald, Elizabeth, 117, 118, 123, 128, 182
 A Simple Story, 118, 128
 Lover's Vows, 123
 Nature and Art, 128
Independent Theatre Society, 184
industrialisation, 216
infanticide, 184, 195
Inglelow, Jean, 168
Iota
 A Yellow Aster, 193
Irigaray, Luce, 222, 236, 239, 250
 Speculum of the Other Woman, 244
Irish women writers, 246, 248

Irving, Henry, 184
Italian Risorgimento, 194

Jacobean period, 4, 48, 62
Jacobin, 145n
James II, 65
James, P. D.
 An Unsuitable Job for a Woman, 254
Jamie, Kathleen, 248
Jennings, Elizabeth, 241, 242
 'In a Garden', 242
Jennings, Gertrude
 A Woman's Influence, 196
Jennings, Paula
 'Lesbian', 248
Jewel, John, 39
Jewsbury, Geraldine, 152
 The Half Sisters, 152
 Zoe, 152
Joan of Arc, 26, 32
Johnson, Samuel, 113
Jones, Gwyneth, 255
Jones, Richard, 42
Jonson, Ben, 51
Joseph, Jenny, 241
 'Persephone', 242
journalism, 151, 152, 178, 180, 195
journals, 95, 151, 205
 suffrage journals, 195
Joyce, James, 3, 217
 Ulysses, 204, 213–14
Julian of Norwich, 10, 16, 19, 20, 21–2, 23,
  24, 32 26, 33
 Revelations of Divine Love, 16, 21–2

Kaplan, Cora, 254, 255
Kay, Jackie, 255, 256, 257
 The Adoption Papers, 257
Kazantzis, Judith, 247, 248
Keats, John, 3, 122, 141
Kela, Thomas, 30
Kempe, Margery, 10, 12–13, 16, 17, 18,
  19–21, 23, 24, 25, 26, 27, 32, 33n
 The Book of Margery Kempe, 12–13, 16,
  17, 33n
Kenney, Annie
 Memories of a Militant, 197
Kermode, Frank
 The Sense of an Ending, 244, 257
Killigrew, 68
Koteliansky, S.S., 226
Krafft-Ebing, Richard von, 221

Kristeva, Julia, 212, 244, 250
Kyme, Thomas, 39

Lancashire cotton famine, 170
Landon, Laetitia ('L.E.L.'), 123, 141, 143–4,
    169–70
  'Gifts Misused', 144
  'Stanzas on the Death of Mrs Hemans',
    143–4
  The Improvisatrice, 169
landscapes, 215, 236, 242, 244, 257
  'female landscape', 236, 258
Lane, John, 182, 183
Langham Place Group, 170
language, 212, 224, 256, 256
  'man-made', 245
Lanyer, Aemilia, 48–50, 60, 62
  Salve Deus Rex Judaeorum, 48–50
Larrington, Carolyne, 15, 16, 17
Latin, 16, 17, 113
law, 15, 126
Lawes, Henry, 75
Lawrence, D.H., 188, 199n
Le Roman de la Rose, 27
Leapor, Mary, 109–12
  An Epistle to a Lady, 110
  Crumble-Hall, 110
  'Essay on Woman', 110
  'The Epistle of Deborah Dough', 111–2
Leavis, F. R., 145n, 162
Lee, Hannah, 182
Lee, Sophia, 182
Lehmann, Rosamond, 229, 238–9, 254
  The Echoing Grove, 238–9
Leighton, Angela, 169, 193
Lennox, Charlotte, 95–6, 113
  The Female Quixote, 95–6, 113
lesbianism, 76, 172, 192, 220–4, 228, 239,
    248, 252, 252–3
  lesbian writers, 2, 192, 220–4, 250, 252–3
Lesley-Jones, Veronica, 231
Lessing, Doris, 243–4, 255
  Canopus in Argos, 255
  Memoirs of a Survivor, 255
  The Diary of Jane Somers, 252
  The Golden Notebook, 237, 243–4, 246
L'Estrange, Roger, 77
letters, 95, 108–9, 224
Lettres Portugaises, 107
Levertov, Denise, 241
  'The Mutes', 242–3
Lewes, George Henry, 154, 155, 164

'Gentle Hint to Writing Women',150
Lewis, Gwyneth
  'Welsh Espionage', 257
Lilburne, John, 66
Lilith, 242
Linton, Eliza Lynn, 152, 154
  The New Woman in Haste and Leisure, 193
literacy, 95
  and women, 9, 17–18, 95
  and middle classes, 5
literary history, 241
literary production
  male and female patterns, 150
Lively, Penelope
  Moon Tiger, 258
Lochead, Liz, 248
  'Poppies', 249
Locke, John, 99
Lodge, Thomas, 51
love, 56, 57–8, 71–74, 101, 107, 143, 155,
    164, 166, 189, 190, 241
  courtly love, 11–12, 13, 29, 30–1, 32, 33,
    49, 56, 72
  'free love', 188–9
  love poetry, 42, 73
  neo-Platonic love, 49, 58, 75
  Romantic love, 253
Lukács, Georg
  The Meaning of Contemporary Realism, 227
Lyttleton, Edith
  Warp and Woof, 195
Lytton, Bulwer
  Pelham, 157
Lytton, Constance, 197

Macauley, Catharine, 124
Macauley, Rose, 243
  The Towers of Trebizond, 239
  The World My Wilderness, 238
madness, 180, 238, 240, 243–4
magazines, 156
  fiction magazines, 179
  literary magazines, 151
  women's magazines, 95, 179
Mainwaring, George, 43
Makin, Bathsua, 66, 87n
Manley, Delarivier, 101–2, 106
  Almyna, 102
  Memoirs of Europe, 101, 106
  Queen Zarah, 101, 106
  The Lost Lover, 101
  The New Atlantis, 101, 106

The Royal Mischief, 102
Mansfield, Katherine, 205, 206–8, 215–16,
219, 220, 225–7, 231n
'At the Bay', 226
Journal, 207–8
'Prelude', 215, 216, 226
'The Doll's House', 226
'The Tiredness of Rosabel', 206–7
Mar, Lady, 109
Marcus, Jane, 228
marriage, 12, 15, 29, 31, 66, 71–4, 79, 82, 85,
100, 101, 108, 114, 124, 130, 131,
132, 134, 136, 160, 166, 168, 171,
178, 179, 179, 185, 186, 188, 189–92,
196, 198, 220, 220, 229, 236, 240,
246, 247
the 'marriage problem', 168
widowhood, 66
Martineau, Harriet, 152, 158–9
Deerbrook, 160
Illustrations of Political Economy, 152,
158–9
Illustrations of Taxation, 152
Marvell, Andrew, 84
Marx, Eleanor, 186
Marxist criticism, 97
Mary Magdalene, 252
Mary of Oignies, 19, 20, 22
Mary, Queen, 107
Mary, the Virgin, 23, 25, 48, 50
masculinity, 221, 230, 251, 258
Masham, Lady Damaris, 100
'masquerade', 209–10, 230, 251
mass culture, 206
Massingberd, Emily, 179
maternal, the, 216
'maternal genealogy', 236, 239
maternity, 223, 246
see also motherhood
Matheolus, 27, 28
Maxwell, William, 152
McCrory, Moy, 246
McGuckian, Mebh, 248
'From the Dressing-Room', 249
Meade, L. T.
A Sweet Girl Graduate, 178
medical profession, 205
Medieval women, 3–4, Ch. 1 9–36 *passim*
melodrama, 167–8
memoir, 197, 224
memory, 224, 225, 257
Men and Women's Club, 179, 185, 198n

Meredith, Isabel (Helen and Olivia Rossetti)
A Girl Among the Anarchists, 199n
metafiction, 246
metre
iambic pentameter, 104
iambic tetrameter, 104
Meynell, Alice, 193–4, 196
'The Modern Mother', 193–4
Middle Ages, Ch. 1 9–36 *passim*
militancy, 205
Millett, Kate, 1
Sexual Politics, 247, 252
Milton, John
Paradise Lost, 49, 67, 165
Mitchell, Elma, 248
'Thoughts After Ruskin', 249
Mitchell, Juliet
Psychoanalysis and Feminism, 247
'Women: The Longest Revolution', 247
modernism, 3, 6, Ch. 8 203–234 *passim*
modernist novel, 188
modernist period, Ch. 8 203–234 *passim*
Modleski, Tania, 167, 236
Moers, Ellen, 1, 134, 236, 247
Mohin, Lilian
One Foot on the Mountain, 247–8, 253
Mollwo, Adrienne
A Fair Suffragette, 196
Montagu, Lady Mary Wortley, 95, 100,
108–9
Simplicity, A Comedy, 108
The Nonsense of Common Sense, 108
morality, 133, 255
and the woman writer, 106
More, Hannah, 118, 124, 136–7, 140
Cheap Repository Tracts, 136
Coelebs in Search of a Wife, 130
*Strictures on the Modern System of
Education*, 125, 136
'The Gin Shop', 136–7
More, Thomas, 37
Mornay, Philippe de, 46
Morning Chronicle, 152
Morning Post, 138
Morris, Pam, 1, 2
Morrison, Toni
Beloved, 256
mother, 242
'mother-daughter plot', 215–16,
231n
mother-daughter relationship, 222, 230
search for, 238

motherhood, 15, 21, 22, 32, 134, 180, 185, 186, 190, 193–4, 196, 210, 216, 230, 237, 242, 246, 256
'Movement' poets, 242
Mudie, Charles Edward, 156
Mudie's Select Library, 156
Munda, Constantia, 59, 61
Murdoch, Iris, 245, 246
   A Severed Head, 245
   'Against Dryness: A Polemical Sketch', 245
   The Black Prince, 245
   Under the Net, 245
Murry, John Middleton, 226, 231n
muse, the, 115, 242
myth, 7, 211–16, 235, 242, 251, 258, 259
   cultural myths, 134, 235, 240, 251, 255, 259
   Greek myths, 213, 255

Namjoshi, Suniti, 255
   Feminist Fables, 255
narrative poems, 171
narrative strategy, 187, 195, 236
National Union of Women's Suffrage Societies (NUWSS), 195
Nesbit, E., 198
New Age, 205
New Criticism, 203
New Freewoman, The, 205
New Historicist criticism, 97
New Woman, 6, 185–94, 199n
   drama, 185–6
   novels, 185–194
   short stories, 189
   writers, 181, 185–194, 198
Newnham college, 177, 205
Nichols, Grace
   i is a long memoried woman, 256–7
nineteenth century, 5, Ch. 6 149–76 *passim*
North British Review, 170
novel
   development of, 94, 106, 181, 194
   female novelists, 106, 116, 153, 181, 194
   production of, 106, 181
   see also 'Condition of England' novel, detective novel, domestic fiction, Gothic novel, modernist novel, romantic novel, sensation fiction, sentimental novel, serialised novel, 'silver-fork' novel, social protest fiction, Victorian novel
nursing, 205

O'Brien, Edna, 245–6
   Girl With Green Eyes, 245–6
Odle, Alan, 231
old age, 239, 252
Oliphant, Margaret, 152, 154, 160, 167, 189
   'Chronicles of Carlingford', 160
   Salem Chapel, 160
Onlywomen, 249
Opie, Amelia
   Adeline Mowbray, 130–1
Orage, A.R., 205
oral traditions, 252, 255, 256
O'Rourke, Rebecca, 248
   Jumping the Cracks, 255
orphans, 160, 172n, 163
Osborne, Dorothy, 68, 86, 87n
'Other', the, 98
Ouida, (Mary Louise de la Ramée), 166

Palmer, Paulina, 235, 250
Pandora, 249
Pankhurst, Christabel, 197
   'The Great Scourage and How to End it', 197
   Unshackled, 197
Pankhursts, the, 197
Paris, 220
Parliament, 65
   women's petitions to, 66
Parr, Catherine, 39
Parr, Susanna, 4, 67, 69–70
   Susanna's Apology Against the Elders, 69–70
Paston, John II, 30–1
Paston, John III, 30–1
Paston letters, 30–1, 33
Paston, Margaret, 30–1
Paston, Margery, 31
patriarchy, 4, 32, 33, 48, 96, 128, 166, 214, 215, 236, 252, 255, 259
   critique of, 247
patronage, 50–1, 62
Pearse, Gabriella, 256
Pepys, Samuel, 73, 84, 87n
periodicals
   eighteenth century, 108
   nineteenth century, 150, 151
   modernist, 205
   1890s, 179

Pethick-Lawrences, the, 197
Petrarch, 46, 57, 58
Petroff, Elizabeth, 10, 16, 19
Phibbs, Mrs Harlow
   The Mothers' Meeting, 196
Phibbs, L. S.
   Jim's Leg, 196
Philips, James, 74
Philips, Katherine ('Orinda'), 67, 68, 74–6,
   87n, 88n, 104, 106
   'Friendship's Mystery . . .', 75
   'Orinda to Lucasia', 68, 75–6
   'To my excellent Lucasia . . . ', 76
Picasso, Pablo
   Les Demoiselles d'Avignon, 204
Pinero, Arthur Wing
   The Notorious Mrs Ebbsmith, 186
Pioneer Club, 179, 185, 198n
Pitt-Kethley, Fiona, 3
Pix, Mary, 101
   The Innocent Mistress, 101
   The Beau Defeated, 101
Pizan, Christine de, 4, 15, 26–9, 31, 32, 33
   'Ditié de Jehanne d'Arc', 26
   The Book of the City of Ladies, 15, 16,
      27–9
   The Treasure of the City of Ladies, 29
Planché, Eliza, 182
Planché, J. R., 182
Plath, Sylvia, 240–1, 242
   Ariel, 237, 240
   'Daddy', 241
   'Lady Lazarus', 240–1
   'The Applicant', 240
   'Tulips', 240
'Poem for Jacqueline Hill', 251
poet
   'poetess', 169
   woman, 169, 171, 226, 240
polemic, 130, 135
politics
   and women's writing, 68–71, 99, 104, 106,
      108, 123, 132, 158, 164, 170, 195,
      197, 248
Polwhele, Elizabeth, 66
   The Frolicks, 66
Poor Clares, 14
Pope, Alexander, 109, 110
   'Epistle to a Lady', 110
   Epistle to Arbuthnot, 111
   Essay on Criticism, 106
   Rape of the Lock, 110

The Dunciad, 106
Popish Plot, 83
popular literature, 206
Porete, Marguerite, 10, 18, 32
   Le Mirouer des Simples Ames, 10
post-colonial theory, 244
Pound, Ezra, 203, 222
presses
   suffrage, 196
   women's, 249–50
Proctor, Adelaide, 170
   Legends and Lyrics, 170
professional authorship, 172, 181, 204
   and women, 149, 152
professions, 205
prostitution, 195, 219, 220, 250–1
pseudonyms, 183–4
psychoanalysis, 222, 224
publishing, 95, 122, 150, 179
   and the stage, 198–9n
   state control of, 65
   women and publication, 67, 99, 122,
      149–51, 179, 181, 182, 196, 205, 253
   women's publishing, 249–50
   see also feminist publishing
Punch, 185
Pym, Barbara, 237

Quaker movement, 69, 70
Quilligan, Maureen, 28

race, 97, 178, 244, 256
Radcliffe, Ann, 5, 128–30
   The Castles of Athlin and Dunbayne, 118
   The Italian, 128, 129
   The Mysteries of Udolpho, 128–129
Radcliffe, Mary Ann, 125
   The Female Advocate, 125
Raine, Kathleen, 241, 242
rape, 29, 128, 250
rationality, 127, 133
reader
   address to the female reader, 108
   female reading public, 153, 181
   middle-class reader, 157
reading, 95
   novel reading, 156
   re-reading, 235–6
realism, 118, 161, 181, 185, 227, 243, 246, 255
   historical realism, 228–9
   social realism, 194
   see also domestic realism

realist fiction, 227–31, 246, 250
Reeve, Clara, 118
  The Progress of Romance, 118
Reformation, 4, Ch. 2 37–64 *passim*
relations between the sexes, 188, 189, 192, 242
relations between women, 171, 192, 210, 238
  see also friendship
religion, 158
  women's writing on, 68–71, 241, 245
Renaissance, 4, Ch. 2 37–64 *passim*
Restoration, Ch. 3 65–93 passim, 94, 102
reviewing, 151–2
Rhys, Jean, 219–220, 236, 238, 254
  'Vienne', 220
  Wide Sargasso Sea, 237, 243, 244
Rich, Adrienne, 6, 220, 235, 248
Richardson, Dorothy, 205, 208–10, 214, 220, 229, 231n
  Pilgrimage, 6, 205, 208–10, 219, 225
  'Women and the Future', 209
Richardson, Samuel, 106, 116
  Clarissa Harlowe, 113
  Pamela, 113
Riley, Joan
  The Unbelonging, 256
Rivers, W.H.R., 258
Riviere, Joan, 209
Roberts, Michèle, 247, 252
  Daughters of the House, 252
  The Wild Girl, 252
Robins, Elizabeth, 183–4, 199n
  A Dark Lantern, 198n
  Alan's Wife, 184, 191, 195
  George Mandeville's Husband, 183–4
  'Miss de Maupassant', 183
  The Convert, 195, 197
  The Open Question, 195
  Votes for Women, 194–5, 196, 197
  Where Are You Going To . . .?, 195
Robinson, Mary, 125, 128, 130, 138–9, 140
  Captivity . . ., 138
  'January', 139
  Letter to the Women of England . . ., 125
  Lyrical Tales, 138
  Poems, 138
  'Stanzas' (1797), 139
  'Stanzas . . . 1792', 138
  'The Birthday', 139
  The Natural Daughter, 128
  'To the Poet Coleridge', 138
  'Winkfield Plain', 139

Rochester, Earl of, 94
Rogers, Jane
  Mr Wroe's Virgins, 257
romance, 194, 229, 238, 245, 253, 258, 259
  French, 107, 113
  ideology, 236, 237, 238, 254
  lesbian romance, 253, 254
  literature, 4, 13, 38, 45, 54, 55, 56
  plot, 236, 237, 238, 239, 243, 244, 245, 252
  popular romance, 206–7, 229, 230, 236
  romantic fiction, 180, 194, 253–4
Romantic period, 3, 5, Ch. 5 122–148 *passim*
Romanticism, 114, 116, 118, Ch. 5 122–48 *passim*
Rose, Jacqueline, 240, 241
Rossetti, Christina, 169, 170, 171–2
  Goblin Market, 171–2
Rousseau, Jean-Jacques
  Emile, 130
  Julie, 114
  La Nouvelle Héloise, 127
Rule, Jane, 221, 239, 247
Rumens, Carol
  Making for the Open, 248–9
Ryley, Madeliane Lucette, 198
  Jedbury Junior, 198

Sage, Lorna, 235, 243
St Audrey, 16
St Bridget, *see* Bridget of Sweden
St Catherine of Alexandria, 16
St John, Christopher
  How the Vote Was Won, 196
St Katherine, 25
St Margaret, 25
St Paul, 40, 41, 60, 69, 70
Salter, Thomas, 38
Saturday Review, 152
Saxton, Josephine, 255
Schreiner, Olive, 181, 186–8
  The Story of an African Farm, 181, 184, 186–8, 199n
science fiction, 135, 253, 255
Scott, Sir Walter, 123, 153
Scottish women writers, 248, 257
Second World War, 214, 218, 238
Sedgwick, Eve Kosofsky, 229
sensation fiction, 157, 166–8
sensibility
  cult of, 170
sentimental novel, 113, 114, 117

sentimental tradition, 204
sentimentality, 95
separate spheres, 179, 180, 205
serialised novel, 156
seventeenth century, 4, 37, Ch. 3 65–93
    passim
Seward, Anna, 135, 140
sewing, 105
sex, 15, 129, 178, 185, 194, 245, 258
    see also relations between the sexes
sexual difference, 209, 215, 217, 221, 226,
    249
sexual harassment, 196
sexuality, 79, 220–4, 236, 245, 250, 252, 258
    female, 13, 59, 81, 106, 126, 127–8, 185,
        186, 194, 198, 206, 220–224
    male, 197, 198
Shakespeare, William, 55
    Romeo and Juliet, 81
    Twelfth Night, 85
    Othello, 88n
Sharp, Evelyn
    Rebel Women, 196
Sharp, Jane, 86
Shaw, G.B., 198
    Mrs Warren's Profession, 186
Sheba, 249
shell-shock, 258
Shelley, Mary, 134–5
    Frankenstein, 134–5, 254
    The Last Man, 135
    Valperga, 135
Shelley, Percy Bysshe, 122
Sheridan, Frances, 113
    Memoirs of Miss Sidney Bidulph, 112–13,
        114
Showalter, Elaine, 1, 67, 68, 167, 185, 197,
    236, 238, 247, 258
Siddons, Sarah, 123
Sidney, Mary, Countess of Pembroke, 46–7,
    54
    'A Dialogue between two shepherds', 46
    Psalms, 46–7
Sidney, Philip, 46, 47, 55
    'Astrophel and Stella', 57
    The Countess of Pembroke's Arcadia, 54, 55
'silver-fork' novel, 157
Sinclair, May, 198
    Life and Death of Harriett Frean, 207
    The Creators, 6, 198
single women, 170, 179, 205
    see also 'surplus women'

sisterhood, 20, 185,194, 252, 255
    see also friendship
sisters, 189, 223, 239
slavery, 80, 136, 145n, 170, 171, 256,
    258
    'white slave trade', 195
Slovo, Gillian, 254
smallpox, 108
Smith, Charlotte, 5, 114, 117, 118, 123, 128,
    139- 40, 140
    Beachy Head, 139, 140
    Desmond, 128
    Elegiac Sonnets, 123, 139
    Emmeline, 117
    The Emigrants, 139, 140
Smith, Joan, 254
    Why Aren't They Screaming?, 255
Smith, Sidonie, 20
Smith, Stevie, 241, 242
    'I rode With my Darling', 242
Smith, W.H., 156, 182
social protest fiction, 158–9, 167
Society of Authors, 181, 182
Socrates, 113
Southey, Robert, 149
Sowerby, Githa
    Rutherford and Son, 192
Sowernam, Ester, 59
Spacks, Patricia Meyer, 247
Spanish Civil War, 228–9
Spark, Muriel, 244–5, 246
    The Driver's Seat, 244
    The Prime of Miss Jean Brodie, 245
Spectator, The, 94, 108
Speght, Rachel, 59–62
    A Dreame . . ., 60–1
    A Mouzell for Melastomus, 59–60, 61–2
    Mortalities Memorandum . . ., 60–2
Spender, Dale, 3, 245
spinsters, 186, 228
    see also single women
Steedman, Carolyn
    Landscape for a Good Woman, 237
Steele, Richard, 94
Stevenson, Anne, 241, 242
    'Correspondances', 242
    'Generations', 242
Stoneman, Patsy, 236, 237, 238
Stopes, Marie
    Married Love, 216
Strahan, Alexander, 152
Stuckley, 69

subjectivity, 6, 47, 57, 207, 207–11, 213, 218,
        219, 224, 255
    female subjectivity, 4, 11, 32, 48, 56, 58,
        59, 85, 170, 207–11, 218, 219, 247,
        248
sublime, 114, 129–30
suffrage, the, 180, 194–7
    movement, 179, 194–7, 205–6
    writing, 194–7
    suffragettes, 206
    United Suffragists, The, 196
Suffragette, The, 179, 195
suffragist drama, 196
suicide, 186, 230, 240
'surplus women', 170, 179
sweated labour, 195
Swetnam, Joseph, 59, 60, 62
Swinburne, Algernon Charles
    'Itylus', 223
Symbolism, 226
Symonds, Deb, 248

Talleyrand, Périgord, 124
Tatler, The, 94, 108
Taylor, Elizabeth, 236
    Palladian, 237–8
Taylor, Jane, 141
    Essays in Rhyme on Morals and Manners,
        141
Taylor, Jeremy, 74
Temple, William, 68
Tennyson, Alfred, Lord, 170
Thackeray, William Makepeace, 227
    Punch's Prize Novelists, 157
    Vanity Fair, 157
The Liberty Belle, 170
theatre
    and women, 101, 118, 182–3, 184, 196,
        199n
'Theatre of Ideas', 196
Thomas, Elizabeth, 100
Tighe, Mary, 141
    Psyche, 141
Todhunter, John
    The Black Cat, 186
Tonna, Charlotte Elizabeth
    Helen Fleetwood . . ., 158
tradition, 169
    female, 2, 26, 28, 32, 33n, 169, 236, 245
    'great tradition', 162
    male, 164–5
translation, 25, 38–9, 45, 46, 48, 95

Trapnel, Anna, 67, 70
    Her Report and Plea, 70
travel literature, 123
Trollope, Anthony, 153
Trollope, Frances Elizabeth
    Michael Armstrong . . ., 158
Trotter, Catherine, 101
    Agnes de Castro, 101
    Olinda's Adventures, 101
    The Fatal Friendship, 101
    The Unhappy Penitant, 101
Trotula texts, 16
Trye, Mary, 86
Tudor, Mary, 38
twentieth century, Ch. 8 203–34 *passim*,
        Ch. 9 235–263 *passim*
Tyler, Margaret, 39, 45
    A mirrour of princely deeds and knighthood,
        45

urbanization, 216–20
utopias, 194, 255, 259

Vaughan, Henry, 74, 75
venereal disease, 190, 195, 197
Vicinus, Martha, 168, 178
Victorian period, Ch. 6 149–76 *passim*
Victorian novel, 153–68
violence against women, 250–1, 256
Virago, 249
Vives, Juan Luis
    Instructions of a Christian Woman, 37–8
Vote, The, 196
Votes for Women, 179, 195
Voynich, Ethel
    The Gadfly, 194

Walker, Alice
    The Color Purple, 256
Walkley, A.B., 184
Wallace, Jo-Ann, 204
Wandor, Michelene, 247
war, 214–15, 238, 248
    see also civil war, First World War,
        Second World War
Ward, Mrs Humphry, 194
    Delia Blanchflower, 197
Warner, Sylvia Townsend, 227–9
    'Cottage Mantleshelf', 228
    'In this Midwinter', 228
    Lolly Willowes, 228
    'Red Front', 228

Summer Will Show, 6, 228–9
Weaver, Harriet Shaw, 205
Webster, Augusta, 170
  A Woman Sold and Other Poems, 170
  Portraits, 170
Webster, Ben, 182
Weldon, Fay, 245, 250, 255
  Down Among the Women, 250
  Female Friends, 252
  The Life and Loves of a She Devil, 254
Weldon, Georgina, 195
  Not Alone, 195
Welsh women poets, 257
Wentworth, Anne, 72
  Vindication, 72
Wentworth, Vera
  The Allegory, 196
West, Jane, 130
  The Advantages of Education, 130
West, Rebecca, 214, 227, 238, 239
  Cousin Rosamund, 239
  The Fountain Overflows, 239
  The Return of the Soldier, 214
  This Real Night, 239
Westminster Review, 152, 154
White, Antonia, 239–40, 243
  Beyond the Glass, 239–40
  Frost in May, 239
  The Lost Traveller, 239–40
  The Sugar House, 239–40
Whitney, Isabella, 39, 42–5
  A sweet Nosgay . . ., 43–4
  Copy of a letter . . ., 42–3
  'Wyll and Testament', 44–5
Wilde, Oscar, 226, 227
Williams, Helen Maria, 140
Williams, Raymond, 178
Wilson, Elizabeth, 237
Winchilsea, Countess of, *see* Finch, Anne
Winterson, Jeanette
  Oranges are not the Only Fruit, 253, 258
  Written on the Body, 239
Wittig, Monique, 2
Wolley, Hannah, 86
Wollstonecraft, Mary, 5, 117, 118, 124–5, 126–7 128, 130, 131, 132, 134, 134, 139, 144
  Mary: A Fiction, 118
  The Wrongs of Woman, 126–7
  Vindication of the Rights of Women, 124–5, 126, 127, 136

Woman Question, the, 170, 178–80, 204
womanhood, 188
womanliness, 149, 161, 162, 164, 186, 193, 210
  see also femininity
Women Writers Suffrage League, 195
Women's Dreadnought, The, 196
Women's Franchise, The, 195
Women's Freedom League, 195, 196
Women's Movement, 235, 184, 194–7, 247
  see also feminist movement
Women's Press, the, 196
Women's Press, The, 249
Women's Social and Political Union (WSPU), 195, 205
Women's World, 179
Wood, Ellen (Mrs Henry), 152
  East Lynne, 166
Woolf, Virginia, 67, 161, 164, 177, 205, 209, 210- 12, 214–15, 218–19, 220, 224, 226, 227, 229, 231n
  'A Sketch of the Past', 224
  A Room of One's Own, 1, 84, 149, 150, 154, 212, 236
  Between the Acts, 212, 218
  Jacob's Room, 210, 214–15
  Mrs Dalloway, 6, 210, 214, 219
  Orlando, 211–12, 251
  'Street Haunting . . .', 218–19
  The Waves, 214
  The Years, 214, 219
  Three Guineas, 214
  To the Lighthouse, 210–11, 214, 215, 224
Wordsworth, Dorothy, 125–6, 145n
  Journals, 125–6
Wordsworth, William, 3, 122, 139
  'Extempore Effusion upon the Death of James Hogg', 169
  Lyrical Ballads, 136, 141, 145n
  'Ode: Intimations of Immortality', 247
  Prelude, 140
work, 179, 186, 196, 205, 206, 219, 247
Wroth, Lady Mary, 48, 54–9
  'Pamphilius to Amphilanthus', 57–8
  Urania, 54–7, 62
Wyatt, Thomas, 47
Wycherley, William, 94
  The Country Wife, 81

Xenophon, 113

Yaegar, Patricia, 129
Yearsley, Ann, 109, 137–8, 140
  'On Mrs Montagu', 137
  'Remonstrance in the Platonic Shade . . .',
    137
  'The Indifferent Shepherdess to Colin',
    137

The Rural Lyre, 137
Yeats, W.B., 3
Yellow Book, The, 179, 182
Yorke, Liz, 235–6, 241, 242, 247, 259
'Yorkshire Ripper' (Peter Sutcliffe), 250, 251

Zlosnick, Sue, 236, 244